Where Joy Resides

WHERE JOY RESIDES

*A Christopher Isherwood
Reader edited by Don Bachardy
and James P. White with an
introduction by Gore Vidal*

*The Noonday Press
Farrar, Straus and Giroux
New York*

And the true realism, always and everywhere, is

that of the poets: to find out where joy resides,

and give it a voice . . . For to miss the joy is

to miss all.

From "The Lantern-Bearers" by Robert Louis Stevenson,

as quoted by Christopher Isherwood in his commonplace book

Contents

Introduction
by Gore Vidal

IN 1954 I HAD LUNCH with Christopher Isherwood at MGM. He told me that he had just written a film for Lana Turner. The subject? Diane de Poitiers. When I laughed, he shook his head. "Lana can do it," he said grimly. Later, as we walked about the lot and I told him that I hoped to get a job as a writer at the studio since I could no longer live on my royalties as a novelist (and would not teach), Christopher gave me as melancholy a look as those bright—even harsh—blue eyes could affect. "Don't," he said with great intensity, posing against the train beneath whose wheels Greta Garbo as Anna Karenina made her last dive, "become a hack like me." But we both knew that this was play-acting. Like his friend Aldous Huxley (like William Faulkner and many others), he had been able to write to order for movies while never ceasing to do his own work in his own way. Those whom Hollywood destroyed were never worth saving. Not only had Isherwood written successfully for the camera, he had been, notoriously, in his true art, *the* camera.

"I am a camera." With those four words at the beginning of the novel *Goodbye to Berlin* (1939), Christopher Isherwood became famous. Because of those four words he has been written of (and sometimes written off) as a naturalistic writer, a recorder of surfaces, a film director *manqué*. Although it is true that, up to a point, Isherwood often appears to be recording perhaps too impartially the lights, the shadows, the lions that come within the area of his vision, he is never without surprises; in the course of what looks to be an undemanding narrative, the author will suddenly produce a Polaroid shot of the reader reading, an alarming effect achieved by the sly use of the second person pronoun. You never know quite where *you* stand in relation to an Isherwood work.

During the half century that Christopher Isherwood was more or less at the center of Anglo-American literature, he has been much scrutinized by friends, acquaintances, purveyors of book-chat. As memoirs and biographies now accumulate, Isherwood keeps cropping up as a principal figure, and if he does not always seem in character, it is because he is not an easy character to fix upon the page. Also, he has so beautifully invented himself in the Berlin stories, *Lions and Shadows, Down There on a Visit*, and *Christopher and His Kind*, that anyone who wants to re-reveal him has his work cut out for him. After all, nothing is harder to reflect than a mirror.

To date, the best-developed portrait of Isherwood occurs in Stephen Spender's autobiography, *World Within World* (1951). Like Isherwood, Spender was a part of that upper-middle-class generation which came of age just after World War I. For the lucky few able to go to the right schools and universities, postwar England was still a small and self-contained society where everyone knew everyone else: an extension of school. But something disagreeable had happened at school just before the Isherwoods and Spenders came on stage. World War I had killed off the better part of a generation of graduates, and among the graduated dead was Isherwood's father. There was a long shadow over the young . . . of dead fathers, brothers; also of dead or dying attitudes. Rebellion was in the air. New things were promised.

In every generation there are certain figures who are who they are at an early age: stars *in ovo*. People want to know them; imitate them; destroy them. Isherwood was such a creature and Stephen Spender fell under his spell even before they met.

At nineteen Spender was an undergraduate at Oxford; another undergraduate was the twenty-one-year-old W. H. Auden. Isherwood himself (three years Auden's senior) was already out in the world; he had got himself sent down from Cambridge by sending up a written examination. He had deliberately broken out of the safe, cozy university world, and the brilliant but cautious Auden revered him. Spender writes how, "according to Auden, [Isherwood] held no opinions whatever about anything. He was wholly and simply interested in people. He did not like or dislike them, judge them favorably or unfavorably. He simply regarded them as material for his Work. At the same time, he was the Critic in whom Auden had absolute trust. If Isherwood disliked a poem, Auden destroyed it without demur."

Auden was not above torturing the young Spender: "Auden withheld the privilege of meeting Isherwood from me." Writing twenty years later, Spender cannot resist adding, "Isherwood was not famous at this time. He had published one novel, *All the Conspirators*, for which he had received an advance of £30 from his publishers, and which had been not very favorably reviewed." But Isherwood was already a legend, as Spender concedes, and worldly success has nothing to do with legends. Eventually Auden brought them together. Spender was not disappointed:

He simplified all the problems which entangled me, merely by describing his own life and his own attitudes towards these things. . . . Isherwood had a peculiarity of being attractively disgusted and amiably bitter. . . . But there was a positive as well as negative side to his beliefs. He spoke of being Cured and Saved with as much intensity as any Salvationist.

In *The Whispering Gallery*, the publisher and critic John Lehmann describes his first meeting with Spender in 1930 and how he "talked a great deal about Auden, who shared (and indeed had inspired) so many of his views, and also about a certain young novelist called Christopher Isherwood, who, he told me, had settled in Berlin in stark poverty and was an even greater rebel against the England we lived in than he was." When Lehmann went to work for Leonard and Virginia Woolf at the Hogarth Press, he got them to publish Isherwood's second novel, *The Memorial*.

Lehmann noted that the generation's Novelist was

much shorter than myself, he nevertheless had a power of dominating which small people of outstanding intellectual or imaginative equipment often possess. One of my favourite private fancies has always been that the most ruthless war that underlies our civilized existence . . . is the war between the tall and the short.

Even so, "It was impossible not to be drawn to him. . . . And yet for some months after our first meeting . . . our relations remained rather formal: perhaps it was the sense of alarm that seemed to hang in the air when his smile was switched off, a suspicion he seemed to radiate that one might after all be in league with the 'enemy,' a phrase which covered everything he had, with a pure hatred, cut himself off from in English life."

In 1931 a cold transatlantic eye was turned upon both Isherwood and Spender. The twenty-year-old Paul Bowles presented himself to Isherwood in Berlin. "When I came to Isherwood," Bowles records in *Without Stopping,* "he said he would take me himself to meet Spender." Bowles did not approve of Spender's looking and acting the part of a poet: "Whether Spender wrote poetry or not seemed relatively unimportant; that at all costs the fact should not be evident was what should have mattered to him." Bowles acknowledges that this primness reflected the attitudes of his puritan family and background. "I soon found that Isherwood with Spender was a very different person from Isherwood by himself." But then the camera and its director are bound to alter according to light, weather, cast. "Together they were overwhelmingly British, two members of a secret society constantly making references to esoteric data not available to outsiders." This strikes me as an accurate and poignant description of the difference between American and English writers. The English tend to play off (and with) one another; while the Americans are, if not Waldenized solitaries, Darwinized predators constantly preying upon one another. I think it significant that when the excellent American writer Paul Bowles came to write *his* autobiography, he chose a prose style not unlike that of Julius Caesar's report on how he laid waste Gaul.

"At all our meetings I felt that I was being treated with good-humored condescension. They accepted Aaron [Copland], but they did not accept me because they considered me too young and uninteresting; I never learned the reason, if there was one, for this exclusion by common consent." Bowles describes a British girl he met with Isherwood. She was called Jean Ross "(When Christopher wrote about her later, he called her Sally Bowles)."

Christopher and His Kind describes Isherwood's life from 1929 to 1939. The narrative (based on diaries and written, generally, in the third person) takes up where *Lions and Shadows* ends, with "twenty-four-year-old Christopher's departure from England on March 14, 1929, to visit Berlin for the first time in his life." The book ends a decade later when Isherwood emigrates to the United States. Of *Lions and Shadows*, Isherwood says that it describes his "life between the ages of seventeen and twenty-four. It is not truly autobiographical, however. The author conceals important facts about himself . . . and gives his characters fictitious names." But "The book I am now going to write will be as frank and factual as I can make it, especially as far as I myself am concerned." He means to be sexually candid; and he is. He is also that rarest of creatures, the objective narcissist; he sees himself altogether plain and does not hesitate to record for us the lines that the face in the mirror has accumulated, the odd shadow that flaws character.

As I now reread the two memoirs in sequence, it is odd how little Isherwood changed in a half century. The style is much the same throughout. The shift from first to third person does not much alter the way he has of looking at things and it is, of course, the *precise* way in which Isherwood perceives the concrete world that makes all the difference. He is particularly good at noting a physical appearance that suggests, through his selection of nouns, verbs, a psychic description. This is from *Lions and Shadows*:

[Chalmers] had grown a small moustache and looked exactly my idea of a young Montmartre poet, more French than the French. Now he caught sight of us, and greeted me with a slight wave of the hand, so very typical of him, tentative, diffident, semi-ironical, like a parody of itself. Chalmers expressed himself habitually in fragments of gestures, abortive movements, half-spoken sentences.

Then the same sharp eye is turned upon the narrator:

Descending the staircase to the dining-room, I was Christopher Isherwood no longer, but a satanically proud, icy, impenetrable demon; an all-knowing, all-pardoning saviour of mankind; a martyr-evangelist of the tea-table, from whom the most atrocious drawing-room tortures could wring no more than a polite proffer of the buttered scones.

This particular *auteur du cinéma* seldom shoots a scene without placing somewhere on the set a mirror that will record the *auteur* in the act of filming.

At the time of the publication of *Lions and Shadows* in 1938, Isherwood was thirty-four years old. He had published three novels: *All the Conspirators, The Memorial, Mr. Norris Changes Trains*. With Auden he had written the plays *The Dog beneath the Skin* and *The Ascent of F6*. Finally, most important of all, the finest of his creations had made a first appearance in *Mr. Norris Changes Trains*; with no great fuss or apparent strain, Isherwood had invented Isherwood. The Isherwood of the Berlin stories is a somewhat anodyne and enigmatic narrator. He is looking carefully at life. He does not commit himself to much of anything. Yet what might have been a limitation in a narrator, the author, rather mysteriously, made a virtue of.

Spender describes Isherwood in Berlin as occasionally "depressive, silent, or petulant. Sometimes he would sit in a room with Sally Bowles or Mr. Norris without saying a word, as though refusing to bring his characters to life." But they were very much *his* characters. He lived "surrounded by the models for his creations, like one of those portraits of a writer by a bad painter, in which the writer is depicted meditating in his chair whilst the characters of his novels radiate round him under a glowing cloud of dirty varnish." Isherwood had rejected not only the familiar, cozy world of Cambridge and London's literary life but also the world of self-conscious aestheticism. He chose to live as a proletarian in Berlin, where, Spender tells us, "He was comparatively poor and almost unrecognized. His novel, *All the Conspirators*, had been remaindered," Spender notes yet again. Nevertheless, Spender realized that Isherwood

was more than a young rebel passing through a phase of revolt against parents, conventional morality, and orthodox religion. . . . He was on the side of the forces which make a work of art, even more than he was interested in art itself. . . . His hatred of institutions of learning, and even of the reputation attached to some past work of art, was really hatred of the fact that they came between people and their direct unprejudiced approach to one another.

2.

ART AND SEX: the two themes intertwine in Isherwood's memoirs, but in the first volume we do not know what the sex was all about: the reticences of the thirties forbade candor. In *Christopher and His Kind*, Isherwood filled in the blanks; he is explicit about both sex and love.

"The book I am now going to write will be as frank and factual as I can make it, especially as far as I myself am concerned." Then the writer shifts to the third person: "At school, Christopher had fallen in love with many boys and been yearningly romantic about them. At college he had at last managed to get into bed with one. This was due entirely to the initiative of his partner, who, when Christopher became scared and started to raise objections, locked the door, and sat down firmly on Christopher's lap." For an American twenty-two years younger than Christopher, the late development of the English of that epoch is astonishing. In Washington, D.C., puberty arrived at ten, eleven, twelve, and sex was riotous and inventive between consenting paeds. Yet Tennessee Williams (fourteen years my senior) reports in his *Memoirs* that neither homo- nor heterosexuality began for him until his late twenties. On the other hand, he did not go to a mono-sexual school as I did, as Isherwood and his kind did.

Isherwood describes his experiments with heterosexuality: "She was five or six years older than [Christopher], easygoing, stylish, hu-morous. . . . He was surprised and amused to find how easily he could relate his usual holds and movements to this unusual partner. He felt curiosity and the fun of playing a new game. He also felt a lust which was largely narcissistic." Then: "He asked himself: Do I now want to go to bed with more women and girls? Of course not, as long as I can have boys. Why do I prefer boys? Because of their shape and their voices and their smell and the way they move. And boys can be romantic. I can put them into my myth and fall in love with them. Girls can be absolutely beautiful but never romantic. In fact, their utter lack of romance is what I find most likable about them." There is a clear-eyed normality (if not great accuracy) about all this.

Then Isherwood moves from the personal to the general and notes the lunatic pressure that society exerts on everyone to be heterosexual, to deny at all costs a contrary nature. Since heterosexual relations proved to be easy for Isherwood, he could have joined the majority. But he was stopped by Isherwood the rebel, the Protestant saint who declared with the fury of a Martin Luther: "Even if my nature were like theirs, I should still have to fight them, in one way or another. If boys didn't exist, I should have to invent them." Isherwood's war on what he has called, so aptly, "the heterosexual dictatorship" was unremitting and admirable.

Meanwhile, Isherwood the writer was developing. It is during this period that the Berlin stories were written; also, *Lions and Shadows.* Also, the collaboration with Auden on the last of the verse plays. Finally, there is the inevitable fall into the movies . . . something that was bound to happen. In *Lions and Shadows* Isherwood describes how "I had always been fascinated by films. . . . I was a born film fan. . . . The reason for this had, I think, very little to do with 'Art' at all; I was, and still am, endlessly interested in the outward appearance of people—their facial expressions, their gestures, their walk, their nervous tricks. . . . The cinema puts people under a microscope: you can stare at them, you can examine them as though they were insects."

Isherwood was invited to write a screenplay for the director "Berthold Viertel [who] appears as Friedrich Bergmann in the novelette called *Prater Violet,* which was published twelve years later." Isherwood and the colorful Viertel hit it off and together worked on a film called *Little Friend.* From that time on, the best prose writer in English supported himself by writing movies. In fact, the first Isherwood work that I encountered was not a novel but a film that he wrote called *Rage in Heaven*: at sixteen I thought it splendid. "The moon!" intoned the nutty Robert Montgomery. "It's staring at me, like a great Eye." Ingrid Bergman shuddered. So did I.

It is hard now for the young who are interested in literature (a tiny minority compared to the young who are interested in that flattest and easiest and laziest of art forms: the movies) to realize that Isherwood was once considered "a hope of English fiction" by Cyril Connolly, and a master by those of us who grew up in World War II. I think the relative neglect of Isherwood's work is, partly, the result of his expatriation. With Auden, he emigrated to the United States just before the war began, and there was a good deal of bitter feeling at the time (they were clumsily parodied by the unspeakable Evelyn Waugh in *Put Out More Flags*). Ultimately, Auden's reputation was hardly affected. But then poets are licensed to be mad, bad, and dangerous to read, while prose writers are expected to be, if not responsible, predictable.

In America Isherwood was drawn first to the Quakers; then to Vedanta. Later, he became a militant spokesman of Gay Liberation. If his defense of Christopher's kind is sometimes shrill . . . well, there is a good deal to be shrill about in a society so deeply and so mindlessly "homophobic." In any case, none of Isherwood's moral preoccupations is apt to endear him to a literary establishment that is, variously, academic, Jewish/Christian, middle-class, and heterosexual. Yet he wrote his best book in the United States, the novel A *Single Man*.

3.

AS I READ THROUGH this selection of Isherwood's work, I was struck by how self-effacing he is despite, paradoxically, a good deal of self-scrutiny. He gives us no sense of what Isherwood meant to the generation after his own and I wonder now if he himself had any idea of how great a space he occupied in the imagination of my generation, where Auden–Isherwood, like some strange heraldic beast of minatory excellence, had swooped down upon the United States and there nested amongst us, part of us but always Other. "I met Isherwood," young men would say with awe in the New York of the war years. To the question "What was he like?" they would talk and talk. Apparently, he was like no other.

In 1947, when I wrote *The City and the Pillar*, I sent it to him for a comment. In due course a letter came from Hollywood. He praised the book, somewhat guardedly. Later I asked if I could use a quotation from his letter for the dust jacket. A one-word telegram arrived: "Certainly." So my third and most "controversial" novel was launched with poor Christopher all over the front of the dust jacket. He was a trouper about it.

In the summer of 1948, famous and unknown (a curious business that Isherwood has dealt with marvelously *vis-à-vis* himself), I was walking down the Boulevard St.-Germain, filled with a sense of my own glory and all atingle with absolute self-pity. Suddenly, I saw Isherwood and a friend seated at the Café Flore. So famous was he that we all knew exactly what he looked like. I presented myself. A friendship began that ended only with his death. He dedicated *A Single Man* to me. I dedicated *Myra Breckinridge* to him—an asymmetrical tit-for-tat. I lived for periods in Los Angeles and often came to the Santa Monica house where Christopher lived with Don Bachardy. Many splendid times were had—now all a blur, as each of us was usually too drunk to recall what was said the next morning. Fortunately, our keeper, Don, kept a journal that may reveal the splendor of our dialogue, the sound of tinkling glass and maniacal laughter and that witty story told for the third time in almost as many minutes.

It seems to me that throughout Christopher's life and work—and he made the two the same—he never ceased to attempt the impossible: to say exactly what a thing was and how it struck him in such a way that the reader might grasp it as he himself did, writer and reader as one in the ultimate collusive act of understanding. Cyril Connolly noted Christopher's belief that "the writer must conform to the language which is understood by the greatest number of people, to the vernacular, but his talent as a novelist will appear in the exactness of his observation, the justice of his situations, and in the construction of his book." Also, life.

Christopher was in character to the end. I paid a last visit as he was dying. He was small, shrunken, all beak like a new-hatched eagle. He rolled his head back and forth on the pillow to relieve the pain. He smiled a great deal; he nodded off from time to time; then woke up and fixed one with those still-sharp eyes, and murmured a word or two.

I sat on the edge of the bed and kept up a stream of chatter like a radio switched on. He listened to me, rather as one does to a radio while thinking of other matters. He had long since made his peace with England and the English. But I had just come from London with numerous complaints of English fecklessness—what would happen when the North Sea oil was gone? They have no plans! I cried. It's just like the grasshopper and the ant, and *they* are hopeless grasshoppers, a nation of grasshoppers. The eyes opened on that. At last, I had his full, focused attention, and he spoke his last complete sentence to me—in the form of a rhetorical question, needless to say. Not for nothing had he swum with swamis yet kept that magic touch. "So," he demanded, "what is wrong with grasshoppers?"

GOODBYE TO BERLIN

(1939)

[A *Berlin Diary* (*Autumn 1930*) and *Sally Bowles* are episodes from Christopher Isherwood's fourth novel, *Goodbye to Berlin*. Adapted by John van Druten into a play, *I Am a Camera*, which was then made into a film, this novel is also the basis for the stage musical *Cabaret* and a musical film of the same name. Along with Isherwood's previous novel, *Mr. Norris Changes Trains*, also set in Berlin shortly before Hitler took power, *Goodbye to Berlin* confirmed his reputation as a major new novelist of the 1930s.]

A Berlin Diary
(Autumn 1930)

FROM MY WINDOW, the deep solemn massive street. Cellar-shops where the lamps burn all day, under the shadow of top-heavy balconied façades, dirty plaster frontages embossed with scroll-work and heraldic devices. The whole district is like this: street leading into street of houses like shabby monumental safes crammed with the tarnished valuables and second-hand furniture of a bankrupt middle class.

I am a camera with its shutter open, quite passive, recording, not thinking. Recording the man shaving at the window opposite and the woman in the kimono washing her hair. Some day, all this will have to be developed, carefully printed, fixed.

At eight o'clock in the evening the house-doors will be locked. The children are having supper. The shops are shut. The electric-sign is switched on over the night-bell of the little hotel on the corner, where you can hire a room by the hour. And soon the whistling will begin. Young men are calling their girls. Standing down there in the cold, they whistle up at the lighted windows of warm rooms where the beds are already turned down for the night. They want to be let in. Their signals echo down the deep hollow street, lascivious and private and sad. Because of the whistling, I do not care to stay here in the evenings. It reminds me that I am in a foreign city, alone, far from home. Sometimes I determine not to listen to it, pick up a book, try to read. But soon a call is sure to sound, so piercing, so insistent, so despairingly human, that at last I have to get up and peep through the slats of the venetian blind to make quite sure that it is not—as I know very well it could not possibly be—for me.

The extraordinary smell in this room when the stove is lighted and the window shut; not altogether unpleasant, a mixture of incense and stale buns. The tall tiled stove, gorgeously coloured, like an altar. The washstand like a Gothic shrine. The cupboard also is Gothic, with carved cathedral windows: Bismarck faces the King of Prussia in stained glass. My best chair would do for a bishop's throne. In the corner, three sham mediæval halberds (from a theatrical touring company?) are fastened together to form a hatstand. Frl. Schroeder unscrews the heads of the halberds and polishes them from time to time. They are heavy and sharp enough to kill.

Everything in the room is like that: unnecessarily solid, abnormally heavy and dangerously sharp. Here, at the writing-table, I am confronted by a phalanx of metal objects—a pair of candlesticks shaped like entwined serpents, an ashtray from which emerges the head of a crocodile, a paper-knife copied from a Florentine dagger, a brass dolphin holding on the end of its tail a small broken clock. What becomes of such things? How could they ever be destroyed? They will probably remain intact for thousands of years: people will treasure them in museums. Or perhaps they will merely be melted down for munitions in a war. Every morning, Frl. Schroeder arranges them very carefully in certain unvarying positions: there they stand, like an uncompromising statement of her views on Capital and Society, Religion and Sex.

All day long she goes padding about the large dingy flat. Shapeless but alert, she waddles from room to room, in carpet slippers and a flowered dressing-gown pinned ingeniously together, so that not an inch of petticoat or bodice is to be seen, flicking with her duster, peeping, spying, poking her short pointed nose into the cupboards and luggage of her lodgers. She has dark, bright, inquisitive eyes and pretty waved brown hair of which she is proud. She must be about fifty-five years old.

Long ago, before the War and the Inflation, she used to be comparatively well off. She went to the Baltic for her summer holidays and kept a maid to do the housework. For the last thirty years she has lived here and taken in lodgers. She started doing it because she liked to have company.

" 'Lina,' my friends used to say to me, 'however can you? How can you bear to have strange people living in your rooms and spoiling your furniture, especially when you've got the money to be independent?' And I'd always give them the same answer. '*My* lodgers aren't lodgers,' I used to say. 'They're my guests.' "

"You see, Herr Issyvoo, in those days I could afford to be very particular about the sort of people who came to live here. I could pick and choose. I only took them really well connected and well educated—proper gentlefolk (like yourself, Herr Issyvoo). I had a Freiherr once, and a Rittmeister and a Professor. They often gave me presents— a bottle of cognac or a box of chocolates or some flowers. And when one of them went away for his holidays he'd always send me a card— from London, it might be, or Paris, or Baden-Baden. Ever such pretty cards I used to get. . . ."

And now Frl. Schroeder has not even got a room of her own. She has to sleep in the living-room, behind a screen, on a small sofa with broken springs. As in so many of the older Berlin flats, our living-room connects the front part of the house with the back. The lodgers who live on the front have to pass through the living-room on their way to the bathroom, so that Frl. Schroeder is often disturbed during the night. "But I drop off again at once. It doesn't worry me. I'm much too tired." She has to do all the housework herself and it takes up most of her day. "Twenty years ago, if anybody had told me to scrub my own floors, I'd have slapped his face for him. But you get used to it. You can get used to anything. Why, I remember the time when I'd have sooner cut off my right hand than empty this chamber. . . . And now," says Frl. Schroeder, suiting the action to the word, "my goodness! It's no more to me than pouring out a cup of tea!"

She is fond of pointing out to me the various marks and stains left by lodgers who have inhabited this room:

"Yes, Herr Issyvoo, I've got something to remember each of them by. . . . Look there, on the rug—I've sent it to the cleaners I don't know how often but nothing will get it out—that's where Herr Noeske was sick after his birthday party. What in the world can he have been eating, to make a mess like that? He'd come to Berlin to study, you know. His parents lived in Brandenburg—a first-class family; oh, I assure you! They had pots of money! His Herr Papa was a surgeon, and of course he wanted his boy to follow in his footsteps. . . . What a charming young man! 'Herr Noeske,' I used to say to him, 'excuse me, but you must really work harder—you with all your brains! Think of your Herr Papa and your Frau Mama; it isn't fair to them to waste their good money like that. Why, if you were to drop it in the Spree it would be better. At least it would make a splash!' I was like a mother to him. And always, when he'd got himself into some scrape—he was terribly thoughtless—he'd come straight to me: 'Schroederschen,' he used to say, 'please don't be angry with me. . . . We were playing cards last night and I lost the whole of this month's allowance. I daren't tell Father. . . .' And then he'd look at me with those great big eyes of his. I knew exactly what he was after, the scamp! But I hadn't the heart to refuse. So I'd sit down and write a letter to his Frau Mama and beg her to forgive him just that once and send some more money. And she always would. . . . Of course, as a woman, I knew how to appeal to a mother's feelings, although I've never had any children of my own. . . . What are you smiling at, Herr Issyvoo? Well, well! Mistakes will happen, you know!"

"And that's where the Herr Rittmeister always upset his coffee over the wall-paper. He used to sit there on the couch with his fiancée. 'Herr Rittmeister,' I used to say to him, 'do please drink your coffee at the table. If you'll excuse my saying so, there's plenty of time for the other thing afterwards. . . .' But no, he always would sit on the couch. And then, sure enough, when he began to get a bit excited in his feelings, over went the coffee-cups. . . . Such a handsome gentleman! His Frau Mama and his sister came to visit us sometimes. They liked coming up to Berlin. 'Fräulein Schroeder,' they used to tell me, 'you don't know how lucky you are to be living here, right in the middle of things. We're only country cousins—we envy you! And now tell us all the latest Court scandals!' Of course, they were only joking.

They had the sweetest little house, not far from Halberstadt, in the Harz. They used to show me pictures of it. A perfect dream!"

"You see those ink-stains on the carpet? That's where Herr Professor Koch used to shake his fountain-pen. I told him of it a hundred times. In the end, I even laid sheets of blotting-paper on the floor around his chair. He was so absent-minded. . . . Such a dear old gentleman! And so simple. I was very fond of him. If I mended a shirt for him or darned his socks, he'd thank me with the tears in his eyes. He liked a bit of fun, too. Sometimes, when he heard me coming, he'd turn out the light and hide behind the door; and then he'd roar like a lion to frighten me. Just like a child. . . ."

Frl. Schroeder can go on like this, without repeating herself, by the hour. When I have been listening to her for some time, I find myself relapsing into a curious trance-like state of depression. I begin to feel profoundly unhappy. Where are all those lodgers now? Where, in another ten years, shall I be, myself? Certainly not here. How many seas and frontiers shall I have to cross to reach that distant day; how far shall I have to travel, on foot, on horseback, by car, push-bike, aeroplane, steamer, train, lift, moving-staircase and tram? How much money shall I need for that enormous journey? How much food must I gradually, wearily consume on my way? How many pairs of shoes shall I wear out? How many thousands of cigarettes shall I smoke? How many cups of tea shall I drink and how many glasses of beer? What an awful tasteless prospect! And yet—to have to die. . . . A sudden vague pang of apprehension grips my bowels and I have to excuse myself in order to go to the lavatory.

Hearing that I was once a medical student, she confides to me that she is very unhappy because of the size of her bosom. She suffers from palpitations and is sure that these must be caused by the strain on her heart. She wonders if she should have an operation. Some of her acquaintances advise her to, others are against it:

"Oh dear, it's such a weight to have to carry about with you! And just think—Herr Issyvoo: I used to be as slim as you are!"

"I suppose you had a great many admirers, Frl. Schroeder?"

Yes, she has had dozens. But only one Friend. He was a married man, living apart from his wife, who would not divorce him.

"We were together eleven years. Then he died of pneumonia. Sometimes I wake up in the night when it's cold and wish he was there. You never seem to get really warm, sleeping alone."

There are four other lodgers in this flat. Next door to me, in the big front-room, is Frl. Kost. In the room opposite, overlooking the courtyard, is Frl. Mayr. At the back, beyond the living-room, is Bobby. And behind Bobby's room, over the bathroom, at the top of a ladder, is a tiny attic which Frl. Schroeder refers to, for some occult reason, as "The Swedish Pavilion." This she lets, at twenty marks a month, to a commercial traveller who is out all day and most of the night. I occasionally come upon him on Sunday mornings, in the kitchen, shuffling about in his vest and trousers, apologetically hunting for a box of matches.

Bobby is a mixer at a west-end bar called the Troika. I don't know his real name. He has adopted this one because English Christian names are fashionable just now in the Berlin demi-monde. He is a pale worried-looking smartly dressed young man with thin sleek black hair. During the early afternoon, just after he has got out of bed, he walks about the flat in shirt-sleeves, wearing a hair-net.

Frl. Schroeder and Bobby are on intimate terms. He tickles her and slaps her bottom; she hits him over the head with a frying-pan or a mop. The first time I surprised them scuffling like this, they were both rather embarrassed. Now they take my presence as a matter of course.

Frl. Kost is a blonde florid girl with large silly blue eyes. When we meet, coming to and from the bathroom in our dressing-gowns, she modestly avoids my glance. She is plump but has a good figure.

One day I asked Frl. Schroeder straight out: What was Frl. Kost's profession?

"Profession? Ha, ha, that's good! That's just the word for it! Oh, yes, she's got a fine profession. Like this—"

And with the air of doing something extremely comic, she began waddling across the kitchen like a duck, mincingly holding a duster between her finger and thumb. Just by the door, she twirled trium-phantly round, flourishing the duster as though it were a silk hand-kerchief, and kissed her hand to me mockingly:

"Ja, ja, Herr Issyvoo! That's how they do it!"

"I don't quite understand, Frl. Schroeder. Do you mean that she's a tight-rope walker?"

"He, he, he! Very good indeed, Herr Issyvoo! Yes, that's right! That's it! She walks along the line for her living. That just describes her!"

One evening, soon after this, I met Frl. Kost on the stairs, with a Japanese. Frl. Schroeder explained to me later that he is one of Frl. Kost's best customers. She asked Frl. Kost how they spent the time together when not actually in bed, for the Japanese can speak hardly any German.

"Oh, well," said Frl. Kost, "we play the gramophone together, you know, and eat chocolates, and then we laugh a lot. He's very fond of laughing. . . ."

Frl. Schroeder really quite likes Frl. Kost and certainly hasn't any moral objections to her trade: nevertheless, when she is angry because Frl. Kost has broken the spout of the teapot or omitted to make crosses for her telephone-calls on the slate in the living-room, then invariably she exclaims:

"But after all, what else can you expect from a woman of that sort, a common prostitute! Why, Herr Issyvoo, do you know what she used to be? A servant girl! And then she got to be on intimate terms with her employer and one fine day, of course, she found herself in certain circumstances. . . . And when that little difficulty was removed, she had to go trot-trot. . . ."

Frl. Mayr is a music-hall *jodlerin*—one of the best, so Frl. Schroeder reverently assures me, in the whole of Germany. Frl. Schroeder doesn't altogether like Frl. Mayr, but she stands in great awe of her; as well she may. Frl. Mayr has a bull-dog jaw, enormous arms and coarse string-coloured hair. She speaks a Bavarian dialect with peculiarly aggressive emphasis. When at home, she sits up like a war-horse at the living-room table, helping Frl. Schroeder to lay cards. They are both adept fortune-tellers and neither would dream of beginning the day without consulting the omens. The chief thing they both want to know at present is: when will Frl. Mayr get another engagement? This question interests Frl. Schroeder quite as much as Frl. Mayr, because Frl. Mayr is behind-hand with the rent.

At the corner of the Motzstrasse, when the weather is fine, there stands a shabby pop-eyed man beside a portable canvas booth. On the sides of the booth are pinned astrological diagrams and autographed letters of recommendation from satisfied clients. Frl. Schroeder goes to consult him whenever she can afford the mark for his fee. In fact, he plays a most important part in her life. Her behaviour towards him is a mixture of cajolery and threats. If the good things he promises her come true she will kiss him, she says, invite him to dinner, buy him a gold watch: if they don't, she will throttle him, box his ears, report him to the police. Among other prophecies, the astrologer has told her that she will win some money in the Prussian State Lottery. So far, she has had no luck. But she is always discussing what she will do with her winnings. We are all to have presents, of course. I am to get a hat, because Frl. Schroeder thinks it very improper that a gentleman of my education should go about without one.

When not engaged in laying cards, Frl. Mayr drinks tea and lectures Frl. Schroeder on her past theatrical triumphs:

"And the Manager said to me: 'Fritzi, Heaven must have sent you here! My leading lady's fallen ill. You're to leave for Copenhagen to-night.' And what's more, he wouldn't take no for an answer. 'Fritzi,' he said (he always called me that), 'Fritzi, you aren't going to let an old friend down?' And so I went. . . ." Frl. Mayr sips her tea reminiscently: "A charming man. And so well-bred." She smiles: "Familiar . . . but he always knew how to behave himself."

Frl. Schroeder nods eagerly, drinking in every word, revelling in it:

"I suppose some of those managers must be cheeky devils? (Have some more sausage, Frl. Mayr?)"

"(Thank you, Frl. Schroeder; just a little morsel.) Yes, some of them . . . you wouldn't believe! But I could always take care of myself. Even when I was quite a slip of a girl. . . ."

The muscles of Frl. Mayr's nude fleshy arms ripple unappetisingly. She sticks out her chin:

"I'm a Bavarian; and a Bavarian never forgets an injury."

Coming into the living-room yesterday evening, I found Frl. Schroeder and Frl. Mayr lying flat on their stomachs with their ears pressed to the carpet. At intervals, they exchanged grins of delight or joyfully pinched each other, with simultaneous exclamations of *Ssh!*

"Hark!" whispered Frl. Schroeder, "he's smashing all the furniture!"

"He's beating her black and blue!" exclaimed Fr. Mayr, in raptures.

"Bang! Just listen to that!"

"Ssh! Ssh!"

"Ssh!"

Frl. Schroeder was quite beside herself. When I asked what was the matter, she clambered to her feet, waddled forward and, taking me round the waist, danced a little waltz with me: "Herr Issyvoo! Herr Issyvoo! Herr Issyvoo!" until she was breathless.

"But whatever has happened?" I asked.

"Ssh!" commanded Frl. Mayr from the floor. "Ssh! They've started again!"

In the flat directly beneath ours lives a certain Frau Glanterneck. She is a Galician Jewess, in itself a reason why Frl. Mayr should be her enemy: for Frl. Mayr, needless to say, is an ardent Nazi. And, quite apart from this, it seems that Frau Glanterneck and Frl. Mayr once had words on the stairs about Frl. Mayr's yodelling. Frau Glanterneck, perhaps because she is a non-Aryan, said that she preferred the noises made by cats. Thereby, she insulted not merely Frl. Mayr, but all Bavarian, all German women: and it was Frl. Mayr's pleasant duty to avenge them.

About a fortnight ago, it became known among the neighbours that Frau Glanterneck, who is sixty years old and as ugly as a witch, had been advertising in the newspaper for a husband. What was more, an applicant had already appeared: a widowed butcher from Halle. He had seen Frau Glanterneck and was nevertheless prepared to marry her. Here was Frl. Mayr's chance. By roundabout inquiries, she discovered the butcher's name and address and wrote him an anonymous letter. Was he aware that Frau Glanterneck had (*a*) bugs in her flat, (*b*) been arrested for fraud and released on the ground that she was insane, (*c*) leased out her own bedroom for immoral purposes, and (*d*) slept in the bed afterwards without changing the sheets? And now the butcher had arrived to confront Frau Glanterneck with the letter.

One could hear both of them quite distinctly: the growling of the enraged Prussian and the shrill screaming of the Jewess. Now and then came the thud of a fist against wood and, occasionally, the crash of glass. The row lasted over an hour.

This morning we hear that the neighbours have complained to the portress of the disturbance and that Frau Glanterneck is to be seen with a black eye. The marriage is off.

The inhabitants of this street know me by sight already. At the grocer's, people no longer turn their heads on hearing my English accent as I order a pound of butter. At the street corner, after dark, the three whores no longer whisper throatily: "Komm, Süsser!" as I pass.

The three whores are all plainly over fifty years old. They do not attempt to conceal their age. They are not noticeably rouged or powdered. They wear baggy old fur coats and longish skirts and matronly hats. I happened to mention them to Bobby and he explained to me that there is a recognized demand for the comfortable type of woman. Many middle-aged men prefer them to girls. They even attract boys in their 'teens. A boy, explained Bobby, feels shy with a girl of his own age but not with a woman old enough to be his mother. Like most barmen, Bobby is a great expert on sexual questions.

The other evening, I went to call on him during business hours.

It was still very early, about nine o'clock, when I arrived at the Troika. The place was much larger and grander than I had expected. A commissionaire braided like an archduke regarded my hatless head with suspicion until I spoke to him in English. A smart cloak-room girl insisted on taking my overcoat, which hides the worst stains on my baggy flannel trousers. A page-boy, seated on the counter, didn't rise to open the inner door. Bobby, to my relief, was at his place behind a blue and silver bar. I made towards him as towards an old friend. He greeted me most amiably:

"Good evening, Mr. Isherwood. Very glad to see you here."

I ordered a beer and settled myself on a stool in the corner. With my back to the wall, I could survey the whole room.

"How's business?" I asked.

Bobby's care-worn, powdered, night-dweller's face became grave.

He inclined his head towards me, over the bar, with confidential flattering seriousness:

"Not much good, Mr. Isherwood. The kind of public we have nowadays . . . you wouldn't believe it! Why, a year ago, we'd have turned them away at the door. They order a beer and think they've got the right to sit here the whole evening."

Bobby spoke with extreme bitterness. I began to feel uncomfortable:

"What'll you drink?" I asked, guiltily gulping down my beer; and added, lest there should be any misunderstanding: "I'd like a whisky and soda."

Bobby said he'd have one, too.

The room was nearly empty. I looked the few guests over, trying to see them through Bobby's disillusioned eyes. There were three attractive, well-dressed girls sitting at the bar: the one nearest to me was particularly elegant, she had quite a cosmopolitan air. But during a lull in the conversation, I caught fragments of her talk with the other barman. She spoke broad Berlin dialect. She was tired and bored; her mouth dropped. A young man approached her and joined in the discussion; a handsome broad-shouldered boy in a well-cut dinner-jacket, who might well have been an English public-school prefect on holiday.

"*Nee, nee*," I heard him say. "*Bei mir nicht!*" He grinned and made a curt, brutal gesture of the streets.

Over in the corner sat a page-boy, talking to the little old lavatory attendant in his white jacket. The boy said something, laughed and broke off suddenly into a huge yawn. The three musicians on their platform were chatting, evidently unwilling to begin until they had an audience worth playing to. At one of the tables, I thought I saw a genuine guest, a stout man with a moustache. After a moment, however, I caught his eye, he made me a little bow and I knew that he must be the manager.

The door opened. Two men and two women came in. The women were elderly, had thick legs, cropped hair and costly evening-gowns. The men were lethargic, pale, probably Dutch. Here, unmistakably, was Money. In an instant, the Troika was transformed. The manager, the cigarette-boy and the lavatory attendant rose simultaneously to their feet. The lavatory attendant disappeared. The manager said something in a furious undertone to the cigarette-boy, who also disappeared. He then advanced, bowing and smiling, to the guests' table and shook hands with the two men. The cigarette-boy reappeared with his tray, followed by a waiter who hurried forward with the wine-list. Meanwhile, the three-man orchestra struck up briskly. The girls at the bar turned on their stools, smiling a not-too-direct invitation. The gigolos advanced to them as if to complete strangers, bowed formally and asked, in cultured tones, for the pleasure of a dance. The page-boy, spruce, discreetly grinning, swaying from the waist like a flower, crossed the room with his tray of cigarettes: *"Zigarren! Zigaretten!"* His voice was mocking, clear-pitched like an actor's. And in the same tone, yet more loudly, mockingly, joyfully, so that we could all hear, the waiter ordered from Bobby: "Heidsick Monopol!"

With absurd, solicitous gravity, the dancers performed their intricate evolutions, showing in their every movement a consciousness of the part they were playing. And the saxophonist, letting his instrument swing loose from the ribbon around his neck, advanced to the edge of the platform with his little megaphone:

> *Sie werden lachen,*
> *Ich lieb'*
> *Meine eigene Frau. . . .*

He sang with a knowing leer, including us all in the conspiracy, charging his voice with innuendo, rolling his eyes in an epileptic pantomime of extreme joy. Bobby, suave, sleek, five years younger, handled the bottle. And meanwhile the two flaccid gentlemen chatted to each other, probably about business, without a glance at the nightlife they had called into being; while their women sat silent, looking neglected, puzzled, uncomfortable and very bored.

Frl. Hippi Bernstein, my first pupil, lives in the Grünewald, in a house built almost entirely of glass. Most of the richest Berlin families inhabit the Grünewald. It is difficult to understand why. Their villas, in all known styles of expensive ugliness, ranging from the eccentric-rococo folly to the cubist flat-roofed steel-and-glass box, are crowded together in this dank, dreary pinewood. Few of them can afford large gardens, for the ground is fabulously dear: their only view is of their neighbour's back-yard, each one protected by a wire fence and a savage dog. Terror of burglary and revolution has reduced these miserable people to a state of siege. They have neither privacy nor sunshine. The district is really a millionaire's slum.

When I rang the bell at the garden gate, a young footman came out with a key from the house, followed by a large growling Alsatian.

"He won't bite you while I'm here," the footman reassured me, grinning.

The hall of the Bernsteins' house has metal-studded doors and a steamer clock fasted to the wall with bolt-heads. There are modernist lamps, designed to look like pressure-gauges, thermometers and switch-board dials. But the furniture doesn't match the house and its fittings. The place is like a power-station which the engineers have tried to make comfortable with chairs and tables from an old-fashioned, highly respectable boarding-house. On the austere metal walls hang highly varnished nineteenth-century landscapes in massive gold frames. Herr Bernstein probably ordered the villa from a popular *avant-garde* architect in a moment of recklessness; was horrified at the result and tried to cover it up as much as possible with the family belongings.

Frl. Hippi is a fat pretty girl, about nineteen years old, with glossy chestnut hair, good teeth and big cow-eyes. She has a lazy, jolly, self-indulgent laugh and a well-formed bust. She speaks schoolgirl English with a slight American accent, quite nicely, to her own complete satisfaction. She has clearly no intention of doing any work. When I tried weakly to suggest a plan for our lessons, she kept interrupting to offer me chocolates, coffee, cigarettes: "Excuse me a minute, there isn't some fruit," she smiled, picking up the receiver of the house-telephone: "Anna, please bring some oranges."

When the maid arrived with the oranges, I was forced, despite my protests, to make a regular meal, with a plate, knife and fork. This destroyed the last pretence of the teacher-pupil relationship. I felt like a policeman being given a meal in the kitchen by an attractive cook. Frl. Hippi sat watching me eat, with her good-natured, lazy smile:

"Tell me, please, why you come to Germany?"

She is inquisitive about me, but only like a cow idly poking with its head between the bars of a gate. She doesn't particularly want the gate to open. I said that I found Germany very interesting:

"The political and economic situation," I improvised authoritatively, in my schoolmaster voice, "is more interesting in Germany than in any other European country."

"Except Russia, of course," I added experimentally.

But Frl. Hippi didn't react. She just blandly smiled:

"I think it shall be dull for you here? You do not have many friends in Berlin, no?"

"No. Not many."

This seemed to please and amuse her:

"You don't know some nice girls?"

Here the buzzer of the house-telephone sounded. Lazily smiling, she picked up the receiver, but appeared not to listen to the tinny voice which issued from it. I could hear quite distinctly the real voice of Frau Bernstein, Hippi's mother, speaking from the next room.

"Have you left your *red* book in here?" repeated Frl. Hippi mockingly and smiling at me as though this were a joke which I must share: "No, I don't see it. It must be down in the study. Ring up Daddy. Yes, he's working there." In dumb show, she offered me another orange. I shook my head politely. We both smiled: "Mummy, what have we got for lunch to-day? Yes? Really? Splendid!"

She hung up the receiver and returned to her cross-examination:

"Do you not know no nice girls?"

"*Any* nice girls. . . ." I corrected evasively. But Frl. Hippi merely smiled, waiting for the answer to her question.

"Yes. One," I had at length to add, thinking of Frl. Kost.

"Only one?" She raised her eyebrows in comic surprise. "And tell me, please, do you find German girls different than English girls?"

I blushed. "Do you find German girls . . ." I began to correct her and stopped, realizing just in time that I wasn't absolutely sure whether one says *different from* or *different to*.

"Do you find German girls different than English girls?" she repeated, with smiling persistence.

I blushed deeper than ever. "Yes. Very different," I said boldly.

"How are they different?"

Mercifully the telephone buzzed again. This was somebody from the kitchen, to say that lunch would be an hour earlier than usual. Herr Bernstein was going to the city that afternoon.

"I am so sorry," said Frl. Hippi, rising, "but for to-day we must finish. And we shall see us again on Friday? Then goodbye, Mr. Isherwood. And I thank you very much."

She fished in her bag and handed me an envelope which I stuck awkwardly into my pocket and tore open only when I was out of sight of the Bernsteins' house. It contained a five-mark piece. I threw it into the air, missed it, found it after five minutes' hunt, buried in sand, and ran all the way to the tram-stop, singing and kicking stones about the road. I felt extraordinarily guilty and elated, as though I'd successfully committed a small theft.

It is a mere waste of time even pretending to teach Frl. Hippi anything. If she doesn't know a word, she says it in German. If I correct her, she repeats it in German. I am glad, of course, that she's so lazy and only afraid that Frau Bernstein may discover how little progress her daughter is making. But this is very unlikely. Most rich people, once they have decided to trust you at all, can be imposed upon to almost any extent. The only real problem for the private tutor is to get inside the front-door.

As for Hippi, she seems to enjoy my visits. From something she said the other day, I gather she boasts to her school friends that she has got a genuine English teacher. We understand each other very well. I am bribed with fruit not to be tiresome about the English language: she, for her part, tells her parents that I am the best teacher she ever had. We gossip in German about the things which interest her. And every three or four minutes, we are interrupted while she plays her part in the family game of exchanging entirely unimportant messages over the house-telephone.

Hippi never worries about the future. Like everyone else in Berlin, she refers continually to the political situation, but only briefly, with a conventional melancholy, as when one speaks of religion. It is quite unreal to her. She means to go to the university, travel about, have a jolly good time and eventually, of course, marry. She already has a great many boy friends. We spend a lot of time talking about them.

One has a wonderful car. Another has an aeroplane. Another has fought seven duels. Another has discovered a knack of putting out street-lamps by giving them a smart kick in a certain spot. One night, on the way back from a dance, Hippi and he put out all the street-lamps in the neighbourhood.

To-day, lunch was early at the Bernsteins'; so I was invited to it, instead of giving my "lesson." The whole family was present: Frau Bernstein, stout and placid; Herr Bernstein, small and shaky and sly. There was also a younger sister, a school-girl of twelve, very fat. She ate and ate, quite unmoved by Hippi's jokes and warnings that she'd burst. They all seem very fond of each other, in their cosy, stuffy way. There was a little domestic argument, because Herr Bernstein didn't want his wife to go shopping in the car that afternoon. During the last few days, there has been a lot of Nazi rioting in the city.

"You can go in the tram," said Herr Bernstein. "I will not have them throwing stones at my beautiful car."

"And suppose they throw stones at me?" asked Frau Bernstein good-humouredly.

"Ach, what does that matter? If they throw stones at you, I will buy you a sticking-plaster for your head. It will cost me only five groschen. But if they throw stones at my car, it will cost me perhaps five hundred marks."

And so the matter was settled. Herr Bernstein then turned his attention to me:

"You can't complain that we treat you badly here, young man, eh? Not only do we give you a nice dinner, but we pay for you eating it!"

I saw from Hippi's expression that this was going a bit far, even for the Bernstein sense of humour; so I laughed and said:

"Will you pay me a mark extra for every helping I eat?"

This amused Herr Bernstein very much; but he was careful to show that he knew I hadn't meant it seriously.

During the last week, our household has been plunged into a terrific row.

It began when Frl. Kost came to Frl. Schroeder and announced that fifty marks had been stolen from her room. She was very much upset; especially, she explained, as this was the money she'd put aside towards the rent and the telephone bill. The fifty-mark note had been lying in the drawer of the cupboard, just inside the door of Frl. Kost's room.

Frl. Schroeder's immediate suggestion was, not unnaturally, that the money had been stolen by one of Frl. Kost's customers. Frl. Kost said that this was quite impossible, as none of them had visited her during the last three days. Moreover, she added, *her* friends were all absolutely above suspicion. They were well-to-do gentlemen, to whom a miserable fifty-mark note was a mere bagatelle. This annoyed Frl. Schroeder very much indeed:

"I suppose she's trying to make out that one of *us* did it! Of all the cheek! Why, Herr Issyvoo, will you believe me, I could have chopped her into little pieces!"

"Yes, Frl. Schroeder. I'm sure you could."

Frl. Schroeder then developed the theory that the money hadn't been stolen at all and that this was just a trick of Frl. Kost's to avoid paying the rent. She hinted so much to Frl. Kost, who was furious. Frl. Kost said that, in any case, she'd raise the money in a few days: which she already has. She also gave notice to leave her room at the end of the month.

Meanwhile, I have discovered, quite by accident, that Frl. Kost has been having an affair with Bobby. As I came in, one evening, I happened to notice that there was no light in Frl. Kost's room. You can always see this, because there is a frosted glass pane in her door to light the hall of the flat. Later, as I lay in bed reading, I heard Frl. Kost's door open and Bobby's voice, laughing and whispering. After much creaking of boards and muffled laughter, Bobby tiptoed out of the flat, shutting the door as quietly as possible behind him. A moment later, he re-entered with a great deal of noise and went straight through into the living-room, where I heard him wishing Frl. Schroeder good-night.

If Frl. Schroeder doesn't actually know of this, she at least suspects it. This explains her fury against Frl. Kost: for the truth is, she is terribly jealous. The most grotesque and embarrassing incidents have been taking place. One morning, when I wanted to visit the bathroom,

Frl. Kost was using it already. Frl. Schroeder rushed to the door before I could stop her and ordered Frl. Kost to come out at once: and when Frl. Kost naturally didn't obey, Frl. Schroeder began, despite my protests, hammering on the door with her fists. "Come out of my bathroom!" she screamed. "Come out this minute, or I'll call the police to fetch you out!"

After this she burst into tears. The crying brought on palpitations. Bobby had to carry her to the sofa, gasping and sobbing. While we were all standing round, rather helpless, Frl. Mayr appeared in the doorway with a face like a hangman and said, in a terrible voice, to Frl. Kost: "Think yourself lucky, my girl, if you haven't murdered her!" She then took complete charge of the situation, ordered us all out of the room and sent me down to the grocer's for a bottle of Baldrian Drops. When I returned, she was seated beside the sofa, stroking Frl. Schroeder's hand and murmuring, in her most tragic tones: "Lina, my poor little child . . . what have they done to you?"

Sally Bowles

ONE AFTERNOON, early in October, I was invited to black coffee at Fritz Wendel's flat. Fritz always invited you to "black coffee," with emphasis on the black. He was very proud of his coffee. People used to say that it was the strongest in Berlin.

Fritz himself was dressed in his usual coffee-party costume—a very thick white yachting sweater and very light blue flannel trousers. He greeted me with his full-lipped, luscious smile:

" 'lo, Chris!"

"Hullo, Fritz. How are you?"

"Fine." He bent over the coffee-machine, his sleek black hair unplastering itself from his scalp and falling in richly scented locks over his eyes. "This darn thing doesn't go," he added.

"How's business?" I asked.

"Lousy and terrible." Fritz grinned richly. "Or I pull off a new deal in the next month or I go as a gigolo."

"*Either* . . . or . . .," I corrected, from force of professional habit.

"I'm speaking a lousy English just now," drawled Fritz, with great self-satisfaction. "Sally says maybe she'll give me a few lessons."

"Who's Sally?"

"Why, I forgot. You don't know Sally. Too bad of me. Eventually she's coming around here this afternoon."

"Is she nice?"

Fritz rolled his naughty black eyes, handing me a rum-moistened cigarette from his patent tin:

"*Mar*-vellous!" he drawled. "Eventually I believe I'm getting crazy about her."

"And who is she? What does she do?"

"She's an English girl, an actress: sings at the Lady Windermere— hot stuff, believe me!"

"That doesn't sound much like an English girl, I must say."

"Eventually she's got a bit of French in her. Her mother was French."

A few minutes later, Sally herself arrived.

"Am I terribly late, Fritz darling?"

"Only half of an hour, I suppose," Fritz drawled, beaming with proprietary pleasure. "May I introduce Mr. Isherwood—Miss Bowles? Mr. Isherwood is commonly known as Chris."

"I'm not," I said. "Fritz is about the only person who's ever called me Chris in my life."

Sally laughed. She was dressed in black silk, with a small cape over her shoulders and a little cap like a page-boy's stuck jauntily on one side of her head:

"Do you mind if I use your telephone, sweet?"

"Sure. Go right ahead." Fritz caught my eye. "Come into the other room, Chris. I want to show you something." He was evidently longing to hear my first impressions of Sally, his new acquisition.

"For heaven's sake, don't leave me alone with this man!" she exclaimed. "Or he'll seduce me down the telephone. He's most terribly passionate."

As she dialled the number, I noticed that her finger-nails were painted emerald green, a colour unfortunately chosen, for it called attention to her hands, which were much stained by cigarette-smoking and as dirty as a little girl's. She was dark enough to be Fritz's sister. Her face was long and thin, powdered dead white. She had very large brown eyes which should have been darker, to match her hair and the pencil she used for her eyebrows.

"Hilloo," she cooed, pursing her brilliant cherry lips as though

she were going to kiss the mouthpiece: "Ist dass Du, mein Liebling?"
Her mouth opened in a fatuously sweet smile. Fritz and I sat watching
her, like a performance at the theatre. "Was wollen wir machen,
Morgen Abend? Oh, wie wunderbar. . . . Nein, nein, ich werde
bleiben Heute Abend zu Hause. Ja, ja, ich werde wirklich bleiben zu
Hause. . . . Auf Wiedersehen, mein Liebling . . ."

She hung up the receiver and turned to us triumphantly.

"That's the man I slept with last night," she announced. "He
makes love marvellously. He's an absolute genius at business and he's
terribly rich—" She came and sat down on the sofa beside Fritz, sinking
back into the cushions with a sigh: "Give me some coffee, will you,
darling? I'm simply dying of thirst."

And soon we were on to Fritz's favourite topic: he pronounced
it Larv.

"On the average," he told us, "I'm having a big affair every two
years."

"And how long is it since you had your last?" Sally asked.

"Exactly one year and eleven months!" Fritz gave her his naugh-
tiest glance.

"How marvellous!" Sally puckered up her nose and laughed a
silvery little stage-laugh: "*Doo* tell me—what was the last one like?"

This, of course, started Fritz off on a complete autobiography.
We had the story of his seduction in Paris, details of a holiday flirtation
at Las Palmas, the four chief New York romances, a disappointment
in Chicago and a conquest in Boston; then back to Paris for a little
recreation, a very beautiful episode in Vienna, to London to be consoled and, finally, Berlin.

"You know, Fritz darling," said Sally, puckering up her nose at
me, "*I* believe the trouble with you is that you've never really found
the right woman."

"Maybe that's true—" Fritz took this idea very seriously. His black
eyes became liquid and sentimental: "Maybe I'm still looking for my
ideal. . . ."

"But you'll find her one day, I'm absolutely certain you will."
Sally included me, with a glance, in the game of laughing at Fritz.

"You think so?" Fritz grinned lusciously, sparkling at her.

"Don't *you* think so?" Sally appealed to me.

"I'm sure I don't know," I said. "Because I've never been able to discover what Fritz's ideal is."

For some reason, this seemed to please Fritz. He took it as a kind of testimonial: "And Chris knows me pretty well," he chimed in. "If Chris doesn't know, well, I guess no one does."

Then it was time for Sally to go.

"I'm supposed to meet a man at the Adlon at five," she explained. "And it's six already! Never mind, it'll do the old swine good to wait. He wants me to be his mistress, but I've told him I'm damned if I will till he's paid all my debts. Why are men always such beasts?" Opening her bag, she rapidly retouched her lips and eyebrows: "Oh, by the way, Fritz darling, could you be a perfect angel and lend me ten marks? I haven't got a bean for a taxi."

"Why sure!" Fritz put his hand into his pocket and paid up without hesitation, like a hero.

Sally turned to me: "I say, will you come and have tea with me sometime? Give me your telephone number. I'll ring you up."

I suppose, I thought, she imagines I've got cash. Well, this will be a lesson to her, once for all. I wrote my number in her tiny leather book. Fritz saw her out.

"Well!" he came bounding back into the room and gleefully shut the door: "What do you think of her, Chris? Didn't I tell you she was a good-looker?"

"You did indeed!"

"I'm getting crazier about her each time I see her!" With a sigh of pleasure, he helped himself to a cigarette: "More coffee, Chris?"

"No, thank you very much."

"You know, Chris, I think she took a fancy to you, too!"

"Oh, rot!"

"Honestly, I do!" Fritz seemed pleased. "Eventually I guess we'll be seeing a lot of her from now on!"

When I got back to Frl. Schroeder's, I felt so giddy that I had to lie down for half an hour on my bed. Fritz's black coffee was as poisonous as ever.

.   .   .

A few days later, he took me to hear Sally sing.

The Lady Windermere (which now, I hear, no longer exists) was an arty "informal" bar, just off the Tauentzienstrasse, which the proprietor had evidently tried to make look as much as possible like Montparnasse. The walls were covered with sketches on menu-cards, caricatures and signed theatrical photographs—("To the one and only Lady Windermere." "To Johnny, with all my heart.") The Fan itself, four times life size, was displayed above the bar. There was a big piano on a platform in the middle of the room.

I was curious to see how Sally would behave. I had imagined her, for some reason, rather nervous, but she wasn't, in the least. She had a surprisingly deep husky voice. She sang badly, without any expression, her hands hanging down at her sides—yet her performance was, in its own way, effective because of her startling appearance and her air of not caring a curse what people thought of her. Her arms hanging carelessly limp, and a take-it-or-leave-it grin on her face, she sang:

> *Now I know why Mother*
> *Told me to be true;*
> *She meant me for Someone*
> *Exactly like you.*

There was quite a lot of applause. The pianist, a handsome young man with blond wavy hair, stood up and solemnly kissed Sally's hand. Then she sang two more songs, one in French and the other in German. These weren't so well received.

After the singing, there was a good deal more hand-kissing and a general movement towards the bar. Sally seemed to know everybody in the place. She called them all Thou and Darling. For a would-be demi-mondaine, she seemed to have surprisingly little business sense or tact. She wasted a lot of time making advances to an elderly gentleman who would obviously have preferred a chat with the barman. Later, we all got rather drunk. Then Sally had to go off to an appointment, and the manager came and sat at our table. He and Fritz;

talked English Peerage. Fritz was in his element. I decided, as so often before, never to visit a place of this sort again.

Then Sally rang up, as she had promised, to invite me to tea.

She lived a long way down the Kurfürstendamm on the last dreary stretch which rises to Halensee. I was shown into a big gloomy half-furnished room by a fat untidy landlady with a pouchy sagging jowl like a toad. There was a broken-down sofa in one corner and a faded picture of an eighteenth-century battle, with the wounded reclining on their elbows in graceful attitudes, admiring the prancings of Frederick the Great's horse.

"Oh, hullo, Chris darling!" cried Sally from the doorway. "How sweet of you to come! I was feeling most terribly lonely. I've been crying on Frau Karpf's chest. Nicht wahr, Frau Karpf?" She appealed to the toad landlady, "ich habe geweint auf Dein Brust." Frau Karpf shook her bosom in a toad-like chuckle.

"Would you rather have coffee, Chris, or tea?" Sally continued. "You can have either. Only I don't recommend the tea much. I don't know what Frau Karpf does to it; I think she empties all the kitchen slops together into a jug and boils them up with the tea-leaves."

"I'll have coffee, then."

"Frau Karpf, Leibling, willst Du sein ein Engel und bring zwei Tassen von Kaffee?" Sally's German was not merely incorrect; it was all her own. She pronounced every word in a mincing, specially "foreign" manner. You could tell that she was speaking a foreign language from her expression alone. "Chris darling, will you be an angel and draw the curtains?"

I did so, although it was still quite light outside. Sally, meanwhile, had switched on the table-lamp. As I turned from the window, she curled herself up delicately on the sofa like a cat, and, opening her bag, felt for a cigarette. But hardly was the pose complete before she'd jumped to her feet again:

"Would you like a Prairie Oyster?" She produced glasses, eggs and a bottle of Worcester sauce from the boot-cupboard under the dismantled washstand: "I practically live on them." Dexterously, she broke the eggs into the glasses, added the sauce and stirred up the mixture with the end of a fountain-pen: "They're about all I can afford." She was back on the sofa again, daintily curled up.

She was wearing the same black dress to-day, but without the cape. Instead, she had a little white collar and white cuffs. They produced a kind of theatrically chaste effect, like a nun in grand opera. "What are you laughing at, Chris?" she asked.

"I don't know," I said. But still I couldn't stop grinning. There was, at that moment, something so extraordinarily comic in Sally's appearance. She was really beautiful, with her little dark head, big eyes and finely arched nose—and so absurdly conscious of all these features. There she lay, as complacently feminine as a turtle-dove, with her poised self-conscious head and daintily arranged hands.

"Chris, you swine, do tell me why you're laughing?"

"I really haven't the faintest idea."

At this, she began to laugh, too: "You are mad, you know!"

"Have you been here long?" I asked, looking round the large gloomy room.

"Ever since I arrived in Berlin. Let's see—that was about two months ago."

I asked what had made her decide to come out to Germany at all. Had she come alone? No, she'd come with a girl friend. An actress. Older than Sally. The girl had been to Berlin before. She'd told Sally that they'd certainly be able to get work with the Ufa. So Sally borrowed ten pounds from a nice old gentleman and joined her.

She hadn't told her parents anything about it until the two of them had actually arrived in Germany: "I wish you'd met Diana. She was the most marvellous gold-digger you can imagine. She'd get hold of men anywhere—it didn't matter whether she could speak their language or not. She made me nearly die of laughing. I absolutely adored her."

But when they'd been together in Berlin three weeks and no job had appeared, Diana had got hold of a banker, who'd taken her off with him to Paris.

"And left you here alone? I must say I think that was pretty rotten of her."

"Oh, I don't know. . . . Everyone's got to look after themselves. I expect, in her place, I'd have done the same."

"I bet you wouldn't!"

"Anyhow, I'm all right. I can always get along alone."

"How old are you, Sally?"

"Nineteen."

"Good God! And I thought you were about twenty-five!"

"I know. Everyone does."

Frau Karpf came shuffling in with two cups of coffee on a tarnished metal tray.

"Oh, Frau Karpf, Leibling, wie wunderbar von Dich!"

"Whatever makes you stay in this house?" I asked, when the landlady had gone out: "I'm sure you could get a much nicer room than this."

"Yes, I know I could."

"Well then, why don't you?"

"Oh, I don't know. I'm lazy, I suppose."

"What do you have to pay here?"

"Eighty marks a month."

"With breakfast included?"

"No—I don't think so."

"You don't *think* so?" I exclaimed severely. "But surely you must know for certain?"

Sally took this meekly: "Yes, it's stupid of me, I suppose. But, you see, I just give the old girl money when I've got some. So it's rather difficult to reckon it all up exactly."

"But, good heavens, Sally—I only pay fifty a month for my room, with breakfast, and it's ever so much nicer than this one!"

Sally nodded, but continued apologetically: "And another thing is, you see, Christopher darling, I don't quite know what Frau Karpf would do if I were to leave her. I'm sure she'd never get another lodger. Nobody else would be able to stand her face and her smell and everything. As it is, she owes three months' rent. They'd turn her out at once if they knew she hadn't any lodgers: and if they do that, she says she'll commit suicide."

"All the same, I don't see why you should sacrifice yourself for her."

"I'm not sacrificing myself, really. I quite like being here, you know. Frau Karpf and I understand each other. She's more or less what I'll be in thirty years' time. A respectable sort of landlady would probably turn me out after a week."

"My landlady wouldn't turn you out."

Sally smiled vaguely, screwing up her nose: "How do you like the coffee, Chris darling?"

"I prefer it to Fritz's," I said evasively.

Sally laughed: "Isn't Fritz marvellous? I adore him. I adore the way he says, 'I give a damn.' "

" 'Hell, I give a damn.' " I tried to imitate Fritz. We both laughed. Sally lit another cigarette: she smoked the whole time. I noticed how old her hands looked in the lamplight. They were nervous, veined and very thin—the hands of a middle-aged woman. The green finger-nails seemed not to belong to them at all; to have settled on them by chance—like hard, bright, ugly little beetles. "It's a funny thing," she added meditatively, "Fritz and I have never slept together, you know." She paused, asked with interest: "Did you think we had?"

"Well, yes—I suppose I did."

"We haven't. Not once . . ." she yawned. "And now I don't suppose we ever shall."

We smoked for some minutes in silence. Then Sally began to tell me about her family. She was the daughter of a Lancashire mill-owner. Her mother was a Miss Bowles, an heiress with an estate, and so, when she and Mr. Jackson were married, they joined their names together: "Daddy's a terrible snob, although he pretends not to be. My real name's Jackson-Bowles; but, of course, I can't possibly call myself that on the stage. People would think I was crazy."

"I thought Fritz told me your mother was French?"

"No, of course not!" Sally seemed quite annoyed. "Fritz is an idiot. He's always inventing things."

Sally had one sister, named Betty. "She's an absolute angel. I adore her. She's seventeen, but she's still most terribly innocent. Mummy's bringing her up to be very county. Betty would nearly die if she knew what an old whore I am. She knows absolutely nothing whatever about men."

"But why aren't you county, too, Sally?"

"I don't know. I suppose that's Daddy's side of the family coming out. You'd love Daddy. He doesn't care a damn for anyone. He's the most marvellous business man. And about once a month he gets absolutely dead tight and horrifies all Mummy's smart friends. It was he who said I could go to London and learn acting."

"You must have left school very young?"

"Yes. I couldn't bear school. I got myself expelled."

"However did you do that?"

"I told the headmistress I was going to have a baby."

"Oh, rot, Sally, you didn't!"

"I did, honestly! There was the most terrible commotion. They got a doctor to examine me, and sent for my parents. When they found out there was nothing the matter, they were most frightfully disappointed. The headmistress said that a girl who could even think of anything so disgusting couldn't possibly be allowed to stay on and corrupt the other girls. So I got my own way. And then I pestered Daddy till he said I might go to London."

Sally had settled down in London, at a hostel, with other girl students. There, in spite of supervision, she had managed to spend large portions of the night at young men's flats: "The first man who seduced me had no idea I was a virgin until I told him afterwards. He was marvellous. I adored him. He was an absolute genius at comedy parts. He's sure to be terribly famous, one day."

After a time, Sally had got crowd-work in films, and finally a small part in a touring company. Then she had met Diana.

"And how much longer shall you stay in Berlin?" I asked.

"Heaven knows. This job at the Lady Windermere only lasts another week. I got it through a man I met at the Eden Bar. But he's gone off to Vienna now. I must ring up the Ufa people again, I suppose. And then there's an awful old Jew who takes me out sometimes. He's always promising to get me a contract; but he only wants to sleep with me, the old swine. I think the men in this country are awful. They've none of them got any money, and they expect you to let them seduce you if they give you a box of chocolates."

"How on earth are you going to manage when this job comes to an end?"

"Oh well, I get a small allowance from home, you know. Not that that'll last much longer. Mummy's already threatened to stop it if I don't come back to England soon. . . . Of course, they think I'm here with a girl friend. If Mummy knew I was on my own, she'd simply pass right out. Anyhow, I'll get enough to support myself somehow, soon. I loathe taking money from them. Daddy's business is in a frightfully bad way now, from the slump."

"I say, Sally—if you ever really get into a mess I wish you'd let me know."

Sally laughed: "That's terribly sweet of you, Chris. But I don't sponge on my friends."

"Isn't Fritz your friend?" It had jumped out of my mouth. But Sally didn't seem to mind a bit.

"Oh yes, I'm awfully fond of Fritz, of course. But he's got pots of cash. Somehow, when people have cash, you feel differently about them—I don't know why."

"And how do you know I haven't got pots of cash, too?"

"You?" Sally burst out laughing. "Why, I knew you were hard-up the first moment I set eyes on you!"

The afternoon Sally came to tea with me, Frl. Schroeder was beside herself with excitement. She put on her best dress for the occasion and waved her hair. When the door-bell rang, she threw open the door with a flourish: "Herr Issyvoo," she announced, winking knowingly at me and speaking very loud, "there's a lady to see you!"

I then formally introduced Sally and Frl. Schroeder to each other. Frl. Schroeder was overflowing with politeness: she addressed Sally repeatedly as "Gnädiges Fräulein." Sally, with her page-boy cap stuck over one ear, laughed her silvery laugh and sat down elegantly on the sofa. Frl. Schroeder hovered about her in unfeigned admiration and amazement. She had evidently never seen anyone like Sally before. When she brought in the tea there were, in place of the usual little chunks of pale unappetising pastry, a plateful of jam tarts arranged in the shape of a star. I noticed also that Frl. Schroeder had provided us with two tiny paper serviettes, perforated at the edges to resemble lace. (When, later, I complimented her on these preparations, she told me that she had always used the serviettes when the Herr Rittmeister had had his fiancée to tea. "Oh, yes, Herr Issyvoo. You can depend on me! I know what pleases a young lady!")

"Do you mind if I lie down on your sofa, darling?" Sally asked, as soon as we were alone.

"No, of course not."

Sally pulled off her cap, swung her little velvet shoes up on to the sofa, opened her bag and began powdering: "I'm most terribly tired. I didn't sleep a wink last night. I've got a marvellous new lover."

I began to put out the tea. Sally gave me a sidelong glance:

"Do I shock you when I talk like that, Christopher darling?"

"Not in the least."

"But you don't like it?"

"It's no business of mine." I handed her the tea-glass.

"Oh, for God's sake," cried Sally, "don't start being English! Of course it's your business what you think!"

"Well then, if you want to know, it rather bores me."

This annoyed her even more than I had intended. Her tone changed: she said coldly: "I thought you'd understand." She sighed: "But I forgot—you're a man."

"I'm sorry, Sally. I can't help being a man, of course. . . . But please don't be angry with me. I only meant that when you talk like that it's really just nervousness. You're naturally rather shy with strangers, I think: so you've got into this trick of trying to bounce them into approving or disapproving of you, violently. I know, because I try it myself, sometimes. . . . Only I wish you wouldn't try it on me, because it just doesn't work and it only makes me feel embarrassed. If you go to bed with every single man in Berlin and come and tell me about it each time, you still won't convince me that you're *La Dame aux Camélias*—because, really and truly, you know, you aren't."

"No . . . I suppose I'm not—" Sally's voice was carefully impersonal. She was beginning to enjoy this conversation. I had succeeded in flattering her in some new way: "Then what *am* I, exactly, Christopher darling?"

"You're the daughter of Mr. and Mrs. Jackson-Bowles."

Sally sipped her tea: "Yes . . . I think I see what you mean. . . . Perhaps you're right. . . . Then you think I ought to give up having lovers altogether?"

"Certainly I don't. As long as you're sure you're really enjoying yourself."

"Of course," said Sally gravely, after a pause, "I'd never let love interfere with my work. Work comes before everything. . . . But I don't believe that a woman can be a great actress who hasn't had any love-affairs—" She broke off suddenly: "What are you laughing at, Chris?"

"I'm not laughing."

"You're always laughing at me. Do you think I'm the most ghastly idiot?"

"No, Sally. I don't think you're an idiot at all. It's quite true, I *was* laughing. People I like often make me want to laugh at them. I don't know why."

"Then you do like me, Christopher darling?"

"Yes, of course I like you, Sally. What did you think?"

"But you're not in love with me, are you?"

"No. I'm not in love with you."

"I'm awfully glad. I've wanted you to like me ever since we first met. But I'm glad you're not in love with me, because, somehow, I couldn't possibly be in love with you—so, if you had been, everything would have been spoilt."

"Well then, that's very lucky, isn't it?"

"Yes, very . . ." Sally hesitated. "There's something I want to confess to you, Chris darling. . . . I'm not sure if you'll understand or not."

"Remember, I'm only a man, Sally."

Sally laughed: "It's the most idiotic little thing. But somehow, I'd hate it if you found out without my telling you. . . . You know, the other day, you said Fritz had told you my mother was French?"

"Yes, I remember."

"And I said he must have invented it? Well, he hadn't. . . . You see, I'd told him she was."

"But why on earth did you do that?"

We both began to laugh. "Goodness knows," said Sally. "I suppose I wanted to impress him."

"But what is there impressive in having a French mother?"

"I'm a bit mad like that sometimes, Chris. You must be patient with me."

"All right, Sally, I'll be patient."

"And you'll swear on your honour not to tell Fritz?"

"I swear."

"If you do, you swine," exclaimed Sally, laughing and picking up the paper-knife dagger from my writing-table, "I'll cut your throat!"

Afterwards, I asked Frl. Schroeder what she'd thought of Sally. She was in raptures: "Like a picture, Herr Issyvoo! And so elegant: such beautiful hands and feet! One can see that she belongs to the very best society. . . . You know, Herr Issyvoo, I should never have expected you to have a lady friend like that! You always seem so quiet. . . ."

"Ah, well, Frl. Schroeder, it's often the quiet ones—"

She went off into her little scream of laughter, swaying backwards and forwards on her short legs:

"Quite right, Herr Issyvoo! Quite right!"

On New Year's Eve, Sally came to live at Frl. Schroeder's.

It had all been arranged at the last moment. Sally, her suspicions sharpened by my repeated warnings, had caught out Frau Karpf in a particularly gross and clumsy piece of swindling. So she had hardened her heart and given notice. She was to have Frl. Kost's old room. Frl. Schroeder was, of course, enchanted.

We all had our Sylvester Abend dinner at home: Frl. Schroeder, Frl. Mayr, Sally, Bobby, a mixer colleague from the Troika and myself. It was a great success. Bobby, already restored to favour, flirted daringly with Frl. Schroeder. Frl. Mayr and Sally, talking as one great artiste to another, discussed the possibilities of music-hall work in England. Sally told some really startling lies, which she obviously for the moment half-believed, about how she'd appeared at the Palladium and the London Coliseum. Frl. Mayr capped them with a story of how she'd been drawn through the streets of Munich in a carriage by excited students. From this point it did not take Sally long to persuade Frl. Mayr to sing *Sennerin Abschied von der Alm*, which, after claret cup and a bottle of very inexpensive cognac, so exactly suited my mood that I shed a few tears. We all joined in the repeats and the final, ear-splitting *Fuch-he!* Then Sally sang "I've got those Little Boy Blues" with so much expression that Bobby's mixer colleague, taking it personally, seized her round the waist and had to be restrained by Bobby, who reminded him firmly that it was time to be getting along to business.

Sally and I went with them to the Troika, where we met Fritz. With him was Klaus Linke, the young pianist who used to accompany Sally when she sang at the Lady Windermere. Later, Fritz and I went off alone. Fritz seemed rather depressed: he wouldn't tell me why. Some girls did classical figure-tableaux behind gauze. And then there was a big dancing-hall with telephones on the tables. We had the usual kind of conversations: "Pardon me, Madame, I feel sure from your voice that you're a fascinating little blonde with long black eye-lashes—just my type. How did I know? Aha, that's my secret! Yes—quite right: I'm tall, dark, broad-shouldered, military appearance, and the tiniest little moustache. . . . You don't believe me? Then come and see for yourself!" The couples were dancing with hands on each other's hips, yelling in each other's faces, streaming with sweat. An orchestra in Bavarian costume whooped and drank and perspired beer. The place stank like a zoo. After this, I think I strayed off alone and wandered for hours and hours through a jungle of paper streamers. Next morning, when I woke, the bed was full of them.

I had been up and dressed for some time when Sally returned home. She came straight into my room, looking tired but very pleased with herself.

"Hullo, darling! What time is it?"

"Nearly lunch-time."

"I say, is it really? How marvellous! I'm practically starving. I've had nothing for breakfast but a cup of coffee. . . ." She paused expectantly, waiting for my next question.

"Where have you been?" I asked.

"But, darling," Sally opened her eyes very wide in affected surprise: "I thought you knew!"

"I haven't the least idea."

"Nonsense!"

"Really I haven't, Sally."

"Oh, Christopher darling, how can you be such a liar! Why, it was obvious that you'd planned the whole thing! The way you got rid of Fritz—he looked so cross! Klaus and I nearly died of laughing."

All the same, she wasn't quite at her ease. For the first time, I saw her blush.

"Have you got a cigarette, Chris?"

I gave her one and lit the match. She blew out a long cloud of smoke and walked slowly to the window:

"I'm most terribly in love with him."

She turned, frowning slightly; crossed to the sofa and curled herself up carefully, arranging her hands and feet: "At least, I think I am," she added.

I allowed a respectful pause to elapse before asking: "And is Klaus in love with you?"

"He absolutely adores me." Sally was very serious indeed. She smoked for several minutes: "He says he fell in love with me the first time we met, at the Lady Windermere. But as long as we were working together, he didn't dare to say anything. He was afraid it might put me off my singing. . . . He says that, before he met me, he'd no idea what a marvellously beautiful thing a woman's body is. He's only had about three women before, in his life . . ."

I lit a cigarette.

"Of course, Chris, I don't suppose you really understand. . . . It's awfully hard to explain. . . ."

"I'm sure it is."

"I'm seeing him again at four o'clock." Sally's tone was slightly defiant.

"In that case, you'd better get some sleep. I'll ask Frl. Schroeder to scramble you some eggs; or I'll do them myself if she's still too drunk. You get into bed. You can eat them there."

"Thanks, Chris darling. You are an angel." Sally yawned. "What on earth I should do without you, I don't know."

After this, Sally and Klaus saw each other every day. They generally met at our house; and, once, Klaus stayed the whole night. Frl. Schroeder didn't say much to me about it, but I could see that she was rather shocked. Not that she disapproved of Klaus: she thought him very attractive. But she regarded Sally as my property, and it shocked her to see me standing so tamely to one side. I am sure, however, that if I hadn't known about the affair, and if Sally had really been deceiving me, Frl. Schroeder would have assisted at the conspiracy with the greatest relish.

Meanwhile, Klaus and I were a little shy of each other. When we happened to meet on the stairs, we bowed coldly, like enemies.

About the middle of January, Klaus left suddenly, for England. Quite unexpectedly he had got the offer of a very good job, synchronizing music for the films. The afternoon he came to say goodbye there was a positively surgical atmosphere in the flat, as though Sally were undergoing a dangerous operation. Frl. Schroeder and Frl. Mayr sat in the living-room and laid cards. The results, Frl. Schroeder later assured me, couldn't have been better. The eight of clubs had appeared three times in a favourable conjunction.

Sally spent the whole of the next day curled up on the sofa in her room, with pencil and paper on her lap. She was writing poems. She wouldn't let me see them. She smoked cigarette after cigarette, and mixed Prairie Oysters, but refused to eat more than a few mouthfuls of Frl. Schroeder's omelette.

"Can't I bring you something in, Sally?"

"No thanks, Chris darling. I just don't want to eat anything at all. I feel all marvellous and ethereal, as if I was a kind of most wonderful saint, or something. You've no idea how glorious it feels. . . . Have a chocolate, darling? Klaus gave me three boxes. If I eat any more, I shall be sick."

"Thank you."

"I don't suppose I shall ever marry him. It would ruin our careers. You see, Christopher, he adores me so terribly that it wouldn't be good for him to always have me hanging about."

"You might marry after you're both famous."

Sally considered this:

"No. . . . That would spoil everything. We should be trying all the time to live up to our old selves, if you know what I mean. And we should both be different. . . . He was so marvellously primitive: just like a faun. He made me feel like a most marvellous nymph, or something, miles away from anywhere, in the middle of the forest."

The first letter from Klaus duly arrived. We had all been anxiously awaiting it; and Frl. Schroeder woke me up specially early to tell me that it had come. Perhaps she was afraid that she would never get a chance of reading it herself and relied on me to tell her the contents. If so, her fears were groundless. Sally not only showed the letter to Frl. Schroeder, Frl. Mayr, Bobby and myself, she even read selections from it aloud in the presence of the porter's wife, who had come up to collect the rent.

From the first, the letter left a nasty taste in my mouth. Its whole tone was egotistical and a bit patronizing. Klaus didn't like London, he said. He felt lonely there. The food disagreed with him. And the people at the studio treated him with lack of consideration. He wished Sally were with him: she could have helped him in many ways. However, now that he was in England, he would try to make the best of it. He would work hard and earn money; and Sally was to work hard too. Work would cheer her up and keep her from getting depressed. At the end of the letter came various endearments, rather too slickly applied. Reading them, one felt: he's written this kind of thing several times before.

Sally was delighted, however. Klaus' exhortation made such an impression upon her that she at once rang up several film companies, a theatrical agency and half a dozen of her "business" acquaintances. Nothing definite came of all this, it is true; but she remained very optimistic throughout the next twenty-four hours—even her dreams, she told me, had been full of contracts and four-figure cheques: "It's the most marvellous feeling, Chris. I know I'm going right ahead now and going to become the most wonderful actress in the world."

One morning, about a week after this, I went into Sally's room and found her holding a letter in her hand. I recognized Klaus' hand-writing at once.

"Good morning, Chris darling."

"Good morning, Sally."

"How did you sleep?" Her tone was unnaturally bright and chatty.

"All right, thanks. How did you?"

"Fairly all right. . . . Filthy weather, isn't it?"

"Yes." I walked over to the window to look. It was.

Sally smiled conversationally: "Do you know what this swine's gone and done?"

"What swine?" I wasn't going to be caught out.

"Oh Chris! For God's sake, don't be so dense!"

"I'm very sorry. I'm afraid I'm a bit slow in the uptake this morning."

"I can't be bothered to explain, darling." Sally held out the letter. "Here, read this, will you? Of all the blasted impudence! Read it aloud. I want to hear how it sounds."

"Mein liebes, armes Kind," the letter began. Klaus called Sally his poor dear child because, as he explained, he was afraid that what he had to tell her would make her terribly unhappy. Nevertheless, he must say it: he must tell her that he had come to a decision. She mustn't imagine that this had been easy for him: it had been very difficult and painful. All the same, he knew he was right. In a word, they must part.

"I see now," wrote Klaus, "that I behaved very selfishly. I thought only of my own pleasure. But now I realize that I must have had a bad influence on you. My dear little girl, you have adored me too much. If we should continue to be together, you would soon have no will and no mind of your own." Klaus went on to advise Sally to live for her work. "Work is the only thing which matters, as I myself have found." He was very much concerned that Sally shouldn't upset herself unduly: "You must be brave, Sally, my poor darling child."

Right at the end of the letter, it all came out:

"I was invited a few nights ago to a party at the house of Lady Klein, a leader of the English aristocracy. I met there a very beautiful and intelligent young English girl named Miss Gore-Eckersley. She is related to an English lord whose name I couldn't quite hear—you will probably know which one I mean. We have met twice since then and had wonderful conversations about many things. I do not think I have ever met a girl who could understand my mind so well as she does—"

"That's a new one on me," broke in Sally bitterly, with a short laugh: "I never suspected the boy of having a mind at all."

At this moment we were interrupted by Frl. Schroeder, who had come, sniffing secrets, to ask if Sally would like a bath. I left them together to make the most of the occasion.

"I can't be angry with the fool," said Sally, later in the day, pacing up and down the room and furiously smoking: "I just feel sorry for him in a motherly sort of way. But what on earth'll happen to *his* work, if he chucks himself at these women's heads, I can't imagine."

She made another turn of the room:

"I think if he'd been having a proper affair with another woman, and had only told me about it after it'd been going on for a long time, I'd have minded more. But this girl! Why, I don't suppose she's even his mistress."

"Obviously not," I agreed. "I say, shall we have a Prairie Oyster?"

"How marvellous you are, Chris! You always think of just the right thing. I wish I could fall in love with you. Klaus isn't worth your little finger."

"I know he isn't."

"The blasted cheek," exclaimed Sally gulping the Worcester sauce and licking her upper lip, "of his saying I adored him! . . . The worst of it is, I did!"

That evening I went into her room and found her with pen and paper before her:

"I've written about a million letters to him and torn them all up."

"It's no good, Sally. Let's go to the cinema."

"Right you are, Chris darling." Sally wiped her eyes with the corner of her tiny handkerchief: "It's no use bothering, is it?"

"Not a bit of use."

"And now I jolly well *will* be a great actress—just to show him!"

"That's the spirit!"

We went to a little cinema in the Bülowstrasse, where they were showing a film about a girl who sacrificed her stage career for the sake of a Great Love, Home and Children. We laughed so much that we had to leave before the end.

"I feel ever so much better now," said Sally, as we were coming away.

"I'm glad."

"Perhaps, after all, I can't have been properly in love with him.
. . . What do you think?"

"It's rather difficult for me to say."

"I've often thought I was in love with a man, and then I found
I wasn't. But this time," Sally's voice was regretful, "I really did feel
sure of it. . . . And now, somehow, everything seems to have got a
bit confused. . . ."

"Perhaps you're suffering from shock," I suggested.

Sally was very pleased with this idea: "Do you know, I expect I
am! . . . You know, Chris, you do understand women most marvellously: better than any man I've ever met. . . . I'm sure that some day
you'll write the most marvellous novel which'll sell simply millions of
copies."

"Thank you for believing in me, Sally!"

"Do you believe in me, too, Chris?"

"Of course I do."

"No, but honestly?"

"Well . . . I'm quite certain you'll make a terrific success at
something—only I'm not sure what it'll be. . . . I mean, there's so
many things you could do if you tried, aren't there?"

"I suppose there are." Sally became thoughtful. "At least, sometimes I feel like that. . . . And sometimes I feel I'm no damn' use at
anything. . . . Why, I can't even keep a man faithful to me for the
inside of a month."

"Oh, Sally, don't let's start all that again!"

"All right, Chris—we won't start all that. Let's go and have a
drink."

During the weeks that followed, Sally and I were together most
of the day. Curled up on the sofa in the big dingy room, she smoked,
drank Prairie Oysters, talked endlessly of the future. When the weather
was fine, and I hadn't any lessons to give, we strolled as far as the
Wittenbergplatz and sat on a bench in the sunshine, discussing the
people who went past. Everybody stared at Sally, in her canary-yellow
beret and shabby fur coat, like the skin of a mangy old dog.

"I wonder," she was fond of remarking, "what they'd say if they knew that we two old tramps were going to be the most marvellous novelist and the greatest actress in the world."

"They'd probably be very much surprised."

"I expect we shall look back on this time when we're driving about in our Mercedes, and think: After all, it wasn't such bad fun!"

"It wouldn't be such bad fun if we had that Mercedes now."

We talked continually about wealth, fame, huge contracts for Sally, record-breaking sales for the novels I should one day write. "I think," said Sally, "it must be marvellous to be a novelist. You're frightfully dreamy and unpractical and unbusiness-like, and people imagine they can fairly swindle you as much as they want—and then you sit down and write a book about them which fairly shows them what swine they all are, and it's the most terrific success and you make pots of money."

"I expect the trouble with me is that I'm not quite dreamy enough. . . ."

". . . if only I could get a really rich man as my lover. Let's see. . . . I shouldn't want more than three thousand a year, and a flat and a decent car. I'd do anything, just now, to get rich. If you're rich you can afford to stand out for a really good contract; you don't have to snap up the first offer you get. . . . Of course, I'd be absolutely faithful to the man who kept me—"

Sally said things like this very seriously and evidently believed she meant them. She was in a curious state of mind, restless and nervy. Often she flew into a temper for no special reason. She talked incessantly about getting work, but made no effort to do so. Her allowance hadn't been stopped, so far, however, and we were living very cheaply, since Sally no longer cared to go out in the evenings or to see other people at all. Once, Fritz came to tea. I left them alone together afterwards to go and write a letter. When I came back Fritz had gone and Sally was in tears:

"That man *bores* me so!" she sobbed. "I hate him! I should like to kill him!"

But in a few minutes she was quite calm again. I started to mix the inevitable Prairie Oyster. Sally, curled up on the sofa, was thoughtfully smoking:

"I wonder," she said suddenly, "if I'm going to have a baby."

"Good God!" I nearly dropped the glass: "Do you really think you are?"

"I don't know. With me it's so difficult to tell: I'm so irregular . . . I've felt sick sometimes. It's probably something I've eaten. . . ."

"But hadn't you better see a doctor?"

"Oh, I suppose so." Sally yawned listlessly. "There's no hurry."

"Of course there's a hurry! You'll go and see a doctor to-morrow!"

"Look here, Chris, who the hell do you think you're ordering about? I wish now I hadn't said anything about it at all!" Sally was on the point of bursting into tears again.

"Oh, all right! All right!" I hastily tried to calm her. "Do just what you like. It's no business of mine."

"Sorry, darling. I didn't mean to be snappy. I'll see how I feel in the morning. Perhaps I will go and see that doctor, after all."

But of course, she didn't. Next day, indeed, she seemed much brighter: "Let's go out this evening, Chris. I'm getting sick of this room. Let's go and see some life!"

"Right you are, Sally. Where would you like to go?"

"Let's go to the Troika and talk to that old idiot Bobby. Perhaps he'll stand us a drink—you never know!"

Bobby didn't stand us any drinks; but Sally's suggestion proved to have been a good one, nevertheless. For it was while sitting at the bar of the Troika that we first got into conversation with Clive.

From that moment onwards we were with him almost continuously; either separately or together. I never once saw him sober. Clive told us that he drank half a bottle of whisky before breakfast, and I had no reason to disbelieve him. He often began to explain to us why he drank so much—it was because he was very unhappy. But why he was so unhappy I never found out, because Sally always interrupted to say that it was time to be going out or moving on to the next place or smoking a cigarette or having another glass of whisky. She was drinking nearly as much whisky as Clive himself. It never seemed to make her really drunk, but sometimes her eyes looked awful, as though they had been boiled. Every day the layer of make-up on her face seemed to get thicker.

Clive was a very big man, good-looking in a heavy Roman way, and just beginning to get fat. He had about him that sad, American air of vagueness which is always attractive; doubly attractive in one who possessed so much money. He was vague, wistful, a bit lost: dimly anxious to have a good time and uncertain how to set about getting it. He seemed never to be quite sure whether he was really enjoying himself, whether what we were doing was *really* fun. He had constantly to be reassured. *Was* this the genuine article? *Was* this the real guaranteed height of a Good Time? It was? Yes, yes, of course—it was marvellous! It was great! Ha, ha, ha! His big school-boyish laugh rolled out, re-echoed, became rather forced and died away abruptly on that puzzled note of enquiry. He couldn't venture a step without our support. Yet, even as he appealed to us, I thought I could sometimes detect odd sly flashes of sarcasm. What did he really think of us?

Every morning, Clive sent round a hired car to fetch us to the hotel where he was staying. The chauffeur always brought with him a wonderful bouquet of flowers, ordered from the most expensive flower-shop in the Linden. One morning I had a lesson to give and arranged with Sally to join them later. On arriving at the hotel, I found that Clive and Sally had left early to fly to Dresden. There was a note from Clive, apologizing profusely and inviting me to lunch at the hotel restaurant, by myself, as his guest. But I didn't. I was afraid of that look in the head waiter's eye. In the evening, when Clive and Sally returned, Clive had brought me a present: it was a parcel of six silk shirts. "He wanted to get you a gold cigarette case," Sally whispered in my ear, "but I told him shirts would be better. Yours are in such a state. . . . Besides, we've got to go slow at present. We don't want him to think we're gold-diggers. . . ."

I accepted them gratefully. What else could I do? Clive had corrupted us utterly. It was understood that he was going to put up the money to launch Sally upon a stage career. He often spoke of this, in a thoroughly nice way, as though it were a very trivial matter, to be settled, without fuss, between friends. But no sooner had he touched on the subject than his attention seemed to wander off again—his thoughts were as easily distracted as those of a child. Sometimes Sally was very hard put to it, I could see, to hide her impatience. "Just leave us alone for a bit now, darling," she would whisper to me, "Clive and I are going to talk business." But however tactfully Sally tried to bring him to the point, she never quite succeeded. When I rejoined them, half an hour later, I would find Clive smiling and sipping his whisky; and Sally also smiling, to conceal her extreme irritation.

"I adore him," Sally told me, repeatedly and very solemnly, whenever we were alone together. She was intensely earnest in believing this. It was like a dogma in a newly adopted religious creed: Sally adores Clive. It is a very solemn undertaking to adore a millionaire. Sally's features began to assume, with increasing frequency, the rapt expression of the theatrical nun. And indeed, when Clive, with his charming vagueness, gave a particularly flagrant professional beggar a twenty-mark note, we would exchange glances of genuine awe. The waste of so much good money affected us both like something inspired, a kind of miracle.

There came an afternoon when Clive seemed more nearly sober than usual. He began to make plans. In a few days we were all three of us to leave Berlin, for good. The Orient Express would take us to Athens. Thence, we should fly to Egypt. From Egypt to Marseilles. From Marseilles, by boat to South America. Then Tahiti. Singapore. Japan. Clive pronounced the names as though they had been stations on the Wannsee railway, quite as a matter of course: he had been there already. He knew it all. His matter-of-fact boredom gradually infused reality into the preposterous conversation. After all, he could do it. I began seriously to believe that he meant to do it. With a mere gesture of his wealth, he could alter the whole course of our lives.

What would become of us? Once started, we should never go back. We could never leave him. Sally, of course, he would marry. I should occupy an ill-defined position: a kind of private secretary without duties. With a flash of vision, I saw myself ten years hence, in flannels and black and white shoes, gone heavier round the jowl and a bit glassy, pouring out a drink in the lounge of a Californian hotel.

"Come and cast an eye at the funeral," Clive was saying.

"What funeral, darling?" Sally asked, patiently. This was a new kind of interruption.

"Why, say, haven't you noticed it?" Clive laughed. "It's a most elegant funeral. It's been going past for the last hour."

We all three went out on to the balcony of Clive's room. Sure enough, the street below was full of people. They were burying Hermann Müller. Ranks of pale steadfast clerks, government officials, trade union secretaries—the whole drab weary pageant of Prussian Social Democracy—trudged past under their banners towards the silhouetted arches of the Brandenburger Tor, from which the long black streamers stirred slowly in an evening breeze.

"Say, who was this guy, anyway?" asked Clive, looking down. "I guess he must have been a big swell?"

"God knows," Sally answered, yawning. "Look, Clive darling, isn't it a marvellous sunset?"

She was quite right. We had nothing to do with those Germans down there, marching, or with the dead man in the coffin, or with the words on the banners. In a few days, I thought, we shall have forfeited all kinship with ninety-nine per cent of the population of the world, with the men and women who earn their living, who insure their lives, who are anxious about the future of their children. Perhaps in the Middle Ages people felt like this, when they believed themselves to have sold their souls to the Devil. It was a curious, exhilarating, not unpleasant sensation: but, at the same time, I felt slightly scared. Yes, I said to myself, I've done it, now. I am lost.

Next morning, we arrived at the hotel at the usual time. The porter eyed us, I thought, rather queerly.

"Whom did you wish to see, Madam?"

The question seemed so extraordinary that we both laughed.

"Why, number 365, of course," Sally answered. "Who did you think? Don't you know us by this time?"

"I'm afraid you can't do that, Madam. The gentleman in 365 left early this morning."

"Left? You mean he's gone out for the day? That's funny! What time will he be back?"

"He didn't say anything about coming back, Madam. He was travelling to Budapest."

As we stood there goggling at him, a waiter hurried up with a note.

"Dear Sally and Chris," it said, "I can't stick this darned town any longer, so am off. Hoping to see you sometime, Clive."

"(These are in case I forgot anything.)"

In the envelope were three hundred-mark notes. These, the fading flowers, Sally's four pairs of shoes and two hats (bought in Dresden) and my six shirts were our total assets from Clive's visit. At first, Sally was very angry. Then we both began to laugh:

"Well, Chris, I'm afraid we're not much use as gold-diggers, are we, darling?"

We spent most of the day discussing whether Clive's departure was a premeditated trick. I was inclined to think it wasn't. I imagined him leaving every new town and every new set of acquaintances in much the same sort of way. I sympathized with him, a good deal.

Then came the question of what was to be done with the money. Sally decided to put by two hundred and fifty marks for some new clothes: fifty marks we would blow that evening.

But blowing the fifty marks wasn't as much fun as we'd imagined it would be. Sally felt ill and couldn't eat the wonderful dinner we'd ordered. We were both depressed.

"You know, Chris, I'm beginning to think that men are always going to leave me. The more I think about it, the more men I re-member who have. It's ghastly, really."

"I'll never leave you, Sally."

"Won't you, darling? . . . But seriously, I believe I'm a sort of Ideal Woman, if you know what I mean. I'm the sort of woman who can take men away from their wives, but I could never keep anybody for long. And that's because I'm the type which every man imagines he wants, until he gets me; and then he finds he doesn't really, after all."

"Well, you'd rather be that than the Ugly Duckling with the Heart of Gold, wouldn't you?"

". . . I could kick myself, the way I behaved to Clive. I ought never to have bothered him about money, the way I did. I expect he thought I was just a common little whore, like all the others. And I really did adore him—in a way. . . . If I'd married him, I'd have made a man out of him. I'd have got him to give up drinking."

"You set him such a good example."

We both laughed.

"The old swine might at least have left me with a decent cheque."

"Never mind, darling. There's more where he came from."

"I don't care," said Sally. "I'm sick of being a whore. I'll never look at a man with money again."

Next morning, Sally felt very ill. We both put it down to the drink. She stayed in bed the whole morning and when she got up she fainted. I wanted her to see a doctor straight away, but she wouldn't. About tea-time, she fainted again and looked so bad afterwards that Frl. Schroeder and I sent for a doctor without consulting her at all.

The doctor, when he arrived, stayed a long time. Frl. Schroeder and I sat waiting in the living-room to hear his diagnosis. But, very much to our surprise, he left the flat suddenly, in a great hurry, without even looking in to wish us good afternoon. I went at once to Sally's room. Sally was sitting up in bed, with a rather fixed grin on her face:

"Well, Christopher darling, I've been made an April Fool of."

"What do you mean?"

Sally tried to laugh:

"He says I'm going to have a baby."

"Oh my God!"

"Don't look so scared, darling! I've been more or less expecting it, you know."

"It's Klaus's, I suppose?"

"Yes."

"And what are you going to do about it?"

"Not have it, of course." Sally reached for a cigarette. I sat stupidly staring at my shoes.

"Will the doctor . . ."

"No, he won't. I asked him straight out. He was terribly shocked. I said: 'My dear man, what do you imagine would happen to the unfortunate child if it was born? Do I look as if I'd make a good mother?' "

"And what did he say to that?"

"He seemed to think it was quite beside the point. The only thing which matters to him is his professional reputation."

"Well then, we've got to find someone without a professional reputation, that's all."

"I should think," said Sally, "we'd better ask Frl. Schroeder."

So Frl. Schroeder was consulted. She took it very well: she was alarmed but extremely practical. Yes, she knew of somebody. A friend of a friend's friend had once had difficulties. And the doctor was a fully qualified man, very clever indeed. The only trouble was, he might be rather expensive.

"Thank goodness," Sally interjected, "we haven't spent all that swine Clive's money!"

"I must say, I think Klaus ought—"

"Look here, Chris. Let me tell you this once for all: if I catch you writing to Klaus about this business, I'll never forgive you and I'll never speak to you again!"

"Oh, very well . . . Of course I won't. It was just a suggestion, that's all."

I didn't like the doctor. He kept stroking and pinching Sally's arm and pawing her hand. However, he seemed the right man for the job. Sally was to go into his private nursing-home as soon as there was a vacancy for her. Everything was perfectly official and above-board. In a few polished sentences, the dapper little doctor dispelled the least whiff of sinister illegality. Sally's state of health, he explained, made it quite impossible for her to undergo the risks of childbirth: there would be a certificate to that effect. Needless to say, the certificate would cost a lot of money. So would the nursing-home and so would the operation itself. The doctor wanted two hundred and fifty marks down before he would make any arrangements at all. In the end, we beat him down to two hundred. Sally wanted the extra fifty, she explained to me later, to get some new night-dresses.

At last, it was spring. The cafés were putting up wooden platforms on the pavement and the ice-cream shops were opening, with their rainbow-wheels. We drove to the nursing-home in an open taxi. Because of the lovely weather, Sally was in better spirits than I had seen her in for weeks. But Frl. Schroeder, though she bravely tried to smile, was on the verge of tears. "The doctor isn't a Jew, I hope?" Frl. Mayr asked me sternly. "Don't you let one of those filthy Jews touch her. They always try to get a job of that kind, the beasts!"

Sally had a nice room, clean and cheerful, with a balcony. I called there again in the evening. Lying there in bed without her make-up, she looked years younger, like a little girl:

"Hullo, darling. . . . They haven't killed me yet, you see. But they've been doing their best to. . . . Isn't this a funny place? . . . I wish that pig Klaus could see me. . . . This is what comes of not understanding his *mind*. . . ."

She was a bit feverish and laughed a great deal. One of the nurses came in for a moment, as if looking for something, and went out again almost immediately.

"She was dying to get a peep at you," Sally explained. "You see, I told her you were the father. You don't mind, do you, darling . . ."

"Not at all. It's a compliment."

"It makes everything so much simpler. Otherwise, if there's no one, they think it so odd. And I don't care for being sort of looked down on and pitied as the poor betrayed girl who gets abandoned by her lover. It isn't particularly flattering for me, is it? So I told her we were most terribly in love but fearfully hard up, so that we couldn't afford to marry, and how we dreamed of the time when we'd both be rich and famous and then we'd have a family of ten, just to make up for this one. The nurse was awfully touched, poor girl. In fact, she wept. To-night, when she's on duty, she's going to show me pictures of *her* young man. Isn't it sweet?"

Next day, Frl. Schroeder and I went round to the nursing-home together. We found Sally lying flat, with the bedclothes up to her chin:

"Oh, hullo, you two! Won't you sit down? What time is it?" She turned uneasily in bed and rubbed her eyes: "Where did all these flowers come from?"

"We brought them."

"How marvellous of you!" Sally smiled vacantly. "Sorry to be such a fool to-day. . . . It's this bloody chloroform. . . . My head's full of it."

We only stayed a few minutes. On the way home, Frl. Schroeder

was terribly upset: "Will you believe it, Herr Issyvoo, I couldn't take
it more to heart if it was my own daughter? Why, when I see the poor
child suffering like that, I'd rather it was myself lying there in her
place—I would indeed!"

Next day Sally was much better. We all went to visit her: Frl.
Schroeder, Frl. Mayr, Bobby and Fritz. Fritz, of course, hadn't the
faintest idea what had really happened. Sally, he had been told, was
being operated upon for a small internal ulcer. As always is the way
with people when they aren't in the know, he made all kinds of
unintentional and startlingly apt references to storks, gooseberry-
bushes, perambulators and babies generally; and even recounted a
special new item of scandal about a well-known Berlin society lady
who was said to have undergone a recent illegal operation. Sally and
I avoided each other's eyes.

On the evening of the next day, I visited her at the nursing-home
for the last time. She was to leave in the morning. She was alone and
we sat together on the balcony. She seemed more or less all right now
and could walk about the room.

"I told the Sister I didn't want to see anybody to-day except you."
Sally yawned languidly. "People make me feel so tired."

"Would you rather I went away too?"

"Oh no," said Sally, without much enthusiasm, "if you go, one
of the nurses will only come in and begin to chatter; and if I'm not
lively and bright with her, they'll say I have to stay in this hellish place
a couple of extra days, and I couldn't stand that."

She stared out moodily over the quiet street:

"You know, Chris, in some ways I wish I'd had that kid. . . . It
would have been rather marvellous to have had it. The last day or
two, I've been sort of feeling what it would be like to be a mother.
Do you know, last night, I sat here for a long time by myself and held
this cushion in my arms and imagined it was my baby? And I felt a
most marvellous sort of shut-off feeling from all the rest of the world.
I imagined how it'd grow up and how I'd work for it, and how, after
I'd put it to bed at nights, I'd go out and make love to filthy old men
to get money to pay for its food and clothes. . . . It's all very well for
you to grin like that, Chris . . . I did really!"

"Well, why don't you marry and have one?"

"I don't know. . . . I feel as if I'd lost faith in men. I just haven't any use for them at all. . . . Even you, Christopher, if you were to go out into the street now and be run over by a taxi. . . . I should be sorry in a way, of course, but I shouldn't really *care* a damn."

"Thank you, Sally."

We both laughed.

"I didn't mean that, of course, darling—at least, not personally. You mustn't mind what I say while I'm like this. I get all sorts of crazy ideas into my head. Having babies makes you feel awfully primitive, like a sort of wild animal or something, defending its young. Only the trouble is, I haven't any young to defend. . . . I expect that's what makes me so frightfully bad-tempered to everybody just now."

It was partly as the result of this conversation that I suddenly decided, that evening, to cancel all my lessons, leave Berlin as soon as possible, go to some place on the Baltic and try to start working. Since Christmas, I had hardly written a word.

Sally, when I told her my idea, was rather relieved, I think. We both needed a change. We talked vaguely of her joining me later; but, even then, I felt that she wouldn't. Her plans were very uncertain. Later, she might go to Paris, or to the Alps, or to the South of France, she said—if she could get the cash. "But probably," she added, "I shall just stay on here. I should be quite happy. I seem to have got sort of used to this place."

I returned to Berlin towards the middle of July.

All this time I had heard nothing of Sally, beyond half a dozen post-cards, exchanged during the first month of my absence. I wasn't much surprised to find she'd left her room in our flat:

"Of course, I quite understand her going. I couldn't make her as comfortable as she'd the right to expect; especially as we haven't any running water in the bedrooms." Poor Frl. Schroeder's eyes had filled with tears. "But it was a terrible disappointment to me, all the same. . . . Frl. Bowles behaved very handsomely, I can't complain about that. She insisted on paying for her room until the end of July. I was entitled to the money, of course, because she didn't give notice until the twenty-first—but I'd never have mentioned it. . . . She was such a charming young lady—"

"Have you got her address?"

"Oh yes, and the telephone number. You'll be ringing her up, of course. She'll be delighted to see you. . . . The other gentlemen came and went, but you were her real friend, Herr Issyvoo. You know, I always used to hope that you two would get married. You'd have made an ideal couple. You always had such a good steady influence on her, and she used to brighten you up a bit when you got too deep in your books and studies. . . . Oh yes, Herr Issyvoo, you may laugh— but you never can tell! Perhaps it isn't too late yet!"

Next morning, Frl. Schroeder woke me in great excitement:

"Herr Issyvoo, what do you think! They've shut the Darmstädter und National! There'll be thousands ruined, I shouldn't wonder! The milkman says we'll have civil war in a fortnight! Whatever do you say to that!"

As soon as I'd got dressed, I went down into the street. Sure enough, there was a crowd outside the branch bank on the Nollen-dorfplatz corner, a lot of men with leather satchels and women with string-bags—women like Frl. Schroeder herself. The iron lattices were drawn down over the bank windows. Most of the people were staring intently and rather stupidly at the locked door. In the middle of the door was fixed a small notice, beautifully printed in Gothic type, like a page from a classic author. The notice said that the Reichspresident had guaranteed the deposits. Everything was quite all right. Only the bank wasn't going to open.

A little boy was playing with a hoop amongst the crowd. The hoop ran against a woman's legs. She flew out at him at once: "Du, sei bloss nicht so frech! Cheeky little brat! What do you want here!" Another woman joined in, attacking the scared boy: "Get out! You can't understand it, can you?" And another asked, in furious sarcasm: "Have you got your money in the bank too, perhaps?" The boy fled before their pent-up, exploding rage.

In the afternoon it was very hot. The details of the new emergency decrees were in the early evening papers—terse, governmentally in-spired. One alarmist headline stood out boldly, barred with blood-red ink: "Everything Collapses!" A Nazi journalist reminded his readers that to-morrow, the fourteenth of July, was a day of national rejoicing in France; and doubtless, he added, the French would rejoice with especial fervour this year, at the prospect of Germany's downfall. Going into an outfitter's, I bought myself a pair of ready-made flannel trousers for twelve marks fifty—a gesture of confidence by England. Then I got into the Underground to go and visit Sally.

She was living in a block of three-room flats, designed as an Artists' Colony, not far from the Breitenbachplatz. When I rang the bell, she opened the door to me herself:

"Hillooo, Chris, you old swine!"

"Hullo, Sally darling!"

"How are you? . . . Be careful, darling, you'll make me untidy. I've got to go out in a few minutes."

I had never seen her all in white before. It suited her. But her face looked thinner and older. Her hair was cut in a new way and beautifully waved.

"You're very smart," I said.

"Am I?" Sally smiled her pleased, dreamy, self-conscious smile. I followed her into the sitting-room of the flat. One wall was entirely window. There was some cherry-coloured wooden furniture and a very low divan with gaudy fringed cushions. A fluffy white miniature dog jumped to its feet and yapped. Sally picked it up and went through the gestures of kissing it, just not touching it with her lips:

"Freddi, mein Liebling, Du bist *soo* süss!"

"Yours?" I asked, noticing the improvement in her German accent.

"No. He belongs to Gerda, the girl I share this flat with."

"Have you known her long?"

"Only a week or two."

"What's she like?"

"Not bad. As stingy as hell. I have to pay for practically everything."

"It's nice here."

"Do you think so? Yes, I suppose it's all right. Better than that hole in the Nollendorfstrasse, anyhow."

"What made you leave? Did you and Frl. Schroeder have a row?"

"No, not exactly. Only I got so sick of hearing her talk. She nearly talked my head off. She's an awful old bore, really."

"She's very fond of you."

Sally shrugged her shoulders with a slight impatient listless movement. Throughout this conversation, I noticed that she avoided my eyes. There was a long pause. I felt puzzled and vaguely embarrassed. I began to wonder how soon I could make an excuse to go.

Then the telephone bell rang. Sally yawned, pulled the instrument across on to her lap:

"Hilloo, who's there? Yes, it's me. . . . No. . . . No. . . . I've really no idea. . . . *Really* I haven't! I'm to guess?" Her nose wrinkled: "Is it Erwin? No? Paul? No? Wait a minute. . . . Let me see. . . ."

"And now, darling, I must fly!" cried Sally, when, at last, the conversation was over: "I'm about two hours late already!"

"Got a new boy friend?"

But Sally ignored my grin. She lit a cigarette with a faint expression of distaste.

"I've got to see a man on business," she said briefly.

"And when shall we meet again?"

"I'll have to see, darling. . . . I've got such a lot on, just at present. . . . I shall be out in the country all day to-morrow, and probably the day after. . . . I'll let you know. . . . I may be going to Frankfurt quite soon."

"Have you got a job there?"

"No. Not exactly." Sally's voice was brief, dismissing this subject. "I've decided not to try for any film work until the autumn, anyhow. I shall take a thorough rest."

"You seem to have made a lot of new friends."

Again, Sally's manner became vague, carefully casual:

"Yes, I suppose I have. . . . It's probably a reaction from all those months at Frl. Schroeder's, when I never saw a soul."

"Well," I couldn't resist a malicious grin. "I hope for your sake that none of your new friends have got their money in the Darmstädter und National."

"Why?" She was interested at once. "What's the matter with it?"

"Do you really mean to say you haven't heard?"

"Of course not. I never read the papers, and I haven't been out to-day, yet."

I told her the news of the crisis. At the end of it, she was looking quite scared.

"But why on earth," she exclaimed impatiently, "didn't you tell me all this before? It may be serious."

"I'm sorry, Sally. I took it for granted that you'd know already . . . especially as you seem to be moving in financial circles, now-adays—"

But she ignored this little dig. She was frowning, deep in her own thoughts:

"If it was *very* serious, Leo would have rung up and told me . . ." she murmured at length. And this reflection appeared to ease her mind considerably.

We walked out together to the corner of the street, where Sally picked up a taxi.

"It's an awful nuisance living so far off," she said. "I'm probably going to get a car soon."

"By the way," she added just as we were parting, "what was it like on Ruegen?"

"I bathed a lot."

"Well, goodbye, darling. I'll see you sometime."

"Goodbye, Sally. Enjoy yourself."

About a week after this, Sally rang me up:

"Can you come round at once, Chris? It's very important. I want you to do me a favour."

This time, also, I found Sally alone in the flat.

"Do you want to earn some money, darling?" she greeted me.

"Of course."

"Splendid! You see, it's like this. . . ." She was in a fluffy pink dressing-wrap and inclined to be breathless: "There's a man I know who's starting a magazine. It's going to be most terribly highbrow and artistic, with lots of marvellous modern photographs, ink-pots and girls' heads upside down—you know the sort of thing. . . . The point is, each number is going to take a special country and kind of review it, with articles about the manners and customs, and all that. . . . Well, the first country they're going to do is England and they want me to write an article on the English Girl. . . . Of course, I haven't the foggiest idea what to say, so what I thought was: you could write the article in my name and get the money—I only want not to disoblige this man who's editing the paper, because he may be terribly useful to me in other ways, later on. . . ."

"All right, I'll try."

"Oh, marvellous!"

"How soon do you want it done?"

"You see, darling, that's the whole point. I must have it at once. . . . Otherwise it's no earthly use, because I promised it four days ago and I simply must give it him this evening. . . . It needn't be very long. About five hundred words."

"Well, I'll do my best. . . ."

"Good. That's wonderful. . . . Sit down wherever you like. Here's some paper. You've got a pen? Oh, and here's a dictionary, in case there's a word you can't spell. . . . I'll just be having my bath."

When, three-quarters of an hour later, Sally came in dressed for the day, I had finished. Frankly, I was rather pleased with my effort.

She read it through carefully, a slow frown gathering between her beautifully pencilled eyebrows. When she had finished, she laid down the manuscript with a sigh:

"I'm sorry, Chris. It won't do at all."

"Won't do?" I was genuinely taken aback.

"Of course, I dare say it's very good from a literary point of view, and all that. . . ."

"Well then, what's wrong with it?"

"It's not nearly snappy enough." Sally was quite final. "It's not the kind of thing this man wants, at all."

I shrugged my shoulders: "I'm sorry, Sally. I did my best. But journalism isn't really in my line, you know."

There was a resentful pause. My vanity was piqued.

"My goodness, I know who'll do it for me if I ask him!" cried Sally, suddenly jumping up. "Why on earth didn't I think of him before?" She grabbed the telephone and dialled a number: "Oh, hilloo, Kurt darling. . . ."

In three minutes, she had explained all about the article. Replacing the receiver on its stand, she announced triumphantly: "That's marvellous! He's going to do it at once. . . ." She paused impressively and added: "That was Kurt Rosenthal."

"Who's he?"

"You've never heard of him?" This annoyed Sally; she pretended to be immensely surprised: "I thought you took an interest in the cinema? He's miles the best young scenario writer. He earns pots of money. He's only doing this as a favour to me, of course. . . . He says he'll dictate it to his secretary while he's shaving and then send it straight round to the editor's flat. . . . He's marvellous!"

"Are you sure it'll be what the editor wants, this time?"

"Of course it will! Kurt's an absolute genius. He can do anything. Just now, he's writing a novel in his spare time. He's so fearfully busy, he can only dictate it while he's having breakfast. He showed me the first few chapters, the other day. Honestly, I think it's easily the best novel I've ever read."

"Indeed?"

"That's the sort of writer I admire," Sally continued. She was careful to avoid my eye. "He's terribly ambitious and he works the whole time; and he can write anything—anything you like: scenarios, novels, plays, poetry, advertisements. . . . He's not a bit stuck-up about it either. Not like these young men who, because they've written one book, start talking about Art and imagining they're the most wonderful authors in the world. . . . They make me sick. . . ."

Irritated as I was with her, I couldn't help laughing:

"Since when have you disapproved of me so violently, Sally?"

"I don't disapprove of you"—but she couldn't look me in the face—"not exactly."

"I merely make you sick?"

"I don't know what it is. . . . You seem to have changed, somehow. . . ."

"How have I changed?"

"It's difficult to explain. . . . You don't seem to have any energy or want to get anywhere. You're so dilettante. It annoys me."

"I'm sorry." But my would-be facetious tone sounded rather forced. Sally frowned down at her tiny black shoes.

"You must remember I'm a woman, Christopher. All women like men to be strong and decided and following out their careers. A woman wants to be motherly to a man and protect his weak side, but he must have a strong side too, which she can respect. . . . If you ever care for a woman, I don't advise you to let her see that you've got no ambition. Otherwise she'll get to despise you."

"Yes, I see. . . . And that's the principle on which you choose your friends—your *new* friends?"

She flared up at this:

"It's very easy for you to sneer at my friends for having good business heads. If they've got money, it's because they've worked for it. . . . I suppose you consider yourself better than they are?"

"Yes, Sally, since you ask me—if they're at all as I imagine them—I do."

"There you go, Christopher! That's typical of you. That's what annoys me about you: you're conceited and lazy. If you say things like that, you ought to be able to prove them."

"How does one prove that one's better than somebody else? Besides, that's not what I said. I said I considered myself better—it's simply a matter of taste."

Sally made no reply. She lit a cigarette, slightly frowning.

"You say I seem to have changed," I continued. "To be quite frank, I've been thinking the same thing about *you.*"

Sally didn't seem surprised: "Have you, Christopher? Perhaps you're right. I don't know. . . . Or perhaps we've neither of us changed. Perhaps we're just seeing each other as we really are. We're awfully different in lots of ways, you know."

"Yes, I've noticed that."

"I think," said Sally, smoking meditatively, her eyes on her shoes, "that we may have sort of outgrown each other, a bit."

"Perhaps we have. . . ." I smiled: Sally's real meaning was so obvious: "At any rate, we needn't quarrel about it, need we?"

"Of course not, darling."

There was a pause. Then I said that I must be going. We were both rather embarrassed, now, and extra polite.

"Are you certain you won't have a cup of coffee?"

"No, thanks awfully."

"Have some tea? It's specially good. I got it as a present."

"No, thanks very much indeed, Sally. I really must be getting along."

"Must you?" She sounded, after all, rather relieved. "Be sure and ring me up some time soon, won't you?"

"Yes, rather."

It wasn't until I had actually left the house and was walking quickly away up the street that I realized how angry and ashamed I felt. What an utter little bitch she is, I thought. After all, I told myself, it's only what I've always known she was like—right from the start. No, that wasn't true: I hadn't known it. I'd flattered myself—why not be frank about it?—that she was fond of me. Well, I'd been wrong, it seemed; but could I blame her for that? Yet I did blame her, I was furious with her; nothing would have pleased me more, at that moment, than to see her soundly whipped. Indeed, I was so absurdly upset that I began to wonder whether I hadn't, all this time, in my own peculiar way, been in love with Sally myself.

But no, it wasn't love either—it was worse. It was the cheapest, most childish kind of wounded vanity. Not that I cared a curse what she thought of my article—well, just a little, perhaps, but only a very little; my literary self-conceit was proof against anything *she* could say—it was her criticism of myself. The awful sexual flair women have for taking the stuffing out of a man! It was no use telling myself that Sally had the vocabulary and mentality of a twelve-year-old schoolgirl, that she was altogether comic and preposterous; it was no use—I only knew that I'd been somehow made to feel a sham. Wasn't I a bit of a sham anyway—though not for her ridiculous reasons—with my arty talk to lady pupils and my newly-acquired parlour-socialism? Yes, I was. But she knew nothing about that. I could quite easily have impressed her. That was the most humiliating part of the whole business; I had mis-managed our interview from the very beginning. I had blushed and squabbled, instead of being wonderful, convincing, superior, fatherly, mature. I had tried to compete with her beastly little Kurt on his own ground; just the very thing, of course, which Sally had wanted and expected me to do! After all these months, I had made the one really fatal mistake—I had let her see that I was not only incompetent but jealous. Yes, vulgarly jealous. I could have kicked myself. The mere thought made me prickly with shame from head to foot.

Well, the mischief was done, now. There was only one thing for it, and that was to forget the whole affair. And of course it would be impossible for me ever to see Sally again.

It must have been about ten days after this that I was visited, one morning, by a small pale dark-haired young man who spoke American fluently with a slight foreign accent. His name, he told me, was George P. Sandars. He had seen my English-teaching advertisement in the B.Z. am Mittag.

"When would you like to begin?" I asked him.

But the young man shook his head hastily. Oh no, he hadn't come to take lessons, at all. Rather disappointed, I waited politely for him to explain the reason of his visit. He seemed in no hurry to do this. Instead, he accepted a cigarette, sat down and began to talk chattily about the States. Had I ever been to Chicago? No? Well, had I heard of James L. Schraube? I hadn't? The young man uttered a faint sigh. He had the air of being very patient with me, and with the world in general. He had evidently been over the same ground with a good many other people already. James L. Schraube, he explained, was a very big man in Chicago: he owned a whole chain of restaurants and several cinemas. He had two large country houses and a yacht on Lake Michigan. And he possessed no less than four cars. By this time, I was beginning to drum with my fingers on the table. A pained expression passed over the young man's face. He excused himself for taking up my valuable time; he had only told me about Mr. Schraube, he said, because he thought I might be interested—his tone implied a gentle rebuke—and because Mr. Schraube, had I known him, would certainly have vouched for his friend Sandars' respectability. However . . . it couldn't be helped . . . well, would I lend him two hundred marks? He needed the money in order to start a business; it was a unique opportunity, which he would miss altogether if he didn't find the money before to-morrow morning. He would pay me back within three days. If I gave him the money now he would return that same evening with papers to prove that the whole thing was perfectly genuine.

No? Ah well. . . . He didn't seem unduly surprised. He rose to go at once, like a business man who has wasted a valuable twenty minutes on a prospective customer: the loss, he contrived politely to imply, was mine, not his. Already at the door, he paused for a moment: Did I happen, by any chance, to know some film actresses? He was travelling, as a sideline, in a new kind of face-cream specially invented to keep the skin from getting dried up by the studio lights. It was being used by all the Hollywood stars already, but in Europe it was still quite unknown. If he could find half a dozen actresses to use and recommend it, they should have free sample jars and permanent supplies at half-price.

After a moment's hesitation, I gave him Sally's address. I don't know quite why I did it. Partly, of course, to get rid of the young man, who showed signs of wishing to sit down again and continue our conversation. Partly, perhaps, out of malice. It would do Sally no harm to have to put up with his chatter for an hour or two: she had told me that she liked men with ambition. Perhaps she would even get a jar of the face-cream—if it existed at all. And if he touched her for the two hundred marks—well, that wouldn't matter so very much, either. He couldn't deceive a baby.

"But whatever you do," I warned him, "don't say that I sent you."

He agreed to this at once, with a slight smile. He must have had his own explanation of my request, for he didn't appear to find it in the least strange. He raised his hat politely as he went downstairs. By the next morning, I had forgotten about his visit altogether.

A few days later, Sally herself rang me up. I had been called away in the middle of a lesson to answer the telephone and was very ungracious.

"Oh, is that you, Christopher darling?"

"Yes. It's me."

"I say, can you come round and see me at once?"

"No."

"Oh. . . ." My refusal evidently gave Sally a shock. There was a little pause, then she continued, in a tone of unwonted humility: "I suppose you're most terribly busy?"

"Yes. I am."

"Well . . . would you mind frightfully if I came round to see you?"

"What about?"

"Darling"—Sally sounded positively desperate—"I can't possibly explain to you over the telephone. . . . It's something really serious."

"Oh, I see"—I tried to make this as nasty as possible—"another magazine article, I suppose?"

Nevertheless, as soon as I'd said it, we both had to laugh.

"Chris, you are a brute!" Sally tinkled gaily along the wire: then checked herself abruptly: "No, darling—this time I promise you: it's most terribly serious, really and truly it is." She paused; then impressively added: "And you're the only person who can possibly help."

"Oh, all right. . . ." I was more than half melted already. "Come in an hour."

"Well, darling, I'll begin at the very beginning, shall I? . . . Yesterday morning, a man rang me up and asked if he could come round and see me. He said it was on very important business; and as he seemed to know my name and everything of course I said: Yes, certainly, come at once. . . . So he came. He told me his name was Rakowski—Paul Rakowski—and that he was a European agent of Metro-Goldwyn-Mayer and that he'd come to make me an offer. He said they were looking out for an English actress who spoke German to act in a comedy film they were going to shoot on the Italian Riviera. He was most frightfully convincing about it all; he told me who the director was and the camera-man and the art-director and who'd written the script. Naturally, I hadn't heard of any of them before. But that didn't seem so surprising: in fact, it really made it sound much more real, because most people would have chosen one of the names you see in the newspapers. . . . Anyhow, he said that, now he'd seen me, he was sure I'd be just the person for the part, and he could practically promise it to me, as long as the test was all right . . . so of course I was simply thrilled and I asked when the test would be and he said not for a day or two, as he had to make arrangements with the Ufa people. . . . So then we began to talk about Hollywood and he told me all kinds of stories—I suppose they *could* have been things he'd read in fan magazines, but somehow I'm pretty sure they weren't— and then he told me how they make sound-effects and how they do the trick-work; he was really most awfully interesting and he certainly must have been inside a great many studios. . . . Anyhow, when we'd finished talking about Hollywood, he started to tell me about the rest of America and the people he knew, and about the gangsters and about New York. He said he'd only just arrived from there and all his luggage was still in the customs at Hamburg. As a matter of fact, I *had* been thinking to myself that it seemed rather queer he was so shabbily dressed; but after he said that, of course, I thought it was quite natural. . . . Well—now you must promise not to laugh at this part of the story, Chris, or I simply shan't be able to tell you—presently he started making the most passionate love to me. At first I was rather angry with him, for sort of mixing business with pleasure; but then, after a bit, I didn't mind so much: he was quite attractive, in a Russian kind of way. . . . And the end of it was, he invited me to have dinner with him; so we went to Horcher's and had one of the most marvellous dinners I've ever had in my life (that's one consolation); only, when the bill came, he said 'Oh, by the way, darling, could you lend me three hundred marks until to-morrow? I've only got dollar bills on me, and I'll have to get them changed at the Bank.' So, of course, I gave them to him: as bad luck would have it, I had quite a lot of money on me, that evening. . . . And then he said: 'Let's have a bottle of champagne to celebrate your film contract.' So I agreed, and I suppose by that time I must have been pretty tight because when he asked me to spend the night with him, I said Yes. We went to one of those little hotels in the Augsburgerstrasse—I forget its name, but I can find it again, easily. . . . It was the most ghastly hole. . . . Anyhow, I don't remember much more about what happened that evening. It was early this morning that I started to think about things properly, while he was still asleep; and I began to wonder if everything was really quite all right. . . . I hadn't noticed his underclothes before: they gave me a bit of a shock. You'd expect an important film man to wear silk next his skin, wouldn't you? Well, his were the most extraordinary kind of stuff like camel-hair or something; they looked as if they might have belonged to John the Baptist. And then he had a regular Woolworth's tin clip for his tie. It wasn't so much that his things were shabby; but you could see they'd never been any good, even when they were new. . . . I was just making up my mind to get out of bed and take a look inside his pockets, when he woke up and it was too late. So we ordered breakfast. . . . I don't know if he thought I was madly in love with him by this time and wouldn't notice, or whether he just couldn't be bothered to go on pretending, but this morning he was like a completely different person—just a common little guttersnipe. He ate his jam off the blade of his knife, and of course most of it went on to the sheets. And he sucked the insides out of the eggs with a most terrific squelching noise. I couldn't help laughing at him, and that made him quite cross. . . . Then he said: 'I must have beer!' Well, I said, all right; ring down to the office and ask for some. To tell you the truth, I was beginning to be a bit frightened of him. He'd started to scowl in the most cave-mannish way; I felt sure he must be mad. So I thought I'd humour him as much as I could. . . . Anyhow, he seemed to think I'd made quite a good suggestion, and he picked up the telephone and had a long conversation and got awfully angry, because he said they refused to send beer up to the rooms. I realize now that he must have been holding the hook all the time and just acting; but he did it most awfully well, and anyhow I was much too scared to notice things much. I thought he'd probably start murdering me because he couldn't get his beer. . . . However, he took it quite quietly. He said he must get dressed and go downstairs and fetch it himself. All right, I said. . . . Well, I waited and waited and he didn't come back. So at last I rang the bell and asked the maid if she'd seen him go out. And she said: 'Oh yes, the gentleman paid the bill and went away about an hour ago. . . . He said you weren't to be disturbed.' I was so surprised, I just said: 'Oh, right, thanks. . . .' The funny thing was, I'd so absolutely made up my mind by this time that he was a looney that I'd stopped suspecting him of being a swindler. Perhaps that was what he wanted. . . . Anyhow, he wasn't such a looney, after all, because, when I looked in my bag, I found he'd helped himself to all the rest of my money, as well as the change from the three hundred marks I'd lent him the night before. . . . What really annoys me about the whole business is that I bet he thinks I'll be ashamed to go to the police. Well, I'll just show him he's wrong—"

"I say, Sally, what exactly did this young man look like?"

"He was about your height. Pale. Dark. You could tell he wasn't a born American; he spoke with a foreign accent—"

"Can you remember if he mentioned a man named Schraube, who lives in Chicago?"

"Let's see . . . Yes, of course he did! He talked about him a lot. . . . But, Chris, how on earth did you know?"

"Well, it's like this. . . . Look here, Sally, I've got a most awful confession to make to you. . . . I don't know if you'll ever forgive me. . . ."

We went to the Alexanderplatz that same afternoon.

The interview was even more embarrassing than I had expected. For myself at any rate. Sally, if she felt ،ncomfortable, did not show it by so much as the movement of an eyelid. She detailed the facts of the case to the two bespectacled police officials with such brisk bright matter-of-factness that one might have supposed she had come to complain about a strayed lapdog or an umbrella lost in a bus. The two officials—both obviously fathers of families—were at first inclined to be shocked. They dipped their pens excessively in the violet ink, made nervous inhibited circular movements with their elbows, before beginning to write, and were very curt and gruff.

"Now about this hotel," said the elder of them sternly: "I suppose you knew, before going there, that it was an hotel of a certain kind?"

"Well, you didn't expect us to go to the Bristol, did you?" Sally's tone was very mild and reasonable: "They wouldn't have let us in there without luggage, anyway."

"Ah, so you had no luggage?" The younger one pounced upon this fact triumphantly, as of supreme importance. His violet copper-plate police-hand began to travel steadily across a ruled sheet of foolscap paper. Deeply inspired by his theme, he paid not the slightest attention to Sally's retort:

"I don't usually pack a suitcase when a man asks me out to dinner."

The elder one caught the point, however, at once:

"So it wasn't till you were at the restaurant that this young man invited you to—er—accompany him to the hotel?"

"It wasn't till after dinner."

"My dear young lady," the elder one sat back in his chair, very much the sarcastic father, "may I enquire whether it is your usual custom to accept invitations of this kind from perfect strangers?"

Sally smiled sweetly. She was innocence and candour itself:

"But, you see, Herr Kommissar, he wasn't a perfect stranger. He was my fiancé."

That made both of them sit up with a jerk. The younger one even made a small blot in the middle of his virgin page—the only blot, perhaps, to be found in all the spotless dossiers of the Polizeipräsidium.

"You mean to tell me, Frl. Bowles"—but in spite of his gruffness, there was already a gleam in the elder one's eye—"You mean to tell me that you became engaged to this man when you'd only known him a single afternoon?"

"Certainly."

"Isn't that, well—rather unusual?"

"I suppose it is," Sally seriously agreed. "But nowadays, you know, a girl can't afford to keep a man waiting. If he asks her once and she refuses him, he may try somebody else. It's all these surplus women—"

At this, the elder official frankly exploded. Pushing back his chair, he laughed himself quite purple in the face. It was nearly a minute before he could speak at all. The young one was much more decorous; he produced a large handkerchief and pretended to blow his nose. But the nose-blowing developed into a kind of sneeze which became a guffaw; and soon he too had abandoned all attempt to take Sally seriously. The rest of the interview was conducted with comic-opera informality, accompanied by ponderous essays in gallantry. The elder official, particularly, became quite daring; I think they were both sorry that I was present. They wanted her to themselves.

"Now don't you worry, Frl. Bowles," they told her, patting her hand at parting, "we'll find him for you, if we have to turn Berlin inside out to do it!"

. . .

"Well!" I exclaimed admiringly, as soon as we were out of earshot, "you do know how to handle them, I must say!"

Sally smiled dreamily: she was feeling very pleased with herself: "How do you mean, exactly, darling?"

"You know as well as I do—getting them to laugh like that: telling them he was your fiancé! It was really inspired!"

But Sally didn't laugh. Instead, she coloured a little, looking down at her feet. A comically guilty, childish expression came over her face:

"You see, Chris, it happened to be quite true—"

"True!"

"Yes, darling." Now, for the first time, Sally was really embarrassed: she began speaking very fast: "I simply couldn't tell you this morning: after everything that's happened, it would have sounded too idiotic for words. . . . He asked me to marry him while we were at the restaurant, and I said Yes. . . . You see, I thought that, being in films, he was probably quite used to quick engagements, like that: after all, in Hollywood, it's quite the usual thing. . . . And, as he was an American, I thought we could get divorced again easily, any time we wanted to. . . . And it would have been a good thing for my career— I mean, if he'd been genuine—wouldn't it? . . . We were to have got married to-day, if it could have been managed. . . . It seems funny to think of, now—"

"But Sally!" I stood still. I gaped at her. I had to laugh: "Well really . . . You know, you're the most extraordinary creature I ever met in my life!"

Sally giggled a little, like a naughty child which has unintentionally succeeded in amusing the grown-ups:

"I always told you I was a bit mad, didn't I? Now perhaps you'll believe it—"

It was more than a week before the police could give us any news. Then, one morning, two detectives called to see me. A young man answering to our description had been traced and was under observation. The police knew his address, but wanted me to identify him before making the arrest. Would I come round with them at once to a snack-bar in the Kleiststrasse? He was to be seen there, about this time, almost every day. I should be able to point him out to them in the crowd and leave again at once, without any fuss or unpleasantness.

I didn't like the idea much, but there was no getting out of it now. The snack-bar, when we arrived, was crowded, for this was the lunch-hour. I caught sight of the young man almost immediately: he was standing at the counter, by the tea-urn, cup in hand. Seen thus, alone and off his guard, he seemed rather pathetic: he looked shabbier and far younger—a mere boy. I very nearly said: "He isn't here." But what would have been the use? They'd have got him, anyway. "Yes, that's him," I told the detectives. "Over there." They nodded. I turned and hurried away down the street, feeling guilty and telling myself: I'll never help the police again.

A few days later, Sally came round to tell me the rest of the story: "I had to see him, of course. . . . I felt an awful brute; he looked so wretched. All he said was: 'I thought you were my friend.' I'd have told him he could keep the money, but he'd spent it all, anyway. . . . The police said he really had been to the States, but he isn't American; he's a Pole. . . . He won't be prosecuted, that's one comfort. The doctor's seen him and he's going to be sent to a home. I hope they treat him decently there. . . ."

"So he was a looney, after all?"

"I suppose so. A sort of mild one. . . ." Sally smiled. "Not very flattering to me, is it? Oh, and Chris, do you know how old he was? You'd never guess!"

"Round about twenty, I should think."

"Sixteen!"

"Oh, rot!"

"Yes, honestly. . . . The case would have to have been tried in the Children's Court!"

We both laughed. "You know, Sally," I said, "what I really like about you is that you're so awfully easy to take in. People who never get taken in are so dreary."

"So you still like me, Chris darling?"

"Yes, Sally. I still like you."

"I was afraid you'd be angry with me—about the other day."

"I was. Very."

"But you're not, now?"

"No . . . I don't think so."

"It's no good my trying to apologize, or explain, or anything. . . . I get like that, sometimes. . . . I expect you understand, don't you, Chris?"

"Yes," I said. "I expect I do."

I have never seen her since. About a fortnight later, just when I was thinking I ought really to ring her up, I got a post-card from Paris: "Arrived here last night. Will write properly to-morrow. Heaps of love." No letter followed. A month after this, another post-card arrived from Rome, giving no address: "Am writing in a day or two," it said. That was six years ago.

So now I am writing to her.

When you read this, Sally—if you ever do—please accept it as a tribute, the sincerest I can pay, to yourself and to our friendship.

And send me another post-card.

PRATER VIOLET

(1945)

[*Prater Violet*, one of the rare successful novels about film-
making, drew on Isherwood's experience of writing a film
in London. It was his first novel written in
the United States.]

"MR. ISHERWOOD?"

"Speaking."

"Mr. Christopher Isherwood?"

"That's me."

"You know, we've been trying to contact you ever since yesterday afternoon." The voice at the other end of the wire was a bit reproachful.

"I was out."

"You were out?" (Not altogether convinced.)

"Yes."

"Oh . . . I see . . ." (A pause, to consider this. Then, suddenly suspicious.) "That's funny, though . . . Your number was always engaged. All the time."

"Who are you?" I asked, my tone getting an edge on it.

"Imperial Bulldog."

"I beg your pardon?"

"Imperial Bulldog Pictures. I'm speaking for Mr. Chatsworth. . . . By the way, were you in Blackpool any time during 1930?"

"There must be some mistake . . ." I got ready to hang up on him. "I've never been to Blackpool in my life."

"Splendid!" The voice uttered a brisk little business laugh. "Then you never saw a show called *Prater Violet*?"

"Never. But what's that got to do with . . . ?"

"It folded up after three nights. But Mr. Chatsworth likes the music, and he thinks we can use most of the lyrics. . . . Your agent says you know all about Vienna."

"Vienna? I was only there once. For a week."

"Only a week?" The voice became quite peevish. "But that's impossible, surely? We were given to understand you'd *lived* there."

"He must have meant Berlin."

"Oh, Berlin? Well, that's pretty much the same kind of set-up, isn't it? Mr. Chatsworth wanted someone with the continental touch. I understand you speak German? That'll come in handy. We're getting Friedrich Bergmann over from Vienna, to direct."

"Oh."

"Friedrich Bergmann, you know."

"Never heard of him."

"That's funny. He's worked in Berlin a lot, too. Weren't you in pictures, over there?"

"I've never been in pictures anywhere."

"You haven't?" For a moment, the voice was audibly dismayed. Then it brightened. "Oh, well . . . It'll be all the same to Mr. Chatsworth, I imagine. He often uses writers who haven't had any experience. If I were you, I wouldn't worry . . ."

"Look here," I interrupted, "what is it that makes you think I have the very slightest interest in taking this job at all?"

"Oh . . . Well, you see, Mr. Isherwood, I'm afraid that's not my department. . . ." The voice began to speak very rapidly and to grow fainter. "No doubt Mr. Katz will be talking things over with your agent. I'm sure we'll be able to come to some arrangement. I'll keep in touch with you. Goodbye . . ."

"I say, wait a minute. . . ."

He was off the line. I jiggled the phone for a moment, stupidly, with vague indignation. Then I picked up the directory, found Imperial Bulldog's number, dialed the first letter, stopped. I walked across to the dining-room door. My mother and my younger brother, Richard, were still sitting at breakfast. I stood just inside the doorway and lit a cigarette, not looking at them, very casual.

"Was that Stephen?" my mother asked. She generally knew when I needed a cue line.

"No." I blew out a lot of smoke, frowning at the mantelpiece clock. "Only some movie people."

"Movie people!" Richard put down his cup with a clatter. "Oh, Christopher! How exciting!"

This made me frown harder.

After a suitable pause, my mother asked, with extreme tact, "Did they want you to write something?"

"Apparently," I drawled, almost too bored to speak.

"Oh, Christopher, how thrilling that sounds! What's the film going to be about? Or mustn't you tell us?"

"I didn't ask."

"Oh, I see. . . . When are you going to start?"

"I'm not. I turned it down."

"You turned it down? Oh . . . What a pity!"

"Well, practically . . ."

"Why? Didn't they offer you enough money?"

"We didn't talk about money," I told Richard, with a slight suggestion of reproof.

"No, of course you wouldn't. Your agent does all that, doesn't he? He'll know how to squeeze the last drop out of them. How much shall you ask for?"

"I've told you once. I refused to do it."

There was another pause. Then my mother said, in her most carefully conversational manner, "Really, the films nowadays seem to get stupider and stupider. No wonder they can't persuade any good writers to come and work for them, no matter what they offer."

I didn't answer. I felt my frown relax a little.

"I expect they'll be calling you again in a few minutes," said Richard, hopefully.

"Why on earth should they?"

"Well, they must want you awfully badly, or they wouldn't have rung up so early in the morning. Besides, movie people never take 'no' for an answer, do they?"

"I dare say they're trying the next one on their list already." I yawned, rather unconvincingly. "Ah, well, I suppose I'd better go and wrestle with chapter eleven."

"I do admire the way you take everything so calmly," Richard said, with that utter lack of sarcasm which sometimes makes his remarks sound like lines from Sophocles. "If it was me, I know I'd be so excited I wouldn't be able to write a word all day."

I mumbled, "See you later," yawned again, stretched myself, and began a turn toward the door, which was checked by my own unwillingness, leaving me facing the sideboard. I started to fiddle with the key of the spoon drawer, locking, unlocking, locking. Then I blew my nose.

"Have another cup of tea before you go?" my mother asked, after watching this performance with a faint smile.

"Oh, do, Christopher! It's still scalding hot."

Without answering, I sat down in my chair at the table. The morning paper still lay where I had let it fall, half an hour ago, crumpled and limp, as if bled of its news. Germany's withdrawal from the League was still the favorite topic. An expert predicted a preventive war against Hitler some time next year, when the Maginot Line would be impregnable. Goebbels told the German people that their vote on November the twelfth would be either Yes or Yes. Governor Ruby Laffoon of Kentucky had given a colonel's commission to Mae West.

"Cousin Edith's dentist," said my mother, as she passed me the teacup, "seems to be quite convinced Hitler's going to invade Austria soon."

"Oh, indeed?" I took a big sip of tea and sat back, feeling suddenly in a very good humor. "Well, no doubt the *dental* profession has sources of information denied to the rest of us. But I must say, in my ignorance, I entirely fail to see how . . ."

I was off. My mother poured fresh cups of tea for Richard and herself. They exchanged milk and sugar with smiling pantomime and settled back comfortably in their chairs, like people in a restaurant when the orchestra strikes up a tune which everybody knows by heart.

Within ten minutes, I had set up and knocked down every argument the dentist could possibly have been expected to produce, and many that he couldn't. I used a lot of my favorite words: Gauleiter, solidarity, démarche, dialectic, Gleichschaltung, infiltration, An schluss, realism, tranche, cadre. Then, after pausing to light another cigarette and get my breath, I started to sketch, none too briefly, the history of National Socialism since the Munich Putsch.

The telephone rang.

"What a bore!" said Richard, politely. "That stupid thing always interrupts just when you're telling us something interesting. Don't let's answer it. They'll soon get tired. . . ."

I had jumped up, nearly knocking over my chair, and was out in the hall already, grabbing for the instrument.

"Hullo . . ." I gasped.

There was no answer. But I could hear that the receiver was off at the other end—distant voices, seemingly in a violent argument, with a background of wireless music.

"Hullo?" I repeated.

The voices moved away a little.

"Hullo!" I yelled.

Perhaps they heard me. The sounds of talking and music were suddenly cut right out, as though a hand had covered the mouthpiece.

"To hell with you all," I told them.

The mouthpiece was uncovered long enough for me to hear a man's voice, with a thick, growling foreign accent, say, "It's all too idiotic for words."

"Hullo!" I yelled. "Hullo! Hullo! Hullo! Hullo! Hullo!"

"Wait," said the foreign voice, very curt, as if speaking to a nagging child.

"I bloody well won't wait!" I shouted at him. And this sounded so silly that I started to laugh.

The hand came off the mouthpiece again, releasing a rush of talk and music which sounded as though it had been dammed up during the interval, it was so loud.

"Hullo," said the foreign voice, rapidly and impatiently. "Hullo, hullo!"

"Hullo?"

"Hullo? Here Dr. Bergmann."

"Good morning, Dr. Bergmann."

"Yes? Good morning. Hullo? Hullo, I would like to speak to Mr. Isherwood, please, at once."

"Speaking."

"Mr. Kreestoffer Ischervood . . ." Dr. Bergmann said this with great care and emphasis. He must have been reading the name from a notebook.

"Here I am."

"*Ja, ja* . . ." Bergmann was obviously nearing the end of his patience. "I wish to speak to Mr. Isherwood personally. Please bring him."

"I'm Christopher Isherwood," I said, in German. "It was me talking to you all the time."

"Ah—*you* are Mr. Isherwood! Marvelous! Why did you not say so at once? And you speak my language? Bravo! *Endlich ein vernünftiger Mensch!* You cannot imagine how I am glad to hear your voice! Tell me, my dear friend, can you come to me immediately?"

I turned cautious at once. "You mean, today?"

"I mean now, as immediately as possible, this instant."

"I'm awfully busy this morning . . ." I began, hesitantly. But Dr. Bergmann cut me short with a sigh which was nearer to a loud, long groan.

"It's too stupid. Terrible. I give up."

"I think I could manage this afternoon, perhaps. . . ."

Bergmann disregarded this completely. "Hopeless," he muttered to himself. "All alone in this damned idiotic city. Nobody understands a single word. Terrible. Nothing to do."

"Couldn't you," I suggested, "come here?"

"No, no. Nothing to do. Never mind. It's all too difficult. *Scheusslich.*"

There was a pause of extreme tension. I sucked my lip. I thought of chapter eleven. I felt myself weakening. Oh, damn the man!

At length, I asked unwillingly, "Where are you?"

I heard him turn to someone, and growl belligerently, "Where am I?" There was an answer I couldn't catch. Then Bergmann's growl, "Don't understand a word. You tell him."

A new voice, reassuringly Cockney:

"Hullo, sir. This is Cowan's Hotel, in Bishopsgate. We're just across from the station. You can't miss it."

"Thanks," I said. "I'll be right along. Good-b—"

I heard Bergmann's hasty, "Moment! Moment!" After what sounded like a brief but furious struggle, he got possession of the instrument and emitted a deep, snorting breath. "Tell me, my friend, when will you be here?"

"Oh, in about an hour."

"An *hour*? That is very long. How will you come?"

"By Underground."

"Would it not be better to take a taxi?"

"No, it wouldn't," I answered firmly, as I mentally reckoned up the cost of a fare from Kensington to Liverpool Street Station: "No better."

"Why would it not be better?"

"It would be just as slow as the Underground. All the traffic, you know."

"Ah, the traffic. Terrible." A deep, deep snort, as of a dying whale about to sink to the bottom of the ocean forever.

"Don't worry," I told him cheerfully. I felt quite kindly toward him, now that I had won my point about the taxi. "I'll be with you very soon."

Bergmann groaned faintly. I knew that he didn't believe me.

"Goodbye, my friend."

"*Auf Wiedersehen* . . . No, I can't say that, can I? I haven't seen you yet."

But he had hung up on me already.

"Was that the movie people again?" Richard asked, as I looked into the dining room.

"No. Well, yes, in a way. Tell you everything later. I've got to rush. Oh, and Mummy, I *might* be a little late for lunch. . . ."

Cowan's Hotel was *not* just across from the station. No place ever is, when they tell you that. I arrived in a bad temper, having been twice misdirected and once nearly knocked down by a bus. Also, I was out of breath. Despite my resolve to take Bergmann calmly, I had run all the way from the Underground.

It was quite a small place. The porter was standing at the door, as I came panting up. Evidently he'd been on the lookout for me.

"It's Mr. Usherwood, isn't it? The Doctor'll be glad to see you.

He's been having a lot of vexation. Arrived a day before he was expected. Some mistake. No one to meet him at the boat. Trouble with
his passport. Trouble with the Customs. Lost a suitcase. A regular
mix-up. It happens that way, sometimes."

"Where is he now? Upstairs?"

"No, sir. Just popped out for some cigarettes. Didn't seem to fancy
what we had. You get to like those continental kinds, I suppose, if
you're used to them. They're milder."

"All right. I'll wait."

"If you'll excuse me, you'd better go after him. You know what
foreign gentlemen are, being strange to the city. They'll lose themselves
in the middle of Trafalgar Square. Not that I won't say we wouldn't
be the same, in their place. I'm sure I don't know what's become of
him. He's been gone above twenty minutes already."

"Which way?"

"Round the corner, to your left. Three doors down. You'll be
sure to catch him."

"What does he look like?"

My question seemed to amuse the porter. "Oh, you'll know him
all right when you see him, sir. You couldn't mistake him in a million."

The girl at the little tobacconist's was equally chatty. There was
no need for me to try to describe Dr. Bergmann. His visit had made
a great impression.

"Quite a character, isn't he?" she giggled. "Asked me what I
thought about, being here all day long. I don't have much time to
think, I told him. . . . Then we got to talking about dreams."

Bergmann had told her of a doctor, somewhere abroad, who said
that your dreams don't mean what you think they mean. He had
seemed to regard this as a great scientific discovery, which had amused
the girl and made her feel somewhat superior, because she'd always
known that. She had a book at home which used to belong to her
aunt. It was called *The Queen of Sheba's Dream Dictionary*, and it
had been written long before this foreign doctor was born.

"It's ever so interesting. Suppose you dream of sausages—that's
a quarrel. Unless you're eating them. Then it's love, or good health,
the same as sneezing and mushrooms. The other night, I dreamed I
was taking off my stockings and, sure enough, the very next morning,

my brother sent me a postal order for five and six. Of course, they don't always come true like that. Not at once . . ."

Here I managed to interrupt, and ask her if she knew where Bergmann had gone.

He had wanted some magazine or other, she told me. So she'd sent him over to Mitchell's. It was down at the other end of the street. I couldn't miss it.

"And you'd better take him his cigarettes," she added. "He left them lying here on the counter."

Mitchell's, also, remembered the foreign gentleman, but less favorably than the girl at the tobacconist's. There seemed to have been a bit of an argument. Bergmann had asked for *The New World-Stage*, and had become quite indignant when the boy naturally supposed it was a theatrical magazine, and had offered him *The Stage* or *The Era* instead. "Hopeless. Nothing to do," I could imagine him groaning. At length, he had condescended to explain that *The New World-Stage* was about politics, and in German. The boy had advised him to try the bookstall inside the station.

It was at this point that I lost my head. The whole business was degenerating into a man-hunt, and I could only run, like a bloodhound, from clue to clue. It wasn't until I had arrived, gasping, in front of the bookstall that I realized how silly I'd been. The bookstall attendants were much too busy to have noticed anybody with a foreign accent; there had probably been several, anyway, within the past half hour. I glanced wildly around, accosted two likely-looking strangers, who regarded me with insulted suspicion, and then hurried back to the hotel.

Again, the porter was waiting for me.

"Bad luck, sir." His manner was that of a sympathetic spectator toward the last man in an obstacle race.

"What do you mean? Isn't he here yet?"

"Come and gone again. Wasn't a minute after you left. 'Where is he?' he asks, same as you. Then the phone rings. It was a gentleman from the studio. We'd been trying to get him all morning. Wanted the Doctor to come out there, right away, as quick as he could. I said you'd be back, but he wouldn't wait. He's like that, sir—all impatience. So I put him in a taxi."

"Didn't he leave any message?"

"Yes, sir. You was to meet them for lunch, at the Café Royal. One o'clock sharp."

"Well, I'm damned."

I went into the lobby, sat down in a chair and wiped my forehead. That settled it. Who in hell did they think they were? Well, this would be a lesson to me. One thing was certain: they wouldn't hear from me again. Not if they came to the house and sat on the doorstep all day long.

I found them in the Grill Room.

I was ten minutes late, a little concession to my injured vanity. The headwaiter knew Mr. Chatsworth and pointed him out to me. I paused to get a first impression before approaching their table.

A gray bushy head, with its back to me, confronted a big pink moon-face, thin, sleek, fair hair, heavy tortoise-shell glasses. The gray head was thrust forward intently. The pink face lolled back, wide open to all the world.

"Between you and me," it was saying, "there's just one thing the matter with them. They've got no *savoir vivre*."

The pale round eyes, magnified by their lenses, moved largely over the room, included me without surprise: "It's Mr. Isherwood, isn't it? Very glad you could come. I don't think you two know each other?"

He didn't rise. But Bergmann jerked to his feet with startling suddenness, like Punch in a show. "A tragic Punch," I said to myself. I couldn't help smiling as we shook hands, because our introduction seemed so superfluous. There are meetings which are like recognitions—this was one of them. Of course we knew each other. The name, the voice, the features were inessential, I knew that face. It was the face of a political situation, an epoch. The face of Central Europe.

Bergmann, I am sure, was aware of what I was thinking. "How do you do, *sir*?" He gave the last word a slight, ironic emphasis. We stood there, for a moment, looking at each other.

"Sit down," Mr. Chatsworth told us, good-humoredly.

He raised his voice. "*Garçon, la carte pour monsieur!*" Several people looked around. "You'd better have the Tournedos Chasseur," he added.

I chose Sole Bonne Femme, which I don't like, because it was the first thing I saw, and because I was determined to show Chatsworth that I had a will of my own. He had already ordered champagne. "Never drink anything else before sunset." There was a little place in Soho, he informed us, where he kept his own claret. "Picked up six dozen at an auction last week. I bet my butler I'd find him something better than we had in the cellar. The blighter's so damned superior, but he had to admit I was right. Made him pay up, too."

Bergmann grunted faintly. He had transferred his attention to Chatsworth, now, and was watching him with an intensity which would have reduced most people to embarrassed silence within thirty seconds. Having eaten up his meat with a sort of frantic nervous impatience, he was smoking. Chatsworth ate leisurely, but with great decision, pausing after each mouthful to make a new pronouncement. Bergmann's strong, hairy, ringless hand rested on the table. He held his cigarette like an accusing forefinger, pointed straight at Chatsworth's heart. His head was magnificent, and massive as sculptured granite. The head of a Roman emperor, with dark old Asiatic eyes. His stiff drab suit didn't fit him. His shirt collar was too tight. His tie was askew and clumsily knotted. Out of the corner of my eye, I studied the big firm chin, the grim compressed line of the mouth, the harsh furrows cutting down from the imperious nose, the bushy black hair in the nostrils. The face was the face of an emperor, but the eyes were the dark mocking eyes of his slave—the slave who ironically obeyed, watched, humored and judged the master who could never understand him; the slave upon whom the master depended utterly for his amusement, for his instruction, for the sanction of his power; the slave who wrote the fables of beasts and men.

From wine, Chatsworth had passed, by a natural sequence of ideas, to the Riviera. Did Bergmann know Monte Carlo? Bergmann grunted negatively. "I don't mind telling you," said Chatsworth, "that Monte's my spiritual home. Never cared much about Cannes. Monte's got a *je ne sais quoi*, something all its own. I make a point of getting down there for ten days every winter. Doesn't matter how busy I am.

I just pull up stakes and go. I look at it this way; it's an investment. If I didn't have my time at Monte, I just couldn't stand this bloody London fog and drizzle. I'd come down with the flu, or something. Be in bed for a month. I'm bloody well doing the studio a favor; that's what I tell them. *Garçon!*"

Pausing to order Crêpes Suzette, without consulting either of us, Chatsworth went on to explain that he wasn't a gambler, really. "Have to do enough gambling in the motion-picture business, anyway. Roulette's a damn silly game. Only fit for suckers and old women. I like chemmy, though. Lost a couple of thousand last year. My wife prefers bridge. I tell her that's her bloody insularity."

I wondered if Bergmann's English was equal to understanding all this. His expression was getting more and more enigmatic. Even Chatsworth seemed to be aware of it. He was becoming a little unsure of his audience. He tried another opening, which began by congratulating the headwaiter on the Crêpes Suzette. "Give Alphonse my compliments, and tell him he's excelled himself." The headwaiter, who evidently knew just how to handle Chatsworth, bowed deeply. "For you, monsieur, we take a leetle beet extra trouble. We know you are connoisseur. You can appreciate."

Chatsworth fairly beamed. "My wife tells me I'm a bloody Red. Can't help it. It just makes me sick, the way most people treat servants. No consideration. Especially chauffeurs. You'd think they weren't human beings. Some of these damned snobs'll work a man to death. Get him up at all hours. He daren't call his soul his own. I can't afford it, but I keep three: two for day and the other fellow for the night. My wife's always after me to sack one of them. 'Either we have three,' I tell her, 'or you drive yourself.' And she'll never do that. All women are bloody bad drivers. But at least she admits it."

Coffee was served, and Chatsworth produced a formidable red morocco-leather case of beautiful workmanship, as big as a pocket Testament, which contained his cigars. They cost five and sixpence each, he informed us. I refused, but Bergmann took one, lighting it with his grimmest frown. "Once you've got a taste for them, you'll never smoke anything else," Chatsworth warned him, and added graciously, "I'll send you a box tomorrow."

The cigar somehow completed Chatsworth. As he puffed it, he

seemed to grow larger than life size. His pale eyes shone with a prophetic light.

"For years, I've had one great ambition. You'll laugh at me.
Everybody does. They say I'm crazy. But I don't care." He paused.
Then announced solemnly, "*Tosca*. With Garbo."

Bergmann turned, and gave me a rapid, enigmatic glance. Then
he exhaled, with such force that Chatsworth's cigar smoke was blown
back around his head. Chatsworth looked pleased. Evidently this was
the right kind of reaction.

"Without music, of course. I'd do it absolutely straight." He
paused again, apparently waiting for our protest. There was none.

"It's one of the greatest stories in the world. People don't realize
that. Christ, it's magnificent."

Another impressive pause.

"And do you know who I want to write it?" Chatsworth's tone
prepared us for the biggest shock of all.

Silence.

"Somerset Maugham."

Utter silence, broken only by Bergmann's breathing.

Chatsworth sat back, with the air of a man who makes his ultimatum. "If I can't get Maugham, I won't do it at all."

"Have you asked him?" I wanted to inquire, but the question
sounded unworthy of the occasion. I met Chatsworth's solemn eye,
and forced a weak, nervous smile.

However, the smile seemed to please Chatsworth. He interpreted
it in his own way, and unexpectedly beamed back at me.

"I bet I know what Isherwood's thinking," he told Bergmann.
"He's right, too, blast him. I quite admit it. I'm a bloody intellectual
snob."

Bergmann suddenly looked up at me. At last, I said to myself,
he is going to speak. The black eyes sparkled, the lips curved to the
form of a word, the hands sketched the outline of a gesture. Then I
heard Chatsworth say, "Hullo, Sandy."

I turned, and there, standing beside the table, incredibly, was
Ashmeade. An Ashmeade nearly ten years older, but wonderfully little
changed; still handsome, auburn-haired and graceful; still dressed with
casual undergraduate elegance in sports coat, silk pullover and flannel

bags. "Sandy's our story editor," Chatsworth was telling Bergmann. "Obstinate as a mule. He'd rewrite Shakespeare, if he didn't like the script."

Ashmeade smiled his smooth, pussycat smile. "Hullo, Isherwood," he said softly, in an amused voice.

Our eyes met. "What the hell are you doing here?" I wanted to ask him. I was really quite shocked. Ashmeade, the poet. Ashmeade, the star of the Marlowe Society. Obviously, he was aware of what I was thinking. His light golden eyes smilingly refused to admit anything, to exchange any conspiratorial signal.

"You two know each other?" Chatsworth asked.

"We were at Cambridge together," I said briefly, not taking my eyes from Ashmeade's, challenging him.

"Cambridge, eh?" Chatsworth was obviously impressed. I could feel that my stock had risen several points. "Well, you two will have a lot to talk about."

I looked squarely at Ashmeade, daring him to contradict this. Ashmeade simply smiled, from behind his decorative mask.

"Time to be getting back to the studio," Chatsworth announced, rising and stretching himself. "Dr. Bergmann's coming along with us, Sandy. Have that Rosemary Lee picture run for him, will you? What the hell's it called?"

"*Moon over Monaco*," said Ashmeade, as one says *Hamlet*, casually, without quotation marks.

Bergmann stood up with a deep, tragic grunt.

"It's a nasty bit of work," Chatsworth told him cheerfully, "but you'll get an idea what she's like."

We all moved toward the door. Bergmann looked very short and massive, marching between Chatsworth's comfortable bulk and Ashmeade's willowy tallness. I followed, feeling excluded and slightly sulky.

Chatsworth waved the attendant aside with a lordly gesture and himself helped Bergmann into his overcoat. It was like dressing up a Roman statue. Bergmann's hat was a joke in the worst taste. Much too small, it perched absurdly on his bushy gray curls, and Bergmann's face looked grimly out from under it, with the expression of an emperor taken captive and guyed by the rebellious mob. Ashmeade, of course, wore neither hat nor coat. He carried a slim umbrella, perfectly rolled. Outside, Chatsworth's Rolls-Royce, complete with chauffeur, was waiting—all light gray, to match his own loose-fitting, well-cut clothes.

"Better get plenty of sleep tonight, Isherwood," he advised me graciously. "We're going to work you hard."

Ashmeade said nothing. He smiled, and followed Chatsworth into the car.

Bergmann paused, took my hand. A smile of extraordinary charm, of intimacy, came over his face. He was standing very close to me.

"Goodbye, Mr. Isherwood," he said, in German. "I shall call you tomorrow morning." His voice dropped; he looked deeply, affectionately, into my eyes. "I am sure we shall be very happy together. You know, already, I feel absolutely no shame before you. We are like two married men who meet in a whorehouse."

When I got home, my mother and Richard were in the drawing room waiting for me.

"Well!"

"Any success?"

"What was it like?"

"Did you meet him?"

I dropped into a chair. "Yes," I said, "I met him."

"And—is everything all right?"

"How do you mean, all right?"

"Are you going to take the job?"

"I don't know. . . . Well, yes . . . Yes, I suppose I am."

One of Chatsworth's underlings had installed Bergmann in a service flat in Knightsbridge, not far from Hyde Park Corner. I found him there next morning, at the top of several steep flights of stairs. Even before we could see each other, he began to hail me from above. "Come up! Higher! Higher! Courage! Not yet! Where are you? Don't weaken! Aha! At last! *Servus*, my friend!"

"Well?" I asked, as we shook hands. "How do you like it here?"

"Terrible!" Bergmann twinkled at me comically from under his black bush of eyebrow. "It's an inferno! You have made the *as*-cent to hell."

This morning, he was no longer an emperor but an old clown, shock-headed, in his gaudy silk dressing gown. Tragicomic, like all clowns, when you see them resting backstage after the show.

He laid his hand on my arm. "First, tell me one thing, please. Is your whole city as horrible as this?"

"Horrible? Why, this is the best part of it! Wait till you see our slums, and the suburbs."

Bergmann grinned. "You console me enormously."

He led the way into the flat. The small living room was tropically hot, under a heavy cloud of cigarette smoke. It reeked of fresh paint. The whole place was littered with clothes, papers and books, in explosive disorder, like the debris around a volcano.

Bergmann called, "Mademoiselle!" and a girl came out of the inner room. She had fair smooth hair, brushed plainly back from her temples, and a quiet oval face, which would have looked pretty, if her chin hadn't been too pointed. She wore rimless glasses and the wrong shade of lipstick. She was dressed in the neat jacket and skirt of a stenographer.

"Dorothy, I introduce you to Mr. Isherwood. Dorothy is my secretary, the most beautiful of all the gifts given me by the munificent Mr. Chatsworth. You see, Dorothy, Mr. Isherwood is the good Virgil who has come to guide me through this Anglo-Saxon comedy."

Dorothy smiled the smile of a new secretary—a bit bewildered still, but prepared for anything in the way of lunatic employers.

"And please suppress that fire," Bergmann added. "It definitely kills me."

Dorothy knelt down and turned off the gas fire, which had been roaring away in a corner. "Do you want me now," she asked, very businesslike, "or shall I be getting on with the letters?"

"We always want you, my darling. Without you, we could not exist for one moment. You are our Beatrice. But first, Mr. Virgil and I have to become acquainted. Or rather, he must become acquainted with me. For, you see," Bergmann continued, as Dorothy left the room, "I know everything about you already."

"You do?"

"Certainly. Everything that is important. Wait. I shall show you something."

Raising his forefinger, smilingly, to indicate that I must be patient, he began to rummage among the clothes and scattered papers. I watched with growing curiosity, as Bergmann's search became increasingly furious. Now and then, he would discover some object, evidently not the right one, hold it up before him for a moment, like a nasty-smelling dead rat, and toss it aside again with a snort of disgust or some exclamation such as "Abominable!" "*Scheusslich!*" "Too silly for words!" I watched him unearth, in this way, a fat black notebook, a shaving mirror, a bottle of hair tonic and an abdominal belt. Finally, under a pile of shirts, he found a copy of *Mein Kampf* which he kissed, before throwing it into the wastepaper basket. "I love him!" he told me, making a wry, comical face.

The search spread into the bedroom. I could hear him plunging about, snorting and breathing hard, as I stood by the mantelpiece, looking at the photographs of a large, blond, humorous woman and a thin, dark, rather frightened girl. Next, the bathroom was explored. A couple of wet towels were flung out into the passage. Then Bergmann uttered a triumphant "Aha!" He strode back into the living room, waving a book above his head. It was my novel *The Memorial*.

"So! Here we are! You see? I read it at midnight. And again this morning, in my bath."

I was absurdly pleased and flattered. "Well," I tried to sound casual, "how did you like it?"

"I found it grandiose."

"It ought to have been much better. I'm afraid I . . ."

"You are wrong," Bergmann told me, quite severely. He began to turn the pages. "This scene—he tries to make a suicide. It is genial." He frowned solemnly, as if daring me to contradict him. "This I find clearly genial."

I laughed and blushed. Bergmann watched me, smiling, like a proud parent who listens to his son being praised by the headmaster. Then he patted me on the shoulder.

"Look, if you do not believe me. I will show you. This I wrote this morning, after reading your book." He began to fumble in his pockets. As there were only seven of them, it didn't take him long.

He pulled out a crumpled sheet of paper. "My first poem in English. To an English poet."

I took it and read:

When I am a boy, my mother tells to me
It is lucky to wake up when the morning is bright
And first of all hear a lark sing.

Now I am not longer a boy, and I wake. The morning is dark.
I hear a bird singing with unknown name
In a strange country language, but it is luck, I think.

Who is he, this singer, who does not fear the gray city?
Will they drown him soon, the poor Shelley?
Will Byron's hangmen teach him how one limps?
I hope they will not, because he makes me happy.

"Why," I said, "it's beautiful!"

"You like it?" Bergmann was so delighted that he began rubbing his hands. "But you must correct the English, please."

"Certainly not. I like it the way it is."

"Already I think I have a feeling for the language," said Bergmann, with modest satisfaction. "I shall write many English poems."

"May I keep this one?"

"Really? You want it?" he beamed. "Then I shall inscribe it for you."

He took out his fountain pen and wrote: "For Christopher, from Friedrich, his fellow prisoner."

I laid the poem carefully on the mantelpiece. It seemed to be the only safe place in the room. "Is this your wife?" I asked, looking at the photographs.

"Yes. And that is Inge, my daughter. You like her?"

"She has beautiful eyes."

"She is a pianist. Very talented."

"Are they in Vienna?"

"Unfortunately. Yes. I am most anxious for them. Austria is no longer safe. The plague is spreading. I wished them to come with me, but my wife has to look after her mother. It's not so easy." Bergmann sighed deeply. Then, with a sharp glance at me, "You are not married." It sounded like an accusation.

"How did you know?"

"I know these things. . . . You live with your parents?"

"With my mother and brother. My father's dead."

Bergmann grunted and nodded. He was like a doctor who finds his most pessimistic diagnosis is confirmed. "You are a typical mother's son. It is the English tragedy."

I laughed. "Quite a lot of Englishmen do get married, you know."

"They marry their mothers. It is a disaster. It will lead to the destruction of Europe."

"I must say, I don't quite see . . ."

"It will lead definitely to the destruction of Europe. I have written the first chapters of a novel about this. It is called *The Diary of an Etonian Oedipus.*" Bergmann suddenly gave me a charming smile. "But do not worry. We shall change all that."

"All right," I grinned. "I won't worry."

Bergmann lit a cigarette, and blew a cloud of smoke into which he almost disappeared.

"And now," he announced, "the horrible but unavoidable moment has come when we have to talk about this crime we are about to commit: this public outrage, this enormous nuisance, this scandal, this blasphemy. . . . You have read the original script?"

"They sent a messenger round with it, last night."

"And . . .?" Bergmann watched me keenly, waiting for my answer.

"It's even worse than I expected."

"Marvelous! Excellent! You see, I am such a horrible old sinner that nothing is ever as *bad* as I expect. But you are surprised. You are shocked. That is because you are innocent. It is this innocence which I need absolutely to help me, the innocence of Alyosha Karamazov. I shall proceed to corrupt you. I shall teach you everything from the very beginning. . . . Do you know what the film is?" Bergmann cupped his hands, lovingly, as if around an exquisite flower. "The film is an infernal machine. Once it is ignited and set in motion, it revolves with an enormous dynamism. It cannot pause. It cannot apologize. It cannot retract anything. It cannot wait for you to understand it. It cannot explain itself. It simply ripens to its inevitable explosion. This explosion we have to prepare, like anarchists, with the utmost ingenuity and malice. . . . While you were in Germany did you ever see *Frau Nussbaum's letzter Tag?*"

"Indeed I did. Three or four times."

Bergmann beamed. "I directed it."

"No? Really?"

"You didn't know?"

"I'm afraid I never read the credits. . . . Why, that was one of the best German pictures!"

Bergmann nodded, delighted, accepting this as a matter of course. "You must tell that to Umbrella."

"Umbrella?"

"The Beau Brummel who appeared to us yesterday at lunch."

"Oh, Ashmeade . . ."

Bergmann looked concerned. "He is a great friend of yours?"

"No," I grinned. "Not exactly."

"You see, this umbrella of his I find extremely symbolic. It is the British respectability which thinks: 'I have my traditions, and they will protect me. Nothing unpleasant, nothing ungentlemanly can possibly happen within my private park.' This respectable umbrella is the Englishman's magic wand, with which he will try to wave Hitler out of existence. When Hitler declines rudely to disappear, the Englishman will open his umbrella and say, 'After all, what do I care for a little rain?' But the rain will be a rain of bombs and blood. The umbrella is not bomb-proof."

"Don't underrate the umbrella," I said. "It has often been used successfully, by governesses against bulls. It has a very sharp point."

"You are wrong. The umbrella is useless. . . . Do you know Goethe?"

"Only a little."

"Wait. I shall read you something. Wait. Wait."

"The whole *beauty* of the film," I announced to my mother and Richard next morning at breakfast, "is that it has a certain fixed *speed*. The way you see it is mechanically conditioned. I mean, take a painting—you can just glance at it, or you can stare at the left-hand top corner for half an hour. Same thing with a book. The author can't stop you from skimming it, or starting at the last chapter and reading backwards. The point is, you choose your approach. When you go into a cinema, it's different. There's the film, and you have to look at it as the director wants you to look at it. He makes his points, one after another, and he allows you a certain number of seconds or minutes to grasp each one. If you miss anything, he won't repeat himself, and he won't stop to explain. He can't. He's started something, and he has to go through with it. . . . You see, the film is really like a sort of infernal machine . . ."

I stopped abruptly, with my hands in the air. I had caught myself in the middle of one of Bergmann's most characteristic gestures.

I had always had a pretty good opinion of myself as a writer. But, during those first days with Bergmann, it was lowered considerably. I had flattered myself that I had imagination, that I could invent dialogue, that I could develop a character. I had believed that I could describe almost anything, just as a competent artist can draw you an old man's face, or a table, or a tree.

Well, it seemed that I was wrong.

The period is early twentieth century, some time before the 1914 war. It is a warm spring evening in the Vienna Prater. The dancehalls are lighted up. The coffee houses are full. The bands blare. Fireworks are bursting above the trees. The swings are swinging. The roundabouts are revolving. There are freak shows, gypsies telling fortunes, boys playing the concertina. Crowds of people are eating, drinking beer, wandering along the paths beside the river. The drunks sing noisily. The lovers, arm in arm, stroll whispering in the shadow of the elms and the silver poplars.

There is a girl named Toni, who sells violets. Everybody knows her, and she has a word for everybody. She laughs and jokes as she offers the flowers. An officer tries to kiss her; she slips away from him good-humoredly. An old lady has lost her dog; she is sympathetic. An indignant, tyrannical gentleman is looking for his daughter; Toni knows where she is, and with whom, but she won't tell.

Then, as she wanders down the alleys carrying her basket, light-hearted and fancy-free, she comes face to face with a handsome boy in the dress of a student. He tells her, truthfully, that his name is Rudolf. But he is not what he seems. He is really the Crown Prince of Borodania.

All this I was to describe. "Do not concern yourself with the shots," Bergmann had told me. "Just write dialogue. Create atmosphere. Give the camera something to listen to and look at."

I couldn't. I couldn't. My impotence nearly reduced me to tears. It was all so simple, surely? There is Toni's father, for instance. He is fat and jolly, and he has a stall where he sells *Wiener Wuerstchen*. He talks to his customers. He talks to Toni. Toni talks to the customers. They reply. It is all very gay, amusing, delightful. But what the hell do they actually say?

I didn't know. I couldn't write it. That was the brutal truth—I couldn't draw a table. I tried to take refuge in my pride. After all, this was movie work, hack work. It was something essentially false, cheap, vulgar. It was beneath me. I ought never to have become involved in it, under the influence of Bergmann's dangerous charm, and for the sake of the almost incredible twenty pounds a week which Imperial Bulldog was prepared, quite as a matter of course, to pay me. I was betraying my art. No wonder it was so difficult.

Nonsense. I didn't really believe that, either. It isn't vulgar to be able to make people talk. An old man selling sausages isn't vulgar, except in the original meaning of the word, "belonging to the common people." Shakespeare would have known how he spoke. Tolstoy would have known. I didn't know because, for all my parlor socialism, I was a snob. I didn't know how anybody spoke, except public-school boys and neurotic bohemians.

I fell back, in my despair, upon memories of other movies. I tried to be smart, facetious. I made involved, wordy jokes. I wrote a page of dialogue which led nowhere and only succeeded in establishing the fact that an anonymous minor character was having an affair with somebody else's wife. As for Rudolf, the incognito Prince, he talked like the lowest common denominator of all the worst musical comedies I had ever seen. I hardly dared to show my wretched attempts to Bergmann at all.

He read them through with furrowed brows and a short profound grunt; but he didn't seem either dismayed or surprised. "Let me tell you something, Master," he began, as he dropped my manuscript casually into the wastepaper basket, "the film is a symphony. Each movement is written in a certain key. There is a note which has to be chosen and struck immediately. It is characteristic of the whole. It commands the attention."

Sitting very close to me, and pausing only to draw long breaths from his cigarette, he started to describe the opening sequence. It was astounding. Everything came to life. The trees began to tremble in the evening breeze, the music was heard, the roundabouts were set in motion. And the people talked. Bergmann improvised their conversation, partly in German, partly in ridiculous English; and it was vivid and real. His eyes sparkled, his gestures grew more exaggerated, he mimicked, he clowned. I began to laugh. Bergmann smiled delightedly at his own invention. It was all so simple, so effective, so obvious. Why hadn't I thought of it myself?

Bergmann gave me a little pat on the shoulder. "It's nice, isn't it?"

"It's wonderful! I'll note that down before I forget."

Immediately, he was very serious. "No, no. It is wrong. All wrong. I only wanted to give you some idea . . . No, that won't do. Wait. We must consider . . ."

Clouds followed the sunshine. Bergmann scowled grimly as he passed into philosophical analysis. He gave me ten excellent reasons why the whole thing was impossible. They, too, were obvious. Why hadn't I thought of them? Bergmann sighed. "It's not so easy . . ." He lit another cigarette. "Not so easy," he muttered. "Wait. Wait. Let us see . . ."

He rose and paced the carpet, breathing hard, his hands folded severely behind his back, his face shut against the outside world, implacably, like a prison door. Then a thought struck him. He stopped, amused by it. He smiled.

"You know what my wife tells me when I have these difficulties? 'Friedrich,' she says, 'Go and write your poems. When I have cooked the dinner, I will invent this idiotic story for you. After all, prostitution is a woman's business.' "

. . .

That was what Bergmann was like on his good days; the days when I was Alyosha Karamazov, or, as he told Dorothy, like Balaam's ass, "who *once* said a marvelous line." My incompetence merely stimulated him to more brilliant flights of imagination. He sparkled with epigrams, he beamed, he really amazed himself. On such days, we suited each other perfectly. Bergmann didn't really need a collaborator at all. But he needed stimulation and sympathy; he needed someone he could talk German to. He needed an audience.

His wife wrote to him every day, Inge two or three times a week. He read me extracts from their letters, full of household, theatrical and political gossip; and these led to anecdotes, about Inge's first concert, about his mother-in-law, about German and Austrian actors, and the plays and films he had directed. He would spend a whole hour describing how he had produced *Macbeth* in Dresden, with masks, in the style of a Greek tragedy. A morning would go by while he recited his poems, or told me of his last days in Berlin, in the spring of that year, when the Storm Troopers were roving the streets like bandits, and his wife had saved him from several dangerous situations by a quick answer or a joke. Although Bergmann was an Austrian, he had been advised to give up his job and leave Germany in a hurry. They had lost most of their money in consequence. "And so, when Chatsworth's offer came, you see, I could not afford to refuse. There was no alternative. I had my doubts about this artificial Violet, from the very first. Even across half of Europe, it didn't smell so good. . . . Never mind, I said to myself. Here is a problem. Every problem has its solution. We will do what we can. We will not despair. Who knows? Perhaps, after all, we shall present Mr. Chatsworth with a charming nosegay, a nice little surprise."

Bergmann wanted all my time, all my company, all my attention. During those first weeks, our working day steadily increased in length, until I had to make a stand and insist on going home to supper. He seemed determined to possess me utterly. He pursued me with questions, about my friends, my interests, my habits, my love life. The weekends, especially, were the object of his endless, jealous curiosity. What did I do? Whom did I see? Did I live like a monk? "Is it Mr. W.H. you seek, or the Dark Lady of the Sonnets?" But I was equally obstinate. I wouldn't tell him. I teased him with smiles and hints.

Foiled, he turned his attention to Dorothy. Younger and less experienced, she was no match for his inquisitiveness. One morning, I arrived to find her in tears. She rose abruptly and hurried into the next room. "She has her struggle," Bergmann told me, with a certain grim satisfaction. "It's not so easy." Dorothy, it appeared, had a boy friend, an older man, who was married. He didn't seem able to make up his mind which of the two women he liked better; just now, he had gone back to his wife. His name was Clem. He was a car salesman. He had taken Dorothy to Brighton for weekends. Dorothy also had a lover of her own age, a radio engineer, nice and steady, who wanted to marry her. But the radio engineer lacked glamour; he couldn't compete with the fatal appeal of Clem, who wore a little black mustache.

Bergmann's interest in all this was positively ghoulish. In addition, he knew everything about Dorothy's father, another sinister influence, and about her aunt, who worked at an undertaker's, and was having an affair with her brother-in-law. At first, I could hardly believe that Dorothy had really brought herself to reveal such intimate details, and suspected Bergmann of having invented the whole story. She seemed such a shy, reserved girl. But soon they were actually speaking of Clem in my presence. When Dorothy cried, Bergmann would pat her on the shoulder, like God Himself, and murmur, "That's all right, my child. Nothing to do. It will pass."

He was fond of lecturing me on Love. "When a woman is awakened, when she gets the man she wants, she is amazing, amazing. You have no idea . . . Sensuality is a whole separate world. What we see on the outside, what comes up to the surface—it's nothing. Love is like a mine. You go deeper and deeper. There are passages, caves, whole strata. You discover entire geological eras. You find things, little objects, which enable you to reconstruct her life, her other lovers, things she does not even know about herself, things you must never tell her that you know . . .

"You see," Bergmann continued, "women are absolutely necessary to a man; especially to a man who lives in ideas, in the creation of moods and thoughts. He needs them, like bread. I do not mean for the coitus; that is not so important, at my age. One lives more in the fantasy. But one needs their aura, their ambience, their perfume. Women always recognize a man who wants this thing from them. They feel it at once, and they come to him, like horses." Bergmann paused, grinning. "You see, I am an old Jewish Socrates who preaches to the Youth. One day, they will give me the hemlock."

In the hot little room, our life together seemed curiously isolated. The three of us formed a self-contained world, independent of London, of Europe, of 1933. Dorothy, the representative of Woman, did her best to keep the home in some kind of order, but her efforts were not very successful. Her schemes for arranging Bergmann's huge litter of papers only caused worse confusion. As he could never describe exactly what it was that he was looking for, she could never tell him where she had put it. This sent him into frenzies of frustration. "Terrible, terrible. This definitely kills me. Too idiotic for words." And he would relapse into grumpy silence.

Then there was the problem of meals. The house had a restaurant service, theoretically. It could produce bitter coffee, very strong black tea, congealed eggs, sodden toast and a gluey chop, followed by some nameless kind of yellow pudding. The food took an almost incredible time to arrive. As Bergmann said, when you ordered breakfast, it was best to ask for what you wanted at lunch, because it would be four hours before you got it. So we lived chiefly on cigarettes.

At least twice a week, there was a Black Day. I would enter the flat to find Bergmann in complete despair. He hadn't slept all night, the story was hopeless, Dorothy was crying. The best way of dealing with this situation was to make Bergmann come out with me to lunch. Our nearest restaurant was a big gloomy place on the top floor of a department store. We ate early, when there were very few other customers, sitting together at a table in the darkest corner, next to a rather sinister grandfather clock, which reminded Bergmann of the story by Edgar Allan Poe.

"It ticks every moment," he told me. "Death comes nearer. Syphilis. Poverty. Consumption. Cancer discovered too late. My art no good, a failure, a damn flop. War. Poison gas. We are dying with our heads together in the oven."

And then he would begin to describe the coming war. The attack

on Vienna, Prague, London and Paris, without warning, by thousands
of planes, dropping bombs filled with deadly bacilli; the conquest of
Europe in a week; the subjugation of Asia, Africa, the Americas; the
massacre of the Jews, the execution of intellectuals, the herding of
non-Nordic women into enormous state brothels; the burning of paintings and books, the grinding of statues into powder; the mass steril-
ization of the unfit, mass murder of the elderly, mass conditioning of
the young; the reduction of France and the Balkan countries to wil-
derness, in order to make national parks for the Hitler Jugend; the
establishment of Brown Art, Brown Literature, Brown Music, Brown
Philosophy, Brown Science and the Hitler Religion, with its Vatican
at Munich and its Lourdes at Berchtesgaden: a cult based upon the
most complex system of dogmas concerning the real nature of the
Fuehrer, the utterances of *Mein Kampf,* the ten thousand Bolshevist
heresies, the sacrament of Blood and Soil, and upon elaborate rituals
of mystic union with the Homeland, involving human sacrifice and
the baptism of steel.

"All these people," Bergmann continued, "will be dead. All of
them . . . No, there is one . . ." He pointed to a fat, inoffensive man
sitting alone in a distant corner. "He will survive. He is the kind that
will do anything, anything to be allowed to live. He will invite the
conquerors to his home, force his wife to cook for them and serve the
dinner on his bended knees. He will denounce his mother. He will
offer his sister to a common soldier. He will act as a spy in prisons.
He will spit on the Sacrament. He will hold down his daughter while
they rape her. And, as a reward for this, he will be given a job as
bootblack in a public lavatory, and he will lick the dirt from people's
shoes with his tongue . . ." Bergmann shook his head sadly. "Too
bad. I do not envy him."

This kind of talk had a strange effect on me. Like all my friends,
I said I believed that a European war was coming soon. I believed it
as one believes that one will die, and yet I didn't believe. For the
coming war was as unreal to me as death itself. It was unreal because
I couldn't imagine anything beyond it; I refused to imagine anything;
just as a spectator refuses to imagine what is behind the scenery in a
theatre. The outbreak of war, like the moment of death, crossed my
perspective of the future like a wall; it marked the instant, total end

of my imagined world. I thought about this wall from time to time, with acute depression and a flutter of fear at the solar plexus. Then, again, I forgot or ignored it. Also, just as when one thinks of one's own death, I secretly whispered to myself, "Who knows? Maybe we shall get around it somehow. Maybe it will never happen."

Bergmann's apocalyptic pictures of universal doom made the prospect of war more unreal than ever, and so they never failed to cheer me up. I suppose they worked like that for him, too; probably that was why he dwelt upon them so gleefully. And, while he was in the midst of the horrors, his glance around the room generally discovered a girl or woman who interested him, and diverted the stream of his imagination toward more agreeable subjects.

His favorite was the manageress of the restaurant, a handsome blonde with a very sweet motherly smile, about thirty years old. Bergmann approved of her highly. "I have only to look at her," he told me, "to know that she is satisfied. Deeply satisfied. Some man has made her happy. For her, there is no longer any search. She has found what we are all looking for. She understands all of us. She does not need books, or theories, or philosophy, or priests. She understands Michelangelo, Beethoven, Christ, Lenin—even Hitler. And she is afraid of nothing, nothing. . . . Such a woman is my religion."

The manageress would always have a special smile for Bergmann when we came in; and, during the meal, she would walk over to our table and ask if everything was all right. "Everything is all right, my darling," Bergmann would reply; "thanks to God, but chiefly to you. You restore our confidence in ourselves."

I don't know exactly what the manageress made of this, but she smiled, in an amused, kindly way. She really was very nice. "You see?" Bergmann would turn to me, after she had gone. "We understand each other perfectly."

And so, our confidence restored by *das ewige Weibliche*, we went back refreshed to tend the poor little *Prater Violet*, wilting in the suffocating atmosphere of our flat.

Meanwhile, in Berlin, the proceedings of the Reichstag Fire Trial continued through October, November and into the first weeks of December. Bergmann followed them passionately. "Do you know what he said yesterday?" he would frequently ask me, when I arrived in the morning for work. "He," of course, was Dimitrov. I did know, having read the newspaper as eagerly as Bergmann himself, but I wouldn't, for the world, have spoiled the performance which followed.

Bergmann enacted the entire drama and represented all the characters. He was Dr. Buenger, the testy, embarrassed President of the Court. He was van der Lubbe, doped and apathetic, with sunken head. He was earnest, harassed Torgler. He was Goering, the straddling military bully, and Goebbels, lizardlike, crooked and adroit. He was fiery Popov and stolid Tanev. And, in the biggest way, he was Dimitrov himself.

Bergmann actually became Dimitrov, with his furiously untidy hair, his grim ironic slit of a mouth, his large gestures, his flashing eyes.

"Is the Herr Reichsminister aware," he thundered, "that those who possess this alleged criminal mentality are today controlling the destinies of a sixth part of the world, namely the Soviet Union—the greatest and best land on earth?"

Then, as Goering, bull-necked, infuriated, he bellowed, "I'll tell you what I'm aware of! I'm aware that you're a communist spy who came to Germany to set the Reichstag on fire. In my eyes, you're nothing but a dirty crook, who ought to be hanging on the gallows!"

Bergmann smiled, a faint, terrible smile. Like a toreador, who never takes his eyes from the enraged and wounded bull, he asked softly, "You are very afraid of my questions, aren't you, Herr Minister?"

Bergmann's face contorted, bulged, seemed to swell into an apoplectic clot of blood. His hand shot out. He yelled like a lunatic, "Get out of here, you crook!"

Bergmann bowed slightly, with ironic dignity. He half turned, as if to withdraw. Then he paused. His eye fell upon the imagined figure of van der Lubbe. His hand was raised, slowly, in a great, historic gesture. He addressed all Europe:

"There stands the miserable Faust. . . . But where is Mephistopheles?"

Then he made his exit.

"You wait!" Bergmann-Goering roared after the retreating figure. "You wait till I get you out of the power of this Court!"

Another scene, which Dorothy and I would often persuade Berg-mann to repeat, was the moment when van der Lubbe is cross-examined. He stands before his accusers, with his huge stooped shoulders and hanging hands, the chin sunken on the chest. He is scarcely human—a wretched, clumsy, tormented animal. The President tries to make him look up. He does not move. The Interpreter tries. Dr. Seuffert tries. There is no response. Then, suddenly, with the harsh authority of an animal trainer, Helldorf barks out, "Head up, man! Quick!"

The head jerks up at once, automatically, as if in obedience to some deeply hidden memory. The clouded eyes wander around the courtroom. Are they searching for somebody? A faint gleam of rec-ognition seems to flicker in them for a moment. And then van der Lubbe begins to laugh. This is really horrible, indecent, terrifying. The heavy body quivers and heaves with noiseless laughter, as if shaken by its death agony. Van der Lubbe laughs and laughs, silently, blindly, his mouth open and dribbling, like an idiot's. Then, with equal sud-denness, the paroxysm ceases. Again, the head falls forward. The grotesque figure stands motionless, guarding its secret, unapproachable as the dead.

"Goodness!" Dorothy would exclaim, with a shiver. "I'm glad I'm not over there! It gives you the creeps, just to think about it. Those Nazis aren't human."

"You are wrong, darling," Bergmann told her, seriously. "That is how they wish you to imagine them, as unconquerable monsters. But they are human, very human, in their weakness. We must not fear them. We must understand them. It is absolutely necessary to understand them, or we are all lost."

Now that Bergmann had become Dimitrov, he was obliged to abandon a great deal of his cynicism. It was no longer in character. Dimitrov had to have a cause to fight for, to make speeches about. And the cause turned out to be *Prater Violet*.

We were at work on the sequence in which Rudolf loses his future kingdom of Borodania through a palace revolution. A wicked Uncle deposes his Father and seizes the throne. Rudolf returns to Vienna, a penniless exile. He is now, in reality, the poor student he pretended to be at the beginning of the story. But Toni, naturally, refuses to believe this. She has been deceived once already. She has trusted him, she has loved him, and he has left her. (Unwillingly, of course; and only because his faithful chamberlain, Count Rosanoff, reminds him with tears of his duty to the Borodanians.) So Rudolf pleads in vain; and Toni angrily dismisses him as an impostor.

We had been through the usual procedure. I had made my lazy, half-hearted attempt at a first draft. Bergmann had put it aside with his brief grunt. And now, with his usual brilliance and wealth of gesture, he had gone over the story for the second time.

But it didn't work. I was feeling temperamental and sulky that day, chiefly because I had a bad cold. My conscience had driven me to Bergmann's flat, and I felt that my sacrifice wasn't being properly appreciated. I had expected to be fussed over and sent home again.

"It's no good," I told him.

Bergmann was belligerent at once. "Why is it no good?"

"I'm afraid it just doesn't interest me."

Bergmann gave a terrible snort. I seldom defied him like this. But I was in a thoroughly obstructive mood. I didn't care if I got fired. I didn't care what happened.

"It's such a bore," I said brutally. "It's so completely unreal. It has no relation to anything that ever happened anywhere. I can't believe a word of it."

For a whole minute, he didn't answer. He paced the carpet, grunting. Dorothy, from her seat at the typewriter, watched him nervously. I expected a major volcanic eruption.

Then Bergmann came right up to me.

"You are wrong," he said.

I looked him in the eye, and forced a smile. But I didn't say anything. I wouldn't give him an opening.

"Totally and principally wrong. It is not uninteresting. It is not unreal. It is of the very greatest interest. It is highly contemporary. And it is of enormous psychological and political significance."

I was startled right out of my sulks.

"Political?" I laughed. "Why, really, Friedrich! How on earth do you make that out?"

"It is political." Bergmann swept into the attack. "And the reason you refuse to see this, the reason you pretend it is uninteresting, is that it directly concerns yourself."

"I must say, I . . ."

"Listen!" Bergmann interrupted, imperiously. "The dilemma of Rudolf is the dilemma of the would-be revolutionary writer or artist, all over Europe. This writer is not to be confused with the true proletarian writer, such as we find in Russia. His economic background is bourgeois. He is accustomed to comfort, a nice home, the care of a devoted slave who is his mother and also his jailer. From the safety and comfort of his home, he permits himself the luxury of a romantic interest in the proletariat. He comes among the workers under false pretenses, and in disguise. He flirts with Toni, the girl of the working class. But it is only a damn lousy act, a heartless masquerade . . ."

"Well, if you like to put it in that way. . . . But what about . . .?"

"Listen! Suddenly Rudolf's home collapses, security collapses. The investments which built his comfortable life are made worthless by inflation. His mother has to scrub doorsteps. The young artist prince, with all his fine ideas, has to face grim reality. The play becomes bitter earnest. His relation to the proletariat is romantic no longer. He now has to make a choice. He is declassed, and he must find a new class. Does he really love Toni? Did his beautiful words mean anything? If so, he must prove that they did. Otherwise . . ."

"Yes, that's all very well, but . . ."

"This symbolic fable," Bergmann continued, with sadistic relish, "is particularly disagreeable to you, because it represents your deepest fear, the nightmare of your own class. In England, the economic catastrophe has not yet occurred. The pound wavered, but it did not utterly fall. Inflation still lies ahead of the English bourgeoisie, but you know in your heart that it is coming, as it came to Germany. And, when it comes, you will have to choose. . . ."

"How do you mean, choose?"

"The declassed intellectual has two choices. If his love for Toni is sincere, if he is loyal to his artistic traditions, the great liberal-revolutionary traditions of the nineteenth century, then he will know where he belongs. He will know how to align himself. He will know who are his real friends and his real enemies." (My eye caught Dorothy's. She was watching us blankly, for Bergmann, as he usually did when excited, had started to talk German.) "Unfortunately, however, he does not always make this choice. Indeed, he seldom makes it. He is unable to cut himself free, sternly, from the bourgeois dream of the Mother, that fatal and comforting dream. He wants to crawl back into the economic safety of the womb. He hates the paternal, revolutionary tradition, which reminds him of his duty as its son. His pretended love for the masses was only a flirtation, after all. He now prefers to join the ranks of the dilettante nihilists, the bohemian outlaws, who believe in nothing, except their own ego, who exist only to kill, to torture, to destroy, to make everyone as miserable as themselves . . ."

"In other words, I'm a Nazi and you're my father?"

We both laughed.

"I only try to analyze certain tendencies," said Bergmann.

"Nevertheless," he added, "there are times when I feel gravely worried about you."

Bergmann worried not only about me, but about the whole of England. Wherever he went, he kept a sharp lookout for what he called "significant phenomena." A phenomenon, I soon discovered, could be practically anything. The fog, for instance. Like nearly all Middle Europeans, he was convinced that fog was our normal weather throughout the year. I would have been sorry to disappoint him; and, as luck would have it, there were several quite thick fogs that winter. Bergmann seemed to imagine that they covered not only London but the entire island; thereby accounting for all our less agreeable racial characteristics, our insularity, our hypocrisy, our political muddling, our prudery and our refusal to face facts. "It is the English themselves who have created this fog. They feed upon it, like a kind of bitter soup which fills them with illusions. It is their national costume, clothing the enormous nakedness of the slums and the scandal of unjust ownership. It is also the jungle within which Jack the Ripper goes about his business of murder in the elegant overcoat of a member of the Stock Exchange."

We started making sightseeing excursions together. Bergmann showed me London: the London he had already created for himself in his own imagination, the dark, intricate, sinister town of Dickens, the old German silent movies, Wedekind and Brecht. He was always the guide, and I the tourist. Whenever I asked where we were going, he would say, "Wait," or "You will see." Often, I think he hadn't the least idea, until we actually arrived.

We visited the Tower, where Bergmann lectured me on English history, comparing the reign of the Tudors to the Hitler regime. He took it for granted that Bacon wrote the Shakespearian plays, in order to make political propaganda, and that Queen Elizabeth was a man. He even had a further theory that Essex was beheaded because he threatened the Monarch with revelations of their homosexual intrigue. I had some difficulty in getting him out of the Bloody Tower, where he was inspired to a lurid reconstruction of the murder of the Little Princes, amazing the other visitors, who merely saw a stocky, shock-headed, middle-aged man pleading for his life to an invisible assassin, in German, with theatrical falsetto accents.

At the Zoo, he identified a baboon, a giraffe and a dromedary with three of our leading politicians, and reproached them publicly for their crimes. In the National Gallery, he explained, with reference to the Rembrandt portraits, his theory of camera angles and the lighting of close-ups, so loudly and convincingly that he drew a crowd away from one of the official lecturers, who was naturally rather annoyed.

Sometimes he persuaded me to go out with him at night. This, at the end of a long day, was very exhausting. But the streets fascinated him, and he never seemed tired or wished to return home. It was embarrassing, too. Bergmann spoke to anybody whose face happened to interest him, with the directness of a child; or he talked about them to me, like a lecturer, so that they were sure to overhear him. One evening, in the bus, there were two lovers. The girl was sitting just in front of us; the young man stood beside her, holding the strap. Bergmann was delighted with them. "See how he stands? They do not even look at each other. They might be strangers. Yet they keep touching, as if by accident. Now watch: their lips are moving. That is how two people talk when they are very happy and alone, in the darkness. Already they are lying in each other's arms in bed. Good night, my dears. We shall not intrude upon your secrets."

Bergmann talked to taxi drivers, to medical students in bars, to elderly colonels returning from their clubs, to clergymen, to Piccadilly tarts, to the boys who hung around the medallion of W. S. Gilbert

on the Embankment. Nobody seemed to mind, or even to misunderstand his intentions. I envied him his freedom—the freedom of a
foreigner. I could have done the same thing, myself, in Vienna or
Berlin. With a foreigner's luck, or intuition, he nearly always succeeded in picking out the unusual individual from the average type:
a constable who did watercolors, a beggar who knew classical Greek.
And this betrayed him into a foreigner's generalizations. In London,
all policemen paint, all the scholars are starving.

The year was drawing to an end. The newspapers were full of
optimism. Things were looking up; this Christmas was to be the greatest
ever. Hitler talked only of peace. The Disarmament Conference had
broken down. The British Government didn't want isolation; equally,
it didn't want to promise military aid to France. When people planned
their next summer's holiday in Europe, they remembered to add, "If
Europe's still there." It was like the superstition of touching wood.

Just before Christmas, Bergmann and I went down to Brighton
for the day. It was the only time we ever left London together. I
remember this as one of the most depressing experiences of my life.
Behind high clouds of white fog, the wintry sun made a pale splash
of gold, far out on the oyster-gray surface of the Channel. We walked
along the pier and stopped to watch a young man in plus-fours with
a fair mangy mustache, who was hitting a punch-ball. "He can't ring
the bell," I said. "None of them can ring it," Bergmann answered
somberly. "That bell will never ring again. They're all done for. Finished." Coming back in the Pullman car, the sea air made us both
doze. I had a peculiarly vivid nightmare about Hitler Germany.

First of all, I dreamed that I was in a courtroom. This, I knew,
was a political trial. Some communists were being sentenced to death.
The State Prosecutor was a hard-faced, middle-aged, blond woman,
with her hair twisted into a knot on the back of her head. She stood
up, gripping one of the accused men by his coat collar, and marched
him down the room toward the judge's desk. As they advanced, she
drew a revolver and shot the communist in the back. His knees sagged
and his chin fell forward; but she dragged him on, until they faced
the judge, and she cried, in a loud voice, "Look! Here is the traitor!"

A girl was sitting beside me, among the spectators. In some way,

I was aware that she was a hospital nurse by profession. As the prosecutor held up the dying man, she rose and ran out of the courtroom in tears. I followed her, down passages and flights of steps, into a cellar, where there were central-heating pipes. The cellar was fitted with bunks, like a barracks. The girl lay down on one of them, sobbing. And then several youths came in. I knew that they belonged to the Hitler Jugend; but, instead of uniforms, they wore bits of bearskin, with belts, helmets and swords, shoddy and theatrical-looking, such as supers might wear in a performance of *The Ring*. Their partly naked bodies were covered with acne and skin rash, and they seemed tired and dispirited. They climbed into their bunks, without taking the least notice of the girl or of me.

Then I was walking up a steep, very narrow street. A Jew came running down toward me, with his wrists thrust into his overcoat pockets. I knew that this was because his hands had been shot off. He had to hide his injuries. If anybody saw them, he would be recognized and lynched.

At the top of the street, I found an old lady, dressed in a kind of uniform, French "horizon blue." She was sniveling and cursing to herself. It was she who had shot off the Jew's hands. She wanted to shoot him again; but her ammunition (which was, I noticed with surprise, only for a .22 rifle) lay scattered on the ground. She couldn't collect it, because she was blind.

Then I went into the British Embassy, where I was welcomed by a cheerful, fatuous, drawling young man, like Wodehouse's Bertie Wooster. He pointed out to me that the walls of the entrance hall were covered with post-impressionist and cubist paintings. "The Ambassador likes them," he explained. "I mean to say, a bit of contrast, what?"

Somehow, I couldn't bring myself to tell this dream to Bergmann. I wasn't in the mood for one of his elaborate and perhaps disagreeably personal interpretations. Also, I had a curious suspicion that he had put the whole thing, telepathically, into my head.

All these months, there hadn't been a single word from Chatsworth.

His silence was magnificent. It seemed to express the most generous kind of confidence. He was giving us an absolutely free hand. Or perhaps he was so busy that he had forgotten about us altogether.

I think he must have written *Prater Violet* on the first leaf of his 1934 calendar. For January had barely begun before we started to get telephone calls from the studio. How was the script coming along?

Bergmann went down to Imperial Bulldog to see him, and came back in a state of considerable self-satisfaction. He gave me to understand that he had been exceedingly diplomatic. Chatsworth's stock rose. He was no longer a vulgarian, but a man of culture and insight. "He appreciates," said Bergmann, "how a director needs time to follow his ideas quietly and lovingly." Bergmann had told the story, no doubt with a most lavish display of gesture and intonation, and Chatsworth had seemed very pleased.

However, this didn't alter the fact that our script was still a torso, or, at best, a living body with mechanical limbs. The final sequence, the whole episode of Toni's revenge on Rudolf with its happy ending, was still wishfully vague. Neither of us really liked the idea of her masquerade, in a blond wig, as the famous opera singer. Not all Bergmann's histrionics, no amount of Freudian analysis or Marxian dialectic could make it anything but very silly.

And perhaps Chatsworth hadn't been so impressed, after all. Because now we started to have visits from Ashmeade. His approach was extremely tactful. It opened with what appeared to be a purely social call. "I happened to be passing," he told us, "so I thought I'd look in. Are you and Isherwood still on speaking terms?"

But Bergmann wasn't deceived. "The Secret Police are on our footprints," he said gloomily. "So . . . Now it begins."

Two days later, Ashmeade returned. This time, he was more frankly inquisitive. He wanted to know all about the last sequence. Bergmann went into his act; he had never been better. Ashmeade looked politely dubious.

Next morning, early, he was on the phone. "I've been thinking it over. I've just had an idea. Suppose Toni knew all the time that Rudolf was the Prince? I mean, right from the beginning."

"No, no, no!" cried Bergmann in despair. "Definitely not!"

When their conversation was over, he was furious. "They have given me this fashionable cretin, this elegant dwarf to sit on my back!

Have we not enough burdens already? Here we are, breaking our heads off fighting for Truth!"

His anger, as always, subsided into philosophic doubt. He could never dismiss any suggestion, however fantastic, without hours of soul-searching. He groaned painfully. "Very well, let us see where this leads us. Wait. Wait. Let us see . . . How would it be if Toni . . . ?"

Another day was lost in speculation.

Ashmeade was indefatigable. Either he telephoned, or he came to visit us, every day. He never minded being snubbed, and his ideas abounded. Bergmann began to entertain the blackest suspicions.

"I see it all. This is a plot. It is a clear sabotage. This diplomatic Umbrella has his instructions. Chatsworth is playing with us. He has decided not to make the picture."

I was inclined to agree with him; and I couldn't altogether blame Chatsworth, either. No doubt, Bergmann's methods were leisurely. Perhaps they were conditioned by habits formed in the old silent days, when the director went into the studio and photographed everything within sight, finally revising his story in the cutting room by a process of selection and elimination. I was seriously afraid that Bergmann would soon reach a state of philosophic equilibrium, in which all possible solutions would seem equally attractive or unattractive, and that we should hang poised in potentiality, until the studio stopped sending us our checks.

Then, one morning, the telephone rang. It was Chatsworth's private secretary. (I recognized the voice which had introduced me to *Prater Violet*, on that last day of what I now looked back to as the pre-Bergmann period of my life.) Would we please both come to the studio as soon as possible, for a script conference?

Bergmann was very grim as he heard the news.

"So. Finally. Chatsworth assumes the black cap. This is the end. The criminals are dragged into court to hear the death sentence. Never mind. Goodbye, Dorothy, my darling. Come, my child. We shall march to the guillotine together."

In those days Imperial Bulldog was still down in Fulham. (They didn't move out to the suburbs until the summer of 1935.) It was quite a long taxi ride. Bergmann's spirits rose as we drove along.

"You have never been inside a film studio before?"

"Only once. Years ago."

"It will interest you, as a phenomenon. You see, the film studio of today is really the palace of the sixteenth century. There one sees what Shakespeare saw: the absolute power of the tyrant, the courtiers, the flatterers, the jesters, the cunningly ambitious intriguers. There are fantastically beautiful women, there are incompetent favorites. There are great men who are suddenly disgraced. There is the most insane extravagance, and unexpected parsimony over a few pence. There is enormous splendor, which is a sham; and also horrible squalor hidden behind the scenery. There are vast schemes, abandoned because of some caprice. There are secrets which everybody knows and no one speaks of. There are even two or three honest advisers. These are the court fools, who speak the deepest wisdom in puns, lest they should be taken seriously. They grimace, and tear their hair privately, and weep."

"You make it sound great fun."

"It is unspeakable," said Bergmann, with relish. "But to us all this does not matter. We have honorably done our task. Now, like Socrates, we pay the penalty of those who tell the truth. We are thrown to the Bulldog to be devoured, and the Umbrella will weep a crocodile tear over our graves."

The outside of the studio was as uninteresting as any modern office building: a big frontage of concrete and glass. Bergmann strode up the steps to the swinging door with such impetus that I couldn't follow him until it had stopped whirling around. He scowled, breathing ferociously, while the doorman took our names, and a clerk telephoned to announce our arrival. I caught his eye and grinned, but he wouldn't smile back. He was obviously planning his final speech for the defense. I had no doubt that it would be a masterpiece.

Chatsworth confronted us, as we entered, across a big desk. The first things I saw were the soles of his shoes and the smoke of his cigar. The shoes stood upright on their heels, elegantly brown and shiny, like a pair of ornaments, next to two bronze horses which were rubbing necks over an inkstand. Sitting apart from him, but still more or less behind the desk, were Ashmeade and a very fat man I didn't know. Our chairs were ready for us, facing them, isolated in the middle of the room. It really looked like a tribunal. I drew nearer to Bergmann, defensively.

"Hullo, you two!" Chatsworth greeted us, very genial. His head was tilted sideways, holding a telephone against his jaw, like a violin. "Be with you in a moment." He spoke into the phone. "Sorry, Dave. Nothing doing. No. I've made up my mind. . . . Well, he may have told you that last week. I hadn't seen it then. It stinks. . . . My dear fellow, I can't help that. I didn't know they'd do such a rotten job. It's bloody awful. . . . Well, tell them anything you like. . . . I don't care if their feelings *are* hurt. They damn well ought to be hurt. . . . No. Goodbye."

Ashmeade was smiling subtly. The fat man looked bored. Chatsworth took his feet off the desk. His big face came up into view.

"I've got some bad news for you," he told us.

I glanced quickly across at Bergmann; but he was watching Chatsworth with the glare of a hypnotist.

"We've just changed our schedule. You'll have to start shooting in two weeks."

"Impossible!" Bergmann discharged the word like a gun.

"Of course it's impossible," said Chatsworth, grinning. "We're impossible people around here. . . . I don't think you know Mr. Harris? He sat up all last night doing designs for your sets. I hope you'll dislike them as much as I do. . . . Oh, another thing: we can't get Rosemary Lee. She's sailing for New York tomorrow. So I talked to Anita Hayden, and she's interested. She's a bitch, but she can sing. In a minute, I want you to come and listen to Pfeffer's arrangement of the score. It's as noisy as hell. I don't mind it, though. . . . I've put Watts on to the lighting. He's our best man. He knows how to catch the mood."

Bergmann grunted dubiously. I smiled. I liked Chatsworth that morning.

"What about the script?" I asked.

"Don't you worry about that, my lad. Never let a script stand in our way, do we, Sandy? Matter of fact, I can lick that ending of yours. Thought about it this morning, while I was shaving. I have a great idea."

Chatsworth paused to relight his cigar.

"I want you to stay with us," he told me, "right through the picture. Just keep your ears and eyes open. Watch the details. Listen for the intonations. You can help a lot. Bergmann isn't used to the language. Besides, there may be rewrites. . . . From now on, I'm giving you two an office here in the building, so I'll have my eye on you. If you want anything, just call me. You'll get all the co-operation you need. . . . Well, I think that takes care of everything. Come along, Doctor. Sandy, will you show Isherwood his new dungeon?"

Thus, as the result of ten minutes' conversation, the whole rhythm of our lives was abruptly changed. For Bergmann, of course, this was nothing new. But I felt dazed. It was as though two hermits had been transported from their cave in the mountains into the middle of a modern railway station. There was no privacy any more. The process of wasting time, which hitherto had been orientally calm and philo-sophical, now became guilty and apprehensive.

Our "dungeon" was a tiny room on the third floor, forlornly bare, with nothing in it but a desk, three chairs and a telephone. The telephone had a very loud bell. When it rang, we both jumped. The window commanded a view of sooty roofs and the gray winter sky. Outside, along the passage, people went back and forth, making what seemed a deliberately unnecessary amount of noise. Often, their bodies bumped against the door; or it opened, and a head was thrust in. "Where's Joe?" a stranger would ask, somewhat reproachfully. Or else he would say, "Oh, sorry . . ." and vanish without explanation. These interruptions made Bergmann desperate. "It is the third degree," he would groan. "They torture us, and we have nothing to confess."

We were seldom together for long. The telephone, or a messenger, would summon Bergmann away to confer with Chatsworth, or the casting director, or Mr. Harris, and I would be left with an unfinished scene and his pessimistic advice "to try and think of something." Usually, I didn't even try. I stared out of the window, or gossiped with Dorothy. We had a tacit understanding that, if anybody looked in, we would immediately pretend to be working. Sometimes Dorothy herself left me. She had plenty of friends in the studio, and would slip away for a chat when the coast seemed clear.

Nevertheless, under the pressure of this crisis, we advanced. Berg-mann was reckless, now. He was ready to pass even the weakest of my suggestions with little more than a sigh. Also, I myself was getting bolder. My conscience no longer bothered me. The dyer's hand was subdued. There were days when I could write page after page with magical facility. It was really quite easy. Toni joked. The Baron made a pun. Toni's father clowned. Some inner inhibition had been removed. This was simply a job. I was doing it as well as I could.

In the meanwhile, whenever I got a chance, I went exploring. Imperial Bulldog had what was probably the oldest studio site in London. It dated back to early silent days, when directors yelled through megaphones to make themselves heard above the carpenters' hammering; and great flocks of dazed, deafened, limping, hungry extras were driven hither and thither by aggressive young assistant directors, who barked at them like sheep dogs. At the time of the panic, when Sound first came to England and nobody's job was safe, Bulldog had carried through a hasty and rather hysterical reconstruction program. The whole place was torn down and rebuilt at top speed, most of it as cheaply as possible. No one knew what was coming next: Taste, perhaps, or Smell, or Stereoscopy, or some device that climbed right down out of the screen and ran around in the audience. Nothing seemed impossible. And, in the interim, it was unwise to spend much money on equipment which might be obsolete within a year.

The result of the rebuilding was a maze of crooked stairways, claustrophobic passages, abrupt dangerous ramps and Alice-in-Wonderland doors. Most of the smaller rooms were overcrowded, underventilated, separated only by plywood partitions and lit by naked bulbs hanging from wires. Everything was provisional, and liable to electrocute you, fall on your head, or come apart in your hand. "Our motto," said Lawrence Dwight, "is: 'If it breaks, it's Bulldog.' "

Lawrence was the head cutter on our picture: a short, muscular, angry-looking young man of about my own age, whose face wore a frown of permanent disgust. We had made friends, chiefly because he had read a story of mine in a magazine, and growled crossly that he liked it. He limped so slightly that I might never have noticed; but, after a few minutes' conversation, he told me abruptly that he had an artificial leg. This he referred to as "my stump." The amputation had followed a motor accident, in which his wife had been killed a month after their marriage.

"We'd just had time to find out that we couldn't stand each other," he told me, angrily watching my face to see if I would be shocked. "I was driving. I suppose I really wanted to murder her."

"I don't know what the hell you imagine you're doing here," he said, a little later. "Selling your soul, I suppose? All you writers have such a bloody romantic attitude. You think you're too good for the movies. Don't you believe it. The movies are too good for you. We don't need any romantic nineteenth-century whores. We need technicians. Thank God, I'm a cutter. I know my job. As a matter of fact, I'm damned good at it. I don't treat film as if it were a bit of my intestine. It's all Chatsworth's fault. He's a romantic, too. He will hire people like you. Thinks he's Lorenzo the Magnificent . . . I bet you despise mathematics? Well, let me tell you something. The movies aren't drama, they aren't literature—they're pure mathematics. Of course, you'll never understand that, as long as you live."

Lawrence took great pleasure in pointing out to me the many inefficiencies of the studio. For instance, there was no proper storage room for scenery. Sets had to be broken up as soon as they had been used; the waste of materials was appalling. And then, Bulldog carried so many passengers. "We could do a much better job with two-thirds of our present staff. All these assistant directors, fussing about and falling over each other . . . They even have what they call dialogue directors. Can you imagine? Some poor stooge who sits around on his fat behind and says 'Yes' whenever anybody looks at him."

I laughed. "That's what I'm going to do."

But Lawrence wasn't in the least embarrassed. "I might have known it," he said disgustedly. "You're just the right type. So bloody tactful."

His deepest scorn was reserved for the Reading Department, officially known as Annex G. The back lot of Imperial Bulldog sloped down to the river. Annex G had originally been a warehouse. It reminded me of a lawyer's office in a Dickens novel. There were cobwebbed shelves, rows and rows of them, right up to the roof; and not a crack anywhere wide enough to insert your little finger. The lower rows were mostly scripts; scripts in duplicate and triplicate, treatments, rough drafts, every scrap of paper on which any Bulldog writer had ever scribbled. Lawrence told me that the rats had gnawed long tunnels through them, from end to end. "They ought to be dumped in the Thames," Lawrence added, "but the River Police would prosecute us for poisoning the water."

And then there were books. These were the novels and plays which the studio had bought to make into pictures. At any rate, that was what they were supposed to be. Had Bulldog ever considered filming *Bradshaw's Railway Timetable for 1911?* Well, perhaps that had come originally from the Research Department. "But will you explain to me," said Lawrence, "why we have twenty-seven copies of *Half Hours with a Microscope,* one of them stolen from the Woking Public Library?"

Rather to my surprise, Lawrence approved of Bergmann and admired him. He had seen several of the pictures Bergmann had directed in Germany; and this, of course, delighted Bergmann, although he would never admit it. Instead, he praised Lawrence's character, calling him *"ein anstaendiger Junge."* Whenever they met, Bergmann addressed him as "Master." After a while, Lawrence started to reciprocate. Whereupon Bergmann, never to be outdone, began to call Lawrence "Grand Master." Lawrence took to calling me "Herr Talk-Director." I called him "Herr Cut-Master."

I was careful, however, not to inform Bergmann of Lawrence's political opinions. "All of this fascist-communist nonsense," said Lawrence, "is so bloody old-fashioned. People rave about the workers. It makes me sick. The workers are just sheep. Always have been. Always will be. They choose to be that way, and why shouldn't they? It's their life. And they dodge a lot of headaches. . . . Take the men at this place. What do they know or care about anything, except getting their pay checks? If any problem arises outside their immediate job, they expect someone else to decide it for them. Quite right, too, from their point of view. A country has to be run by a minority of some sort. The only thing is, we've got to get rid of these damned sentimental politicians. All politicians are amateurs. It's as if we'd handed over the studio to the Publicity Department. The only people who really matter are the technicians. They know what they want."

"And what do they want?"

"They want efficiency."

"What's that?"

"Efficiency is doing a job for the sake of doing a job."

"But why should you do a job, anyway? What's the incentive?"

"The incentive is to fight anarchy. That's all Man lives for. Reclaiming life from its natural muddle. Making patterns."

"Patterns for what?"

"For the sake of patterns. To create meaning. What else is there?"

"And what about the things that won't fit into your patterns?"

"Discard them."

"You mean, kill Jews?"

"Don't try to shock me with your bloody sentimental false analogies. You know perfectly well what I mean. When people refuse to fit into patterns, they discard themselves. That's not my fault. Hitler doesn't make patterns. He's just an opportunist. When you make patterns, you don't persecute. Patterns aren't people."

"Who's being old-fashioned now? That sounds like Art for Art's sake."

"I don't care what it sounds like. . . . Technicians are the only real artists, anyway."

"It's all very well for you to make patterns with your cutting. But what's the use, when you have to work on pictures like *Prater Violet*?"

"That's Chatsworth's worry, and Bergmann's, and yours. If you so-called artists would behave like technicians and get together, and stop playing at being democrats, you'd make the public take the kind of picture you wanted. This business about the box office is just a sentimental democratic fiction. If you stuck together and refused to make anything but, say, abstract films, the public would have to go and see them, and like them. . . . Still, it's no use talking. You'll never have the guts. You'd much rather whine about prostitution, and keep on making *Prater Violets*. And that's why the public despises you, in its heart. It knows damn well it's got you by the short hairs. . . . Only, one thing: don't come to me with your artistic sorrows, because I'm not interested."

We started shooting the picture in the final week of January. I give this approximate date because it is almost the last I shall be able

to remember. What followed is so confused in my memory, so trans-
posed and foreshortened, that I can only describe it synthetically. My
recollection of it has no sequence. It is all of a piece.

Within the great barnlike sound-stage, with its high bare padded
walls, big enough to enclose an airship, there is neither day nor night:
only irregular alternations of activity and silence. Beneath a firmament
of girders and catwalks, out of which the cowled lamps shine coldly
down like planets, stands the inconsequent, half-dismantled architecture of the sets; archways, sections of houses, wood and canvas hills,
huge photographic backdrops, the frontages of streets; a kind of Pom-
peii, but more desolate, more uncanny, because this is, literally, a
half-world, a limbo of mirror-images, a town which has lost its third
dimension. Only the tangle of heavy power cables is solid, and apt to
trip you as you cross the floor. Your footsteps sound unnaturally loud;
you find yourself walking on tiptoe.

In one corner, amidst these ruins, there is life. A single set is
brilliantly illuminated. From the distance, it looks like a shrine, and
the figures standing around it might be worshippers. But it is merely
the living room of Toni's home, complete with period furniture, gaily
colored curtains, a canary cage and a cuckoo clock. The men who
are putting the finishing touches to this charming, life-size doll's house
go about their work with the same matter-of-fact, unsmiling efficiency
which any carpenters and electricians might show in building a garage.

In the middle of the set, patient and anonymous as tailor's dum-
mies, are the actor and actress who are standing in for Arthur Cromwell
and Anita Hayden. Mr. Watts, a thin bald man with gold-rimmed
spectacles, walks restlessly back and forth, regarding them from various
angles. A blue-glass monocle hangs from a ribbon around his neck.
He raises it repeatedly to observe the general effect of the lighting; and
the gesture is incongruously like that of a Regency fop. Beside him is
Fred Murray, red-haired and wearing rubber shoes. Fred is what is
called "the Gaffer," in studio slang. According to our etiquette, Mr.
Watts cannot condescend to give orders directly. He murmurs them
to Fred; and Fred, as if translating into a foreign language, shouts up
to the men who work the lamps on the catwalk, high above.

"Put a silk on that rifle. . . . Take a couple of turns on number
four. . . . Kill that baby."

"I'm ready," says Mr. Watts, at length.

"All right," Fred Murray shouts to his assistants. "Save them." The arcs are switched off and the house lights go on. The set loses its shrinelike glamour. The stand-ins leave their positions. There is an atmosphere of anti-climax, as though we were about to start all over again from the beginning.

"Now then, are we nearly ready?" This is Eliot, the assistant-director. He has a long pointed nose and a public-school accent. He carries a copy of the script, like an emblem of office, in his hand. His manner is bossy, but self-conscious and unsure. I feel sorry for him. His job makes him unpopular. He has to fuss and keep things moving; and he doesn't know how to do it without being aggressive. He doesn't know how to talk to the older men, or the stagehands. He is conscious of his own high-pitched, cultured voice. His shirt collar has too much starch in it.

"What's the hold-up?" Eliot plaintively addresses the world in general. "What about you, Roger?"

Roger, the sound-recordist, curses under his breath. He hates being rushed. "There's a baffle on this mike," he explains, with acid patience. "It's a bloody lively set. . . . Shift your boom a bit more round to the left, Teddy. We'll have to use a flower pot."

The boom moves over, dangling the microphone, like a fishing rod. Teddy, who works it, crosses the set and conceals a second microphone behind a china figure on the table.

Meanwhile, somewhere in the background, I hear Arthur Cromwell calling, "Where's the invaluable Isherwood?" Arthur plays Toni's father. He is a big handsome man who used to be a matinee idol—a real fine old ham. He wants me to hear him in his part. When he forgets a line, he snaps his fingers, without impatience.

"What's the matter, Toni? Isn't it time to go to the Prater?"

"Aren't you going to the Prater today?" I prompt.

"Aren't you going to the Prater today?" But Arthur has some mysterious actor's inhibition about this. "Bit of a mouthful, isn't it? I can't hear myself saying that, somehow. . . . How about 'Why aren't you at the Prater?' "

"All right."

Bergmann calls, "Isherwood!" (Since we have been working in

the studio, he always addresses me by my surname in public.) He marches away from the set with his hands behind his back, not even glancing around to see if I am following. We go through the double doors and out onto the fire-escape. Everybody retires to the fire-escape when they want to talk and smoke, because smoking isn't allowed inside the building. I nod to the doorman, who is reading the *Daily Herald* through his pince-nez. He is a great admirer of Soviet Russia.

Standing on the little iron platform, we can see a glimpse of the chilly gray river beyond the rooftops. The air smells damp and fresh, after being indoors, and there is a breeze which ruffles Bergmann's bushy hair.

"How is the scene? Is it all right like this?"

"Yes, I think so." I try to sound convincing. I feel lazy, this morning, and don't want any trouble. We both examine our copies of the script; or, at least, I pretend to. I have read it so often that the words have lost their meaning.

Bergmann frowns and grunts. "I thought, maybe, if we could find something. It seems so bare, so poor. . . . Couldn't perhaps Toni say, 'I cannot sell the violets of yesterday; they are unfresh?' "

" 'I can't sell yesterday's violets; they wither so quickly.' "

"Good. Good . . . Write that down."

I write it into the script. Eliot appears at the door. "Ready to rehearse now, sir."

"Let us go." Bergmann leads the way back to the set, with Eliot and myself following—a general attended by his staff. Everybody watches us, wondering if anything important has been decided. There is a childish satisfaction in having kept so many people waiting.

Eliot goes over to the door of Anita Hayden's portable dressing room. "Miss Hayden," he says, very self-consciously, "would you come now, please? We're ready."

Anita, looking like a petulant little girl in her short flowered dress, apron and frilly petticoats, emerges and walks onto the set. Like nearly all famous people, she seems a size smaller than her photographs.

I approach her, afraid that this is going to be unpleasant. I try to grin. "Sorry! We've changed a line again."

But Anita, for some reason, is in a good mood.

"Brute!" she exclaims, coquettishly. "Well, come on, let's hear the worst."

Eliot blows his whistle. "Quiet there! Dead quiet! Full rehearsal! Green light!" This last order is for the doorman, who will switch on the sign over the sound-stage door: "Rehearsal. Enter quietly."

At last we are ready. The rehearsal begins.

Toni is standing alone, looking pensively out of the window. It is the day after her meeting with Rudolf. And now she has just received a letter of love and farewell, cryptically worded, because he cannot tell her the whole truth: that he is the Prince and that he has been summoned to Borodania. So Toni is heartbroken and bewildered. Her eyes are full of tears. (This part of the scene is covered by a close-up.)

The door opens. Toni's father comes in.

Father: "What's the matter, Toni? Why aren't you at the Prater?"

Toni (inventing an excuse): "I—I haven't any flowers."

Father: "Did you sell all you had yesterday?"

Toni (with a faraway look in her eyes, which shows that her answer is symbolic): "I can't sell yesterday's violets. They wither so quickly."

She begins to sob, and runs out of the room, banging the door. Her father stands looking after her, in blank surprise. Then he shrugs his shoulders and grimaces, as much as to say that woman's whims are beyond his understanding.

"Cut." Bergmann rises quickly from his chair and goes over to Anita. "Let me tell you something, Madame. The way you throw open that door is great. It is altogether much too great. You give to the movement a theatrical importance beside which the slaughter of Rasputin is just a quick breakfast."

Anita smiles graciously. "Sorry, Friedrich. I *felt* it wasn't right." She *is* in a good mood.

"Let me show you, once . . ." Bergmann stands by the table. His lips tremble, his eyes glisten; he is a beautiful young girl on the verge of tears. "I cannot sell violets of yesterday . . . They wither . . ." He runs, with face averted, from the room. There is a bump, behind the scenes, and a muttered, "*Verflucht!*" He must have tripped over one of the cables. An instant later, Bergmann reappears, grinning, a little out of breath. "You see how I mean? With a certain lightness. Do not hit it too hard."

"Yes," Anita nods seriously, playing up to him. "I *think* I see."

"All right, my darling," Bergmann pats her arm. "We shoot it once."

"Where's Timmy?" Anita demands, in a bored, melodious voice. The make-up man hurries forward. "Timmy darling, is my face all right?"

She submits it to him, as impersonally as one extends a shoe to the bootblack; this anxiously pretty mask which is her job, her source of income, the tool of her trade. Timmy dabs at it expertly. She glances at herself coldly, without vanity, in his pocket mirror. The camera operator's assistant measures the distance from the lens to her nose, with a tape.

A boy named George asks the continuity girl for the number of the scene. It has to be chalked on the board which he will hold in front of the camera, before the take.

Roger calls from the sound booth, "Come in for this one, Chris. I need an alibi." He often says this, jokingly, but with a certain veiled resentment, which is directed chiefly against Eliot. Roger resents any criticism of the sound recording. He is very conscientious about his job.

I go into the sound booth, which is like a telephone box. Eliot begins to shout bossily, "Right! Ready, sir? Ready, Mr. Watts? Bell, please. Doors! Red light!" Then, because some people are still moving about, "Quiet! This is a take!"

Roger picks up the headphones and plugs in to the sound-camera room, which is in a gallery, overlooking the floor. "Ready to go, Jack?" he asks. Two buzzes: the okay signal.

"Are we all set?" asks Eliot. Then, after a moment, "Turn them over."

"Running," the boy at the switchboard tells him.

George steps forward and holds the board up before the camera.

Roger buzzes twice to the sound camera. Two buzzes in reply. Roger buzzes twice to signal Bergmann that Sound is ready.

Clark, the boy who works the clappers, says in a loud voice, "104, take one." He claps the clappers.

Bergmann, sitting grim in his chair, hisses between shut teeth, "Camera!"

I watch him, throughout the take. It isn't necessary to look at the set; the whole scene is reflected in his face. He never shifts his eyes from the actors for an instant. He seems to control every gesture, every intonation, by a sheer effort of hypnotic power. His lips move, his face relaxes and contracts, his body is thrust forward or drawn back in its seat, his hands rise and fall to mark the phases of the action. Now he is coaxing Toni from the window, now warning against too much haste, now encouraging her father, now calling for more expression, now afraid the pause will be missed, now delighted with the tempo, now anxious again, now really alarmed, now reassured, now touched, now pleased, now very pleased, now cautious, now disturbed, now amused. Bergmann's concentration is marvelous in its singleness of purpose. It is the act of creation.

When it is all over, he sighs, as if awaking from sleep. Softly, lovingly, he breathes the word, "Cut."

He turns to the camera operator. "How was it?"

"All right, sir, but I'd like to go again."

Roger gives two buzzes.

"Okay for sound, sir," says Teddy.

Joyce, the continuity girl, checks the footage with the operator. Roger puts his head out of the booth. "Teddy, will you favor round toward Miss Hayden a bit? I'm afraid of that bloody camera."

This problem of camera noise is perpetual. To guard against it, the camera is muffled in a quilt, which makes it look like a pet poodle wearing its winter jacket. Nevertheless, the noise persists. Bergmann never fails to react to it. Sometimes he curses, sometimes he sulks. This morning, however, he is in a clowning mood. He goes over to the camera and throws his arms around it.

"My dear old friend, we make you work so hard! It's too cruel! Mr. Chatsworth should give you a pension, and send you to the meadow to eat grass with the retired racehorses."

Everybody laughs. Bergmann is quite popular on the floor. "He's what I call a regular comedian," the doorman tells me. "This picture will be good, if it's half as funny as he is."

Mr. Watts and the camera operator are discussing how to avoid the mike shadow. Bergmann calls it "the Original Sin of the Talking Pictures." On rare occasions, the microphone itself somehow manages to get into the shot, without anybody noticing it. There is something sinister about it, like Poe's Raven. It is always there, silently listening.

A long buzz from the sound-camera room. Roger puts on the headphones and reports, "Sound-camera reloading, sir." Bergmann gives a grunt and goes off into a corner to dictate a poem to Dorothy. Amidst all this turmoil, he still finds time to compose one, nearly every day. Fred Murray is shouting directions for the readjustment of various lamps on the spot-rail and gantry; the tweets, the snooks and the baby spots. Joyce is typing the continuity report, which contains the exact text of each scene, as acted, with details of footage, screen-time, hours of work and so forth.

"Come on," shouts Eliot. "Aren't we ready, yet?"

Roger calls up to the camera room, "Going again, Jack."

Teddy notices that Eliot is inadvertently standing in front of Roger's window, blocking our view of the set. He grins maliciously, and says, in an obvious parody of Eliot's most officious tone, "Clear the booth, please!" Eliot blushes and moves aside, murmuring, "Sorry." Roger winks at me. Teddy, very pleased with himself, swings the microphone-boom, over whistling, and warning his crew, "Mind your heads, my braves!"

Roger generally lets me ring the bell for silence and make the two-buzz signal. It is one of the few opportunities I get of earning my salary. But, this time, I am mooning. I watch Bergmann telling something funny to Fred Murray, and wonder what it is. Roger has to make the signals himself. "I'm sorry to see a falling off in your wonted efficiency, Chris," he tells me. And he adds, to Teddy, "I was thinking of giving Chris his ticket, but now I shall have to reconsider it."

Roger's nautical expressions date back to the time when he was a radio operator on a merchant ship. He still has something of the ship's officer about him, in his brisk movements, his conscientiousness, his alert, pink, open-air face. He studies yachting magazines in the booth, between takes.

"Quiet! Get settled down. Ready? Turn them over."

"Running."

"104, take two."

"Camera . . ."

"Cut."

"Okay, sir."

"Okay for sound, Mr. Bergmann."

"All right. We print this one."

"Are you going again, sir?"

"We shoot it once more, quickly."

"Right. Come on, now. Let's get this in the can."

But the third take is N.G. Anita fluffs a line. In the middle of the fourth take, the camera jams. The fifth take is all right, and will be printed. My long, idle, tiring morning is over, and it is time for lunch.

There was a choice of three places to eat. Imperial Bulldog had its own canteen on the premises; but this was so crowded with studio workers, secretaries, bit players and extras that you could hardly ever find room to sit down. Then there was a public house, right across the street, where the food was quite good. This was the resort of the intellectuals: the writers, the cutters, the musicians and the members of the Art Department. I always tried to persuade Bergmann to go there; for we invariably had our meals together. But he usually insisted on the third alternative, a big hotel in South Kensington, where the studio executives and directors ate. Bergmann went to the hotel on principle. "One has to show one's self," he told me. "The animals expect to see their trainer." He had a half-humorous, half-serious theory that the powers of Bulldog were eternally plotting against him, and that, if he didn't put in an appearance, they would somehow contrive to liquidate him altogether.

The hotel had an imposing dining room and bad, would-be Continental food. Bergmann would enter it in his grimmest, most majestic mood, his eyebrows drawn down formidably, shooting severe glances to left and right. Catching the eyes of his colleagues, he would bow stiffly, but seldom speak. We had a small table to ourselves; unless, as sometimes happened, we were invited to sit with one of the Bulldog groups.

My chief objection to the hotel, apart from its boredom, was the expense. Earning so much money had made me curiously stingy, and

I grudged spending it on food. So I began to eat less and less, saying that I wasn't hungry. By ordering only a plate of soup or a sweet I managed to cut my bill down to about two shillings a day.

Neither Bergmann nor any of the others seemed to find this remarkable. Many of them had bad digestions, due to their sedentary occupation, and were on a diet. But there was a little waiter who, for some reason, had taken a fancy to me. We always exchanged a few words when I came in. One day, when I was sitting in a large group and had ordered, as usual, the cheapest item on the menu, he came up behind my chair and whispered, "Why not take the Lobster New-burg, sir? The other gentlemen have ordered it. There'll be enough for one extra. I won't charge you anything."

After the bustle of the morning, our afternoon begins in a leisurely, relaxed mood. We have migrated to another sound-stage, where a new set has been built: Toni's bedroom. The first scene to be shot is the one immediately preceding the arrival of Rudolf's letter. Toni is lying in bed, asleep, a smile on her lips. She is dreaming of her lover and yesterday's romantic meeting. Outside, it is a brilliant spring morning. Toni stirs, wakes, stretches herself, jumps out of bed, runs across the room, throws open the window, breathes in the perfume of the flowers delightedly, and bursts into the theme song of the picture.

We can hear Anita practicing it now, with Pfeffer at the piano, somewhere behind the set:

> *Spring wakes,*
> *Winter's dead.*
> *Ice breaks,*
> *Frosts have fled.*
> *Mornings are blue as your eyes,*
> *And from the skies*
> *I hear a lark*
> *Sing . . .*

Anita breaks off, abruptly, "Damn, I missed that beat again. Sorry, darling. Let's try it once more."

Spring wakes,
Winter's dead.
Ice breaks,
Frosts have fled . . .

Meanwhile, the carpenters, with a magnificent disregard for Art, are hammering and chiseling away at the bedroom window-sill. But George, the romantic, hums the tune and smiles dreamily as he writes on his board. George is an Irish boy, dark, good-looking, and full of innocent conceit. He flirts with Dorothy, Joyce and any attractive extras who come around the set. No doubt his fantasy even aspires to Anita herself. Joyce likes him; Dorothy is not impressed. "Kids of his age are more trouble than they're worth," she tells me. "I like a man to be sophisticated, if you know what I mean."

Last year's
Flowers were gay,
But who cares
For yesterday?

George strolls over to Roger, Teddy and myself, grinning and humming. When Anita gets to the refrain, he joins in, so that they sing a kind of long-distance duet:

Flowers must fade, and yet
One I can't forget:
Prater Vi-o-let.

Roger and Teddy clap their hands ironically. George bows, complacently taking the applause for what it is worth, and a bit extra.

"You know," he confides to us, with his artless smile, "I like that old-fashioned stuff. It gets me."

"How's the Great Lover today?" Teddy asks him. "And who's that little piece of goods I saw you with in the canteen?"

George smirks, "Just a friend of mine."

"She looked young enough to be your grand-daughter, you nasty old man."

"Our nurseries are no longer safe," says Roger. "I shall have to clean the family blunderbuss. . . . Which reminds me, Teddy, my boy: when are we going to hear those wedding bells?"

Teddy blushes, and becomes serious at once. His engagement, to a girl in the Art Department, is a standard topic of studio humor.

"As a matter of fact," he tells us gravely, "Mary and I had a talk about it last night. We've agreed to wait a while. I want to work up to a better job. In five years . . ."

"Five years!" I am really shocked. "But Teddy, anything may happen in five years. Suppose there's a war?"

"All the same," says Teddy stolidly, "a chap's got to be able to offer his wife a proper home."

Teddy is like that. No doubt he really will wait, if Mary lets him. He is a steady boy, solid all through. I can see him at forty, at fifty, at sixty, still just the same. He saves his money, and plays rugger on Saturday afternoons. Once a week, he and Fred Murray go to watch the All-In Wrestling at the local baths. They are both ardent fans, and spend a lot of time arguing about the merits of their respective favorites, Norman the Butcher and the Golden Hawk.

> *Flowers must fade, and yet*
> *One I can't forget:*
> *Prater Vi-o-let.*

The carpenters are still working on the window. Bergmann is still downstairs in the projection room, looking at the rushes: the prints of the film that was shot yesterday. Probably we shan't get started for another hour, at least. I wander off by myself to see what is happening on the other stages.

On Stage One, they are building our big restaurant set. This is for the final sequence of the picture. It is here, according to Chatsworth's revised version, that Toni takes her revenge on Rudolf by pretending to be the mistress of the notorious Baron Goldschrank. The Baron, an old admirer, can refuse her nothing, and rather unwillingly agrees to help in the plot. Toni makes a sensational entrance, on his arm, at the top of the staircase, in a blaze of borrowed diamonds. Rudolf, who is present, springs to his feet and strikes the Baron across the mouth. A duel is arranged, there and then; despite the Baron's timidity and Toni's attempted explanations. The Baron, as the injured party, is about to take the first shot, and Rudolf is striking an heroic attitude, when Count Rosanoff rushes in and throws himself between them, exclaiming, "Kill me, but do not dare to harm His Royal Highness!" For the wicked uncle has been overthrown, the King knows all and sends his blessing, and the way is open for Rudolf's return to Borodania with Toni as his bride.

Well, at any rate, the music is quite pretty.

On Stage Three, Eddie Kennedy is directing *Ten's a Honeymoon*. He is a dynamic, red-faced man, with bulging eyes and a wheezy voice, who specializes in American-style farces, full of mugging and slick lines. Having spent a year in Hollywood, he is regarded as an expert. And he certainly dresses the part. He is in his shirtsleeves, with his hat on, and a chewed cigar sticking out of the corner of his big mouth. He calls his actors "laddie" and his actresses "baby" or "sugar." He works very fast, with immense decision, shouting, swearing, bullying, and keeping everybody in a good humor. I stand there a long time, watching the comedian's efforts to rescue a fat lady from a portable Turkish bath. The assistant director tells me proudly that the picture will be finished by the end of this week, five days ahead of schedule.

I come back to our set, to find Bergmann returned and Anita already in bed, under a battery of lights, waiting for a close-up. Roger is talking to Timmy, the make-up man, and Clark.

"Hullo, Chris," Roger greets me. "Anita was asking for you."

"She was?"

"Said she wanted you to get in there and keep her warm. She's lonely."

"Why didn't one of you gentlemen oblige?"

"I wouldn't mind," says Clark. He means it. He is a tall skinny boy with a ferret's eyes and an unpleasantly small mouth.

"She's married, isn't she?" Roger asks.

"Used to be," says Timmy, "to Oliver Gilchrist. They got divorced."

"I don't blame him. She'd be a devil to live with. I know her sort," Roger mimics. " 'Not now, darling. I've got *such* a headache,

and my hair's been waved.' And she tells her girl friends, 'Men all
want the same thing. They're such *brutes.*' "

Timmy rolls his eyes, and sings, sotto voce:

> *Just the same, I'll bet*
> *You're not hard to get:*
> *Prater Vi-o-let.*

"Now then, everybody ready?" shouts Eliot, eyeing us with dis-
approval. "Let's get started."

We scatter to our respective positions.

The close-up takes nearly two hours. Watts fusses endlessly over
the lighting. The camera jams. Anita begins to sulk. Arthur Cromwell
is getting peevish. He has an appointment. Why couldn't they have
shot his scene first? (It belongs to the last sequence, when Toni's father
comes home late and finds that she hasn't returned.) "I think I'm
entitled to some consideration," he tells me, plaintively. "After all,
I've been a star for fifteen years."

In the middle of this, Ashmeade pays us a visit, with Mr. Harris.
They have heard of a place in Essex where it might be possible to
shoot some exteriors for the Prater scenes. Wouldn't Bergmann care
to go down with Harris next weekend and look at it?

But Bergmann is firm. He smiles his blandest, most subtle smile.
"A Sunday without Harris is my religion."

Harris can't very well take offense at this, so he and Ashmeade
have to force a laugh; but they aren't pleased. Bergmann dislikes
Harris, and Harris knows it. (In private, Bergmann calls him "the art-
constrictor.") Ashmeade and Harris retire, baffled.

At five o'clock, the word goes round that we shall be working
late. The union men get paid overtime, but they grumble, like the
rest of us. Clark is particularly bitter; this is the third date he's had to
break with his girl. "Eddie Kennedy's unit," he complains, "hasn't
worked late since the picture started. What we need is more organization." Teddy, who is very loyal to Bergmann, feels that this is going
too far. "Slapstick's different," he points out. "You can't rush this
high-class stuff. It's got to be artistic."

I go to the telephone and dial my home number.

"Hullo."

"Oh, Christopher . . . Does this mean you won't be in to supper again?"

"I'm afraid so."

"And we're having fishcakes!"

After the close-up, there is a tracking-shot, which will take time to prepare. The dolly, on which the camera will retreat before Toni's advance to the bedroom window, is apt to emit loud squeaks, audible to the microphone. It has to be oiled and tested. Roger and I go out to the fire-escape for a smoke. It is quite dark now, but not cold. The electric Bulldog sign casts a red light on the angle of the building.

Roger is feeling depressed.

"I don't know why I hang on to this job," he tells me. "The pay's all right. But it doesn't lead anywhere. . . . Next month, I'll be thirty-four. Know how I spend my evenings, Chris? Designing a boat. I've got it all figured out, even down to the cabin fixtures. It wouldn't cost much to build, either. I've saved a bit."

"What would you do with it?"

"Just sail away."

"Well, why don't you?"

"I don't know. . . . Places are all the same, really. I've been around."

"Haven't you ever thought of getting married?"

"Oh, I tried that, too. When I was a kid . . . She died."

"I'm sorry."

"It wasn't so ruddy wonderful. She was a good girl, though. . . . You know, sometimes I wonder what all this is for. Why not just peacefully end it?"

"We all think that. But we don't do it."

"Surely you're not fool enough to imagine there's anything afterwards?"

"Perhaps. No, I suppose not . . . I don't think it makes much difference."

Now that we have touched rock-bottom, Roger suddenly brightens. "You know what have been the best things in my life, Chris? Good, unexpected lays."

And he tells me the story of a married woman he once met in a hotel in Burton-on-Trent.

At seven-thirty, a boy from the canteen brings up tea and sandwiches. Eating together like this seems to raise the spirits of the entire unit. Anita has finished her scene, and another close-up, and gone home; she can be very co-operative when it suits her. Arthur Cromwell's scene won't take long. We shall be through by nine, after all.

Lawrence Dwight comes up from the cutting room to watch us.

He is scowling, as usual, but I can see that he feels pleased with himself. He has had a good day.

"Good evening, Herr Cut-Master. How are the patterns?"

"The patterns are a damn sight better than you deserve," says Lawrence, "considering the muck you send us. I'm going to make you quite a nice little picture, for which you'll take all the credit."

"That's ghastly decent of you."

Bergmann is pacing the floor, as he often does just before a take. He comes right up to us and stands for a moment, regarding our faces with dark, troubled, unseeing eyes. Then he turns abruptly and walks away in a kind of trance.

"Come on, now," shouts Eliot. "Let's get going. We don't want to be here all night."

"He's wasting his talents," says Lawrence. "What an ideal nursery governess!"

"Dead quiet, please!"

By ten minutes to nine, it is all over. We have shot two thousand feet of film. The day's work represents four minutes and thirty seconds of the completed picture.

"What are you doing this evening?" Lawrence asks.

"Nothing special. Why?"

"Let's go to a movie."

"Poor Dr. Bergmann," said my mother, when I came down to breakfast one morning, in the middle of February. "I'm afraid he'll be very worried about his family."

"What do you mean?"

"They're still in Vienna, aren't they? It seems dreadfully unsettled there, just now."

I picked up the newspaper. The word "Austria" jumped at me from the headlines. I was too excited to read properly. My eye caught bits of sentences, proper names: "At Linz, after heavy fighting . . . Fey . . . Starhemberg . . . martial law . . . hundreds of arrests . . . general strike fails to . . . Viennese workers besieged . . . hunt out socialist hyenas, Dollfuss declares . . ."

I dropped the paper, ran out into the hall, and dialed Bergmann's number. His voice answered as soon as the bell began to ring. "Hullo, yes . . ."

"Hullo, Friedrich."

"Oh . . . Hullo, Christopher." He sounded weary and disappointed. Obviously, he had been expecting some other call.

"Friedrich, I've just read the news . . ."

"Yes." His voice had no expression in it at all.

"Is there anything I can do?"

"There is nothing any of us can do, my child."

"Would you like me to come round?"

Bergmann sighed. "Very well. Yes. If you wish."

I hung up and phoned for a taxi. While I was waiting for it, I hastily swallowed some breakfast. My mother and Richard watched me in silence. Bergmann had become part of their lives, although they had only seen him once, for a few minutes, one day when he came to the house to fetch me. This was a family crisis.

Bergmann was sitting in the living room when I arrived, facing the telephone, his head propped in his hands. I was shocked by his appearance. He looked so tired and old.

"*Servus*," he said. He didn't raise his eyes. I saw that he had been crying.

I sat down at his side and put my arm around him. "Friedrich . . . You mustn't worry. They'll be all right."

"I have been trying to speak to them," Bergmann told me, wearily. "But it is impossible. There is no communication. Just now, I sent a telegram. It will be delayed for many hours. For days, perhaps."

"I'm sure they'll be all right. After all, Vienna is a big city. The fighting's localized, the paper says. Probably it won't last long."

Bergmann shook his head. "This is only the beginning. Now, anything may happen. Hitler has his opportunity. In a few hours, there can be war."

"He wouldn't dare. Mussolini would stop him. Didn't you read what the *Times* correspondent in Rome said about . . . ?"

But he wasn't listening to me. His whole body was trembling. He began to sob, helplessly, covering his face with his hands. At length, he gasped out, "I am so afraid . . ."

"Friedrich, don't. Please don't."

After a moment, he recovered a little. He looked up. He rose to his feet, and began to walk about the room. There was a long silence.

"If by this evening I hear nothing," he told me, suddenly, "I must go to them."

"But, Friedrich . . ."

"What else can I do? I have no choice."

"You wouldn't be able to help them."

Bergmann sighed. "You do not understand. How can I leave them alone at such a time? Already, they have endured so much. . . . You are very kind, Christopher. You are my only friend in this country. But you cannot understand. You have always been safe and protected. Your home has never been threatened. You cannot know what it is like to be an exile, a perpetual stranger. . . . I am bitterly ashamed that I am here, in safety."

"But they wouldn't want you to be with them. Don't you realize, they must be glad you're safe? You might even compromise them. After all, lots of people must know about your political opinions. You might be arrested."

Bergmann shrugged his shoulders. "All that is unimportant. You do not understand."

"Besides," I unwisely continued, "they wouldn't want you to leave the picture."

All Bergmann's pent-up anxiety exploded. "The picture! I shit upon the picture! This heartless filth! This wretched, lying charade! To make such a picture at such a moment is definitely heartless. It is a crime. It definitely aids Dollfuss, and Starhemberg, and Fey and all their gangsters. It covers up the dirty syphilitic sore with rose leaves, with the petals of this hypocritical reactionary violet. It lies and declares that the pretty Danube is blue, when the water is red with blood. . . . I am punished for assisting at this lie. We shall all be punished. . . ."

The telephone rang. Bergmann seized it. "Yes, hullo. Yes . . ." His face darkened. "It is the studio," he told me. "You speak to them."

"Hullo, Mr. Isherwood?" said the voice of Chatsworth's secretary, very brightly. "My word, you're up early this morning! Well, that's splendid—because Mr. Harris is a little bit worried. He's not sure about some details in the next set. Perhaps you could come in a little sooner and talk things over before you start work?"

I covered the mouthpiece with my hand. "Do you want me to tell them you're not well?" I asked Bergmann.

"Moment . . . Wait . . . No. Do not say that." He sighed deeply. "We must go."

It was an awful day. Bergmann went through it in a kind of stupor, and I watched him anxiously, fearing some outburst. During the takes, he sat like a dummy, seeming not to care what happened. If spoken to, he answered briefly and listlessly. He made no criticisms, no objection to anything. Unless Roger or the camera operator said "No," the scene would be printed; and we went on dully to the next.

Everybody in the unit reacted to his mood. Anita made difficulties, Cromwell hammed, Eliot fussed idiotically, the electricians were lazy, Mr. Watts wasted hours on lighting. Only Roger and Teddy were efficient, quiet and considerate. I had tried to explain to them how Bergmann was feeling. Teddy's only comment was, "Rotten luck." But he meant it.

In the evening, just as we were finishing work, a telegram arrived from Vienna: "Don't be silly, Friedrich dear. You know how newspapers exaggerate. Inge is still on holiday in the mountains with friends. I have just made a cake. Mother says it is delicious and sends love. Many kisses."

Bergmann showed it to me, smiling, with tears in his eyes. "She is great," he said. "Definitely great."

But now his personal trouble gave way to political anxiety and anger, which grew from day to day. Throughout Tuesday and Wednesday, the struggle continued. Without definite orders, without leadership, cut off and isolated into small groups, the workers went on fighting. What else could they do? Their homes, the great modern tenements, admired by the whole of Europe as the first architecture of a new and better world, were now described by the Press as "red fortresses"; and the government artillery was shooting them to pieces. The socialist leaders, fearing this emergency, had provided secret stores of arms and ammunition; but the leaders were all arrested now, or in hiding. Nobody knew where the weapons were buried. Desperately, men dug in courtyards and basements, and found nothing. Dollfuss took tea with the Papal Nuncio. Starhemberg saw forty-two corpses laid out in the captured Goethe Hof, and commented: "Far too few!" Berlin looked on, smugly satisfied. Another of its enemies was being destroyed; and Hitler's hands were clean.

Bergmann listened eagerly to every news broadcast, bought every special edition. During those first two days, while the workers still held out, I knew that he was hoping against hope. Perhaps the street fighting would grow into a revolution. Perhaps international Labor would force the Powers to intervene. There was just one little chance—one in a million. And then there was no chance at all.

Bergmann raged in his despair. He wanted to write letters to the conservative Press, protesting against its studied tone of neutrality. The letters were written, but I had to persuade him not to send them. He had no case. The papers were being perfectly fair, according to their own standards. You couldn't expect anything else.

By the beginning of the next week, it was all over, except for the government's vengeance on its prisoners. The workers' tenements were made to fly the white flag. The Engels Hof was renamed the Dollfuss Hof. Every man over eighteen from the Schlinger Hof was in prison, including the sick and the cripples. Terrorism became economical, since a new law stopped the unemployment pay of those who had been arrested. Meanwhile, Frau Dollfuss went among the workers' families, distributing cakes. Dollfuss was sincerely sad: "I hope the blood that flowed in our land will bring people to their senses."

The other centers of resistance, in Graz, Steuer and Linz, were all crushed. Bauer, Deutsch and many others fled into Czechoslovakia. Wallisch, caught near the frontier, was hanged at Loeben, in a brightly lighted courtyard, while his socialist fellow-prisoners looked on. "Long live freedom!" he shouted. The hangman and his assistants pulled him from the scaffold and clung to his legs until he choked.

Bergmann sat in his chair facing the set, grim and silent, like an accusing specter. One morning, Eliot ventured to ask him how he had liked a take.

"I loved it," Bergmann told him, savagely. "I loved it. It was unspeakably horrible. It was the maximum of filth. Never in my whole life have I seen anything so idiotic."

"You want to shoot it again, sir?"

"Yes, by all means. Let us shoot it again. Perhaps we can achieve something worse. I doubt it. But let us try."

Eliot grinned nervously, trying to pass this off as a joke.

"So?" Bergmann turned on him suddenly. "You find this amusing? You do not believe me? Very well—let me see you direct this scene yourself."

Eliot looked scared. "I couldn't do that, sir."

"You mean that you refuse to do it? You definitely refuse? Is that what you mean?"

"No, sir. Of course not. But . . ."

"You prefer that I ask Dorothy to direct this scene?"

"No . . ." Eliot, poor boy, was almost in tears.

"Then obey me!" Bergmann flared at him. "Do what I order!"

All that week, he seemed to be possessed by a devil. He tried to quarrel with everybody, even the loyal Teddy and Roger. We moved to another small set—a room in the Borodanian palace. Harris was present when Bergmann inspected it. I knew there would be trouble.

Bergmann found fault with everything. "In which *stables*," he asked Harris, "did you get these curtains?" Then he discovered that one of the doors wouldn't open.

"Sorry, sir," the carpenter explained, "we didn't have no orders it was to be made practical."

Bergmann snorted frantically. He walked up to the door and gave it a violent kick. We looked on, wondering what was coming. Suddenly, he swung round upon us.

"And there you all stand," he shouted, "grinning at me like evil, stubborn monkeys!"

He stormed out. We avoided each other's eyes. It was ridiculous, of course. But Bergmann's rage was so genuine, and somehow so touching, that nobody wanted to laugh.

An instant later, his tousled head popped in through a window of the set, like an infuriated Punch.

"No!" he cried. "Not monkeys! Donkeys!"

It would have been kindest, perhaps, to shout back at him, to afford him the exquisite relief of a fight. But none of us would do it. Some were sorry for him, some sulky and offended, some embarrassed, some scared. I was a bit scared of him, myself. The others assumed that I could manage him; but they were quite wrong. "You talk to him, Chris," Teddy would tell me. And once he added, with surprising insight, "Talk to him in German. It'll make him feel more at home."

But what was I to say? To have tried to excuse Bergmann's outbursts to himself would merely have made things worse. I knew he was ashamed of them, five minutes later. I only avoided his rage by keeping very close to him. Though he took little notice of me, he needed my presence, as a lonely man needs his dog. There was nothing I could do to help, except to maintain our contact.

I was with him nearly every evening, until he was tired enough to go to bed and lie still. I don't think he slept much. I would have offered to spend the night on the couch in his living room, but I knew he would resent that. I couldn't treat him as an invalid.

One evening, while we were having supper in a restaurant, a man named Patterson came up to our table. He was a journalist, who did a movie gossip column for one of the daily papers, and spent most of his time hunting for news around the studios. He had visited our unit once or twice, to talk to Anita. He was a breezy, stupid, thick-skinned person, whose curiosity knew no inhibitions; in fact, he was very well suited to his job.

"Well, Mr. Bergmann," he began heartily, with the fatal instinct of the very tactless, "what do you think of Austria?"

My heart sank. I tried, weakly, to interrupt and change the subject. But it was already too late. Bergmann stiffened. His eyes flashed. He thrust his head forward across the table, accusingly.

"What do *you* think of Austria, Mr. Patterson?"

The journalist was rather taken aback, as most of them are, when you ask them questions. "Well, as a matter of fact, I . . . It's terrible, of course. . . ."

Bergmann gathered himself together, and struck out at him like a snake. "I will tell you what you think. You think nothing. Nothing whatsoever."

Patterson blinked. But he was too stupid to realize he had better drop the subject. "Of course," he said, "I don't pretend to know much about politics, but . . ."

"This has nothing to do with politics. This has to do with plain human men and women. Not with actresses and indiscreet whores. Not with celluloid. Not with self-advertisement. With flesh and with blood. And you do not think about it. You do not care one damn."

Even now, Patterson wasn't really rattled. "After all, Mr. Bergmann," he said defensively, with his silly, teasing, insensitive smile, "you must remember, it isn't our affair. I mean, you can't really expect people in England to care . . ."

Bergmann's fist hit the table, so that the knives and forks rang. He turned scarlet in the face. He shouted, "I expect everybody to care! Everybody who is not a coward, a moron, a piece of dirt! I expect this whole damned island to care! I will tell you something: if they do not care, they will be made to care. The whole lot of you. You will be bombed and slaughtered and conquered. And do you know what I shall do? I shall sit by and smoke my cigar and laugh. And I shall say, 'Yes, it's terrible; and I do not give a damn. Not *one* damn.' "

Patterson, at last, was looking a bit scared.

"Don't get me wrong, Mr. Bergmann," he said, hastily. "I quite agree with you. I'm on your side entirely. Oh, yes . . . We don't think enough of the other fellow, and that's a fact. . . . Well, I must be toddling along. Glad to have seen you. We must have a talk, some day. . . . Good night."

We were alone. Bergmann was still fuming. He breathed hard, watching me out of the corner of his eye. I knew that he was waiting for me to make some comment.

And I couldn't. That night, as never before, I felt emotionally exhausted. Bergmann's intense, perpetual demand had drained me, it seemed, of the last drop of response. I no longer knew what I felt— only what I was supposed to feel. My only emotion, as always in such moments, was a weak resentment against both sides; against Bergmann, against Patterson, and against myself. "Why can't they leave me alone?" I resentfully exclaimed. But the "I" that thought this was both

Patterson and Bergmann, Englishman and Austrian, islander and continental. It was divided, and hated its division.

Perhaps I had traveled too much, left my heart in too many places. I knew what I was supposed to feel, what it was fashionable for my generation to feel. We cared about everything: fascism in Germany and Italy, the seizure of Manchuria, Indian nationalism, the Irish question, the workers, the Negroes, the Jews. We had spread our feelings over the whole world; and I knew that mine were spread very thin. I cared—oh, yes, I certainly cared—about the Austrian socialists. But did I care as much as I said I did, tried to imagine I did? No, not nearly as much. I felt angry with Patterson; but he, at least, was honest. What is the use of caring at all, if you aren't prepared to dedicate your life, to die? Well, perhaps it was some use. Very, very little.

Bergmann must have known what I was thinking. After a long silence, he said, kindly and gently, "You are tired, my child. Go to bed."

We parted at the restaurant door. I watched him walking away down the street, his head sunk in thought, until he was lost among the crowd.

I had failed him; I knew it. But I could do no more. It was beyond my strength.

That night, I think, he explored the uttermost depths of his loneliness.

Next morning, Ashmeade came onto the set. I wondered why. He seemed to have no special mission. He nodded to Bergmann, but didn't engage him in conversation. For some time, he stood watching, with a faint, secret smile on his lips.

Presently, Bergmann walked off into a corner, to speak to Dorothy. This must have been what Ashmeade was waiting for. He turned to me.

"Oh, Isherwood, can you spare me a minute of your valuable time?"

We strolled away together, toward the other end of the stage.

"You know," Ashmeade told me, in his soft, flattering voice, "Chatsworth's very grateful to you. In fact, we all are."

"Oh, really?" I was cautious, somehow suspecting this opening.

"We quite realize," Ashmeade chose each word, smiling, as if it tasted nice, "that you're in rather a difficult position. I think you've shown a great deal of tact and patience. We appreciate that."

"I'm afraid I don't understand," I said. I knew exactly what he was driving at now. And he knew that I knew. He was enjoying this little game.

"Well, I'm going to be frank with you. This is between ourselves, of course. . . . Chatsworth's getting worried. He simply can't understand Bergmann's attitude."

"How dreadful!" My tone was thoroughly nasty. Ashmeade gave me one of his poker-face looks.

"Everybody's complaining about him," he continued, his voice becoming confidential. "Anita talked to us yesterday. She wants to be released from the picture. We wouldn't agree to it, of course. But you can't blame her. After all, she's a big star. Bergmann treats her like a bit player. . . . It isn't only Anita, either. Harris feels the same way. So does Watts. They're prepared to put up with a good deal of temperament from a director. But there's a limit."

I said nothing. I hated having to agree with Ashmeade.

"You two are still great friends, aren't you?" It sounded like a playful accusation.

"Better than ever," I told him, defiantly.

"Well, can't you give us some idea of what's the matter with him? Isn't he happy here? What's he got against us?"

"Nothing . . . It's hard to explain. . . . You know he's been worried about his family. . . ."

"Oh, yes, this business in Austria . . . But that's all over now, isn't it?"

"On the contrary. It's probably just beginning."

"But I mean, the fighting has stopped. And his family's safe. What more does he want?"

"Look here, Ashmeade," I said. "It's no use our talking about this. You couldn't possibly understand. . . . You want the picture finished. I see that. Just be patient, a little. He'll come round."

"I hope you're right," Ashmeade gave me a playfully wry smile. "It's costing the studio a lot of money."

"He'll come round," I repeated, confidently. "You'll see. I'm sure it's going to be all right."

But I wasn't sure. I wasn't even hopeful. And Ashmeade knew it.

I don't know exactly how the whole thing started. Two days later, I overheard Joyce saying something to Clark about Eddie Kennedy. It would have made no impression on me if they hadn't stopped talking and looked guilty and slightly gleeful as I came up.

Several times that morning, I heard Kennedy's name. Fred Murray said it. Roger was mentioning it in a conversation with Timmy. Prince Rudolf was murmuring it to Count Rosanoff, as they waited to rehearse a scene. They glanced toward Bergmann, and their faces betrayed a discreet satisfaction.

Then, while we were in the sound booth together, Roger said to me, "I suppose you've heard? Eddie Kennedy looked at our rushes this morning."

For the moment, I didn't understand what he meant.

"That's funny," I said. "I was in the projection room myself. I didn't see him."

Roger smiled. "Of course you didn't. He saw them later. After you and Bergmann had gone."

"I wonder why?"

Roger gave me a glance, as though he thought I might be acting innocent. "There's only one explanation, Chris. Figure it out for yourself."

"You mean—they're going to put him on this picture?"

"I don't see what else it can mean."

"Gosh . . ."

"Do you think Bergmann knows?" Roger asked.

I shook my head. "He'd have told me."

"For Christ's sake, Chris, don't tell him I told you this."

"Do you suppose I want to talk about it?"

"I'm sorry for Bergmann," said Roger, thoughtfully. "He's had bad luck here. I don't care if he does sound off sometimes. He's a decent old bird. . . . I wish this didn't have to happen. Besides, Eddie could no more direct this picture than a drunken cow."

My one cowardly idea was: Bergmann has got to hear this from somebody else, and not when I'm around. At lunchtime, I tried to sneak away; but he was watching for me. "Come," he said, "we shall eat at the hotel." This was exactly what I had feared.

Sure enough, Kennedy was there, sitting with Ashmeade. They were deep in conversation. Kennedy seemed to be outlining some plan. He had arranged his knife, fork and spoon in a square, and was demonstrating something with the pepper-pot. Neither of them took any notice of us; but, as we passed, Ashmeade looked at Kennedy and laughed an intimate, flattering laugh. Several of the other Bulldog directors and executives regarded us curiously. I could feel their eyes following our backs.

During the meal, Bergmann was thoughtful and moody. We scarcely spoke. I had to force myself to eat. I felt as if I were going to vomit. Should I tell him? No, I couldn't. I waited for something to happen.

We had nearly finished when Patterson, the journalist, came in.

He greeted everybody, stopping at each group for a joke and a word or two; but I knew instinctively that he was making for our table. His face was beaming, it seemed to me, with the malice of the stupid man who thinks he is going to score a point.

"Well, well, Mr. Bergmann," he began, sitting down without being invited. "What's all this I hear? Is it really true?"

"Is what true?" Bergmann looked at him with distaste.

"About the picture. You're really dropping it?"

"Dropping?"

"Retiring. Giving it up."

For a moment, it seemed that Bergmann still didn't understand him. Then he jerked out, "Who told you this?"

"Oh, well, you know," Patterson looked maliciously coy, "these things get about." He watched Bergmann's face inquisitively. Then he turned to me, with a most unconvincing display of anxiety. "I say, I hope I haven't put my foot in it?"

"I never pay much attention to studio gossip," I said incautiously, in the agony of my embarrassment.

Bergmann turned on me, quite savagely. "You heard this, too?"

"There must be some mistake, of course," Patterson was now

openly malicious, "if *you* know nothing about it, Mr. Bergmann. . . . It's a funny thing, though. I got this from pretty high up. It certainly sounded authentic. Eddie Kennedy was mentioned. . . ."

"Oh, if that's all it was . . ." (I was desperately trying to give Bergmann a chance of pretending he knew this already) "it's quite easily explained. Just because he saw our rushes this morning . . . You know how these things are misrepresented. . . ."

But Bergmann was beyond all diplomacy.

"Kennedy saw the rushes? And I knew nothing about it! Nothing! I wasn't told!" He swung round upon me, again. "You knew this all the time? You were in this conspiracy against me?"

"I—I didn't think it was important. . . ."

"Not important! Oh, no! If I am betrayed and tricked and lied to, it is not in the least important! If my only friend joins the enemy, it is not important!" Suddenly, he turned back to Patterson. "Who told you this?"

"Well, really, Mr. Bergmann—I'm not at liberty to say."

"Of course you are not at liberty to say! These people are your paymasters! Very good: I will tell you who it was. Ashmeade!"

Patterson tried to look inscrutable. He didn't succeed.

"It was Ashmeade!" cried Bergmann, triumphantly. "I knew it!" He spoke so loud that the people at the next table stared at us. "I shall confront him immediately with this impudent lie!"

He jumped to his feet.

"Friedrich!" I grabbed his arm. "Wait. Not now."

My tone must have been commanding in its desperation, for Bergmann hesitated.

"We'll talk to him at the studio," I continued. "It'll be better. Let's think this over first."

Bergmann nodded and sat down again.

"Very well, we shall deal with him later," he agreed, breathing hard. "First, we must see his master. At once. After lunch."

"All right." My one idea was to pacify him. "After lunch."

"I'm afraid I've been the bearer of evil tidings," said Patterson, with a smirk. At that moment, I really hated him.

"Look here," I said, "you aren't going to print any of this?"

"Well . . ." Patterson became cagey, at once. "I'll have to get it confirmed, naturally. . . . If Mr. Bergmann would care to make a statement. . . ."

"He wouldn't," I interrupted, firmly.

"I shall make a statement," said Bergmann. "Undoubtedly I shall make a statement. This is nothing secret. Let the whole world know of this betrayal. I shall write to every newspaper. I shall reveal how a foreign director, a guest in this country, is betrayed. I regard this as a clear stab in the back. It is discrimination. It is persecution. I shall bring an action for damages."

"I'm quite sure," I told Patterson, "that everything will be explained satisfactorily. You'll know by this evening."

Bergmann merely snorted.

"Well," said Patterson, with his teasing smile, "I hope so, I'm sure. . . . Goodbye, Mr. Bergmann." He left us, delightedly. We saw him go straight over to Ashmeade's table.

"That dirty spy," Bergmann hissed. "Now he makes his report."

When we went out of the dining room, a few minutes later, Patterson, Ashmeade and Kennedy were still sitting together. I took Bergmann's arm, resolved, if necessary, to prevent him from speaking to them by force. But he contented himself with saying, very loudly, as we passed, "Judas Iscariot is in council with the High Priests."

Neither Ashmeade nor Patterson looked at us, but Kennedy grinned pleasantly, and called, "Hi, Bergmann. How's everything?"

Bergmann didn't answer.

I had hoped that the taxi ride would have given him time to cool down. But it didn't. As soon as we were back at our office in the studio, he told Dorothy, "Call Mr. Chatsworth, and say I demand to see him immediately."

Dorothy picked up the telephone. She was informed that Chatsworth was still out at lunch. Bergmann grunted dangerously.

Eliot came in.

"All ready to rehearse the restaurant scene, sir."

Bergmann glared at him. "There will be no shooting today."

"No shooting?" Eliot echoed, stupidly.

"You heard what I said."

"But, Mr. Bergmann, we're behind schedule already, and . . ."

"There will be no shooting today!" Bergmann shouted at him. "Is that clear?"

Eliot crumpled. "What time shall I make the call for tomorrow?" he ventured to ask, at length.

"I don't know and I don't care!"

I signaled to Eliot with my eyes to leave us alone. He went out, with a deep sigh.

"Call Chatsworth again," Bergmann ordered.

But Chatsworth was still out. Half an hour later he had returned and gone immediately into conference. An hour later, he was still busy.

"Very well," said Bergmann. "We also can play at this game of rat and mouse. Come, we go home. I shall not return here. Chatsworth shall come to see me, and I shall be too busy. Tell him that."

He struggled furiously into his overcoat. The telephone rang.

"Mr. Chatsworth will see you now," Dorothy reported.

I gasped with relief. Bergmann scowled. He seemed disappointed.

"Come," he said to me.

In Chatsworth's outer office, as ill-luck would have it, there was another delay. This gave Bergmann's temper time to reach boiling point again. He began to mutter to himself. At the end of five minutes, he said, "Enough of this farce. Come. We go."

"Couldn't you . . ." I appealed desperately to the girl at the desk, "couldn't you tell him it's urgent?"

The girl looked embarrassed. "Mr. Chatsworth particularly told me not to disturb him. He's on the line to Paris," she said.

"Enough!" cried Bergmann. "We go!"

"Friedrich! Please wait another minute!"

"You desert me? Splendid! I go alone."

"Oh, very well . . ." I rose unwillingly to my feet.

The inner door opened. It was Ashmeade, grinning all over his face. "Won't you come in, please?" he said.

Bergmann didn't even glance at him. With a fearful snort, like a bull entering the ring, he strode into the room, head lowered. Chatsworth was lolling at his desk, cigar in hand. He flourished it toward the chairs.

"Take a pew, gentlemen!"

But Bergmann didn't sit down. "First," he nearly shouted, "I demand absolutely that this Fouché, this spy, shall leave the room!"

Ashmeade kept on smiling, but I could see that he was disconcerted. Chatsworth looked squarely at Bergmann from behind his thick spectacles.

"Don't be silly," he said, good-humoredly. "Nobody's going to leave any rooms. If you've got something to say, say it. This is as much Sandy's business as mine."

Bergmann growled, "So you protect him?"

"Certainly." Chatsworth was quite unruffled. "I protect all my subordinates. Until they're sacked. And I do the sacking."

"You will not sack me!" Bergmann yelled. "I do not give you that pleasure. I resign!"

"You do, eh? Well, my directors are always resigning. All except the lousy ones, worse luck."

"Such as Mr. Kennedy, for example?"

"Eddie? Oh, he walks out on every picture. He's great."

"You make fun of me!"

"Sorry, old boy. You're being pretty funny yourself, you know."

Bergmann was so angry he couldn't answer. He turned on his heel and made for the door. I stood undecided, watching him.

"Listen," said Chatsworth, with such authority that Bergmann stopped.

"I shall not listen. Not to your insults."

"Nobody's going to insult you. Sit down."

To my amazement, Bergmann did so. My opinion of Chatsworth was rising every moment.

"Listen to me . . ." Chatsworth punctuated his sentences with puffs at his cigar. "You walk off the picture. You break your contract. All right. You know what you're doing, I suppose. That's your affair, and the Legal Department's. But meanwhile, somebody has to shoot this God-damned movie. . . ."

"I am not interested!" Bergmann interrupted. "The picture means nothing to me any more. This is a case of abstract justice. . . ."

"Somebody," Chatsworth continued, imperturbably, "has to shoot this picture. And I have to see that it's shot. . . ."

"My work is spied upon. Behind my back, the rushes are shown to this ignorant cretin. . . ."

"Let's get this straight," said Chatsworth. "Eddie was shown the rushes by Sandy, quite unofficially, because Sandy was worried about the way the picture was going. He wanted an outside opinion. I knew nothing about it. As a matter of fact, Sandy was taking a risk. He was breaking a studio rule. I might have been very angry with him. But, under the circumstances, I think he did perfectly right. . . . I know you've been under the weather lately. I know your wife and daughter were in Vienna during this little spot of bother, and I'm damn sorry. That's why I've kept quiet as long as I have. But I can't throw away the studio's money because of your private sorrows, or mine, or anybody else's. . . ."

"And so you invite this analphabet to take my place?"

"I hadn't got as far as thinking of anybody taking your place. I didn't know you were going to walk out on us."

"And now you set this Kennedy to work, who will carefully annihilate every fragment Isherwood and I have built up, so lovingly, all these months . . ."

"A lot of it's damn good, I admit. . . . But what am I to do? You've left us in the lurch."

(Oh, gosh, I thought, he's smart!)

"Everything destroyed. Obliterated. Reduced to utter nonsense. Terrible. Nothing to do."

"What do you care? You're not interested in the picture."

Bergmann's eyes flashed. "Who says I am not?"

"You did."

"I said nothing of the kind. I said I am not interested in the picture which your Kennedy will make."

"You said you weren't interested. . . . Didn't he, Sandy?"

"It is a lie!" Bergmann glared at Ashmeade. "I could never say such a thing! How could I not be interested? For this picture, I have given everything—all my time, all my thought, all my care, all my strength, since months. Who dares to say I am not interested?"

"Atta boy!" Chatsworth began to laugh very heartily. Getting to his feet, he came around the desk and slapped Bergmann on the shoulder. "That's the spirit! Of course you're interested! I always knew you were. If anybody says you're not, I'll help you beat the hell out of him." He paused, as if struck by a sudden idea. "And now, I'll tell you what: you and I and Isherwood are going down to look at those rushes together. And we won't take Sandy along, either. That'll be his punishment, the dirty dog."

By this time, Chatsworth had walked Bergmann right over to the door. Bergmann looked somewhat dazed. He didn't resist at all. Chatsworth held the door open for us. As I went out, I saw him wink at Ashmeade over his shoulder.

Down in the projection room, they were waiting for us. We sat through the day's rushes. Then Chatsworth said, quite casually, "Suppose we look at everything you've shot these last two weeks?"

My suspicions turned to certainty. I whispered to Lawrence Dwight, "When did Chatsworth arrange for this stuff to be shown?"

"Early this morning," said Lawrence. "Why?"

"Oh, nothing." I smiled to myself in the darkness. So that was that.

When it was all over, and the lights went up, Chatsworth asked, "Well, how does it look?"

"It's terrible," said Bergmann gloomily. "Definitely horrible."

"Oh, now I wouldn't go so far as that," Chatsworth puffed blandly at his cigar. "That scene of Anita's is damn good."

"You are wrong," Bergmann brightened at once. "It is terrible."

"I like your camera angles."

"I hate them. It is so poor, so dull. It is without mood. It is just a lousy newsreel."

"I don't see what you could have done better."

"You do not see," said Bergmann, actually smiling. "But I see. I see clearly. The approach is wrong. My eyes are opened. I have been fumbling in the dark, like an old idiot."

"You think you can cure it?"

"Beginning tomorrow," said Bergmann, with decision, "I reshoot everything. I work night and day. It is perfectly clear to me. We shall keep our schedule. We shall make you a great picture."

"Of course you will!" Chatsworth put his arm around Bergmann's neck. "But you'll have to sell me your new ideas first. . . . Look here, let's have dinner together this evening, the three of us? Then we'll get down to brass tacks."

If I had imagined we kept long hours before, I was wrong. The days which followed were unlike anything else I have ever known. I lost all sense of space and time, I was so tired. Everybody was tired, and yet we worked better than ever before. Even the actors didn't sulk.

Bergmann inspired us all. His absolute certainty swept us along like a torrent. There were hardly any retakes. The necessary script alterations seemed to write themselves. Bergmann knew exactly what he wanted. We took everything in our stride.

Incredibly soon, the last days of shooting arrived. One night (perhaps it was the last night of all; I don't remember) we worked very late, on the big opening scene at the Prater. Bergmann, that evening, was unforgettable. Very haggard, with blazing dark eyes in the furrowed mask of his face, he maneuvered the great crowd this way and that, molded it, reduced it to a single organism, in which every individual had a part. We were exhausted, but we were all laughing. It was like a party, and Bergmann was our host.

When the last take was finished, he came solemnly up to Anita, in front of everybody, and kissed her hand. "Thank you, my darling," he said. "You were great."

Anita loved it. Her eyes filled with tears.

"Friedrich, I'm sorry I was naughty sometimes. I shall never have an experience like this again. I think you're the most wonderful man in the world."

"Well," said Lawrence Dwight, addressing his artificial leg, "now we've seen everything, haven't we, Stump?"

Arthur Cromwell had a flat in Chelsea. Wouldn't we all go round there for a nightcap? Anita said yes. So of course Bergmann and I had to accept. Eliot and Lawrence and Harris joined us. And Bergmann insisted on bringing Dorothy, Teddy and Roger. Then, just as we were starting, Ashmeade appeared.

I was afraid there would be a row—but no. I saw Bergmann stiffen a little. Then Ashmeade took him aside and said something, smiling his subtly flattering smile.

"You go with the others," Bergmann told me. "Ashmeade will drive me in his car. He wants to talk to me."

I don't know what they said to each other; but when we all arrived at Cromwell's flat, it was obvious that a reconciliation had taken place. Bergmann was sparkling, and Ashmeade's smile had become intimate. After a few minutes, I heard him call Bergmann "Friedrich." And, more marvelous still, Bergmann publicly addressed him as "Umbrella."

At the party which followed, Bergmann was terrific. He clowned, he told stories, he sang songs, he imitated German actors, he showed Anita how to dance the *Schuhplattler*. His eyes shone with that last reserve of energy which one puts out in moments of extreme exhaustion, with the aid of a few drinks. And I felt so happy in his success. The way you feel when your father is a success with your friends.

It must have been close on four o'clock when we said good night. Eliot offered us a ride in his car. Bergmann said he preferred to walk.

"I'm coming with you," I told him. I knew that I wouldn't be able to sleep. I was wound up like a watch. In Knightsbridge, I could probably find a taxi to take me home.

It was that hour of the night when the street lamps seem to shine with an unnatural, remote brilliance, like planets on which there is no life. The King's Road was wet-black, and deserted as the moon. It did not belong to the King, or to any human being. The little houses had shut their doors against all strangers and were still, waiting for dawn, bad news and the milk. There was nobody about. Not even a policeman. Not even a cat.

It was that hour of the night at which man's ego almost sleeps. The sense of identity, of possession, of name and address and telephone number grows very faint. It was the hour at which man shivers, pulls up his coat collar, and thinks, "I am a traveler. I have no home."

A traveler, a wanderer. I was aware of Bergmann, my fellow-traveler, pacing beside me: a separate, secret consciousness, locked away within itself, distant as Betelgeuse, yet for a short while, sharing my wanderings. Head thrust forward, hat perched on the thick bush of hair, muffler huddled around the throat under the gray stubble, hands clasped behind the back. Like me, he had his journey to go.

What was he thinking about? *Prater Violet,* his wife, his daughter, myself, Hitler, a poem he would write, his boyhood, or tomorrow morning? How did it feel to be inside that stocky body, to look out of those dark, ancient eyes? How did it feel to be Friedrich Bergmann?

There is one question which we seldom ask each other directly: it is too brutal. And yet it is the only question worth asking our fellow-travelers. What makes you go on living? Why don't you kill yourself? Why is all this bearable? What makes you bear it?

Could I answer that question about myself? No. Yes. Perhaps . . . I supposed, vaguely, that it was a kind of balance, a complex of tensions. You did whatever was next on the list. A meal to be eaten. Chapter eleven to be written. The telephone rings. You go off somewhere in a taxi. There is one's job. There are amusements. There are people. There are books. There are things to be bought in shops. There is always something new. There has to be. Otherwise, the balance would be upset, the tension would break.

It seemed to me that I had always done whatever people recommended. You were born; it was like entering a restaurant. The waiter came forward with a lot of suggestions. You said, "What do you advise?" And you ate it, and supposed you liked it, because it was expensive, or out of season, or had been a favorite of King Edward the Seventh. The waiter had recommended teddy bears, football, cigarettes, motor bikes, whisky, Bach, poker, the culture of Classical Greece. Above all, he had recommended Love: a very strange dish.

Love. At the very word, the taste, the smell of it, something inside me began to throb. Ah yes, Love . . . Love, at the moment, was J.

Love had been J. for the last month—ever since we met at that party. Ever since the letter which had arrived next morning, opening the way to the unhoped-for, the unthinkable, the after-all-quite-thinkable and, as it now seemed, absolutely inevitable success of which my friends were mildly envious. Next week, or as soon as my work for Bulldog was finished, we should go away together. To the South of France, perhaps. And it would be wonderful. We would swim. We would lie in the sun. We would take photographs. We would sit in the café. We would hold hands, at night, looking out over the sea from the balcony of our room. I would be so grateful, so flattered, and I would be damned careful not to show it. I would be anxious. I would be jealous. I would unpack my box of tricks, and exhibit them, once again. And, in the end (the end you never thought about), I would get sick of the tricks, or J. would get sick of them. And very politely, tenderly, nostalgically, flatteringly, we would part. We would part, agreeing to be the greatest friends always. We would part, immune, in future, from that particular toxin, that special twinge of jealous desire, when one of us met the other, with somebody else, at another party.

I was glad I had never told Bergmann about J. He would have taken possession of that, as he did of everything else. But it was still mine, and it would always be. Even when J. and I were only trophies, hung up in the museums of each other's vanity.

After J., there would be K. and L. and M., right down the alphabet. It's no use being sentimentally cynical about this, or cynically sentimental. Because J. isn't really what I want. J. has only the value of being now. J. will pass, the need will remain. The need to get back into the dark, into the bed, into the warm naked embrace, where J. is no more J. than K., L., or M. Where there is nothing but the nearness, and the painful hopelessness of clasping the naked body in your arms. The pain of hunger beneath everything. And the end of all lovemaking, the dreamless sleep after the orgasm, which is like death.

Death, the desired, the feared. The longed-for sleep. The terror of the coming of sleep. Death. War. The vast sleeping city, doomed for the bombs. The roar of oncoming engines. The gunfire. The screams. The houses shattered. Death universal. My own death. Death of the seen and known and tasted and tangible world. Death with its army of fears. Not the acknowledged fears, the fears that are advertised. More dreadful than those: the private fears of childhood. Fear of the height of the high-dive, fear of the farmer's dog and the vicar's pony, fear of cupboards, fear of the dark passage, fear of splitting your fingernail with a chisel. And behind them, most unspeakably terrible of all, the arch-fear: the fear of being afraid.

It can never be escaped—never, never. Not if you run away to the ends of the earth (we had turned into Sloane Street), not if you yell for Mummy, or keep a stiff upper lip, or take to drink or to dope. That fear sits throned in my heart. I carry it about with me, always.

But if it is mine, if it is really within me . . . Then . . . Why, then . . . And, at this moment, but how infinitely faint, how distant, like the high far glimpse of a goat track through the mountains between clouds, I see something else: the way that leads to safety. To where there is no fear, no loneliness, no need of J., K., L., or M. For a second, I glimpse it. For an instant, it is even quite clear. Then the clouds shut down, and a breath off the glacier, icy with the inhuman coldness of the peaks, touches my cheek. "No," I think, "I could never do it. Rather the fear I know, the loneliness I know . . . For to take that other way would mean that I should lose myself. I should no longer be a person. I should no longer be Christopher Isherwood. No, no. That's more terrible than the bombs. More terrible than having no lover. That I can never face."

Perhaps I might have turned to Bergmann and asked, "Who are you? Who am I? What are we doing here?" But actors cannot ask such questions during the performance. We had written each other's parts, Christopher's Friedrich, Friedrich's Christopher, and we had to go on playing them, as long as we were together. The dialogue was crude, the costumes and make-up were more absurd, more of a caricature, than anything in *Prater Violet*: Mother's Boy, the comic Foreigner with the funny accent. Well, that didn't matter. (We had reached Bergmann's door, now.) For, beneath our disguises, and despite all the kind-unkind things we might ever say or think about each other, we knew. Beneath outer consciousness, two other beings, anonymous, impersonal, without labels, had met and recognized each other, and had clasped hands. He was my father. I was his son. And I loved him very much.

Bergmann held out his hand.

"Good night, my child," he said.

He went into the house.

I never saw *Prater Violet*, after all.

It was shown in London, with a great deal of publicity, and got very good notices. ("When we saw your name on the screen," my mother wrote, "we both felt *very* proud, and applauded loudly. Richard kept saying, 'Isn't that *just* like Christopher?' But, I must say, Anita Hayden is hardly one's idea of an *innocent young girl?* She has a charming voice . . .") It went to New York, and the Americans liked it, unusually well for a British picture. It was even shown in Vienna.

Several months later, I got a letter from Lawrence Dwight, who was on holiday in Paris:

A girl I know here came to me in great indignation the other day. She's an earnest Red, and admires the political consciousness of the French workers; but, alas, it seems that the ones in our neighborhood are all going to see *La Violette du Prater*, a horrible British picture which, besides being an insult to the intelligence of a five-year-old child, is definitely counter-revolutionary and ought to be banned. Meanwhile, in the cinema round the corner, a wonderful Russian masterpiece is playing to empty seats.

Incidentally, I've seen the Russian film, myself. It is the usual sex triangle between a girl with thick legs, a boy, and a tractor. As a matter of fact, it's technically superior to anything Bulldog could produce in a hundred years. But you can't expect the poor fools to know that . . .

As for Bergmann, *Prater Violet* got him the offer of a job in Hollywood. He went out there with his family, early in 1935.

EXHUMATIONS

(1966)

[Isherwood describes *Exhumations*, a collection of essays, stories, and verse, as "bits and pieces, fragments of an autobiography which tells itself indirectly, by means of exhibits."]

H. G. Wells

TO WRITE A BIOGRAPHY of Wells is a peculiarly difficult undertaking, as Antonina Vallentin would be the first to admit. "He was so
infinitely sensitive to the changes taking place around us," she says,
in the foreword to her book (*H. G. Wells, Prophet of Our Day*), "so
far ahead of our time and yet so closely, so intensely present in it, that
he sums up its whole content. He *is* the history of our day." That is
precisely the problem—how to determine the relation of a social and
political thinker to an epoch which we cannot yet properly survey,
because we ourselves are still in the middle of it. For this reason alone,
it would seem doubtful that a really adequate biography of Wells is
possible at present. However, Madame Vallentin has certainly made
a courageous try. Her book is always informative, occasionally profound and never dull. It is a valuable guide to the enigmas, the
fascinating but self-contradictory fragments of Wells' own autobiographical work. Daphne Woodward's translation from Madame Vallentin's French original is commendably free from Gallicisms.

Towards the end of his life Wells wrote: "I came up from the
poor in a state of flaming rebellion, most blasphemous and unsaintly."
The phrase jars on one a little; its swagger seems affected. Wells, to
be sure, knew bitter poverty in his youth, semi-starvation and serious
illness. But he doesn't quite fill this suggested role of a proletarian

revolutionary, marching to the barricades with broken chains dangling from his wrists. He was, in fact, the son of a housemaid and a gardener "who had gone into a precarious business as small shopkeepers, not through any urge for independence but because they had lost the employment in which they had been perfectly happy. His mother looked upon 'service,' dependency, as heaven, a haven of security; it represented all she had known of kindness and beauty, the romantic element in her life, the light that still shone through her poverty-stricken days." What Wells "came up from" was, therefore, not the unashamed poverty of the proletariat but the apologetic poverty of the lower middle class, the nineteenth-century heirs of feudal serfdom, with their pitiful yearnings toward "respectability," their clean lace curtains hung to hide bare rooms from prying neighbors. And it was against this concept of respectability, of preordained subservience, of "knowing your place," that he primarily rebelled. He grew up hating, above all things, the feudal philosophy of the Big House, with its smugly defined scale of virtues and values, its fatty conscience and its false God. When Bernard Shaw, on the occasion of Wells' death, remarked that Wells had never been a gentleman, he made a cruel but extremely pertinent observation. For throughout his life, despite wealth and worldwide fame, Wells remained painfully and most aggressively conscious of his origins. He loathed the pretensions of birth and rank and felt himself fully entitled to fight them with any weapons that came to hand. An inverted snob, he seemed sometimes to glory in caddishness. He confronted established authority with that kind of comically cocky, underdog defiance which has been classically represented by Charlie Chaplin. And yet—like the rest of us—he was perversely attracted to what he loathed. Many of the heroines of the novels, and many of the real women he loved, display the aristocratic arrogance, the easy contempt for convention which is so characteristic of a privileged ruling caste.

Wells had no false modesty, but he held some curious and humble views about himself and his talents. He insisted upon his ordinariness. Once, happening to meet Madame Vallentin on the railway station at Nice: " 'It's funny you recognize me,' he said with his crooked smile, 'I'm so exactly like all the middle-class, middle-aged Englishmen who come in swarms to the Riviera.' " Discussing his mental capacities, he declared that "if brains could be put on show, like cats and dogs, he did not believe his own would win even a third prize." This is obviously untrue; but perhaps Wells meant that he lacked a certain quick-witted, superficial cleverness which he greatly admired in others. He had, indeed, that measure of stupidity—or obstinate, plodding slowness—which is an aid, not a hindrance, to clear and careful thinking. The merely clever man brings forth a phrase and mistakes it for an idea. The "stupid" thinker, lacking this agility, never trusts a phrase until he has taken it to pieces; he goes deeper.

Incredible as it sounds, Wells also believed that he lacked vitality. Yet his vitality was the very essence of his genius. His vital appetite for experience and knowledge was prodigious, and he preserved it into his late seventies. He always wrote straight out of his immediate interests and enthusiasms, bubbling over with excitement. He could hardly wait to tell the world what was happening to him, what he was thinking—and, indeed, he had to hurry, or he would be thinking something else. To an altogether extraordinary degree, he had a sense of the present moment, with all its urgency, menace, opportunity and challenge. He was aware of the stars in their courses, the earth turning, time passing, Gandhi spinning, Lenin dying by inches at his desk, Proust (whom he didn't like) writing, the bus-driver's wife cooking supper, China starving, America drunk on bathtub gin, the scientists trying to split the atom, the men of goodwill trying to unite Europe, and the peoples of the world already shivering in the shadow of another war. Not only was he aware of all this—as any ordinary journalist might be—but he reacted to his awareness with passion. He didn't just sit back and watch. He accepted his share of responsibility, of guilt, of duty. What could he do, before it was too late? How could he help? He was prepared to do anything. He bustled hither and thither, with his ready pen and his squeaky voice, joining this movement, resigning from that, minding other people's business, offering suggestions wanted or unwanted, contradicting himself, attacking, accusing. He traveled in many countries, always telling his hosts exactly what he thought of them; he bearded statesmen in their studies, he confronted dictators and generals. He was utterly fearless and reckless, and so clearly above the common motives of ambition and greed that he ended by achieving a privileged position. Like Shaw, he was allowed to write things which no newspaper would dare to publish over any other signature. Unlike Shaw, he made effective use of this privilege. By the time of his death, many of his fellow human beings had dismissed him from their consciences as a nagging and erratic nuisance. It would have been too uncomfortable to listen to him, so they laughed at him and called him absurd. No doubt he often *was* absurd; but his very absurdity put their cowardly apathy to shame.

Wells thought of himself as an historian, an educator, a sociologist, a political pamphleteer, rather than as a literary artist. He was inclined to be impatient with those who believe that style is an end in itself, well worth the practice and effort of a lifetime. "I write, like I walk," he said, "because I want to get somewhere." He was impatient, also, with Henry James, who (while praising him warmly) complained that the heroines of his novels were mere projections of their author's personality: "the ground of the drama is somehow most of all in the adventure for *you*—not to say *of you*, the moral, temperamental, personal, of your setting it forth." Wells felt that the novel in its traditional form was out of date. "It was a fixed frame, apparently established for ever, where individual destinies were played out in an independence that seemed unnatural to the social being of today." He added that the novel "was unlikely to be very important in the intellectual life of future generations. It was quite likely to die out and be replaced by more sincere and revealing biographies and autobiographies." Nevertheless, Wells was capable of fine writing, when he wasn't in too much of a hurry; and, throughout his career, he continued to produce novels.

As a matter of fact, Wells had all the gifts which go to make a "traditional" novelist. He could create solid characters, write lively, naturalistic dialogue, and evoke the atmosphere of houses and places. His humor was Dickensian, lapsing sometimes into facetiousness but bold and warm at its best. These qualities are most apparent in *Kipps*, *Tono-Bungay* and *Mr. Polly*, three books which drew largely upon the experience of Wells' own childhood and adolescence. Wells was always at his most vivid when he returned to that period; no doubt because he could look at it from a distance, objectively. He never gave himself time to do this in dealing with his later life. Everything had to be reported at once, as it happened—like the scribbling of a war correspondent in the midst of a still-smoking battlefield. There was no time to worry about form, or the technical problems of presentation; there was no question of excluding any portions of the given material because they didn't happen to "fit." Every bit of it had to go in.

The majority of Wells' realistic novels (I shall speak of his scientific fantasies later) deal with the impact upon their author of a person, or an idea, or a situation. The person is usually a woman, one of the many in Wells' life, very thinly disguised. The idea or the situation is presented subjectively, just as it struck Wells himself. This initial impact (the impact, for example, of World War I upon Wells in *Mr. Britling Sees It Through*) is the author's point of departure into speculation and theorizing. "What does it mean?" he asks himself aloud, "what do I think about this?" (Wells isn't sure, because he is thinking even as he writes, thrashing the problem out before our eyes.) Along the lines of these speculations, which are like spacious corridors leading off in all directions, wander the minor characters. These are often brilliantly drawn, and their personal circumstances and doings engage our interest, even when they are somewhat irrelevant to the main theme. And then, beyond the open-ended, incomplete structure of the novel, we are aware of the surrounding contemporary world, with all the diversity of its business and its anxieties, ever present on the horizon of the author's consciousness.

It is a measure of Wells' genius that he was able to make these big untidy talkative books so alive and readable. From an artistic standpoint, most of them can only be described as failures; they simply don't "compose." But Wells achieved a larger kind of success; he showed how the tight classic form of the novel might be expanded to include a much wider area of reference. That he himself didn't know when to stop, that he expanded the novel until it burst, is not so important. You can't make experiments without explosions. He remains a great pioneer. The novel-of-ideas is out of fashion at the moment, but it will come back—and when it does, Wells will be reread with admiration and excitement. (Incidentally, Madame Vallentin doesn't say whether he knew *The Magic Mountain*. And one wonders what he would have made of *Doctor Faustus*.)

Several of Wells' realistic novels were hugely popular, at the time of their publication, because of their topicality and the shock value of the problems they discussed. Today, his reputation is based chiefly upon the *Outline of History* and half a dozen of his scientific fantasies. Wells would not regret the survival of the *Outline*; it is a masterpiece. But he might well resent our preference for *The Time Machine, The Island of Doctor Moreau, The Invisible Man, The War of the Worlds, The First Men in the Moon* and *The War in the Air*. No author cares to have his early works (these were all written before 1909) preferred to his later ones; Wells continued to write scientific fantasies throughout his life, but these, like the realistic novels, became increasingly discursive and were never very successful. Besides, he would probably complain that we have failed to understand the inner meaning of the stories themselves. We regard them as enjoyable thrillers—just as we regard *Gulliver's Travels* as a quaint book for children.

We are quite ready to honor Wells as a prophet—but only in a limited and rather ludicrous sense of the word. We marvel that he foretold the invention of television, motion pictures, dishwashing machines, prefabricated houses, helicopters and tanks. But very few of us (as Madame Vallentin points out) appreciate the real significance and drama of Wells' lifelong struggle with the mystery of the future.

When he looked into the future, Wells alternated between extremes of optimism and pessimism. The early scientific fantasies are deeply pessimistic; a fact which we usually overlook. There is the unutterable sadness of the Time Traveller's last glimpse of the dying world; the reversion of Moreau's fabricated humans into beasts; the wretched fate of the Invisible Man. Life and individual genius end in frustration and defeat. Nearly fifty years later, in his book *Mind at the End of its Tether*, Wells repeated this message: "The end of everything we call life is close at hand and cannot be evaded." Yet his own character was essentially optimistic. A natural Utopian, he continued, despite many disappointments, to cling to his vision of a World State; he was still fighting for it in his old age, in the midst of World War II. He believed in world socialism as the only force which could abolish frontiers and rival national sovereignties. "We do not deplore the Russian Revolution as a revolution," he said. "We complain that it was not a good enough revolution and we want a better one."

"In a crowded English or French or German railway carriage of the later nineteenth century, it would have aroused far less hostility to have jeered at God than to have jeered at one of those strange beings, England or France or Germany. . . . (Yet in the background of the consciousness of the world, waiting as silence and moonlight wait above the flares and shouts, the hurdy-gurdys and quarrels of a village fair, is the knowledge that all mankind is one brotherhood, that God is the universal and impartial Father of mankind, and that only in that universal service can mankind find peace, or peace be found for the troubles of the individual soul.)"

Wells' exclusion of this striking passage from the later editions of his *Outline of History* is significant; it marks the end of his "theological excursion," his uneasy phase of public relations with the concept of God. In his youth, Wells hated God and violently denied His existence; for "God," in those days, was the God of the Big House, the feudal Overlord. But *Mr. Britling*, shaken by the horror of the First World War, found that some Ultimate Reality was, after all, necessary to his peace of mind; so Wells rediscovered Him as "the Captain of Mankind," a sort of supernatural President of the future World State. This God appears in two further novels, *The Soul of a Bishop* and *The Undying Fire*; but it is doubtful if Wells found Him either comforting or convincing. Indeed, He appears to be little more than a metaphor. His chief quality is negative; He is fundamentally opposed to His Church and to all organized Religion. He makes a last bow, in the guise of a weary and cynical old man, in *Joan and Peter*, telling the young hero that, if he doesn't like the world, he must change it himself.

Wells' "theological excursion" was doomed to failure because he could never quite escape from the dualistic religious concepts of his upbringing: God high in Heaven and we, His servants, hopelessly far beneath. Such dualism is nauseating to any man of Wells' temperament because it immediately confronts him with his old enemy, established authority. Wells might try to persuade himself that "his" God was different, but he couldn't. The truth was that he didn't really want a Captain of Mankind any more than he had wanted a feudal Overlord. He wasn't a follower. Indeed, he had a horror of "Great men."

Nevertheless—and this is Wells' tragedy—he was always dimly but poignantly aware that something was lacking, some vital spark that would bring his New Utopia to life. Under the influence of Plato's *Republic*, which he had read as a schoolboy, he imagined an Order of Samurai—a group of dedicated and sternly disciplined young people who would give their lives to the work of building the society of the future. His writings on this subject actually inspired the formation of enthusiastic groups which looked to him for leadership. Wells, to his great mortification, was unable to offer them any; he couldn't devise a practical program. "Toward the end of his life he remarked on the fact that just about the time he made this unsuccessful attempt at practical construction, Lenin, 'under the pressure of a more urgent reality,' was quietly and steadily drawing up an 'extraordinarily similar plan'—the Communist party organization." But, even if a revolutionary situation had existed in England at that period, and even if Wells had been a born revolutionary leader, he and his Samurai would have found themselves, sooner or later, in trouble. For a dedicated group demands a faith; without one, it cannot continue to function. Lacking genuinely spiritual inspiration, it will turn to some substitute idolatry, such as nationalism or the cult of a leader; and so the movement defeats itself and the World State can never be founded, much less sustained.

Wells was always proclaiming his faith in the capacities of Man. Yet he refused to take account of Man's highest capacity—that of knowing and drawing strength from what is eternal within himself. Some inhibition or deeply seated fear, it would seem, made Wells unable to accept the validity of the mystical experience, or to recognize its central importance in the scheme of human evolution. Why he couldn't bring himself to do this, despite all his urgent self-questionings, I don't know. Madame Vallentin doesn't tell us. There is no mention of the subject anywhere in her book.

1951

R. L. S.

RANDOM HOUSE has added to its Modern Library Giants the *Selected Writings of Robert Louis Stevenson*, edited, with an informative and fair-minded introduction, by Saxe Commins. This is an astonishingly roomy omnibus, and its contents are as representative as one could wish—*Treasure Island*, *The Master of Ballantrae* and *Weir of Hermiston*, *Dr. Jekyll and Mr. Hyde*, *The Suicide Club*, *The Beach of Falesa*, and seven shorter stories; eight essays and the *Open Letter* about Father Damien; *Travels with a Donkey* and *The Silverado Squatters*; *A Child's Garden of Verses*, five ballads and nine poems. I can hardly blame Mr. Commins for leaving out one of my favorite stories, "The Destroying Angel," since this must be read as part of *The Dynamiter*, an uneven book not worth reprinting in its entirety. I think, however, that he might have included two or three of Stevenson's prayers. Also, since these Modern Library books are designed to be kept, I feel moved to make a general protest against their recently added endpapers. In my opinion, they are messy and undistinguished—quite unworthy to enclose Stevenson, not to mention Augustine and Austen.

Two great legendary figures dominated the literary background of my generation in its youth; the Dying Wanderer and the Martyred Dandy, Stevenson and Oscar Wilde. I don't mean that we necessarily admired either of them very much as writers. But you couldn't deny their personal fascination. Wilde's legend has persisted, almost un-diminished, to the present day—despite every attempted debunking; including Mr. Edmund Wilson's most damaging suggestion that Wilde wasn't a genuine homosexual at all. Stevenson's legend—as distinct from the popularity of his work—seems quite extinguished. Why should this be so?

It is no sufficient explanation to say that Stevenson was a poseur. All legendary figures have been poseurs of one sort or another. But Stevenson's poses now seem fatally lacking in style and conviction. He was half-hearted about them; and he changed them too often. The general effect is confused. As the wanderer, he doesn't achieve the glamour of Byron or George Borrow. As the bohemian, he couldn't survive a single evening with Rimbaud. As the bogus feudal patriarch at Vailima, he pales beside the grand old ham of Yasnaya Polyana. As the moralist, he is never crazy or unreasonable enough to be really impressive. (Tolstoy beats him there, too; Stevenson couldn't con-ceivably have made a remark like "all prostitutes and madmen smoke.") As the invalid, he is far too noble; and we turn with relief to the cozy shamelessness of Proust. Even his antics and caprices seem labored, unfunny and unkind. While at Davos, for example, he sent urgently for the local Anglican clergyman in the middle of the night, allowing him to suppose that he was being called to a deathbed. When the poor man rushed into the room, half-dressed and breathlessly concerned, Stevenson gasped out: "For God's sake, have you a Horace?" Wilde would never have behaved like that.

In order to become a lastingly legendary character, you have to be, or seem to be, all of a piece. You have to have that immediate, total effectiveness of impact which is common to the great figures of literature or the theatre. We say "Ah yes—Byron!" in the same tone as we say "Ah yes—Mr. Micawber!" Forty years ago Stevenson still appeared to be one of these splendid simple human masterpieces— the beloved R.L.S., the world's storyteller who had gladly sacrificed his life to his art and now lay romantically buried on a Samoan moun-taintop, the sailor home from sea. Today, in the clearer perspective of distance, he is seen to be a highly complex creature; courageous but irresponsible, outspoken but disingenuous, strict-principled but self-indulgent; a man of moods rather than of passions, of willfulness rather than of will. And so, in our disappointment, we desert his shrine and are now in danger of forgetting that, if less godlike, he is much more interesting than we had supposed.

It is always hard to guess how much or how little J. M. Barrie meant by anything he wrote; for Barrie is one of the most enigmatic of modern writers. But he was certainly in a position to know Stevenson well. (It was in a letter to Barrie that Stevenson said of his masterful wife: "Hellish energy; can make anything from a house to a row, all fine and large of their kind. . . . A violent friend; a brimstone enemy. . . . Is either loathed or adored; indifference impossible.") And in *Peter Pan* Barrie seems to have created, consciously or subconsciously, a kind of Freudian nightmare about *Treasure Island* and Stevenson himself. Peter Pan–Stevenson is the gallant little boy who plays father to another man's children (Lloyd Osbourne and his sister) while his own development remains mysteriously arrested; he has "decided" not to grow up. Instead, he chooses to inhabit an adventure-book world peopled by Indians and pirates. Wendy, the mother-wife, has her counterpart in Fanny Stevenson, who used to look on indulgently while her young husband sat utterly absorbed in playing soldiers with her son on the floor. Captain Hook is not only a reincarnation of Long John Silver but a dream-version of the swashbuckling, crippled Henley—first extravagantly admired, then angrily renounced—whose "hand of friendship" has been replaced by a deadly weapon. And then there is the crocodile, symbol of sentimental hypocrisy, with its swallowed alarm clock which seems to be saying, "It's later than you think." . . . One wonders how Stevenson would have enjoyed his friend's play, if he had lived to see it performed.

Personally, I never cared much for *Treasure Island*—John Masefield's sea stories appeal to me far more—but it is impossible not to admit that it is a kind of masterpiece. Why is it so successful? Because, I think, it belongs to that very special class of what one may call, without any suggestion of disparagement, superpotboilers. The superpotboiler is the perfect work of synthesis. It is about our daydreams about something. It sums up the totality of our fantasies relating to a certain milieu. It presents to our recognition our own nostalgia, so that we almost feel that we have created it ourselves—as indeed, in a sense, we have. *Treasure Island* isn't simply the account of a particular treasure hunt; it is a definitive statement of the treasure-hunt daydream, and, as such, doubly non-realistic. Other examples of this class are *The Pickwick Papers* (the old-fashioned Christmas), *Carmen* (Spain-as-you-like-it), and *South Pacific* (phallic sailors plus tropical sex). Stevenson tried to produce another superpotboiler, A *Child's Garden of Verses*, about the way grown-ups would like children to feel. As far as I am concerned, he failed—and to fail in this medium is to fail disastrously.

Almost all of Stevenson's stories are set in the past, the eighteenth century or earlier. There is nothing to complain of in this. The greatest novel so far written is an historical novel. But when we describe *Kidnapped*, *Catriona*, *The Master of Ballantrae*, etc., as "romances" we are certainly implying a criticism. For all their carefully accurate documentation, we feel that they have been subtly glamorized and emotionally falsified. Stevenson's trouble was that he was too fond of the Past for its own sake. He loved it and sentimentalized it, just because it wasn't the present. It was his place of refuge from the dull, smug commercialism of nineteenth-century Britain, which he hated with all his heart. No doubt this hatred was also associated with his revolt from his own father, the admirable but narrowly orthodox engineer. Stevenson refused to find romance in the machine (despite a dutiful poem about his father's lighthouses); otherwise, he might have forestalled Kipling. Though a disciple of Balzac—from whom he acquired his fine flair for melodrama—he did not share his master's enthusiasm for the tremendous melodrama of money. Instead, he wished himself back in the age of "velvet and iron."

In view of what has happened and is happening to the modern world, Stevenson's longing to have been a soldier and his cry "Shall we never shed blood?" seem merely morbid; and we excuse him by reminding ourselves that he was a very sick man throughout most of his life. Yet Tennyson, who was in perfect health when he wrote, "Why do they prate of the blessings of peace? We have made them a curse . . . ," would have understood better what he meant. The "peace" of the Victorian Age was a sort of fat after-dinner nap on top of many shelved problems and ignored injustices, and it was natural for an impatient man to want to disturb it, no matter how. Where so many healthier and wiser men failed to estimate the cost of violence, we mustn't be too hard on Stevenson. In his innocence, he was thinking in terms of swords and horses, not jet planes and tanks. He would certainly have found modern war as horrible and sordidly utilitarian as the rest of us do.

Stevenson's only long stories about contemporary London are *The New Arabian Nights* series and *Dr. Jekyll and Mr. Hyde*. The *New Arabian Nights* are charming in their lively artificiality, and one wishes that he had written more of them. He really did manage to create a magic, never-never London, where extraordinary scenes are being enacted behind every curtained window and any cab is ready to whisk you away into an adventure. Stevenson's London has been largely buried, as it were, beneath the more recent and even more magical Londons of Sherlock Holmes and Chesterton's Father Brown; nevertheless, it forms their foundations.

The origins of *Dr. Jekyll and Mr. Hyde* are obscure and fascinating. It is worth discussing them here because they are so closely related to Stevenson's whole predicament as a human being and as an artist. As a very young man, a law student at Edinburgh University, Stevenson had an affair with a girl named Kate Drummond, an innocent, simple person who had drifted into the city from a country home in the Highlands and become involved in its slum nightlife. The affair was a happy one, at any rate from Stevenson's point of view, and he wrote poems to Kate in which he called her "Claire"; poems that were for many years suppressed. Stevenson never forgot Kate. More than ten years later, married and living in the South of France, he decided to write a novel about her. Fanny Stevenson made a terrible scene, declaring that this would ruin his reputation as a clean, wholesome family author, the author of *Treasure Island*. So Stevenson abandoned the novel which would probably have been his best and most adult work, and thereby, it is said, gave Henry James the idea for his *The Author of Beltraffio*. Shortly after this, back in England, Stevenson had a nightmare which inspired him to write *Dr. Jekyll and Mr. Hyde*. Again, Fanny violently objected—because, it has been suggested, the figure of Kate appeared prominently as Jekyll's temptation and Hyde's victim. Be that as it may, Stevenson destroyed his original draft and produced the now published version, from which Kate is entirely absent. (Hollywood, disagreeing with Fanny, has put Kate right back where she belongs, to the considerable improvement of the story.)

Kate or no Kate, we find here the symptoms of a tension which was dominant in Stevenson's character; the struggle between his inherited puritanism and his natural inclinations. Dr. Jekyll is the average sensual man whose sensuality is inhibited by his sense of duty and his regard for the proprieties. "I had learned," he says, "to dwell with pleasure, as a beloved daydream, on the thought of the separation of these elements. If each, I told myself, could be housed in separate identities, life would be relieved of all that was unbearable. . . ." And so he sets himself to discover the drug which will separate him from Mr. Hyde.

Unfortunately, Stevenson's puritanism obscured his psychological insight and caused him to misstate the Jekyll-Hyde problem completely. What he has given us, with Fanny's assistance, is a ridiculous and thumpingly effective melodramatic tract. We all love Mr. Hyde—he is the world's favorite horror-sweetheart—and we roar with joy as he goes skipping off toward the red-light district, trampling on a little girl to show how wicked he is. But he doesn't fool us for an instant. He may be an ugly customer, greedy and brutal and dangerous when roused, but he is no more essentially evil than a big savage dog. The real tragedy of Jekyll—as Stevenson would have seen if he had permitted himself to face it—is that he disowns Hyde, his libido, and calls him evil; just as Stevenson himself was being forced to disown the young man who made love to Kate in the Edinburgh slums. Hyde, driven forth into the streets, becomes a fierce outcast with his hand against every man, but Jekyll, the cruel proud hypocrite wearing a mask of benevolence, is ten thousand times wickeder than he. Perhaps this doesn't matter very much today, when we can enjoy the story as simple entertainment, but the book did a great deal of harm in its time, providing material for fashionable preachers who hailed it in their sermons as a new and edifying proof that Sin is not respectable. If there is a Purgatory for literary characters, Jekyll will have to stay in it until he has hugged Hyde to his bosom and they have gone out on the town together, arm in arm, with all the neighbors watching.

Of the two travel books included in this volume, I much prefer *The Silverado Squatters*, which gives you a vivid glimpse of the Californian backcountry and its inhabitants in the eighteen-eighties. Left all alone with Stevenson and his donkey in the Cévennes, I find myself frequently bored. As a traveling companion he is inclined to be sententious. Imagine being with a man who turns to you in a Trappist monastery and solemnly declares, "And yet, apart from any view of mortification, I can see a certain policy, not only in the exclusion of women, but in this vow of silence"! One can't help wishing that D. H. Lawrence, and not Stevenson, had made this trip. Just think what he would have made of Modestine!

We have a certain prejudice, nowadays, against the middleweight essay; the kind that Stevenson wrote. The middleweight essayist seems to us to be neither serious nor silly enough, and we neglect him for Aldous Huxley or James Thurber. Unjust though this attitude may be, it cannot be denied that Stevenson often gives one the impression of a man playing solitaire, neatly dealing out his opinions with what Chesterton calls "a dainty equity," a little on that side, a little on this. He is too fond of words like "withal" and locutions like "a-tiptoe on the highest point of being." At his worst, he adopts a tone of humorless sprightliness which is tiresome and embarrassing.

Stevenson's greatest defect as a writer is his vanity, and this becomes most evident when he really has something important to say. Throughout the whole of his magnificent and rousing attack on the Reverend Dr. Hyde of Honolulu—the missionary who libeled Father Damien—we are never for a moment allowed to forget Stevenson himself, arising in his righteous anger to defend a poor, dead, saintly priest. "If I have at all learned the trade of using words to convey truth and to arouse emotion, you have at last furnished me with a subject," he tells Dr. Hyde—and one is reminded of some famous and conceited defense counsel warming to his work. It isn't that Stevenson is insincere, but he is a little too pleased with his own sincerity.

The final period of his life—the six years he spent in the South Pacific—gives us some idea of the lines along which his personality and his powers would have developed, if the cerebral hemorrhage hadn't killed him. Toward the end of it, we see him solidly established as an international celebrity and local potentate, the ceremonious Master of Vailima. After all his wanderings, he has found, in Samoa, a sort of tropical-baroque version of the respectability he fled from in his own country. He makes speeches at lavish feasts, composes family prayers, and has his mother sitting as a guest at his table.

What is more, he has at length gratified his ambition to intervene in the sphere of action, though unsuccessfully and on a tiny scale. He has supported one native chieftain against another in a fight for control of the Samoan kingdom. His candidate Mataafa has been defeated and banished, and he has had to accept a truce with the victorious rival; but he has made a public stand as champion of the oppressed and has been treated as a person of political consequence—or at least as a serious nuisance—by the German and British authorities.

Nevertheless, he is melancholy, restless, and terribly homesick for Scotland. (Had he lived, he would probably have returned there sooner or later—his health, his pride, and Fanny permitting. It is possible, also, that he would have gone into politics.) His mind dwells chiefly on Scottish themes. He writes *Catriona* and begins *Weir of Hermiston*.

The extraordinary quality of the *Hermiston* fragment doesn't necessarily prove that this would have been Stevenson's masterpiece. Mr. Commins points out how often his longer books begin strongly and end weakly, in the carelessness of fatigue. But *Hermiston* does show that Stevenson died with his genius unimpaired and growing. Adam Weir, unfinished, is still finer than the wonderful completed portrait of James Durie, in *Ballantrae*. Stevenson could never have created Weir if he hadn't entirely forgiven his own father; the character is too deeply understood to have been conceived in hatred. How his rapidly maturing mind would have come to feel about the Kate Drummond episode, and how he would have resolved these problems in his art, are questions which remain unanswered. But they suggest that we may have lost a much greater writer than the Stevenson we know.

1951

Katherine Mansfield

MISS SYLVIA BERKMAN'S *Katherine Mansfield: A Critical Study*
is a concise, well-documented book which contains much interesting
biographical material and some penetrating judgments. Miss Berkman's style is somewhat lacking in warmth and humor; but I think
that, under the circumstances, these are faults on the right side. For
her approach to her subject is deliberately academic, as befits an Assistant Professor of English at Wellesley College, and she is admirably
determined to weigh and measure accurately what others have over-
praised or undervalued. Where so many have lavishly emoted, Miss
Berkman tidies up the mess with grave commonsense. If she doesn't
communicate the kind of enthusiasm which would send new readers
to Katherine Mansfield, she should at least make every confirmed
admirer pause and reread and ponder. And the resulting reassessment
will certainly be to both the author's and her admirers' advantage.

There are some writers you revere; others you fall in love with.
The loved ones are seldom the greatest; indeed, their very faults are a
part of their charm. For several years I was violently in love with
"Kathy," as my friends and I (who never knew her personally) used to
call her. Then the love affair turned sour and ended in unfair belit-
tlement. I am truly grateful to Miss Berkman for bringing us together

again. From now on, I am sure my affection will be more constant, more intelligent and much less sentimental.

I realize that I loved Mansfield ("Kathy" sounds mawkish now, and "Miss Mansfield" absurdly formal) for her life rather than for her work. I identified myself romantically with her sufferings and her struggle. And today I still find it impossible to think of Mansfield simply as the author of her stories, without relating her to the Journal and the Letters. For she is among the most personal and subjective of all modern writers; and, in her case, fiction and autobiography form a single, indivisible opus.

Katherine Mansfield's life is so fascinating because—despite its surface tangle of moods, impetuous reactions and rash decisions—it presents a very simple symbolic pattern. This is a variant of the Garden of Eden theme. A childhood paradise is lost. An apple of knowledge is eaten, with bitter consequences. And then, under the curse and blessing of that knowledge, comes the attempt to regain the paradise. It is a deeply moving story but not really a tragic one, for it ends in sight of success.

In 1906, after some years of schooling in England, Mansfield returned at the age of eighteen to her native New Zealand. There, amidst the comforts and social activities of her wealthy family home, she at once began to feel restless and miserable. The people she met in Wellington seemed unendurably stuffy and provincial. As a disciple of Oscar Wilde, she longed to demolish "the firm fat framework of their brains" and drown them, for their own good, in "a mad wave of pre-Raphaelitism." She saw herself as the Artist in Exile, alienated by her own finer sensibilities from the vulgar herd. "Here in my room I feel as though I was in London—in London. To write the word makes me feel that I could burst into tears. Isn't it terrible to love anything so much? I do not care at all for men, but *London*—it is Life." Substitute "Moscow" for "London" and this is the cry of Irina in *Three Sisters*. No doubt much of the affinity which Mansfield later felt with Chekhov (whom, of course, she had never met) was based on memories of this period, when she herself had been, most unwillingly, a Chekhov character.

Katherine's father was a generous-minded man who continued to love his daughter even when her conduct puzzled and pained him. Eighteen months after her return home he agreed to let her go back to England in unconditional freedom and with a small living-allowance. She never saw New Zealand again.

But Mansfield's "London" proved to be a mirage; and the first three years of her life in the real city were squalid and disenchanting. Hiding her desperate loneliness behind a mask of intellectual arrogance, she inhabited the trivial bohemia of St. John's Wood and surrounded herself with pitiful, trashy little pretensions of "sophistication." She had a skull decorated with flowers and candles, and a room containing nothing but a Buddha and two black-draped couches. She got involved in messy love affairs and a brief, incompatible marriage. She gave birth to a stillborn illegitimate child. Such behavior is characteristic of a very innocent nature which takes this world's shams at their surface value and learns everything the hard way. Those who have Mansfield's kind of innocence often appear, from the outside, to be more artificial, more cynical, more depraved than the rest of us. Actually, they are purging themselves through excess.

In 1911 Katherine Mansfield met John Middleton Murry, who was later to become her second husband. Their relationship was beset with many difficulties, both financial and temperamental, but it survived them all and remained, until the end, a central, steadying emotional factor in Katherine's life.

For Mansfield the writer, however, the really decisive event was still to come. This was the death of her brother Leslie on the Western Front, in October 1915. Before going over to France with his regiment, Leslie had spent a week's leave at the Murrys' house in London, where the brother and sister had long talks, nostalgically recalling the days of their New Zealand childhood. In retrospect, every detail of it seemed magically beautiful, flawlessly happy. Katherine seems to have forgotten or discounted her more recent boredom and wretchedness in Wellington. She planned eagerly to return with Leslie to New Zealand as soon as the war was over.

When Leslie was killed, that plan was automatically abandoned; but the childhood memories he had aroused seemed to Katherine more precious, more sacred than ever. While still under the immediate and terrible shock of his loss, she wrote in her Journal: "The people . . . whom I wished to bring into my stories don't interest me any more.

The plots of my stories leave me perfectly cold. . . . Now—now I want to write recollections of my own country." And again, addressing her dead brother: "Now, as I write these words and talk of getting down to the New Zealand atmosphere, I see you opposite to me. . . . Ah, my darling, how have I kept away from this tremendous joy? Each time I take up my pen *you* are with me." It was in this mood of spiritual collaboration with Leslie that Mansfield began to write the New Zealand stories which contain so much of her finest work: *Prelude, At the Bay, The Doll's House, The Garden Party, The Stranger.*

In order to re-enter her childhood paradise, Mansfield wanted to turn herself back into a child. And, of course, she couldn't. Whether she liked it or not, she was a beautiful, highly complex woman in her late twenties, with much worldly experience behind her; a woman possessed of (to quote Katherine Anne Porter) "a grim, quiet ruthlessness of judgment, an unsparing and sometimes cruel eye, a natural malicious wit, an intelligent humor." To her undoing, Mansfield began increasingly to hate her own adult personality, dwelling harshly on its defects and rejecting its virtues. Above all, she hated her "cleverness." "I look at the mountains, I try to pray and I think of something *clever*"; her journal is full of such disgusted self-accusations. Mansfield did well to condemn the cheapness and artificiality of which she had sometimes been guilty; but in going to this extreme she was really trying to annihilate herself as a writer and as a human being.

This acute internal conflict could only end in disaster. I myself believe that it was at least partly responsible for the tuberculosis which Mansfield developed in 1918, and which killed her five years later. In the present state of our medical opinion, such conjectures are still usually dismissed as fanciful and ridiculous. But it is worth recalling how Homer Lane, one of the earliest and most daring pioneers of psychosomatic medicine, used to maintain that pulmonary tuberculosis is the characteristic disease of those who desire to escape into their childhood, since the lungs are the first organs used by the newborn baby.

We can never return to the childhood paradise in a state of primitive simplicity. For we have eaten the apple of experience and we cannot unlearn the knowledge it has brought us. What we can do, however, is to reconcile experience with innocence, intellect with instinct; thus we become integrated and able to accept life in its whole-ness. This acceptance is another kind of simplicity. The simplicity of the integrated adult is not the simplicity of the child.

This is what Mansfield slowly started to learn during the last bitter years of her life. She traveled feverishly back and forth between En-gland, Switzerland and the South of France; she suffered the wretched loneliness of the invalid; she had brief hopes of recovery followed by heartbreaking relapses; she consulted many doctors and submitted to drastic treatments. At the end of it all she was no better; and, during the summer of 1922, she came to a revolutionary decision. She would stop going to doctors altogether. She would stop trying to heal her body simply *as* a body. "It seems to me childish and ridiculous to suppose that one can be cured like a cow *if one is not a cow.*" Instead she would put herself in the hands of someone who could heal her divided psyche. Once the spirit had been made whole, she felt the body would imitate its wholeness and grow well.

The healer chosen by Mansfield was Gurdjieff, who at that time was the head of a community near Fontainebleau, outside Paris. In this community a number of men and women practiced a strict routine of manual labor, rhythmic exercises and psychical instruction which was designed to develop a harmonious balance of the intellectual, emotional and spiritual functions. Much has been said against Gurd-jieff, and there is no doubt that he was something of a charlatan. But his basic ideas were perfectly sound, and he certainly helped many of his pupils toward self-integration. Indeed, he was already helping Mansfield. Her last letters are full of faith and exaltation; and the fact that she had begun to question his claims to be an omniscient prophet is a very healthy sign. Had she lived, she would naturally have out-grown Gurdjieff and gone on alone, with increasing self-reliance; but it was he who put her feet upon the path. It was not his fault that she came to him too late, a mortally sick woman. In January 1923, having spent less than three months in the community, she was seized by a violent hemorrhage and died.

In the second part of her book, which deals with Katherine Mans-field's art, Miss Berkman spends a considerable time discussing the resemblances and differences between Mansfield's technique and that of Chekhov and of James Joyce in his pre-*Ulysses* period. Miss Berkman's examples are well chosen; she certainly proves her point. But I can't say that I find this kind of criticism very rewarding; it is really just an amusing game. When all has been said, the fact remains that the literary personalities of Chekhov and Joyce are quite unlike the literary personality of Mansfield. Purely technical comparisons are, at best, extremely superficial.

What is Katherine Mansfield's literary personality? What is the total impression that she makes upon the reader? Such distinguished critics as Eliot, Maurois, Miss Porter and H. E. Bates have described her as "feminine." Both Miss Berkman and I quarrel with that adjective, though for slightly different reasons. In my view, a "feminine" writer is one who writes exclusively out of her experience as a woman; she tells us things that a man could not feel or know. She doesn't necessarily have to write about childbirth or motherhood or the woman's side of marriage, but her perception of the world will be conditioned by the fact that she is biologically female. Anaïs Nin is such a writer. So is Naomi Mitchison. So is Colette. I don't find this quality to any great degree in Katherine Mansfield. Indeed, as I have already suggested, she rather shrank from the recognition of herself as a woman—at any rate, an adult woman. Her view of the sexual relation is distasteful and pessimistic; and one feels that, much as she loves children, she would rather they belonged to someone else.

The word "feminine" is also used in a derogatory sense to describe the kind of writing which is (to quote Mr. Bates) "fluttering, gossipy, breathless." (Stephen Spender once said to me, criticizing a book he didn't like, "It gives me a feeling of earrings.") Mansfield was certainly apt to flutter. She often affects a breathless epistolary style, in which she appears to think she can make words take on deeper meanings by simply writing them in italics. And her coyness at its worst can make you hot with shame. But it must be objected at once that these are not exclusively feminine defects. There is plenty of breathless male gossiping in Henry Miller, and plenty of male coyness in Hemingway.

Miss Berkman seems to me to be much nearer the mark when she calls attention to Mansfield's preoccupation with littleness. In the stories, "tiny" is used over and over again as a synonym for "beautiful" or "exquisite." "This fascination by the very small," Miss Berkman continues, "is a quality found more often in women than in men, but it distinguishes most generally the curious and observant child. . . . The enlargement of perception one receives from Miss Mansfield's finest work is of the kind one gains from association with an imaginative and gifted child, who sees, freshly and sharply, imponderables of meaning within the compass of the small. But she was also a woman who had suffered in the world, and it is not often that the untouched apprehension of the child fuses perfectly with the view acquired through the circumstances of her life."

I would go farther than Miss Berkman. I do not think that the childlike apprehension and the adult view of life were *ever* perfectly fused in any of Katherine Mansfield's stories. In other words, her split psyche produced a split writer—or, as one might put it for the sake of clarity, two separate writers. Mansfield's best work was achieved, it is true, by a collaboration between the writers; but it was an uneasy collaboration, likely to end, at any moment, in a fight and resulting confusion. When one writer pushed the other clear away from the desk and tried to work alone, the product was inferior.

Writer A is the childlike, intuitive Mansfield, the poetess. She is capable of those clairvoyant flashes of perception which one associates particularly with the New Zealand stories. Some creature or object— a flower, a painted teapot, a flying bird—is seen, for an instant, in its own right as a marvel, a microcosm of all creation, and the reader gasps with wonder. These flashes of perception have the quality of genius; but they are, by their very nature, spasmodic. Writer A is a medium, with a medium's lapses. A rather dishonest medium, it must be added; for, when nothing is "coming through," she begins faking, and when she fakes, her tone is false and embarrassingly sentimental. Sometimes, these alternations of poetic truth and sentimental falsehood occur with bewildering frequency; as, for example, in the description of the sunrise which is the opening of At *the Bay.*

Writer B is the critical, witty adult Mansfield, the satirist. She can curb Writer A's sentimentality ruthlessly, whenever Writer A will let her. Writer B can dash off startlingly funny thumbnail portraits, like that of Nurse Andrews in *The Daughters of the Late Colonel.* She can expose the vanity and shallowness of a woman like Isabel in

Marriage à la Mode with a terrible and beautiful justice. Her only trouble is that she is sometimes too brilliant for her own good. She constructs speciously clever plots for stories, and lures Writer A into helping her with them. We read these stories and are, at first, quite dazzled; then, slowly, the doubts begin. For instance, there is poor old Ma Parker, the charlady, who longs to have one good cry over the sadness of her life. At the climax, she realizes that she can't even enjoy this small relief, because there is no place where she won't be disturbed. Again and again Ma Parker's plight has moved me almost to tears; but afterwards, thinking it over—I'm sorry, I just don't believe it. Or take the case of *Poison*, a study in sexual jealousy which is another near-masterpiece. Here a woman, already tired of her lover, is waiting for a letter which will probably call her away to join another man. In order to prepare her lover for this blow, she begins to talk figuratively about the way in which one partner in a relationship will slowly poison the other, with tiny daily doses of suspicion. The metaphor is admirable and intensely dramatic. But then, right at the end, the lover sips his apéritif and says to himself: "Good God! Was it fancy? No, it wasn't fancy. The drink tasted chill, bitter, *queer*." The metaphor is taken literally, so that the lover seems, after all, to be merely play-acting, and the whole situation drops with a bump to the level of a sophisticated parlor game. I am disgusted. Writer B, with her fatal cleverness, has intervened and spoilt everything.

That Katherine Mansfield was well aware of this split in her literary personality is proved by many passages in the journal and the letters. Had she lived to achieve her own psychological integration she would naturally have merged the two writers into one. A would have submitted to B's critical intelligence; B would have learned when not to interfere with A's intuition. Then the sentimentality and the cleverness would have been gradually refined away. That process had already begun when Mansfield died, and one can only end on a note of deep gratitude for what she has actually left us: the best of her stories—fifteen, at the very least—which still, after thirty years, seem as magically vivid as ever. Yes, and not only the stories. Mansfield left us also—in her journal, her letters and her recorded biography— the human example of one who dedicated her whole being and existence to the perfection of her work. Only the greatest men and women have the courage to do this; and the degree of their success is of secondary importance. What matters, what inspires the rest of us, is the intensity of the attempt. And, by that standard, Mansfield need fear no comparisons.

1951

Vivekananda
and Sarah Bernhardt

IN PARIS, during the late summer of 1900, Swami Vivekananda had a conversation with the most famous woman of the Western world. It was probably, but not certainly, their first meeting. The two-volume *Life of Vivekananda*, by his Eastern and Western disciples, refers somewhat vaguely to an earlier occasion, in the United States, on which Bernhardt "sought an interview with him" (that hardly sounds like the imperious Sarah, who had made royalty take its hat off in her presence!) "and expressed her admiration and intense interest in the sublime teaching of the philosophy he so eloquently and truly represented." The date given for this encounter—1895—would seem, in any case, to be wrong. Bernhardt was not in the States that year, though she visited them for a six-month tour in 1896. Moreover, Swamiji himself, writing in 1900 about the people he has met in Paris, particularly mentions that he and Madame Calvé, the singer, were previously acquainted, but speaks of Bernhardt as though they had just been introduced.

His correspondent was Swami Trigunatita, back home in India, and the tone of these travel-letters, which were intended for publication, is instructive, gossipy, explosive, facetious, affectionate and prophetic by turns: they are among the most characteristic things Vivekananda ever wrote. "Madame Bernhardt," he tells his brother-monk, "is an aged lady; but when she steps on the stage after dressing, her imitation of the age and sex of the role she plays is perfect! A girl, or a boy—whatever part you want her to play, she is an exact representation of that. And that wonderful voice! People here say her voice has the ring of silver strings!"

In a couple of months the "aged lady" was going to be fifty-six years old. Even the unkind camera shows us that, "on the stage after dressing," she did not look a day over thirty. Her photograph in the role of *L'Aiglon*, the Duke of Reichstadt, which she played for the first time in March of that year, presents an astonishingly slender and erect little personage in a riding coat and high boots with spurs, neither boy nor girl, woman nor man, sexless, ageless, and altogether impossible by daylight, outside the walls of a theatre. Some later references in another of the letters to the story of Napoleon's tragic son suggest that Vivekananda must almost certainly have seen Sarah in this, her greatest dramatic triumph after *La Dame aux Camélias*.

Bernhardt was then on the final peak of her mountainous career. Her acting was probably better than it had ever been before: better, certainly, than in the nineties, when her hit-or-miss noisiness, ranting and hamming had provoked the brilliant scolding of the young theatre critic Bernard Shaw, and his unfavorable comparisons between her and the more modern restraint of Eleanora Duse. She had disciplined herself, artistically and emotionally. The crazy days of her publicity— of the balloon trip, the coffin, and the shooting of the St. Louis Bay bridge—were far behind her. The shameful tragedy of her marriage with Damala had been ended, long ago, by his death from morphine poisoning. Her extravagance was still immense, but so were her earnings. And the accident in Rio de Janeiro which was to result in her gradual crippling was still five years ahead.

Swamiji seems to have been taken round to visit her in her dressing room at the theatre after a performance. One wonders who introduced them, what word was used to describe the Swami's occupation to the actress, and whether she had already heard of him. "Madame Bernhardt," writes Vivekananda, "has a special regard for India; she tells me again and again that our country is *très ancien, très civilisé*—very ancient and very civilized." There must have been a gleam in Swamiji's eye as he politely received this flattering information.

They talked, as was natural, of the only play Sarah had ever produced with an Indian setting. It was *Izéil*, by Morand and Silvestre, an expensive flop. Bernhardt had always obstinately liked this piece, perhaps because it displayed her undoubted talent for theatrical décor. "She told me that for about a month she had visited every museum and made herself acquainted with the men and women and their dress, the streets and bathing ghats and everything relating to India."

"Madame Bernhardt," the letter concludes, "has a very strong desire to visit India. '*C'est mon rêve*—It is the dream of my life,' she says. Again, the Prince of Wales has promised to take her over to a tiger and elephant hunting excursion. But then, she said, she must spend some two lacs of rupees if she went to India! She is, of course, in no want of money. *La divine Sarah*—the divine Sarah—is her name; how can she want money? She who never travels but by a special train! That pomp and luxury many a prince of Europe cannot afford to indulge in! One can only secure a seat in her performance by paying double the fees, and that a month in advance! Well, she is not going to suffer want of money! But Sarah Bernhardt is given to spending lavishly. Her travel to India is therefore put off for the present."

Underneath these few mock-serious, bantering sentences, one senses the warmth of an immediate sympathy and liking. You can picture Swamiji sitting opposite the vivid, Semitic little French-woman, large and jolly, his amused glance taking in the whole luxurious setting, the jewels, the mirrors, the silks, the cosmetics, the marvelous robes. Here, as in all women everywhere, he saluted his own daughter, sister, mother. Here, as always, he bowed to the eternal Godhead, beneath yet another of those queer disguises which bewilder our wanderings toward Self-realization. Here, also, he surely recognized, to an unusual degree, the virtue he prized so highly: courage. Courage was, perhaps, the one quality which these fantastically dissimilar personalities had in common: the courage which had supported Vivekananda in the blackest hours of spiritual torment, of his Master's loss, of all the early struggles and trials of the Order, and which had never deserted him in the jungle or the mountains or the drawing rooms of American millionaires: the courage which had nerved Sarah in her battles to raise her child, in her work during the siege of Paris, in her defense of Dreyfus, in her return to the stage at the age of seventy-two after the amputation of her right leg. Swamiji must have been aware of this, and loved her for it.

And how did Bernhardt think of him? Perhaps, curiously enough, as a kind of colleague. Had not he, also, appeared triumphantly before the public? Many actors and actresses, including Sarah herself as Joan of Arc, have represented saints—at any rate, to the satisfaction of the audience beyond the footlights. Swamiji, on the other hand, with his superb presence and sonorous voice, might well have been mistaken for a great actor.

In a photograph of this period, we see how the eyes of the young sannyasin, burning almost intolerably with mingled devotion and doubt, have softened and deepened in the face of the mature man. The big lips and the lines spreading from the wide nostrils have a curve of watchful humor, in which there is neither irony, nor bitterness, nor resignation—only a great calm, like the sea, with certainty dawning over it, an absolute, arising sun. "Are you never serious, Swamiji?" somebody asked him, rather reproachfully, and was answered: "Oh, yes. When I have the belly-ache." Even this was an overstatement, for the smiling, joking Vivekananda of 1900 was already a very sick man.

He and Bernhardt never saw each other again. In October the Swami's party left Paris for Austria, the Balkans and Egypt, whence he sailed to India, arriving home at the Belur monastery early in December. Thus ended his last journey to the West. The longer journey, also, was nearly over. One day in July 1902, wishing perhaps to spare his friends the agony of a goodbye, he passed, by stealth, as it were, into *samadhi*, and did not come back.

Sarah survived him by twenty-one years, survived the First World War, lived on into the era of Chaplin and Pickford and the Keystone Cops, appeared in two or three movies herself, and died in action, getting ready to rehearse a new play.

In the half-dozen Bernhardt biographies I have been able to consult, the name of Vivekananda is not even mentioned. In fact, this brief anecdote of their meeting, with its exchange of conventional small talk and politeness, would seem to have no point whatsoever. That is just what makes it so fascinating and so significant. When poets or politicians forgather, we expect epigrams and aphorisms; for talk is their medium of expression. But talk is not, primarily, the medium of the man of illumination. His way of approach is more direct, more subtle and more penetrating. He makes contact with you below the threshold of everyday awareness. No matter whether he speaks of the Prince of Wales, or of God, or only smiles and says nothing, your whole life will be, to some degree, changed from that moment on.

That is why—despite the biographer's silence, and the lack of high-class philosophical conversation—one dare not say that Swamiji's visit made no great or lasting impression upon Sarah. The spotlight of history, which reveals a tiny area of surface action so brightly, cannot help us here. All we can venture to say is this: "One day, the two human mysteries known to the world as Bernhardt and Vivekananda met, exchanged certain signals which we do not understand, and parted, we do not know why. All we *do* know is that their meeting, like every other event in this universe, did not take place by accident."

1945

Hypothesis and Belief

IF A MEMBER of the so-called intellectual class joins any religious group or openly subscribes to its teaching, he will have to prepare himself for a good deal of criticism from his unconverted and more skeptical friends. Some of these may be sympathetic and genuinely interested; others will be covertly satirical, suspicious, or quite frankly hostile and dismayed. It will be suggested to the convert, with a greater or lesser degree of politeness, that he has sold out, betrayed the cause of reason, retreated in cowardice from "the realities of Life," and so forth. Henceforward, his conduct will be narrowly watched for symptoms of pretentiousness, priggishness, prudery and all other forms of puritanism. Certain topics will either be altogether avoided in his presence or they will be presented in the form of a challenge, to see how he will take them.

The convert himself, self-conscious and badly rattled, is almost sure to behave unnaturally. Either he will preach at his old friends and bore them, thus confirming their worst suspicions. Or he will make desperate efforts to reassure them, by his manner and conversation, that he is still "one of the gang." He will be the first to blaspheme, the first to touch upon the delicate subject. And his friends, far from feeling relieved, will be sincerely shocked.

One question, especially, he must learn to expect. It will be asked by the most candid, by those who really want to know: "Yes, of course, I can quite understand why you did it, in a way . . . but tell me, do you actually *believe* all that?" This question is particularly distressing to the convert, because, if he is to be honest, he will have to answer: "No, I don't—yet."

The "all that" to which the questioner refers will vary in detail and mode of formulation, according to the religious group the convert happens to have chosen. In essence, however, it can always be covered by what Aldous Huxley has called "the minimum working hypothesis." This word "hypothesis" is extremely significant, but it will probably be overlooked by the outside observer, who prefers to simplify his picture of the world's religions by regarding their teachings as "creeds" and "dogmas." Nevertheless, a statement of religious doctrine can be properly called a creed only by those who know it to be true. It remains a hypothesis as long as you are not quite sure. Spiritual truth is, by definition, directly revealed and experienced; it cannot be known at second hand. What is revealed truth to a Christ is merely hypothetical truth to the vast majority of his followers; but this need not prevent the followers from trusting in Christ's personal integrity and in the authenticity of his revelation, *as far as Christ himself is concerned.* One can feel sure that Einstein is neither a fraud nor a lunatic, and that he has actually discovered the law of relativity, and still fail, in a certain sense, to "believe" in the conception of Space-Time, just because one has not yet personally understood it.

There is, even nowadays, a good deal of loose and unrealistic talk about "the conflict between religion and science." I call this kind of talk unrealistic because it suggests that "Science," and hence scientists, are one hundred percent materialistic, and that "Religion" is based upon the blind, one hundred percent acceptance of dogmas which are incapable of scientific proof. Modern Science is, of course, very far from being materialistic. In the nineteenth century, it is true, science did pass through a phase of mechanistic materialism. But the scientist himself never has been, and never could be, an absolute materialist. The scientist is a human being. The absolute materialist, if he existed, would have to be some sort of non-human creature, completely lacking the human faculty of intuition, a mere machine for measuring and making calculations. If a human being could become a truly convinced materialist, he would never have the heroism to get up in the morning, shave, and eat his breakfast. His world-picture would be too terrible for even the boldest heart to contemplate; and, within twenty-four hours, he would have committed suicide.

Similarly, a religion based upon blind faith could not possibly survive, as all the world religions have survived, for hundreds and thousands of years. Religion lives, and is revived, from age to age, because of the direct revelation of the few, the saints, who win for themselves a personal knowledge of spiritual reality. Religion survives *in spite* of blind faith, priestly persecution, ecclesiastical politics; in spite of superstition and ignorance amongst the masses of its adherents. Most of us cannot understand this, because our imagination refuses to grasp the gigantic influence and importance of the saint as an historical phenomenon. Whereas the persecution and the ignorance stand out brutally from the pages of history in red and black, plain for all to see. Nine times out of ten, when we use the word "Religion," we are really referring to the crimes or follies committed in religion's name.

There is no conflict between true Religion and true Science, but there is a great deal of bickering between religious dogmatists and scientific pedants. The dogmatist states his case, or rather, presents his dogmatic ultimatum. The scientifically trained pedant reminds him, none too patiently, that his assertions cannot be verified by the microscope, the slide rule, or the laboratory experiment. Therefore, he continues, quite rightly, the dogma is merely another hypothesis. And he will probably add that hypotheses which are incapable of scientific proof do not interest him, anyway. At this point a deadlock is reached, and the two men part in mutual annoyance.

But now let us suppose that, instead of the tiresome, dogmatic convert (who is unconvincing because he has not personally experienced the truth of what he asserts), Christ himself should enter the scientist's laboratory, and make the very same statements which the convert makes. How would the scientist react? If the scientist were a pure, non-human materialist, he would, of course, remain completely unconvinced. But, since he is a creature of emotion and intuition as well as of reason, the chances are that he would be impressed, not rationally but emotionally, by the personality of Christ and the tremendous psychological impact of such a meeting. In spite of his scientific training, he would venture to trust his intuition. He would say to himself: "Although my scientific methods of analysis cannot deal with these statements, my intuition tells me that this man has some authority for his words."

This raises the question of what we may call "the credibility of the witness." The jury in a court of law does not, or should not, judge a case entirely by scientific (i.e. rational) method: it relies, also, on intuition. It decides to believe a witness or not to believe him—sometimes in defiance of considerable circumstantial evidence. There is, also, the factor of corroboration. If two or more witnesses support each other, and make an impression of being truthful, the case is apt to turn in their favor.

When we begin to examine the assertions of the great religious teachers we shall have to behave like jurymen. Reason can help us, no doubt, and it must be brought to bear on the case; but Reason will not take us all the way. It can only deliver a provisional verdict. It can only say: "This is possible," or "Perhaps . . ." Next, we must ask ourselves: "What sort of men are telling us this? Are they charlatans? Do they seem sane? Do their lives bear out the truth of what they preach?" And, again: "Do they, substantially, agree with each other's testimony?" On this second point, however, there can be little argument. The basis of essential agreement between the great religious teachers of the world is very firm, and can easily be demonstrated by documentary evidence. Any student of comparative religion can reconstruct "the minimum working hypothesis." Nevertheless, it is quite possible to decide that Buddha, Christ, Shankara, St. Francis and Ramakrishna were all mad, or self-deluded, and therefore not to be taken seriously. If that is the verdict, then our inquiry ends.

But if the world's teachers were not mad, then, as all must agree, their teaching has universal application, and implies an obligation to put it into practice, in our own lives. And so we are faced by the next question: "Am I dissatisfied with my life as it is at present? And, if so, am I sufficiently dissatisfied to want to do anything about it?"

Here the majority and the minority definitely part company. Buddha said that human life is miserable, but he did not say that everybody thinks it is. Not all the socially underprivileged are dissatisfied, as every reformer knows, to his despair. And this is even truer of spiritual poverty than of economic lack. Life contains a number of vivid sense-pleasures, and the gaps of despondency and boredom between them can be filled more or less adequately by hard work, sleep, the movies, drink and daydreaming. Old age brings lethargy, and morphia will help you at the end. Life is not so bad, if you have plenty of luck, a good physique and not too much imagination. The disciplines proposed by the spiritual teachers are drastic, and the lazy will shrink back from them. They are tedious, also, and this will discourage the impatient. Their immediate results are not showy, and this will deter the ambitious. Their practice is apt to make you appear ridiculous to your neighbors. Vanity, sloth and desire will all intervene to prevent a man from setting his foot upon the path of religious effort.

Disregarding all these obstacles, and they are tremendous, the beginner will have to say to himself: "Well, I am going to try. I believe that my teacher is sane and honest. I do not believe in his teachings with the whole of my mind, and I will not pretend that I do, but I have enough belief to make a start. My reason is not offended. My approach is strictly experimental. I will put myself into his hands, and trust him at least as far as I would trust my doctor. I will try to live the kind of life which he prescribes. If, at the end of three or four years, I can conscientiously say that I have done what was asked of me and had no results whatsoever, then I will give up the whole attempt as a bad job."

1945

Klaus Mann

IT IS VERY EASY to picture him as he was. I see him entering a crowded room, eagerly, with a vague, pleased air. He looks around him curiously, without haste, taking in the furniture and the faces. Recognizing some of them, his pleasure becomes focused and personal. He advances, greets his friends simply and warmly, and is introduced to strangers, accepting them courteously at their surface value. He seems quite without vanity or self-consciousness. Neither frigid nor gushing, he has a certain quiet reserve, a touch of old-world politeness which holds him back from our empty modern familiarity. I cannot imagine him saying "Very happy to know you"—yet perhaps he really *is* happy—much happier, certainly, than most of the people who say it. For it comes naturally to him to like human beings. He approaches them with sympathy and lively interest.

Soon he is talking rapidly, fluently. He moves his head quickly, tilting it from side to side like a bird, and frowning nervously whenever he cannot exactly express himself. Birdlike, he seems to be balancing upon the truth, as if upon a slender, unsteady twig. He is so anxious to say *precisely* what he means. He takes all conversation earnestly, no matter if the topic is light or serious, but always with ease and flexibility. He never lectures you. He listens, answers, discusses. His great charm lay in this openness, this eager, unaffected approach. His quiet, intimate laughter enlivened even the gloomiest subjects. For Klaus never had to pretend to be serious, to pull a long face, like a hypocrite in church. He *was* serious. He minded deeply, he cared passionately, about the tragedies and the great issues of his time—and he took it for granted that *you* cared, too. I do not think I ever heard him utter an insincere remark. Insincerity is a form of laziness, and he was one of the least lazy people I have known.

I suppose that, to outsiders, his life may have seemed comparatively enviable. From his earliest days, he had inhabited the circles of the brilliant and the famous. He had experienced pleasure and success at an age when one is best able to enjoy them. He had traveled widely and continuously—so much so that the huge upheaval of the Emigration seemed, as far as he was concerned, to be no more than an extension of his normal way of living. He was always on the move, in and out of hotel bedrooms, just having arrived, just about to leave, beset by telephone calls, full of appointments. And he was always busy. The whole continuity of his existence was in his work. How I envied him that! I remember once asking him—it was in Copenhagen, I think—what he was writing. He laughed, made a little grimace. "Oh—a pre-war novel." This was in 1934. The joke was so typical of him, of his sane pessimism, and of his courage. Klaus's courage was of the most valuable kind—the kind which is shown in confronting the circumstances of everyday life. It is, by its very nature, unspectacular, anti-heroic. It does not demand great crises of action and danger, though it can face them, too. It shines most brightly in the midst of weariness, boredom, ill health and loneliness. It refuses to despair.

During the last sixteen years of his life, Klaus produced a really impressive body of work—novels, non-fiction books and innumerable articles—under circumstances which would have reduced most writers to impotent silence; he played an active part in the propaganda war against the Nazis; he learnt to write and speak a new language almost perfectly; he served in the American Army. All this he did without complaint, without boasting, with charm and humor. Indeed, he made his whole incredible achievement seem natural and easy. It was not.

His character had a dark underside of melancholy, seldom shown to others. He felt, with an extraordinary intensity, the sadness and cruelty of life, the coldness of the insensitive, the triviality of pseudo-optimists, the pain and nuisance of growing older. He respected, but could not bring himself to share in, the consolations of religious belief. The consolations of blind political hatred—such as they are—were also denied him: he fought injustice unwaveringly, but without hysteria. He must often have been bitterly lonely, despite his many friends and the affection of his large, closely knit family. A wanderer himself, he was temperamentally drawn to other wanderers, the confused, the lost, the astray. I believe that he helped many of them, but they could give him little in return. He found no permanent companion on his journey.

Now he is gone. And I—like others, perhaps—feel guilty. I know now that I took him too much for granted, because he was so self-reliant, so strong. We are all of us ready with our sympathy and support for the charming failures, the amiable misfits, the cowards and the weak. I forgot, as most of us forget, that the brave need reassurance, too. It is not enough simply to love them; they need the expression of our love.

His death is our great loss—the loss of a dear friend and fellow worker, and of a fine artist whose powers were still growing. And yet I cannot think of it as a mere disaster, altogether meaningless and tragic. Klaus had fought and worked so hard, achieved so much, inspired so many people by his example. In forty years he had suffered and experienced enough for a long lifetime. No wonder if he grew utterly weary. He had certainly earned the right to take his rest.

1950

DOWN THERE
ON A VISIT
(1962)

[Published in October 1959 in *The London Magazine*, *Mr.*
Lancaster is the first of four episodes in Isherwood's seventh
novel, *Down There on a Visit*. The use of Isherwood himself
as the narrator is characteristic of much of his fiction.]

Mr. Lancaster

NOW, AT LAST, I'm ready to write about Mr. Lancaster. For years I have been meaning to, but only rather halfheartedly; I never felt I could quite do him justice. Now I see what my mistake was; I always used to think of him as an isolated character. Taken alone, he is less than himself. To present him entirely, I realize I must show how our meeting was the start of a new chapter in my life, indeed a whole series of chapters. And I must go on to describe some of the characters in those chapters. They are all, with one exception, strangers to Mr. Lancaster. (If he could have known what was to become of Waldemar, he would have cast him forth from the office in horror.) If he could ever have met Ambrose, or Geoffrey, or Maria, or Paul—but no, my imagination fails! And yet, through me, all these people are involved with each other, however much they might have hated to think so. And so they are all going to have to share the insult of each other's presence in this book.

In the spring of 1928, when I was twenty-three years old, Mr. Lancaster came to London on a business trip and wrote my mother a note suggesting he should call on us. We had neither of us ever met him. All I knew about him was that he managed the office of a British shipping company in a North German harbor city. And that he was the stepson of my maternal grandmother's brother-in-law; there is perhaps a simpler way of saying this. Even my mother, who delighted in kinship, had to admit that he wasn't, strictly speaking, related to us. But she decided it would be nice if we called him "Cousin Alexander," just to make him feel more at home.

I agreed, although I didn't care a damn what we called him or how he felt about it. As far as I was concerned, everyone over forty belonged, with a mere handful of honorable exceptions, to an alien tribe, hostile by definition but in practice ridiculous rather than formidable. The majority of them I saw as utter grotesques, sententious and gaga, to be regarded with indifference. It was only people of my own age who seemed to me better than half-alive. I was accustomed to say that when we started getting old—a situation which I could theoretically foresee but never quite believe in—I just hoped we would die quickly and without pain.

Mr. Lancaster proved to be every bit as grotesque as I had expected. Nevertheless, hard as I tried, I couldn't be indifferent to him; for, from the moment he arrived, he managed to enrage and humiliate me. (It's obvious to me now that this was quite unintentional; he must have been desperately shy.) He treated me as though I were still a schoolboy, with a jocular, patronizing air. His worst offense was to address me as "Christophilos"—giving the name an affected classical pronunciation which made it sound even more mockingly insulting.

"I'm willing to wager, most excellent Christophilos, that you've never seen the inside of a tramp steamer. No? Then let me counsel you, for the salvation of your immortal soul, let go of your Lady Mother's apron strings for once, and come over to visit us on one of the company's boats. Show us you can rough it. Let's see you eat bacon fat in the middle of a nor'easter, and have to run for the rail while the old salts laugh. It might just possibly make a man out of you."

"I'll be delighted to come," I said, just as nonchalantly as I knew how.

I said it because, at that moment, I loathed Mr. Lancaster and therefore couldn't possibly refuse his challenge. I said it because, at that time, I would have gone anywhere with anyone; I was wild with longing for the whole unvisited world. I said it also because I suspected Mr. Lancaster of bluffing.

I was wrong. About three weeks later, a letter came for me from the London office of his company. It informed me, as a matter already settled, that I should be sailing on such and such a day, on board the company's freighter *Coriolanus*. An employee would be sent to guide me to the ship, if I would meet him at noon outside the dock gates in the West India Dock Road.

Just for a moment, I was disconcerted. But then my fantasy took the situation over. I started to play the lead in an epic drama, adapted freely from Conrad, Kipling, and Browning's "What's become of Waring?" When a girl phoned and asked me if I could come to a cocktail party a week from Wednesday, I replied tersely, with a hint of grimness, "Afraid not. Shan't be here."

"Oh, really? Where *will* you be?"

"Don't know exactly. Somewhere in the middle of the North Sea. On a tramp steamer."

The girl gasped.

Mr. Lancaster and his shipping company didn't fit into my epic. It was humiliating to have to admit that I was only going as far as the north coast of Germany. When speaking to people who didn't know me well, I contrived to suggest that this would be merely the first port of call on an immense and mysterious voyage.

And now before I slip back into the convention of calling this young man "I," let me consider him as a separate being, a stranger almost, setting out on this adventure in a taxi to the docks. For, of course, he *is* almost a stranger to me. I have revised his opinions, changed his accent and his mannerisms, unlearned or exaggerated his prejudices and his habits. We still share the same skeleton, but its outer covering has altered so much that I doubt if he would recognize me on the street. We have in common the label of our name, and a continuity of consciousness; there has been no break in the sequence of daily statements that I am I. But *what* I am has refashioned itself throughout the days and years, until now almost all that remains constant is the mere awareness of being conscious. And that awareness belongs to everybody; it isn't a particular person.

The Christopher who sat in that taxi is, practically speaking, dead; he only remains reflected in the fading memories of us who knew him. I can't revitalize him now. I can only reconstruct him from his remembered acts and words and from the writings he has left us. He embarrasses me often, and so I'm tempted to sneer at him; but I will try not to. I'll try not to apologize for him, either. After all, I owe him some respect. In a sense he is my father, and in another sense my son.

How alone he seems! Not lonely, for he has many friends and he can be lively with them and make them laugh. He is even a sort of leader amongst them. They are apt to look to him to know what they shall think next, what they are to admire and what hate. They regard him as enterprising and aggressive. And yet, in the midst of their company, he is isolated by his self-mistrust, anxiety and dread of the future. His life has been lived, so far, within narrow limits and he is quite naïve about most kinds of experience; he fears it and yet he is wildly eager for it. To reassure himself, he converts it into epic myth as fast as it happens. He is forever play-acting.

Even more than the future, he dreads the past—its prestige, its traditions and their implied challenge and reproach. Perhaps his strongest negative motivation is ancestor-hatred. He has vowed to disappoint, disgrace and disown his ancestors. If I were sneering at him, I should suggest that this is because he fears he will never be able to live up to them; but that would be less than half true. His fury is sincere. He is genuinely a rebel. He knows instinctively that it is only through rebellion that he will ever learn and grow.

He is taking with him on this journey a secret which is like a talisman; it will give him strength as long as he keeps it to himself. Yesterday, his first novel was published—and, of all the people he is about to meet, not one of them knows this! Certainly, the captain and the crew of the *Coriolanus* don't know it; probably no one in the whole of Germany knows. As for Mr. Lancaster, he has already proved himself utterly unworthy of being told; he doesn't know and he never will. Unless, of course, the novel has such a success that he eventually reads about it in a newspaper. . . . But this thought is censored with superstitious haste. No—no—it is bound to fail. All literary critics are corrupt and in the pay of the enemy. . . . And why, anyhow, put your trust in treacherous hopes of this kind, when the world of the epic myth offers unfailing comfort and safety?

That spring, totally disregarded by the crass and conceited littér-ateurs of the time, an event took place which, as we can all agree, looking backward on this, its tenth anniversary, marked the beginning of the modern novel as we know it: All the Conspirators was published. Next day, it was found that Isherwood was no longer in London. He had vanished without a trace or a word. His closest friends were be-wildered and dismayed. There were even fears of his suicide. But then—months later—strange rumors were whispered around the salons—of how, on that same morning, a muffled figure had been glimpsed, board-ing a tramp steamer from a dock on the Isle of Dogs—

No, I will never sneer at him. I will never apologize for him. I am proud to be his father and his son. I think about him and I marvel, but I must beware of romanticizing him. I must remember that much of what looks like courage is nothing but brute ignorance. I keep forgetting that he is as blind to his own future as the dullest of the animals. As blind as I am to mine. His is an extraordinary future in many ways—far happier, luckier, more interesting than most. And yet, if I were he and could see it ahead of me, I'm sure I should exclaim in dismay that it was more than I could possibly cope with.

As it is, he can barely foresee the next five minutes. Everything that is about to happen is strange to him and therefore unpredictable. Now, as the taxi ride comes to an end, I shut down my own foresight and try to look out through his eyes.

The company's employee, a clerk scarcely older than I, named Hicks, met me at the dock gates as arranged. He was not a character I would have chosen for my epic, being spotty-skinned and wan from the sooty glooms and fogs of Fenchurch Street. Also, he was in a fussy hurry, which epic characters never are. "Whew," he exclaimed, glanc-ing at his watch, "we'd better look smart!" He seized hold of the handle of my suitcase and broke into a trot. Since I wouldn't let go and leave him to carry it alone, I had to trot, too. My entrance upon Act One of the drama was lacking in style.

"There she is," said Hicks. "That's her."

The *Coriolanus* was even smaller and dirtier looking than I had expected. The parts of her that weren't black were of a yellowish brown; the same color, I thought—though this may have been merely association of ideas—as vomit. Two cranes were still dangling crates over her deck, which was swarming with dockhands. They were shouting at the top of their voices, to make themselves heard above the rattle of winches and the squawking of the sea gulls that circled overhead.

"But we needn't have hurried!" I said reproachfully to Hicks. He answered indifferently that Captain Dobson liked passengers to be on board in plenty of time. He had lost interest in me already. With a mumbled goodbye, he left me at the gangplank, like a parcel he had delivered and for which he felt no further responsibility.

I elbowed my way aboard, nearly getting myself pushed into the open hold. Captain Dobson saw me from the bridge and came down to greet me. He was a small, fattish man with a weather-scarlet face and the pouched, bulging eyes of a comedian.

"You're going to be sick, you know," he said. "We've had some good men here, but they all failed." I tried to look suitably serious.

Below decks, I found a Chinese cook, a Welsh cabin boy and a steward who looked like a jockey. He had been on the Cunard Line for twelve years, he told me, but liked this better. "You're on your own here." He showed me my cabin. It was tiny as a cupboard and quite airless; the porthole wouldn't unscrew. I went into the saloon, but its long table was occupied by half a dozen clerks, scribbling frantically at cargo lists. I climbed back up on deck again and found a place in the bows where, by making myself very small, I stayed out of everybody's way.

An hour later, we sailed. It took a long time getting out of the dock into the river, for we had to pass through lock gates. Lively slum children hung on them, watching us. One of the cargo clerks came and stood beside me at the rail.

"You'll have it choppy," he said. "She's a regular dancing master." And, without another word, he vaulted athletically over the rail onto the already receding wharf, waved briefly to me, and was gone.

Then we had high tea in the saloon. I made the acquaintance of the mate and the two engineers. We ate soused mackerel and drank the tea out of mugs; it was brassily strong. I went back on deck, to find that a quiet, cloudy evening had set in. We were leaving the city behind us. The docks and the warehouses gave way to cold gray fields and marshes. We passed several lightships. The last of them was called *Barrow Deep*. Captain Dobson passed me and said, "This is the first stage of our daring voyage." In his own way, he was trying to create an epic atmosphere. All right—I awarded him marks for effort.

Back to my cabin, for it was now too dark to see anything. The steward looked in. He had come to propose that I should pay him a pound for my food during the voyage, and eat as much as I liked. I could see he thought this was a stiff bargain, because he was sure I'd be seasick. "There was another gentleman with us a couple of months ago," he told me with relish. "He was taken very bad. You'll knock on the wall if you want anything in the night, won't you, sir?"

I smiled to myself after he had left. For I had a second secret, which I intended to guard as closely as my other. These seafolk were really quite endearingly simple, I thought. They appeared to be absolutely ignorant of the advances of medical science. Naturally, I had taken my precautions. In my pocket was a small cardboard box with capsules in it, wrapped in silver paper. The capsules contained either pink powders or gray powders. You had to take one of each; once before sailing, and thereafter twice a day.

When I woke next morning, the ship was rolling powerfully. Between rolls, she thrust her bows steeply into the air, staggered slightly, fell forward with a crash that shook everything in the cabin. I had just finished swallowing my capsules when the door opened and the steward looked in. I knew from the disappointment in his face what it was he'd been hoping to see.

"I thought you wasn't feeling well, sir," he said reproachfully. "I looked in half an hour ago, and you lay there and didn't say a word."

"I was asleep," I said. "I slept like a log." And I gave this vulture a beaming smile.

At breakfast, the second engineer had his arm in a sling. A pipe had burst in the engines during the night, and he had scalded his hand. Teddy, the Welsh cabin boy, cut up his bacon for him. Teddy was clumsy in doing this, and the second engineer told him sharply to hurry. For this the second engineer was reproved by the first engineer: "You won't half be a bloody old bugger when you're older— my God you will!"

Despite the second engineer's semiheroic injury, I was beginning to lose my sense of the epic quality of this voyage. I had expected to find that the crew of this ship belonged to a race of beings apart— men who lived only for the sea. But, as a matter of fact, none of them quite corresponded to my idea of a seaman. The mate was too handsome, rather like an actor. The engineers might just as well have been working in a factory; they were simply engineers. The steward was like any other kind of professional servant. Captain Dobson wouldn't have looked out of place as the owner of a pub. I had to face the prosaic truth: all kinds of people go to sea.

Actually, their thoughts seemed entirely ashore. They talked about films they had seen. They discussed a recent scandalous divorce case: "She's what you might call a respectable whore." They entertained me by asking riddles: "What is it that a girl of fourteen hasn't got, a girl of sixteen is expecting, and Princess Mary never will get?" Answer: "An insurance card." I told the story about the clergyman, the drunk, and the waifs and strays. When I got to the payoff line: "If you wore your trousers the same way round as your collar . . ." I faltered, not sure that it would be good taste to mimic a Cockney accent, since both engineers had one. However, the story went over quite well. They were all very friendly. But the answer to that constantly repeated young man's question, "What do they really think of me?" seemed to be, as usual, "They don't." They weren't even sufficiently interested in me to be surprised when I took a second helping of bacon, although the ship was going up and down like a seesaw.

All day long we lurched and slithered through the rugged sea. On deck the sea glitter was so brilliant that I felt half stupefied by it. Now that everything was battened down and squared away, the ship seemed to have grown to twice its original size. I walked the empty deck like a prize turkey. Now and then Captain Dobson, who stood benevolently on the bridge smoking a brier pipe and wearing an old felt hat, pointed out passing ships to me. Whenever he did this I felt bound to hurry to the rail and scrutinize them with professional intentness. Later he embarrassed me by bringing me a deck chair and setting it up with his own hands. "Now you'll be as happy as the boy who killed his father," he said. And he added: "I'd like your opinion of this," as he gave me a paperbound book with a sexy picture on the cover. It was called *The Bride of the Brute* and contained a lot of scenes like: "He cupped her ripe breasts in his burning hands, then savagely crushed them together till she cried out in pain and desire." If I had been in London among my friends, we should all have felt bound to make sophisticated fun of this book. It was the sort of book you were supposed to dismiss as ridiculous. But here I could admit to myself that, absurd as it was, it excited me hotly. Captain Dobson took it as a compliment that I read right through the book in an hour. Meanwhile, Teddy served me mugs of tea with large jam puffs.

In the middle of the night I woke, just as if somebody had roused me. Kneeling on my bunk, I peered out through the porthole. And there were the first lights of Germany shining across the black water, blue and green and red.

Next morning we steamed up the river. Captain Dobson drank with the German pilot in the chartroom and became very cheerful. He had exchanged his old felt hat for a smart white cap, which made him look more than ever like a comic music-hall sea dog. We passed barges which were as snug as homes, with gay curtained windows and pots of flowers. Captain Dobson showed me various places of interest along the shore. Pointing to one factory building, he said, "They've got hundreds of girls in there, cleaning the wool. It's so hot, they strip to the waist." He winked. I leered politely.

In the harbor, the *Coriolanus* became tiny again, as she made her way humbly to her berth amidst all the great ships. Captain Dobson shouted greetings to them as we passed, and was greeted in return. He appeared to be universally popular.

When we tied up, our deck was so far below the level of the dock that the gangplank had to be nearly vertical. A police officer, who had come to inspect my passport, hesitated to descend it. Captain Dobson mocked him: "Go 'vay, Tirpitz! Go 'vay!" He had called the pilot "Tirpitz," too, and all the captains of the ships he had hailed. The police officer climbed down cautiously backward, laughing but holding on very tight.

After the stamping of my passport, there were no other formalities. I shook hands with the steward (who was sulking a little; a bad loser), tipped Teddy and waved goodbye to Captain Dobson. "Give my love to the girls!" he shouted from the bridge. The police officer obligingly came with me to the dock gates and put me on a tram which stopped outside Mr. Lancaster's office.

It was an impressive place, even larger than I'd expected, on the ground floor, with revolving glass doors. Half a dozen girls and about twice that many men were at work there. A youth of sixteen ushered me into Mr. Lancaster's private room.

I had remembered Mr. Lancaster as tall, but I had forgotten how very, very tall he was. How tall and how thin. Obeying the strong subconscious physical reaction which is part of every meeting, I defensively became a fraction of a millimeter shorter, broader, more compact, as I shook his bony hand.

"Well, Cousin Alexander, here I am!"

"Christopher," he said, in his deep, languid voice. It was a statement, not an exclamation. I expanded it to mean: Here you are, and it doesn't astonish me in the least.

His head was so small that it seemed feminine. He had very large ears, a broad, wet mustache, and a peevish mouth. He looked sulky, frigid, dyspeptic. His nose was long and red, with a suggestion of moisture at the end of it. And he wore a high, hard collar and awkward black boots. No—I could find no beauty in him. All my earlier impressions were confirmed. I reminded myself with approval of one of my friend Hugh Weston's dicta: "All ugly people are wicked."

"I shall be ready in exactly"— Mr. Lancaster looked at his watch and seemed to make some rapid but complicated calculation—"eighteen minutes." He walked back to his desk.

I sat down on a hard chair in the corner and felt an indignant gloom fill me from my toes to my head. I was violently disappointed. Why? What had I expected? A warm welcome, questions about the voyage, admiration for my freedom from seasickness? Well—yes. I *had* expected that. And I had been a fool, I told myself. I should have known better. Now, here I was, trapped for a week with this frigid old ass.

Mr. Lancaster had begun to write something. Without looking

up, he took a newspaper from the desk and tossed it over to me. It was a London *Times*, three days old.

"Thank you—sir," I said, as spitefully as I dared. It was my declaration of war. Mr. Lancaster didn't react in any way.

Then he began to telephone. He telephoned in English, French, German and Spanish. All these languages he spoke in exactly the same tone and with the same inflections. Every now and then he boomed, and I realized that he was listening to his own voice and liking the way it sounded. It was noticeably ecclesiastical and it also had something of the government minister in it; nothing of the businessman. Several times he became commanding. Once he was almost gracious. He couldn't keep his hands still for a moment, and the least problem made him irritable and excited.

He wasn't ready for more than half an hour.

Then, without warning, he rose, said, "That's all," and walked out, leaving me to follow. All of the adult employees had left the outer office, presumably to get their lunch. The youth was on duty. Mr. Lancaster said something to him in German, from which I learned only that his name was Waldemar. As we went out, I grinned at him, trying instinctively to draw him into a conspiracy against Mr. Lancaster. But he remained expressionless and merely made me a small, stiff German bow. It really shocked me to see an adolescent boy bow like that. Mr. Lancaster certainly broke them in young. Or did he— horrible thought!—class me with Mr. Lancaster and therefore treat me with the same mocking-contemptuous respect? I thought not. Waldemar was probably every bit as stuffy as his employer, and tried to imitate his behavior as a model of gentlemanly deportment.

We took a tram back to Mr. Lancaster's home. It was a warm, humid day of spring. Carrying my suitcase and wearing—in order to transport it—my overcoat made me sweat; but I enjoyed the weather. It disturbed and excited me. I was glad that the tram was crowded— not only because I thus became separated from Mr. Lancaster and didn't have to make conversation with him, but also because I was pressed up close against the bodies of young Germans of my own age, boys and girls; and the nationality barrier between them and me seemed to rub off as the swaying car swung us into a tight-packed huddle. Outside, there were more young people, on bicycles. The schoolboys wore caps with shiny peaks and bright-colored shirts with laces instead of buttons, open at the neck. The gaily painted tram sped clanking and tolling its bell down long streets of white houses, where broad creeper leaves shadowed fronts of embossed stucco, in gardens dense with lilac. We passed a fountain—a sculptured group of Laocoön and his sons writhing in the grip of the snakes. In this sunshine you could almost envy them. For the snakes were vomiting cool water over the hot, naked bodies of the men, and their deadly wrestling match appeared lazy and sensual.

Mr. Lancaster lived in the ground-floor flat of a large house that faced north. Its rooms were high, ugly and airy. They had big white sliding doors which shot open at a touch, with uncanny momentum, making a bang which resounded through the building. The place was furnished in Germanic *art nouveau* style. The chairs, tables, closets and bookcases were grim, angular shapes which seemed to express a hatred of comfort and an inflexible puritanism. An equally grim stenciled frieze of leafless branches ran around the walls of the living room, and the hanging center lamp was an austere sour-green glass lotus bud. The place must have been dreary beyond words in winter; now at least it had the merit of being cool. Mr. Lancaster's only obvious contribution to the décor were a few school and regimental group photographs.

The most arresting of Mr. Lancaster's photographs was a large one showing a vigorous, bearded old man of perhaps seventy-five. What a beard! It was the real article, no longer obtainable, made of sterling silver; the beard of the genuine Victorian paterfamilias. It roared in torrents from his finely arched nostrils and his big-lobed ears, foamed over his cheeks in two tidal waves that collided below his chin to form boiling rapids in which no boat could have lived. What a beard-conscious old beauty—tilting his head up to be admired, with an air of self-indulged caprice!

"My dear old father," said Mr. Lancaster, making it clear, by his memorial tone of voice, that The Beard was now with God. "Before he was sixteen he had rounded the Horn and been north of the Aleutians, right up to the edge of the ice. By the time he was *your* age, Christopher"—this was a faint reproach—"he was second mate, sailing out of Singapore on the China Seas run. He used to translate Xenophon during the typhoons. Taught me everything I know."

Lunch was cold. It consisted of black bread, hard yellow Dutch cheese and various kinds of sausage—the indecently pink kind, the kind that smells gamy, the kind full of lumps of gristle, the kind that looks in cross section like a very old stained-glass window in a church.

Before we had eaten anything, Mr. Lancaster informed me that he didn't approve of after-dinner naps. "When I was managing the company's office at Valparaiso, my second in command was always telling me I ought to take a siesta, like the rest of them did. So I said to him, 'That's the time when the white man steals a march on the dagoes.' "

This, I was to discover, was a characteristic specimen of Mr. Lancaster's line of bold reactionary talk. No doubt, in my case, he was using it for educational reasons, taking it for granted that I must have romantic, liberal views which needed a counterbalance. There he was both right and wrong. I did have liberal views, in a vague, un-thought-out way; but he was quite wrong in thinking that by expressing opposite opinions he could startle me. I should have been startled only if he had agreed with me; as it was, I accepted his prejudices as a matter of course, without curiosity, finding them entirely in character.

Actually, I think, Mr. Lancaster felt himself to be beyond left or right. He took his stand on the infallibility of his experience and his weary knowledge that he had seen everything worth seeing. He was also beyond literature. He told me that he spent his evenings carpentering in a small workshop at the back of the flat—"to keep myself from reading."

"I've got no use for books as books," he announced. "When I've taken what I need out of them, I throw them away. . . . Whenever anyone comes and tells me about some philosophy that's just been discovered, some new idea that's going to change the world, I turn to the classics and see which of the great Greeks expressed it best. . . . Scribbling, in these latter days, is nothing but a nervous disease. And it's spreading everywhere. I don't doubt, my poor Christophilos, that before long you'll have sunk so low as to commit a novel yourself!"

"I've just published one."

The moment I had spoken, I was horrified and ashamed. Not until the words were in my mouth had I known what I was going to say. Mr. Lancaster couldn't have provoked me more artfully into a confession if he'd been a prosecuting lawyer.

The most humiliating aspect of my confession was that it didn't even seem to surprise or interest him in the least. "Send me a copy sometime," he told me blandly. "I'll let you have it back by return post, with all the split infinitives underlined in red pencil and all the non sequiturs in blue." He patted my shoulder; I winced with dislike. "Oh, by the way," he added, "we have a trifling foolish banquet towards—" (He spoke this line in a special, whimsical tone, as if to draw my respectful attention to the fact that here was a quotation from the Divine Swan in playful mood.) "All the local worthies from the shipping companies, the consulates and so forth will be there. I've arranged for you to come."

"No," I said. And I meant it. I had had enough. There was a limit to the amount of my valuable life I could afford to waste on this ignorant, offensive, self-satisfied fool. I would simply walk out on him, at once, this very afternoon. I had some money. I'd go to a travel bureau and find out how much it would cost to get back to England third class by the ordinary, civilized means. If I hadn't enough, I would take a room in a hotel and telegraph my mother for more. It was perfectly easy. Mr. Lancaster wasn't dictator of the world, and there was nothing he could do to stop me. He knew this as well as I did. I wasn't a child. And yet—

And yet—for some absurd, irrational, infuriating, humiliating reason—I was afraid of him! Incredible, but true. So afraid that my defiance made me tremble and my voice turned weak. Mr. Lancaster didn't appear to have heard me.

"It'll be an experience for you," he said, munching his hard old cheese.

"I can't." This time, I spoke much too loudly, because of overcompensation.

"Can't what?"

"Can't come."

"Why not?" His manner was quite indulgent; an adult listening to the excuses of a schoolboy.

"I—I haven't got a dinner jacket." Again, I horrified myself. This betrayal was as involuntary as the other; and, up to the moment of speaking, I'd supposed I was going to tell him I was leaving.

"I didn't expect you would have one," said Mr. Lancaster, imperturbably. "I've already asked my second in command to lend you his. He's about your size, and he has to stay at home tonight. His wife's expecting another baby. Her fifth. They breed like vermin. That's the real menace of the future, Christopher. Not war. Not disease. Starvation. They'll spawn themselves to death. I warned them, back in '21. Wrote a long letter to *The Times*, forecasting the curve of the birth rate. I've been proved right already. But they were afraid. The facts were too terrible. They only printed my first paragraph—" He rose abruptly to his feet. "You can go out and look around town. Be back here at six, sharp. No—better say five fifty-five. I have to work now." And with that, he left me alone.

The banquet was held in some private rooms above a big restaurant in the middle of the city.

As soon as we arrived, Mr. Lancaster's manner became preoccupied. He glanced rapidly away from me in all directions and kept leaving me to go over and speak to groups of guests as they arrived. He wore a greenish-black dinner jacket of pre-1914 cut and carried a white silk handkerchief inside his starched cuff. My own borrowed dinner jacket was definitely too large for me; I felt like an amateur conjurer—but one without any rabbits to produce out of his big pockets.

Mr. Lancaster *was* nervous! He evidently felt a need to explain to me what was worrying him, but he couldn't. He couldn't say anything coherent. He muttered broken sentences, while his eyes wandered around the room.

"You see—this annual meeting. A formality, usually. But this year—certain influences—absolute firmness—make them see clearly what's at stake. Because the alternative is. Same thing everywhere today. Got to be fought. Uncompromisingly. State my position—once and for all. We shall see. I don't quite think they'll dare to—"

Evidently this meeting, whatever it was, would take place at once. For already the guests were moving towards a door at the other end of the room. Without even telling me to wait for him, Mr. Lancaster followed them. I had no alternative but to stay where I was, sitting at the extreme end of one of the settees, facing a large mirror on the wall.

Very very occasionally in the course of your life—goodness knows how or why—a mirror will seem to catch your image and hold it like a camera. Years later, you have only to think of that mirror in order to see yourself just as you appeared in it then. You can even recall the feelings you had as you were looking into it. For example, at the age of nine, I shot a wildly lucky goal in a school football game. When I got back from the field, I looked into a mirror in the changing room, feeling that this improbable athletic success must somehow have altered my appearance. It hadn't; but I still know exactly how I looked and felt. And I know how I looked and felt as I stared into that restaurant mirror.

I see my twenty-three-year-old face regarding me with large, reproachful eyes, from beneath a cowlick of streaky blond hair. A thin, strained face, so touchingly pretty that it might have been photographed and blown up big for a poster appealing on behalf of the world's young: "The old hate us because we're so cute. Won't *you* help?"

And now I experience what that face is experiencing—the sense which the young so constantly have of being deserted. Their god forsakes them many times a day; they are continually crying out in despair from their crosses. It isn't that I feel angry with Mr. Lancaster for having deserted me; I hardly blame him at all. For he seems to me to be an almost impersonal expression, at this moment, of the world's betrayal of the young.

I am in mortal dread of being challenged by the manager of the restaurant or by any one of the various waiters who are hanging around the room, waiting for the banquet to begin. Suppose they ask me what I'm doing here—why, if I'm a bona fide dinner guest, I'm not with the others attending the meeting?

Therefore I concentrate all my will upon the desired condition of not being accosted. Fixing my eyes upon my reflection in the mirror, I try to exclude these men utterly from my consciousness, to eradicate every vestige of a possible telepathic bond between us. It is a tremendous strain. I tremble all over and feel sick to my stomach. Sweat runs down my temples.

The meeting lasted nearly an hour and a half.

The guests returned from it mostly by twos and threes, but Mr. Lancaster was alone. He came straight over to me.

"We've got to eat now," he told me with an air of nervous impatience, just as though I had raised some objection. "I've had them put you next to old Machado. He'll tell you all about Peru. He's their vice-consul here. You speak French, I suppose?"

"Not one word." This was quite untrue. But I wanted to disconcert Mr. Lancaster, and so punish him a little for leaving me alone by making him feel guilty.

But he wasn't even listening. "Good. It'll be an experience for you." And he was off again. I joined the crowd that was now moving into the dining room.

It was a very big place, a real banqueting hall. There were four long tables in it. What was evidently the table of honor was placed along the far wall, under an arrangement of many national flags. At this table I saw Mr. Lancaster already in the act of sitting down. It was equally easy to identify the least important table, right by the door. And, sure enough, one of its place cards had my name on it. On my right I read the name of Emilio Machado; and, a moment later, Sr. Machado himself took his seat at my side. He was a tiny man in his seventies. He had a benevolent mahogany-brown face netted with wrinkles—these were a slightly paler shade of brown—and hung with a drooping white mustache. His lips moved in a rather pathetic, silly smile as he watched the expressions on the faces of some loudly chattering guests across the table, but I didn't have the impression that he wanted to be spoken to.

The dinner, to my surprise, was excellent. (I associated everything in this city so completely with Mr. Lancaster that I was apt to forget he couldn't possibly have had anything to do with the catering.) As soon as the soup course was over, the guests began to toast each other, pair by pair. To do this, a guest would half rise to his feet, glass in hand, and wait until he had succeeded in catching the desired eye. The other guest, when caught, would also rise; glasses would be raised, bows exchanged. It was obvious that this was a serious matter. I felt sure that no toast went unremembered, and that to omit any of them would have led to grave consequences in your subsequent business dealings.

Watching all this toasting made me aware that I myself had nothing to drink. It appeared that the drinks didn't come with the dinner; they had to be ordered separately. In the fuss of changing my clothes, I had forgotten my money; I would have to send the bill over to Mr. Lancaster to be paid. But this didn't bother me. Serve him right, I thought, for his neglect. I made up my mind to speak to Sr. Machado, and ask him to share a bottle of wine with me. He didn't have any, either. I drew a deep breath: "*Si vous voulez, Monsieur, j'aimerais bien boire quelque chose—*"

He didn't hear me. I felt my face getting hot with shame. But now I heard a voice in my other ear: "You are the nephew of Mr. Lancaster, yes?"

I started guiltily. For I had been so absorbed in the problem of communicating with Machado that I'd scarcely noticed my other neighbor. He was a smiling, greedy-faced man, with a gleam in his eye and no chin. His sleek, thin gray hair was brushed immaculately back from his forehead. An unused monocle hung down on a broad silk ribbon against his shirtfront. His mouth pulled down at the corners, giving him a slight resemblance to a shark—but not a very dangerous one; not a man-eater, certainly. Squinting at his place card, I read a Hungarian name which no one but a Hungarian could possibly pronounce.

"I'm not his nephew," I said. "I'm not related to him at all, as a matter of fact."

"You are not?" This delighted the Shark. "You are just friends?"

"I suppose so."

"A frriend?" He rolled the *r* lusciously: "Mr. Lancaster has a yorng frriend!"

I grinned. Already I felt that I knew the Shark very well indeed.

"But he leaves you alone, no? That is not very friendly."

"Well, now I've got you to look after me."

My reply sent the Shark off into peals of screaming laughter. (On second thoughts, he was also partly a parrot.)

"I look after you, yes?" said Parrot-Shark: "Oh, very good! I shall look after you. Do not be afraid of that, please. I shall do it." He beckoned to a waiter. "You will help me drink one great big bottle of wine, yes? Very bad for me, if I must every time drink up all alone."

"Very bad."

"And now tell me, please—you are the friend of Mr. Lancaster, since how long?"

"Since this morning."

"This morning, only!" This didn't really shock Parrot-Shark, as he pretended; but it did puzzle him sincerely. "And he leaves you alone already?"

"Oh, I'm used to that!"

He was looking at me much more inquisitively now, aware, perhaps, that here was something not quite usual, just a bit uncanny, even. Maybe if he could have seen what a very odd young fish he had at the end of his line, he would have fled screaming from the room. However, at this moment the wine arrived, and soon his curiosity was forgotten.

From then on, dinner became quite painless. It was easy enough to keep Parrot-Shark amused, especially after we had finished the first bottle and he had ordered another. At the end of the meal, the lights were turned out and the waiters brought in ice puddings with colored lamps inside them. Then the speeches began. A fat, bald man rose to his feet with the assurance of a celebrity. Parrot-Shark whispered to me that this was the mayor. The mayor told stories. Someone had once explained to me the technique of storytelling in German: you reserve, if possible, the whole point of the story and pack it into the final verb at the end of the last sentence. When you reach this sentence, you pause dramatically, then you cast forth the heavy, clumsy, polysyllabic verb, like a dice thrower, upon the table.

At the end of each story the audience roared and wiped perspiring faces with their handkerchiefs. But, by the time it was Mr. Lancaster's turn to speak, they were getting tired and not so easy to please. His speech was followed by applause that was no more than barely polite.

"Mr. Lancaster is in bad humor tonight," Parrot-Shark told me, with evident sly satisfaction.

"Why is he in a bad humor?"

"Here we have a club for the foreign people who have work in this city. Mr. Lancaster is the president of our club for three years now. Always before, he is elected with no opposition—because he represents so powerful a shipping firm—"

"And this year you elected someone else?"

"Oh no. We elect him. But only after much discussion. We elect him because we are afraid of him."

"Ha, ha! That's very funny!"

"It is true! We are all afraid of Mr. Lancaster. He is our school-master. No—do not tell him that, please! I joke only."

"I'm not afraid of him," I boasted.

"Ah, for you it is different! You also are English. I think when you are Mr. Lancaster's age, people will be afraid of *you*." But Parrot-Shark did not mean this; he didn't believe it for one instant. He patted my hand. "I like every time to tease you a little bit, no?" On this understanding we drank each other's healths and finished a third bottle.

The rest of the evening I remember only rather vaguely. After the speeches, the whole company rose. Some, I suppose, went home. The majority got possession of chairs in the outer room, where they ordered more drinks. Little tables appeared from somewhere to put the drinks on. Those who had nowhere to sit wandered about, on the alert to capture an empty place. The lights seemed very bright. The tremendous clatter of conversation tuned itself down in my ears into a deep, drowsy hum. I was sitting at a table in an alcove. Parrot-Shark was still looking after me, and several of his friends had joined him. I don't think they were all Hungarians—indeed, one of them seemed obviously French and another Scandinavian—but they had the air of belonging together. It was as if they were all members of a secret society, and their talk was full of passwords and smilingly acknowledged countersigns. I felt intuitively that they had all been involved in the opposition to Mr. Lancaster's re-election. They didn't seem very for-midable; it was no wonder that he had defeated them. But they were more dangerous and more determined than they looked. They were smiling enemies, snipers, heel-biters, quick to scurry away, but sure to return.

Machado had long since disappeared. But I kept getting glimpses of Mr. Lancaster. I was surprised to realize that he was every bit as drunk as I was. I had supposed he would be extremely abstinent, either from conviction or caution, or else that he would have a very strong head. We were drinking liqueur brandy, now; I had begun to loll on the table. "Feeling sleepy?" Parrot-Shark asked. "I fix you up, eh?" He called the waiter and gave a detailed order in German, winking at his friends as he did so. They all laughed. I laughed, too. Really and truly, I didn't care what they did with me.

The waiter brought the drink. I sniffed at it. "What is it?" I asked.

"Just a small special medicine, yes?" The faces of Parrot-Shark and his fellow conspirators had moved in very close, now. They formed a circle within which I felt myself hypnotically enclosed. Their eyes followed my every movement with an intentness which pleased and flattered me. It was certainly a change, being at the burning point of such focused attention. I sniffed the drink again. It was some kind of a cocktail; I could distinguish only a musky odor which perhaps contained cloves.

But now something made me turn my head. And there was Mr. Lancaster. My sense of distance had become a bit tricky; he appeared to be about twenty-five yards away and at least twelve feet tall. Actually, he must have been standing right behind my chair. He said sharply, "Don't drink that stuff, Christopher. It's a plot—" (or perhaps, "It's a lot"; I can't be sure).

There was a long pause during which, I suppose, I grinned idiotically. Parrot-Shark said, smiling, "You hear what Herr Lancaster says? You are not to drink it."

"No," I said, "I certainly won't. I won't disoblige my dearest Coz." With these words, I raised the glass to my lips and drained the entire drink. It was like swallowing a skyrocket. The shock made me quite sober for a moment. "That's very interesting," I heard myself saying; "pure reflex action. I mean—you see—if he'd told me *not* to drink it—I mean, I shouldn't—"

My voice trailed off and I just could not be bothered to say any more. Looking up, I was surprised to find that Mr. Lancaster was no longer there. Probably several minutes had gone by.

"He doesn't like you," I abruptly told Parrot-Shark.

Parrot-Shark grinned. "It is because he is afraid that I steal you from him, no?"

"Well, what are you waiting for?" I asked aggressively. "Don't you *want* to steal me?"

"We shall steal you," said Parrot-Shark, but he kept glancing apprehensively toward Mr. Lancaster, who had reappeared in the middle distance. "There is a bar," he whispered to me, "down by the harbor. It is very amusing."

"What do you mean—amusing?"

"You will see."

His words broke the spell. I was suddenly, catastrophically bored. Oh yes, in my own sadistic way, I had been flirting with Parrot-Shark; daring him to overpower my will, to amaze me, to master me, to abduct me. Poor timid creature, he couldn't have abducted a mouse! He had no faith in his own desires. He was fatally lacking in shamelessness. I suppose he thought of himself as a seducer. But his method of seduction had gone out with the nineties. It was like an interminable and very badly written book which I now knew I had never meant to read.

"Amusing?" I said. "*Amusing?*"

With that I rose, in all the dignity of my drunkenness, and walked slowly across to where Mr. Lancaster was sitting. "Take me home," I told him, in a commanding voice. It must have been commanding, because he instantly obeyed!

The next morning, at breakfast, Mr. Lancaster seemed very much under the weather. His poor nose was redder than ever and his face was gray. He sat listlessly at the table and let me get the food from the kitchen. I hummed to myself as I did so. I felt unusually cheerful. I was aware that Mr. Lancaster was watching me.

"I hope you take cold baths, Christopher."

"I took one this morning."

"Good boy! It's one of the habits you can judge a man by."

I wanted to laugh out loud. Because I never took a cold bath unless I had been drunk, and would indeed have thought it shameful and reactionary to take one for any other reason. I agreed with Mr. Lancaster, for once: cold bath taking was a habit you could judge a man by—it marked him as one of the enemy. Nevertheless—I had to confess that part of myself, a spaniel side of me that I deplored, eagerly licked up Mr. Lancaster's misplaced praise!

Altogether, I felt a distinct improvement in our relations; at any rate, on my side. I felt that I had definitely scored over him and could therefore afford to be generous. I had defied him last night about drinking that drink, and had got away with it. I had had a glimpse behind the scenes of his business life and realized that he wasn't quite invulnerable; he was at least subject to petty ambition. Best of all, he had a hangover this morning and I hadn't—well, not much of one.

"I'm afraid I was a little preoccupied, yesterday evening," he said. "I should have taken you aside and explained things to you quietly. It was a very delicate situation. I had to act quickly—" I became aware that Mr. Lancaster didn't really want to tell me about the club and his fight for re-election; it wouldn't have sounded important enough. So he took refuge in grandiose generalizations: "There are evil things abroad in the world. I've been in Russia, and I know. I know Satanists when I see them. And they're getting bolder every year. They no longer crawl the gutters. They sit in the seats of power. I'm going to make a prophecy—listen, I want you to remember this—in ten years from now, this city will be a place you couldn't bring your mother, or your wife, or any pure woman to visit. It will be—I don't say worse, because that would be impossible—but as bad—as bad as Berlin!"

"Is Berlin so bad?" I asked, trying not to sound too interested.

"Christopher—in the whole of *The Thousand and One Nights*, in the most shameless rituals of the Tantras, in the carvings on the Black Pagoda, in the Japanese brothel pictures, in the vilest perversions of the Oriental mind, you couldn't find anything more nauseating than what goes on there, quite openly, every day. That city is doomed, more surely than Sodom ever was. Those people don't even realize how low they have sunk. Evil doesn't know itself there. The most terrible of all devils rules—the devil without a face. You've led a sheltered life, Christopher. Thank God for it. You could never imagine such things."

"No—I'm sure I couldn't," I said meekly. And then and there I made a decision—one that was to have a very important effect on the rest of my life. I decided that, no matter how, I would get to Berlin just as soon as ever I could and that I would stay there a long, long time.

That afternoon Mr. Lancaster arranged that Waldemar should take me to see the sights. We looked at the paintings in the Rathaus and visited the cathedral. Captain Dobson had made me curious to see the Bleikeller, the lead cellar, under it, in which corpses of human beings and animals are preserved. Captain Dobson had described how he had been to see these corpses with his brother: "One of them's a woman, you know. She's wearing a pair of black drawers. So I thought to myself, I'd like to see how things had panned out down there. There was a caretaker on guard, but he'd got his back turned to us. So I said to my brother, just keep an eye on old Tirpitz. And then I lifted them up. And, do you know, there was nothing—nothing at all! The rats must have been at her."

The flesh of the corpses had shriveled on their bones so that they were hardly more than skeletons; it looked like black rubber. There was a caretaker on this occasion, too; but he didn't turn his back and I had no chance of testing Captain Dobson's story. The thought of it made me smile; I wished I could tell it to Waldemar. An American lady who was down in the cellar with us asked me how the corpses had been preserved. When I told her I didn't know, she suggested I should ask Waldemar. I had to explain that I couldn't. Whereupon, she cried to her companion: "Say—isn't this cute? This young man can't speak any German and his friend doesn't speak any English!"

I didn't think it was cute at all. Being with Waldemar embarrassed me. He was probably a nice boy. He was certainly nice looking; in fact he was quite beautiful, in a high-cheekboned, Gothic style. He looked like one of the carved stone angels in the cathedral. No doubt the twelfth-century sculptor had used just such a boy—maybe a direct ancestor of Waldemar—for his model. But an angel isn't a very thrilling companion, especially if he doesn't speak your language; and Waldemar seemed so passive. He just followed me around, without showing any initiative. My guess was that he found me as tiresome as the sights and only consoled himself by reflecting that it would be even more boring back in the office.

.   .   .

The four days which I now spent with Mr. Lancaster seemed like a whole life together. I doubt if I should have gotten to know him any better in four months or four years.

I was bored, of course; but that didn't bother me particularly. (Most of the young are bored most of the time—if they have any spirit at all. That is to say, they are outraged—and quite rightly so—because life isn't as wonderful as they feel it ought to be.)

But I had decided to make the best of Mr. Lancaster. I was ashamed of my adolescent reactions to him that first day. Wasn't I a novelist? At college, my friend Allen Chalmers and I had been fond of exchanging the watchword "All pains!" This was short for Matthew Arnold's line in his sonnet on Shakespeare: "All pains the immortal spirit must endure." We used it to remind each other that, to a writer, everything is potential material and that he has no business quarreling with his bread and butter. Mr. Lancaster, I now reminded myself, was part of "all pains," and I resolved to accept him and study him scientifically.

So the first time I found myself alone in his flat, I searched it carefully for clues. I felt ridiculously guilty doing this. There were no rugs on the floors, and the noise of my footsteps was so loud that I was tempted to take off my shoes. In a corner of the living room stood a pair of skis. They looked somehow so like Mr. Lancaster that they might have been his familiars watching me. I used to make faces at them. I was being watched, anyway, by the photograph of The Beard. How dearly he would have liked to have me aboard his ship, to be ordered aloft in a blizzard off the Horn! When you looked at him and then considered his victim and pupil, Mr. Lancaster, you realized how much the old monster had to answer for.

On the whole, my search was disappointing. I found almost nothing. There was a locked writing desk which might possibly contain secrets; I would watch for a chance to see inside it. Otherwise, all the drawers and cupboards were open. My only discovery of any interest was that Mr. Lancaster kept a British Army captain's uniform in the wardrobe with his other clothes. So he was one of those dreary creatures who made a cult of their war experiences! Well, I might have known it. At least it was something to begin on.

At supper that night—our only eatable meal, since it was cooked by a woman who came in—I got him onto the subject. It certainly wasn't difficult. I barely had to mention the word "war" to start him intoning:

"Loos—Armentières—Ypres—St. Quentin—Compiègne—Abbeville—Épernay—Amiens—Bethune—St. Omer—Arras—" His voice had gone into its ecclesiastical singsong, and I had begun to wonder if he would ever stop. But he did, abruptly. Then, in a much lower voice, he said "Le Cateau," and was silent for several moments. He had pronounced the name in his most specially sacred tone. And now he explained: "It was there that I wrote what I regret to say is one of the very few great lines of poetry on the war." Again, his voice rose into a chant: "Only the monstrous anger of the guns."

"But surely," I involuntarily exclaimed, "that's by—?" Then I quickly checked myself, as I realized the full beauty of this discovery. Mr. Lancaster had genuine delusions of grandeur!

"I could have been a writer," he continued. "I had that power which only the greatest writers have—the power of looking down on all human experience with absolute objectivity." He said this with such conviction that there was something almost spooky about it. I was reminded of the way the dead talk about themselves in Dante.

"Tolstoy had it," Mr. Lancaster mused, "but Tolstoy was dirty. I know, because I've lived in six countries. He couldn't look at a peasant girl without thinking of her breasts under her dress." He paused, to let me recover from the shock of this powerful language. He was in the role of the great novelist now, talking simply and brutally of life as he sees it without fear or desire. "Some day, Christopher, you must go there and see it for yourself. Those steppes stretching thousands of miles beyond the horizon, and all the squalor and the hopelessness. All the terrible rot of sloth. The utter lack of backbone. Then you'll know why Russia is being run today by a pack of atheist Jews. . . . We in England never produced anyone greater than Keats. Keats was a clean-hearted lad, but he couldn't see clearly. He was too sick. You have to have a healthy mind in a healthy body. Oh, I know you young Freudians sneer at such things, but history will prove you wrong. Your generation will pay and pay and pay. The sun's touching the horizon already. It's almost too late. The night of the barbarian is coming on. I could have written all that. I could have warned them. But I'm a man of action, really—

"I'll tell you what, most excellent Christophilos—I'm going to make you a present. I'll give you the idea for a book of short stories that will make your reputation as a writer. It's something that's never been done. No one has dared to do it. Their heads were full of this so-called expressionism. They thought they were being subjective. Pooh! They hadn't the stamina. Their minds were costive. All that they could produce was as dry as sheep droppings—

"You see, these fools imagine that realism is writing *about* emotions. They think they're being very daring because they name things by the catchwords these Freudians have invented. But that's only puritanism turned inside out. The puritans forbid the use of the names; so now the Freudians order the use of the names. That's all. That's the only difference. There's nothing to choose between them. In their dirty little hearts, the Freudians fear the names just as much as the puritans do—because they're still obsessed by this miserable medieval Jewish necromancy—the Rabbi Loew and all that. . . . But the true realism—the kind nobody dares to attempt—has no use for names. The true realism goes behind the names—

"So what I would do is this—"

Here Mr. Lancaster paused impressively, rose, crossed the room, opened a drawer, took out a pipe, filled it, lighted it, shut the drawer, came back to his chair. The process took nearly five minutes. His face remained deadpan throughout it. But I could sense that he was simply delighted to keep me in suspense—and, in spite of myself, I really was.

"What I would do," he at last continued, "is to write a series of stories which do not describe an emotion, but create it. Think of it, Christopher—a story in which the word 'fear' is never mentioned and the emotion of fear is never described, but which *induces* fear in the reader. Can you imagine how terrible that fear would be?

"There'd be a story inducing hunger and thirst. And a story arousing anger. And then there'd be another story—the most terrible of all. Perhaps almost too terrible to write—"

(The story inducing sleep? I didn't say this, but I thought it—very loud.)

"The story," said Mr. Lancaster, speaking very slowly now to get the maximum effect, "which arouses the instinct of—reproduction."

My efforts to view Mr. Lancaster scientifically were not merely for art's sake. I realized by now that he was capable of having a truly shocking effect on my character. It was very dangerous for me to stop regarding him as a grotesque and start thinking of him humanly, because then I should hate him for bullying me. And if I went on hating him and letting myself be bullied by him, I should sink into a vicious, degenerate bitchery; the impotent bitchery of the slave. If there was such a thing as reincarnation—and why not?—I might well have been Mr. Lancaster's slave secretary in the days of classical Rome. We had probably lived out in a tumbledown villa on the wrong side of the Appian Way. I would have been the sort of slave who fancies himself as a poet and philosopher, but is condemned to waste his time transcribing the maunderings of his master and endure his earthshakingly trivial thoughts about the mysteries of nature. My master would have been poor, of course, and stingy, too. I would have had to double my duties, fetching wood and water, and maybe cooking as well. But I would have put on airs with the slaves from the other villas and pretended that I never had to do anything menial. At night I would lie awake planning his murder. But I should never dare go through with it, for fear of being caught and crucified.

No—Mr. Lancaster had to be taken scientifically or not at all. You had to study him like lessons. I actually made notes of his table talk:

"The worst of this work I'm doing now is, it doesn't really use more than a hundredth part of my brain. I get mentally constipated. In the war, my battery major used to set me gunnery problems. I'd solve them in the day. Gave three alternative solutions to each— without mathematics—

"There's one thing, Christopher, that you *must* realize. It is necessary in this world to believe in a positive force of evil. And the joy of life—the *whole* joy of life—is to fight that evil. If we lose sight of that, we lose the meaning of life. We fall into the ghastly despair of Glycon:

Panta gelōs, kī panta konis, kī panta to māden,
panta gar ex alogōn esti ta ginomena. . . .

All is but laughter, dust and nothingness,
All of unreason born. . . .

That's where the Pagans came to an end, the edge of the shoreless
sea. That was all they knew. But we have no excuse to follow them.
For against their negation we can now put Gareth's tremendous affir-
mation, his reply to his mother when she urged him to stay at home
and amuse himself with the distractions of a purposeless life:

Man am I grown, a man's work must I do.
Follow the deer? follow the Christ, the King,
Live pure, speak true, right wrong, follow the King—
Else, wherefore born?

Never forget that, Christopher. Repeat it to yourself every morning,
as you wake up. Else, wherefore born? Never ask, Can we win? Fight,
fight!

Charge once more, then, and be dumb!
Let the victors, when they come,
When the forts of folly fall,
Find thy body by the wall.

None of your clever modern men has Arnold's voice. Meredith had
it. William Watson had it—he was the last. Then the clever-clever
moderns swarmed onto the stage, and we lost the message.

"I could have given it back to them. I could have revived it. But
I heard another call. It was one morning in early summer—at the
edge of the Mer de Glace, just below Mont Blanc. I stood looking out
over that vast dazzling sea of ice, and a voice asked me: Which will
you be? Choose. And I said: Help me to choose. And the voice asked:
Do you want love? And I said: Not at the price of service. And the
voice asked: Do you want wealth? And I said: Not at the price of love.

And the voice asked: Do you want fame? And I said: Not at the price of truth. And then there was a long silence. And I waited, knowing that it would speak again. And at last the voice said: Good, my son. Now I know what to give you—

"You have everything before you. Christopher. Love hasn't come to you, yet. But it will. It comes to all of us. And it only comes once. Make no mistake about that. It comes and it goes. A man must make himself ready for it; and he must know when it comes. Some are unworthy. They degrade themselves and are unfit to receive it. Some hold back from receiving it—call it pride, call it fear—fear of one's own good fortune—who shall judge? Be ready for the moment, Christopher. Be ready—"

One morning, when Mr. Lancaster had started out for the office, I saw that the writing desk he usually kept locked was standing open. As he had left the key, with his key bunch attached to it, sticking in the keyhole, I guessed he would soon discover his mistake and come back. So my investigations had to be quick.

The first thing I found was an army service revolver, evidently another of Mr. Lancaster's sentimental war souvenirs. This couldn't have interested me less; I felt certain the desk must contain some worthier secrets. I leafed through old paid bills and obsolete railway timetables; handled bits of wire, blackened light bulbs, broken picture frames, rusty parts of some small engine, perished rubber bands. It was as if Mr. Lancaster had sternly bundled up all that was untidy in his character and stowed it away here out of sight.

However, in the top drawer—the most prominent and therefore least likely place, I had thought, which was why I looked there last— I found a thick notebook with a shiny black cover. I was thrilled to see that it was full of poetry in Mr. Lancaster's handwriting; a long, narrative poem, apparently. I could do no more than hastily skim through it—lots of nature, of course—mountains, seas, stars, boyhood rambles and ruminations in the manner of Wordsworth—and God— lots and lots of God—and travel—and the war—oh dear, yes, the war—and more travel—hm—hm—hm—aha, what was this? Now we were getting somewhere at last!

And there was One—
Long, long, ago—dear God, how very long—
Who, when the lilac breathed in breathless bloom
And later buds their secrets still withheld
Yet promised to reveal, as soon they must,
Since it was so ordained—as evening came
She too was there, her presence felt ere seen
By him who watched for it. She never knew
What meaning filled the twilight with her step,
What emptiness, for him, the twilight brought
When, soon, she came no more—the ways of Life
Leading her elsewhere. And she never knew,
Going her ways about the world, what deed,
Unknowing, she had done; into what heart
She had brought beauty and left bitter pain.

I can't remember how the lines struck me then, because I regarded them simply and solely as a find. My treasure hunt was successful. I was triumphant. Seizing pencil and paper, I scribbled them down, thinking only of how I would read them aloud to my friends when I got back to London.

I had barely finished my copying when I realized that Mr. Lancaster had re-entered the flat. He had made far less noise than usual. There was no time to cover up the traces of my search. All I could do—and I think it showed great presence of mind—was to drop the notebook into the drawer and take out the revolver. It was at least less embarrassing, I thought, to be caught examining a revolver than an autobiographical poem.

"Put that down!" Mr. Lancaster barked hoarsely.

He had never used that tone to me before; it startled and enraged me. "It isn't loaded," I said. "And, anyhow, I'm not a child." I put the revolver back in the drawer and walked straight out of the room.

(Looking back, I now reinterpret Mr. Lancaster's behavior. I see how his conversation was full of attempts to arouse my interest in him. Didn't he expect, for example, that I'd ask him what it was that that voice on the Mont Blanc glacier had finally given him? Hadn't he even hoped that I'd beg him to tell me about his love life? And wasn't the leaving of the key in his desk a deliberate, if subconscious, attempt to make me read his poem? If I'm right—and I think I am—then my cruelty to Mr. Lancaster was in my lack of curiosity. My would-be scientific study of him was altogether unscientific, because I was sure in advance of what I was going to find—which no scientist should be. I was sure he was a bore.

So, when Mr. Lancaster came in and found me looking at the revolver instead of the notebook, he must have been bitterly disappointed; even if he couldn't have explained to himself why. Hence his outburst of temper.

As for the revolver, maybe he had almost forgotten its existence. And maybe it was actually I who reminded him that it was lying there, all the time, in the bottom drawer, a gross metallic fact in the midst of his world of fantasy.)

Two days before I was due to return to England, Mr. Lancaster took me sailing. He didn't ask me if I wanted to do this; he simply announced his plan and I accepted it. I didn't really care what happened, now. Since the incident of the revolver, our relations were chilly. I was merely counting the hours till I could leave.

We left after the office closed that evening, in his car, to drive out to the village on the river where he kept his boat. On the way, we picked up Sr. Machado. I was glad to have him with us, for I didn't want to spend any more time alone with Mr. Lancaster. Much later, it occurred to me that Machado was probably the only one of Mr. Lancaster's acquaintances left who would agree to come with him on a trip of this kind. No doubt many of them had tried it—once.

The three of us were squeezed into the front seat of Mr. Lancaster's little car, with the outboard engine, under its tarpaulin cover, sitting up in the back. Quite soon we lost our way. Mr. Lancaster, who had forgotten to bring the map, became increasingly jittery as we bumped along a narrow sand road in the twilight, skirting a marsh. Old farmhouses stood half awash amidst water meadows. A crane walked stiffly along the wall of the dike and went flapping away over the lush, wet landscape. I felt a dreamy, romantic contentment steal over me. What did it matter where we were? Why be anywhere in particular? But Mr. Lancaster was frantic.

Just as it began to get really dark, two figures appeared out on the marsh in a punt. Mr. Lancaster stopped the car, ran up on to the dike and hailed them. They were very small and towheaded, a boy and a girl. It was almost incredible that they could manage the punt at all, and this made them seem more like very intelligent animals than terribly stupid children. They stood hand in hand in the punt, staring up at Mr. Lancaster with their big, vacant blue eyes, their mouths open, as if they expected he was going to feed them. Mr. Lancaster addressed them—as he told me later—in High and Low German. He spoke as one speaks to idiots, so slowly and with such elaborate pantomime that even I could understand what he said. But not those children. They just stared and stared. Mr. Lancaster began to shout and wave his arms but they didn't flinch. They were too stupid to be afraid of him. At last he gave it up in despair, turned the car around and drove back the way we had come.

Very late at night we finally arrived at our destination. The place was crowded with holiday-makers, and only one room was vacant at the inn. It must have been one of the best rooms, however, for it had an imposing bed on a dais, as well as a studio couch. The chief decoration was a photogravure of an almost nude woman in an "artistic" pose; this stood on an easel with a piece of figured material like tapestry draped around it. Mr. Lancaster decided that he would sleep on the couch and Sr. Machado on the bed. I was to go back to the cabin of Mr. Lancaster's boat. "It'll be an experience for me," I said sarcastically, before he could say it. But Mr. Lancaster was deaf to sarcasm.

I woke in the early but already brilliant morning, and found myself undecided whether to romanticize my situation or sulk. My situation *was* romantic, I had to admit. Here I was, all alone in this foreign land, in sole occupancy of a sailing boat! No doubt these people were watching me and wondering about me. Although it was barely six o'clock, most of the holiday-makers seemed to be up.

The village was built along the riverbank, with beer gardens running down to the water's edge. The boats were decorated with sprays of poplar at their mastheads; and schoolboys had fastened them to the handlebars of their bikes. On board the boats there were gramophones, and people were playing concertinas and singing. Beer was being drunk and sausages munched, and you could smell the delicious smell of out-of-door coffee. The girls were plump but pretty; the men were cropped blond and piggy-pink. As they sang they shaved or combed their hair, and were temporarily silenced as they brushed their teeth in the river.

All this filled me with joy. But on the debit side of the day there was my stiffness from sleeping curled up on the tiny bunk in the cabin, plus a headache. And there was Mr. Lancaster, who now appeared and was cross because I hadn't tidied the cabin or finished dressing; I was, in fact, sprawling on the deck in the sun. By the time we had had breakfast at the inn and I had become constipated—my usual reaction to having to use strange lavatories and being told to hurry— the sulks were on.

And then the engine was mounted on the boat, but it wouldn't start. A mechanic had to be fetched from the garage; while he was working, quite a large crowd gathered. All that Mr. Lancaster could contribute was his fussing and nagging. Nevertheless, he made the occasion a text for one of his reminiscent sermons: "This reminds me of the war. I remember getting out of a village near Loos just before dawn, because we knew the Hun would start shelling as soon as it got light. I was curious to see how I would stand the strain, because our colonel obviously had the wind up. So I took my pulse. It was *absolutely* normal. I found my brain was functioning so well that, as I was giving orders to my sergeant-major, I visualized a chess problem I'd read in *The Times* a few days before. It was black to play and mate in three moves, and I *saw* the solution, Christopher. I didn't have to think about it at all. I simply looked at it, as you look at the map of a town and say to yourself: 'Well, quite obviously, *that's* the quickest way to the market square.' There couldn't be any question. And I have no doubt whatsoever that I could have played at least half a dozen games simultaneously at that moment, and won all of them. What is it Sophocles says about the greatness of man when his mind rises to its highest in the face of fate—?" And he was off again into a long, straggling string of Greek. How right Hugh Weston was in saying that it is the most hideous of all languages!

At last we were off, heading towards the sea. Mr. Lancaster snapped at me because I dropped some of his fishing gear. I scowled back at him. To snub me and show me my place he then concentrated on Machado, talking to him in Spanish. This was nothing but a relief, as far as I was concerned; but it worried Machado, whose courtly Latin manners demanded that he should communicate with me, now that he was aware of my existence. (I'm sure he simply did not remember we had sat next to each other at that dinner.) So he spoke to me from time to time in French, which I had great difficulty in understanding because of his fearful accent. The worst of Machado's remarks was that they were not only hard to understand but harder still to develop into any kind of conversation. For example, he said: "*Je suppose que le sujet le plus intéressant pour un écrivain, c'est la prostitution.*" To which I could only reply enthusiastically: "*Monsieur, vous avez parfaitement raison.*" And there we stuck.

We were in the estuary now; the river was already very wide. Mr. Lancaster ordered me to steer the boat while he got the fishing rods ready for action. "You've got to be on the alert from the first moment," he told me. "This river's full of sand bars. Careful. Careful! CARE-FUL! Look at the color of that water ahead! Dead slow through here! Steady, now! Steady. Steady. Steady. Steady. *Now*—open her up! OPEN! Quick, man! Port! HARD to port! Do you want to swamp us?" (There was a very mild swell as we left the river mouth; you could hardly even feel the change of motion.) "Away, now. Dead ahead! Hold her two degrees sou'west of the point. Hold her on her course. HOLD HER! Careful, man! Good. *Good!* Oh, good man! *Very* pretty! Well steered, sir! I'm greatly afraid, Christopher, that we're going to make a sailor out of you yet!"

I had done nothing to be praised for, except that I hadn't run us into a buoy as big as a haystack. Mr. Lancaster's enthusiasm was as crazy as his anxiety. Yet once again—as in the case of the cold bath— I was idiotically flattered. Ah, if he had realized how easily manageable I was; how instantly I responded to the crudest compliment! No—even if he had realized it, this would have made no difference in his treatment of me. Flattery was something Mr. Lancaster would never have bestowed upon me; he would have regarded it as bad for my soul.

I suppose he felt no responsibility for Machado's soul. For he began to butter him up in a manner that was absolutely shameless, speaking French, now, for my benefit. He called Machado a "good sport," using the English words and then explaining them in French, until Machado understood and clapped his hands with delight: "Good spot! I—good spot? Oh, yes!"

"Isn't he a dear old man?" said Mr. Lancaster to me, benevolently. "He's three quarters Peruvian Indian, you know. His father probably chewed coca and never wore shoes. That's your real unspoiled dago for you. Doesn't matter what age he is—he always stays a child."

We were now quite far out on the flat shallow sea; the low shore of dunes was already only a pale line between the sparkle of the water and the shine of the sky. White sails were curving all over the seascape. Mr. Lancaster, evidently feeling very pleased with himself, stood in the bows intoning:

> *Pervixi: neque enim fortuna malignior unquam*
> *erepiet nobis quod prior hora dedit.*

I knew, with sudden intense force, just how awful the Odyssey and the voyage of the *Pequod* must have been, and that I would have sooner or later jumped overboard rather than listen to either of those ghastly sea bores, Ulysses and Ahab.

Presently Mr. Lancaster announced that it was time for us to fish. Machado and I were given the rods. We trailed our lines inexpertly in the water. This might have been quite restful, if heaven hadn't rebuked my laziness by performing a most tiresome miracle—nothing less than a miraculous draught. We ran into a school of mackerel!

Mr. Lancaster was absolutely beside himself. "Careful! CARE-FUL, MAN! Easy—easy—easy! Don't let the line slack! You'll lose him! Play him, man! Keep playing him! Fight him! He's a wily devil! He'll trick you yet! Don't look at *me*, man! Watch him! WATCH HIM! Keep your head! Keep calm! NOW—"

All of this was more superfluous than words can tell, for, in fact, there was nothing—absolutely nothing—we could have done to avoid catching those miserable fish—short of throwing the rods away and lying down in the bottom of the boat. Machado wasn't speaking French now, or even Spanish. He emitted what sounded like tribal hunting sounds, maybe in some Indian dialect of the Andes. At first I caught some of their excitement and yanked the fish in as fast as I could. Then I began to get tired. Then rather disgusted. It was so indecently easy. By the time we were through, I think we had at least thirty fish in the boat.

After the catch Mr. Lancaster set himself to clean some of the fish we were to eat, so he didn't pay much attention to Machado. I was steering. Happening to glance over in the old man's direction, I saw that he was leaning right over the side. His back was tense and his legs were stiffly straddled. My first thought was that he was having a stroke. But no—he was pulling desperately at something in the water. He looked as if he were trying to haul up the bottom of the sea. He turned his head toward me, half strangling with the exertion. "*Poisson!*" he gurgled, only it sounded more like "possum!"

Naturally, I jumped to my feet to help him. What was my amazement—and subsequent fury—when I received a violent backhander in the chest from Mr. Lancaster! He knocked me right over backwards, and I sat down very hard. I think if I'd had a knife I'd have whipped it out right then and there, and finished him. As it was, I merely mentally shouted: "Touch me again, you old goat, and I'll throttle you!" Mr. Lancaster, meanwhile, was yelling in my face: "Leave him alone, you silly little fool!" I suppose he saw the blazing hate in my eyes, for he added, somewhat less hysterically, "*Never* help a man when he's landing a fish! NEVER! Don't you even know *that?*"

He turned from me to attend to Machado, who was heaving in his line. Mr. Lancaster knelt beside him, speaking to him in French, soothing him, urging him, entreating him, imploring him to breathe deeply, to relax, to keep up the pressure, gentle and slow. "*Ça va mieux, n'est-ce pas? Ça marche? Mais naturellement—*" He was absurdly like a midwife encouraging a woman in labor. And sure enough, slowly, slowly, with infinite pain, Machado was delivered of an enormous fish—a tuna, Mr. Lancaster said. When he had gaffed it we let it trail in the water behind the boat, to keep it fresh.

Then Mr. Lancaster cooked the mackerel on a spirit stove. I would have liked to be strong-minded and refuse to eat. But I was ragingly hungry. And although Mr. Lancaster, with his usual incompetence, had burned the fish badly, it smelled and tasted delicious. Besides, I was in an awkward position because I couldn't possibly be nasty to Machado, who was in a state of utter triumph and had to be congratulated repeatedly. Quite probably, this would be the last really happy day of his life. I compromised by ignoring Mr. Lancaster. He didn't appear to notice this.

In this mood, we started for home. Mr. Lancaster kept remarking complacently on his own foresight; he had calculated our timetable so that we were going with the tide both ways. But the long, chugging voyage seemed tedious enough, even so. As we got into the river mouth, I was steering again and Mr. Lancaster was nagging at me. We must have been off course, but how was I to know? It was no use trying to follow his pseudonautical directions. I just went ahead by sight.

Suddenly he screamed: "SAND! SAND AHEAD! PUT HER ABOUT! HARD! HARD OVER!"

What happened next was quite unplanned. At least, I had no conscious knowledge of what I was going to do. Nevertheless, I did it. I had the feel of the tiller by this time; I could sense pretty well how much it would stand. All I did was to obey Mr. Lancaster's order just the merest shade too energetically. I swung the tiller hard over—very hard. And with the most exquisitely satisfactory, rending crack, the crosspiece to which the outboard engine was clamped broke off, and the engine fell into the water.

I looked up at Mr. Lancaster and I nearly grinned.

For a moment I thought he would swallow his Adam's apple. "You fool!" he screamed. "You fool! You confounded little idiot!" He stepped over to me, making the boat rock. But I wasn't in the least scared now. I knew he wouldn't—couldn't—hit me. And he didn't.

As a matter of fact, the water was so shallow that we didn't have much trouble in dragging up the engine. But of course there was no question of getting it started again; it needed to be thoroughly cleaned first. So there was nothing for it but to sail back to the village.

The sail lasted all the rest of the day. There was very little wind, and Mr. Lancaster seemed to be making the worst possible use of it, for nearly every boat on the river passed us. He steered, glumly. Machado was peacefully asleep after his exertions. Finally we were taken in tow by a pleasure steamer. Mr. Lancaster had to accept this courtesy because it was beginning to get dark, but I could see how it humiliated him. A man and a woman, neither of them slender or young, were sitting in the stern of the steamer, invisible to the other passengers but right in front of us. Throughout the trip they made love with abandon. And this, too, was a sort of humiliation for Mr. Lancaster, because the lovers evidently felt that his reactions weren't worth bothering about. I felt that I was on the side of the lovers, and smiled at them approvingly; but they weren't bothering about my reactions, either.

As for myself, I was in a wonderful mood. The semideliberate ditching of the outboard engine had discharged all my aggression, like a great orgasm. Now I no longer felt the least resentment against Mr. Lancaster. Indeed, I had stopped thinking about him. My thoughts had gone racing on ahead of my life, of me on this sailing boat; they had left Mr. Lancaster and Germany far behind. They were back in London, in my room, at my desk. But I wasn't even unduly impatient to return there physically, for, meanwhile, I had plenty to think about. After all—despite Mr. Lancaster—this silly day would be memorable to me throughout my life. For, right in the midst of it—maybe at the very instant when that engine had splashed into the water—I had had a visitation. A voice had said: "The two women—the ghosts of the living and the ghosts of the dead—the Memorial." And, in a flash, I had seen it all—the pieces had moved into place—the composition was instantaneously *there*. Dimly, but with intense excitement, I recognized the outline of a new novel.

The day came for my return to England. The *Coriolanus* was sailing in the evening.

That morning Mr. Lancaster informed me, with his usual nonchalance, that Waldemar was to take me to the art gallery. Waldemar and I were to have lunch together—since Mr. Lancaster had a business appointment—and I was to be back at the flat at four fifteen precisely. I made no comment.

But, as soon as Waldemar and I were alone on the gallery steps and Mr. Lancaster had disappeared around the corner, I turned to him and firmly shook my head. "*Nein*," I said.

Waldemar looked puzzled. Pointing to the gallery entrance, he asked: "*Nein?*"

"*Nein*," I repeated, smiling. Then I pantomimed a breast stroke.

Waldemar's face brightened instantly. "*Ach—schwimmen! Sie wollen, dass wir schwimmen gehen?*"

"*Ja*," I nodded. "*Swimmen.*"

Waldemar beamed at me. I had never seen him smile like that before. It changed his whole face. He no longer looked at all angelic.

He took me to a big municipal open-air pool. I had passed this place several times, but with my almost utter lack of German, had never had the nerve to go in there alone. Waldemar didn't seem passive now. He bought our tickets, got me my towel and soap, greeted numerous friends, steered me into the locker room, made me take a shower and showed me how to tie on one of the triangular red bathing slips he had rented. When he undressed, it was as if he took off his entire office personality. It was astonishing how he had managed to disguise his physically mature, animally relaxed brown body in that prim office suit. He no longer behaved to me as if I were forty years old and in league with Mr. Lancaster. We smiled at each other tentatively, then started to wrestle, splashed and ducked each other, swam races. But though we were playing like kids, I was chiefly aware of the fact that he was already a young man.

Presently we were joined by a friend, a boy of his own age named Oskar. Oskar was monkey-faced, impudent, dark and grinning. He spoke fairly fluent English. He was a page, he told me, in one of the large hotels. And I was aware of the page mentality in him; he had been around, he knew the score, and he looked at me speculatively, like one of his hotel guests who might have special requirements he could satisfy in exchange for a tip. He had giggly asides with Waldemar and I knew they were discussing me; but I didn't mind, because Oskar took great trouble to make me feel one of the party.

After swimming, we went to a restaurant for lunch. Both the boys smoked and drank beer. I had the impression that Waldemar was anxious to appear as sophisticated as his friend. By this time, we were calling each other Oskar and Christoph.

Waldemar said something to Oskar and they both roared with laughter.

"What's the joke?" I asked.

"Walli says he thinks his bride will like you," Oskar told me.

"Well—good. Is she coming here?"

"We go to see her. Soon. All right?"

"All right."

"All right!" Waldemar laughed very heartily. He was slightly drunk. He reached across the table and shook my hand hard. Oskar explained: "Walli's bride likes also older gentlemen. Not too old. You—very good! Pretty boy!"

I blushed. A most delicious gradual apprehension began to creep over me.

"You have five marks?"

"Yes." I produced them.

This amused the boys. "No, no—for later."

"But, Oskar"—I felt we were somehow at cross-purposes—"if she's Walli's bride—and, anyhow, isn't he much too young to have a bride?"

"Already at twelve I have a bride. Walli also."

"But—won't he be jealous if I—?"

More laughter. Oskar told me: "We shall not leave you alone with her." I must have looked more and more bewildered, for he patted my hand reassuringly. "You need not be shy, Christoph. First, you watch us. Then you see how easy it is." He translated his joke to Waldemar and they laughed till the tears ran down their faces.

Braut in dictionary German means a bride or fiancée. But boys like Oskar and Waldemar used it to refer to any girl they happened to be going with. This, my first lesson in the language, I learned during that unforgettable, happy, shameless afternoon—an afternoon of closed Venetian blinds, of gramophone music and the slippery sounds of nakedness, of Turkish cigarettes, cushion dust, crude perfume and healthy sweat, of abruptly exploding laughter and wheezing sofa springs.

I didn't return to Mr. Lancaster's flat until nearly six o'clock. I was too dazed with pleasure to have cared if he had scolded me; but he didn't. In fact, he appeared to be back in the mood in which he had received me on the day of my arrival. He just didn't seem particularly interested in my existence. "Give my regards to your mother" was all he said when we parted. I felt hurt by his coldness. However little *I* might care, I was still sincerely surprised when my indifference was returned.

When I got back to London, I found that my novel was indeed a flop. The reviews were even worse than I had expected. My friends loyally closed ranks against the world in its defense, declaring that a masterpiece had been assassinated by the thugs of mediocrity. But I didn't really care. My head was full of my new novel and a crazy new scheme I had of becoming a medical student. And always, in the background, was Berlin. It was calling me every night, and its voice was the harsh sexy voice of the gramophone records I had heard in the bed-sitting room of Waldemar's "bride." Sooner or later, I should get there. I was sure of that. Already I had begun to teach myself German, by one of those learn-it-in-three-months methods. While riding on buses, I recited irregular verbs. To me they were like those incantations in *The Arabian Nights* which will make you master of a paradise of pleasures.

I never sent a copy of *All the Conspirators* to Mr. Lancaster, of course. But I wrote him a thank-you letter—one of those thankless, heartless documents I had been trained since my childhood to compose. He didn't answer it.

When I tried to describe him to my friends, I found I could make very little of him as a significant or even a farcical character. I just did not have the key to him, it seemed. And when I read my copy of his poem to Allen Chalmers, we were both rather embarrassed. It simply wasn't bad enough in the right way. Chalmers had to be polite and pretend that it was much more ridiculous than it actually was.

I also touched on the subject of Mr. Lancaster's love life in talking to my mother. She smiled vaguely and murmured, "Oh, I hardly think *that* was the trouble." I then learned from her what she hadn't thought even worth telling me before—that Mr. Lancaster had actually been married for a few months, after the war, but that his wife had left him and they had separated legally. "Because," said my mother dryly, "Cousin Alexander wasn't—so one was given to understand—at all adequate as a husband." This revelation of Mr. Lancaster's impotence quite shocked me. Not on his account—it was pretty much what I would have expected—but on my mother's. I never fail to be shocked by the ability of even the most ladylike ladies to live in cozy matter-of-fact intimacy with the facts of nature. My mother was surprised and rather pleased by my reaction. She was aware that she had managed for once to say something "modern," though she couldn't altogether understand how she had done it.

I suppose I should gradually have forgotten all about Mr. Lancaster if he hadn't regained my interest in the most dramatic way possible. Toward the end of November that same year he shot himself.

The news came in a letter from Mr. Lancaster's assistant manager, the "second in command" who had lent me his dinner jacket for the banquet. I had met him briefly after that at the office and thanked him. I remembered him only as a florid little Yorkshireman with a broad accent and a capable, good-natured manner.

The letter informed us of the bare facts in a tidy, businesslike style. Mr. Lancaster had shot himself one evening at his flat, but the body had not been discovered until next day. No suicide note had been found, nor any papers "of a personal nature." (He must have burned the notebook with his poem, I supposed.) He had not been unwell at the time. He was in no financial difficulties, and the affairs of the company were giving him no cause for anxiety. The assistant manager concluded with a line of formal condolence with us on our "great loss." No doubt he mistook us for blood relatives, or felt that we had anyhow to represent the family, since there was nobody else to do it.

Mr. Lancaster's act impressed me a great deal. I strongly approved of suicide on principle, because I thought of it as an act of protest against society. I wanted to make a saga around Mr. Lancaster's protest. I wanted to turn him into a romantic figure. But I couldn't. I didn't know how.

The next year I did at last go to Berlin, having thrown up my medical career before it was properly started. And there, some while later, I ran into Waldemar. He had grown bored with his native city and had come to Berlin to seek his fortune.

Waldemar, naturally, knew very little about Mr. Lancaster's death. But he told me something which amazed me. He told me that Mr. Lancaster had often spoken of me, after I had left, to people in the office. Waldemar had heard him say that I had written a book, that it had been a failure in England because the critics were all fools, but that I should certainly be recognized one day as one of the greatest writers of my time. Also, he had always referred to me as his nephew.

"I believe he was really fond of you," said Waldemar, sentimentally. "He never had any son of his own, did he? Who knows, Christoph, if you'd been there to look after him, he might have been alive today!"

If only things were as uncomplicated as that!

I think I see now that Mr. Lancaster's invitation to me was his last attempt to re-establish relations with the outside world. But of course it was already much too late. If my visit had any decisive effect on him, it can only have been to show him what it was that prevented him from having any close contact with anybody. He had lived too long inside his sounding box, listening to his own reverberations, his epic song of himself. He didn't need me. He didn't need any kind of human being; only an imaginary nephew-disciple to play a supporting part in his epic. After my visit he created one.

Then suddenly, I suppose, he ceased to believe in the epic any more. Despair is something horribly simple. And though Mr. Lancaster had been so fond of talking about it, he probably found it absolutely unlike anything he had ever imagined. But, in his case, I hope and believe, it was short-lived. Few of us can bear much pain of this kind and remain conscious. Most of the time, thank goodness, we suffer quite stupidly and unreflectingly, like the animals.

KATHLEEN
AND FRANK
(1971)

[Isherwood chose and commented on selections from his mother's diaries and his father's letters in *Kathleen and Frank*, a chronicle of their Edwardian courtship and marriage. His father, a professional soldier, was reported missing in action on April 28, 1915. This afterword follows a description of the death of his mother in 1960.]

WHEN CHRISTOPHER came back to St. Edmund's in September 1915, after his summer of convalescence, he wore a black crape band around his sleeve. He had now acquired a social status which was respected by everybody in wartime England, including the Crown, the Church and the Press: he was an Orphan of a Dead Hero. At St. Edmund's there were only two or three others who shared this distinction, and at first he was vain of it; it made you, or rather your mourning armband, slightly sacred. The band mustn't on any account be torn or even rumpled, and therefore you yourself couldn't be attacked as long as you were wearing your jacket with the band on it. This taboo had been established by the boys, not the staff. They had done it without any discussion, instinctively, for they had the psychology of primitive tribesmen and could recognize a numen when they saw one. What they couldn't understand was the grown-up concept of grief as a continuing state of mind which had to be maintained, inwardly and outwardly, over a long period; to this they merely paid lip service. When Christopher reappeared amongst them he was greeted with "Bad luck, Isherwood!," which was their formula of condolence and excused them from further sympathy. If Christopher, or any other bereaved boy, happened to remember his loss and was moved to shed a few tears over it, that was something he had to cope with by himself, like an attack of hiccups. If, on the other hand, he felt like ragging, all he needed to do was strip off his jacket and join in the fun; none of his schoolfellows would think this improper.

However, Christopher soon found that being a Sacred Orphan had grave disadvantages—that it was indeed a kind of curse which was going to be upon him, seemingly, for the rest of his life. Henceforward, he was under an obligation to be worthy of Frank, his Hero-Father, at all times and in all ways. Cyril and Rosa were the first to make him aware of this obligation. Later there were many more who tried to do so: people he actually met, and disembodied voices from pulpits, newspapers, books. He began to think of them collectively as The Others.

It was easy for these impressive adults to make a suggestible little boy feel guilty. Yet he soon started to react against his guilt. Timidly and secretly at first, but with passion, with a rage against The Others which possessed him to the marrow of his bones, he rejected their Hero-Father. Such a rejection leads to a much larger one. By denying your duty toward the Hero-Father, you deny the authority of the Flag, the Old School Tie, the Unknown Soldier, The Land That Bore You and the God of Battles. Christopher's realization that he had done this—and that he must tell The Others he had done it—came to him only by degrees and not until he was nearly grown up. The rejection caused him much anxiety at first and some moments of panic; later it gave him immense relief and even a little courage.

Richard too rejected the nursery version of the Hero-Father:

I did so hate being everlastingly reminded of him, when I was young. Everybody kept saying how perfect he was, such a hero and so good at everything. He was always held up as someone you could never hope to be worthy of, and whenever I did anything wrong I was told I was a disgrace to him. You know, I used to have a recurring nightmare that he wasn't dead after all and that he was coming back to live with us! And then I was horrified, and I wanted to run away from home and hide somewhere before he arrived. I used to simply loathe him.

In 1968 Richard read some of Frank's letters which Christopher had just copied. They astonished him, he said; they made Frank seem like somebody quite different—a human being, in fact. Richard was glad to have Frank and the Hero-Father finally disentangled from each other in his mind; but he couldn't be expected to feel strongly about him as a person. He had been less than four years old when Frank was killed, and hardly remembered him at all.

With Christopher it was a different matter. He hadn't grieved much for Frank in 1915, but that was because he had then regarded Frank's death chiefly as an injury done to Kathleen. He had also been jealous of Frank when he came between him and Kathleen by dying and thus monopolizing her emotions. And then the Hero-Father had come between him and Frank. Nevertheless, the Frank he had known was still in his memory: the Frank who had told stories and drawn drawings for him and taught him the magic of make-believe. He wasn't going to surrender his Frank to The Others. They could keep their Hero-Father. He would create a father figure of his own, the anti-heroic hero he now needed—and therefore declared Frank to have been.

This wasn't difficult. Nothing had to be invented. Christopher had only to select certain of Frank's characteristics, doings and sayings (which meant censoring the rest) and make a person out of them, giving it Frank's body and voice.

The Anti-Heroic Hero always appears in uniform, because this is his disguise; he isn't really a soldier. He is an artist who has renounced his painting, music and writing in order to dedicate his life to an antimilitary masquerade. He lives this masquerade right through, day by day to the end, and crowns his performance by actually getting himself killed in battle. By thus fooling everybody (except Christopher) into believing he is the Hero-Father, he demonstrates the absurdity of the military mystique and its solemn cult of War and Death.

When one understands this, one sees that all his behavior is intentionally subversive. He shows his contempt for army documents by doing comic sketches on them, and for his dignity as an officer by knitting in the midst of a bombardment. He tells Christopher that his sword is useless except for toasting bread and that he never fires his revolver because he can't hit anything with it and hates the bang it makes. There was a report, which Christopher accepted because he wanted to believe it, that Frank had last been seen signaling directions to his men with a short swagger cane as he led them into action.

Christopher made this symbolic: The Anti-Heroic Hero mocks the loud Wagnerian Hero-Death by flourishing a stick like a baton at it, as if conducting an opera.

In November 1935, while he was staying in Brussels, Christopher decided, on a sudden impulse, to visit Ypres. Kathleen had occasionally hinted that it would be "nice" if he did. And he himself had always felt a curiosity, slightly mixed with fear, about Frank's deathplace. Afterward he wrote in his diary:

Roeslare is a sordid little cobbled town; it is here that you begin to smell the War. The girl at the café said she hoped there'd be another war soon, as then they'd earn some money. We drove in a bus over the plain to Ypres. Almost all the houses are new and bright pink—here and there the darker bricks mark the outlines of a former ruin. There are no trenches to be seen, only fragments of concrete gun-emplacements and pillboxes, among the fields.

The towers of Ypres, which looked grand in the distance against the sunset, in the cup of the plain, are new and quite meaningless, like London County Council architecture, when you see them close. The Menin Gate— ugly enough, in any case, to be an entrance for the Wembley Exhibition— is made merely absurd by being piled up against the end of the street, on to which it doesn't fit. We searched for Daddy's name and finally found it, high up in a corner, heading a list of Addenda. The town is certainly "forever England"—the England of sordid little teashops, faked souvenirs and touts.

Christopher's visit to Ypres had been on November 11; he can't now remember if this was by accident or design, but the violence of his reactions may have been partly due to the date, for he always hated Armistice Day and thought of it as being preeminently The Day of The Others.

So this was the vulgar sarcophagus in which they imagined they held Frank enshrined! Christopher declared that it was empty. No Hero-Ghost could ever come forth from it to delight them by disowning his unworthy son. The real Frank was beyond their reach. And, far from disowning his son, he gave him his blessing. Christopher had proof of this, in Frank's own handwriting.

Kathleen probably showed Christopher Frank's letters of March 15 and April 9 soon after she received them, at Ventnor in 1915. If she did, it isn't surprising that they made no great impression on him at that time. Frank was still alive then, and Christopher had yet to be confronted with the Hero-Father. It was only much later that he began to see their enormous value to himself, as a statement of Frank's last wishes and a speech for his defense: "I don't think it matters very much what Christopher learns as long as he remains himself and keeps his individuality and develops on his own lines . . ." (Christopher censored the rest of the sentence, about his laziness.) "The whole point of sending him to school was . . . to make him like other boys . . . I for one would much rather have him as he is."

Christopher interpreted this freely as *"Don't* follow in my footsteps! Be all the things I never was. Do all the things I never did and would have liked to do—including the things I was afraid of doing, if you can guess what they were! Be anything except the son The Others tell you you ought to be. I *should* be ashamed of that kind of son. I want an Anti-Son. I want him to horrify The Others and disgrace my name in their eyes. I shall look on and applaud!"

A Hero-Father leaves behind him a Holy Widow-Mother, who shames her children by her sacred grief. Like Charles the First, she teaches them to "remember!," which actually means "avenge!" Kathleen was sometimes pressured by The Others into playing this role, for she too was intimidated by them. It was therefore the duty of the Anti-Son to rescue Kathleen from them, by pouring scorn on the Holy Widow role whenever she tried to assume it.

As Holy Widow, Kathleen had to believe that Frank's death had been an irreparable loss to Christopher and Richard. As Anti-Son, Christopher had to challenge this. He did so quite sincerely, for he was convinced that Richard and he had both been better off without Frank as they grew up. Speaking for himself, he could say that all he really required was his *idea* of a father—the Anti-Heroic Hero. If you are in temporary need of an adviser, an inspirer or a backer, a willing substitute-father can usually be found; it is a mutually agreeable relationship, easily terminated. No, to be honest, he hadn't needed Frank.

And what kind of a father would Frank have been in his fifties and sixties, if he had survived to become a brigadier general and the commandant of Kneller Hall? He might have tried hard to understand Christopher as a young man of the Freudian twenties, but how could he possibly have succeeded, with all his prejudices, his snobbery, his "Early English" attitudes? At best they might have agreed to differ like gentlemen, after Christopher had wasted years of precious youth-time breaking the dreadful news slowly to Frank about boy-love—then later about marxism, and finally pacifism. It was more likely that Frank would have forgotten he had ever wanted Christopher to "develop on his own lines"; that he would have ended by disowning this Anti-Son.

But Christopher did need Kathleen. Frank had been right about him in saying that his danger was laziness; he had to have an opponent to prod him continually into revolt. The Others were no good for this, because they lacked conviction. Their religion and their moral indignation were fundamentally hypocritical. As opponents, they were hopelessly unserious. And the contempt you finally learned to feel for them didn't strengthen you, it merely made you cynical and therefore weaker.

Kathleen's opposition, on the other hand, was serious. It sprang from the depths of her nature—even when her cause was absurd and indefensible. For example, one morning in January 1928 she had looked up from reading the newspaper and remarked, "I can't think why they want to bury that ridiculous Thomas Hardy in the Abbey." Christopher was so furious with her that he got up and left the room, to her genuine dismay. In general she deferred to Christopher's opinions about writers, and she knew that he admired this one greatly. Also, she would have been the first to agree that one shouldn't insult the newly dead. Yet some ancient prejudice against Hardy—maybe dating back to the public attacks on *Jude the Obscure* in 1895—had suddenly asserted itself, sweeping all other considerations aside!

It was wonderful how naturally they disagreed. Christopher used to say that if Kathleen and he had landed on an alien planet where there were two political parties about which they knew nothing, the Uggs and the Oggs, she would have instantly chosen one of them and he the other, simply by reacting to the sound of their names.

Kathleen's opposition was rooted in obstinacy; as she grew older, obstinacy became the form in which her astonishing vitality most often expressed itself. Her skepticism was obstinate; she could never *quite* take anything for a fact, and this she showed by the almost daily use of "it seems" and "it appears" in her diary. Her sense of duty was obstinate. Her patriotism was obstinate. Her religious belief was obstinate. Even her mourning for Frank was obstinate—and much admired by everybody, except Christopher. He wanted her either to remarry, so that he would feel no more responsibility for her, or else to forget Frank and submit to him, Christopher, in all things, so that they might be friends. What Christopher didn't realize until many years later was that, in either of these events, the loss would have been his: he would have lost the counterforce which gave him strength.

It was Kathleen, more than anybody else, who saved him from becoming a mother's boy, a churchgoer, an academic, a conservative, a patriot and a respectable citizen. His friends were all rebels in their different ways, they set him an example and gave him plenty of encouragement; but without Kathleen's counterpressure and the rage it inspired in him, he might still have wavered and lapsed. It was she who made the snug home-womb uninhabitable, despite his desire to hide in it. It was she who thrust the Church upon him as an intolerable loyalty-test, thus making sure he wouldn't betray his own beliefs by accepting its security. It was she who stopped him from pretending to himself that he could be happy in the academic world, by confronting him with her dream-portrait of Christopher as a delightful dead-alive don. Her talk about the necessity of choosing a career which "led somewhere" drove him to venture into the studios of Chelsea and the slums of Berlin, despite his timid misgivings. Her peculiarly feminine patriotism disgusted him with England, the Motherland, thus causing him to be attracted to Germany, the Fatherland which had killed the Hero-Father. When he defiantly told her he was homosexual, she didn't seem at all upset. But this, he suspected, was because she simply didn't believe that a relationship without a woman in it could be serious, or indeed anything more than an infantile game. He sensed her assurance that he would one day have children, *her* grandchildren—never mind what became of the wretched cheated wife! This arrogant demand of hers would have been enough to deter Christopher from the cowardly crime of an unnatural respectable-mock marriage, if he had ever felt tempted to commit it.

Kathleen, he knew, felt their quarrels deeply and grieved over them in private. Yet he didn't feel guilty. He could see that they gave her strength as well as himself. And she and he remained intimate in their opposition. He continued to tell her in detail about every book he was planning or had begun to work on. She was always a member of his private audience. One of the aims of his writing—never quite achieved—was to seduce her into liking it in spite of herself.

His final ritual act of breaking free from her was to become a citizen of the United States, thus separating himself from Mother and Motherland at one stroke. But this was equally a recognition of the fact that the days of his opposition to Kathleen were over. Ironically, his life in the States had involved him more and more in activities which she would be able to approve of, at least partially. By teaching in colleges he had become an academic, even if he had also become a clown. By embracing Vedanta he had joined the ranks of the religious, even while remaining anti-church. By opposing those fellow citizens whom he regarded as a menace to his adopted country he had turned into a patriot, even though his enemies did all the flag-waving. So, when he later came back to England on visits, Kathleen and he had more common ground to meet on than ever before. When they were about to part for the last time, in 1959, she told him she was glad he had settled in America, because he had evidently found happiness there. This was a tremendous concession on her part, and it moved him very much. He took it as her blessing.

About 1960, Christopher began to consider a project which he called *The Autobiography of My Books*; it was to be a discussion, as objective as possible, of the relation between his own life and the subject matter of his books. The questions asked would be: To what extent do these books describe their writer's life? In what ways and for what reasons do they distort or hide facts about it? How far do the writer's father- and mother-characters resemble his own parents? What are the main themes of these books and how do they relate to the writer's personal problems? And so on.

Before starting to write this *Autobiography*, Christopher tried thinking out loud about it by giving a series of lectures. But the lectures showed him he didn't know his subject sufficiently well. He needed to study his Family and his own childhood in depth. So he began by questioning Richard and later borrowed from him Kathleen's diaries and Frank's letters, which Richard had kept at Wyberslegh.

While reading through these, Christopher saw how heredity and kinship create a woven fabric; its patterns vary, but its strands are the same throughout. Impossible to say exactly where Kathleen and Frank end and Richard and Christopher begin; they merge into each other. It is easy to dismiss this as a commonplace literary metaphor; hard to accept it as literal truth in relation to oneself. Christopher has found that he is far more closely interwoven with Kathleen and Frank than he had supposed, or liked to believe.

And as he went on reading he made another discovery. If these diaries and letters were part of his project, he was part of theirs—for they in themselves were a project, too. Its nature was revealed by those coy but broad hints dropped by Kathleen and by Frank: "Perhaps someone will be glad of it, some day," "What a pity your husband's life is never likely to be written!," "I hope posterity when they read this won't think I am grumbling."

So now Christopher's project has become theirs; their demand to be recorded is met by his eagerness to record. For once the Anti-Son is in perfect harmony with his Parents, for he can say, "Our will be done!" *Kathleen and Frank* will seem at first to be their story rather than his. But the reader should remember *The Adventures of Mummy and Daddy*, that lost childhood work, and Kathleen's ironical comment on it (November 6, 1909). Perhaps, on closer examination, this book too may prove to be chiefly about Christopher.

LIONS
AND SHADOWS
(1938)

[W. H. Auden and Isherwood were friends from childhood, when both attended St. Edmund's School in Surrey. This excerpt from *Lions and Shadows* characterizes Auden as a young artist and describes the early friendship of the two men.]

AT MY PREPARATORY SCHOOL, during the last two years of the War, there had been a boy named Hugh Weston. Weston—nicknamed "Dodo Minor" because of the solemn and somewhat birdlike appearance of his bespectacled elder brother—was a sturdy, podgy little boy, whose normal expression was the misleadingly ferocious frown common to people with very short sight. Both the brothers had hair like bleached straw and thick, coarse-looking, curiously white flesh, as though every drop of blood had been pumped out of their bodies—their family was of Icelandic descent.

Although Weston was three years younger than myself, he had reached the top form before I left the school. He was precociously clever, untidy, lazy and, with the masters, inclined to be insolent. His ambition was to become a mining engineer; and his playbox was full of thick scientific books on geology and metals and machines, borrowed from his father's library. His father was a doctor: Weston had discovered, very early in life, the key to the bookcase which contained anatomical manuals with coloured German plates. To several of us, including myself, he confided the first naughty stupendous breath-taking hints about the facts of sex. I remember him chiefly for his naughtiness, his insolence, his smirking tantalizing air of knowing disreputable and exciting secrets. With his hinted forbidden knowledge and stock of mispronounced scientific words, portentously uttered, he enjoyed among us, his semi-savage credulous schoolfellows, the status of a kind of witch-doctor. I see him drawing an indecent picture on the upper fourth form black-board, his stumpy fingers, with their blunt bitten nails, covered in ink: I see him boxing, with his ferocious frown, against a boy twice his size; I see him frowning as he sings opposite me in the choir, surpliced, in an enormous Eton collar, above which his great red flaps of ears stand out, on either side of his narrow scowling pudding-white face. In our dormitory religious arguments, which were frequent, I hear him heatedly exclaiming against churches in which the cross was merely painted on the wall behind the altar: they ought, he said, to be burnt down and their vicars put into prison. His people, we gathered, were high Anglican. As a descendant of a Roundhead judge, I felt bound in honour to disagree with him, and sometimes said so: but I could never work up much enthusiasm, even in those argumentative days, for ritualistic questions.

Weston and I met again, by purest chance, seven years later. Just before Christmas, 1925, a mutual acquaintance brought him in to tea. I found him very little changed. True, he had grown enormously; but his small pale yellow eyes were still screwed painfully together in the same short-sighted scowl and his stumpy immature fingers were still nail-bitten and stained—nicotine was now mixed with the ink. He was expensively but untidily dressed in a chocolate-brown suit which needed pressing, complete with one of the new fashionable double-breasted waistcoats. His coarse woollen socks were tumbled, all any-how, around his babyishly shapeless naked ankles. One of the laces was broken in his elegant brown shoes. While I and his introducer talked he sat silent, aggressively smoking a large pipe with a severe childish frown. Clumsy and severe, he hooked a blunt dirty finger round the tops of several of the books in my shelves, over-balancing them on to his lap and then, when his casual curiosity was satisfied, dropping them face downwards open on the floor—serenely uncon-scious of my outraged glances.

But when my acquaintance, who had another engagement, had gone, Weston dropped some of his aggressive academic gaucherie: we began to chatter and gossip: the preparatory-school atmosphere reas-serted itself. We revived the old jokes; we imitated Pillar cutting bread at supper: ("Here you are! Here you are! Help coming, Waters! Pang-slayers coming! Only one more moment before that terrible hunger is satisfied! Fight it down, Waters! Fight it down!") We remembered how Spem used to pinch our arms for not knowing the irregular verbs and punish us with compulsory fir-cone gathering. We tried to reconstruct the big scene from Reggy's drama, *The Waves*, in which the villain is confronted by the ghost of the murdered boy, seated in the opposite chair: ("The waves . . . the waves . . . can't you hear them calling? Get down, *carrse* you, get down! Ha, ha—I'm not afraid! Who says I'm afraid? Don't stare at me, *carrse* you, with those great eyes of yours. . . . I never feared you living; and I'm demned if I fear you now you're—*dead*! Ha, ha! Ha, ha! Ha ha ha ha ha ha ha!") Weston was brilliant at doing one of Pa's sermons: how he wiped his glasses, how he coughed, how he clicked his fingers when somebody in chapel fell asleep: ("Sn Edmund's Day. . . . Sn Edmund's Day. . . . Whur ders it *mean*? Nert—whur did it mean to *them, then, theah*? Bert—whur ders it mean to *ers, heah, nerw*?") We laughed so much that I had to lend Weston a handkerchief to dry his eyes.

Just as he was going, we started to talk about writing. Weston told me that he wrote poetry nowadays: he was deliberately a little over-casual in making this announcement. I was very much surprised, even rather disconcerted. That a person like Weston (as I pictured him) should write poems upset my notions of the fitness of things. Deeper than all I. A. Richards' newly implanted theories lay the inveterate prejudices of the classical- against the modern-sider. People who un-derstood machinery, I still secretly felt, were doomed illiterates: I had an instantaneous mental picture of some childish, touchingly crude verses, waveringly inscribed, with frequent blots and spelling mistakes, on a sheet of smudgy graph-paper. A bit patronizingly, I asked if I might see some of them. Weston was pleased, I thought. But he agreed ungraciously—"Right you are, if you really want to"—his bad manners returning at once with his shyness. We parted hastily and curtly, quite as though we might never bother to see each other again.

A big envelope full of manuscript arrived, a few mornings later, by post. The handwriting, certainly, was all I had expected, and worse. Indeed, there were whole lines which I have never been able to de-cipher, to this day. But the surprise which awaited me was in the poems themselves: they were neither startlingly good nor startlingly bad; they were something much odder—efficient, imitative and extremely competent. Competence was the last quality I had been prepared for in Weston's work: he had struck me as being an essentially slap-dash person. As for the imitation, it needed no expert to detect two major influences: Hardy and Edward Thomas. I might have found Frost there, too; but, in those days, I hadn't read him.

Here are four which I now think the best—chiefly because they most successfully resemble their originals:

THE TRACTION ENGINE

Its days are over now; no farmyard airs
Will quiver hot above its chimney-stack; the fairs
It dragged from green to green are not what they have been
In previous years.

Here now it lies, unsheltered, undesired,
Its engine rusted fast, its boiler mossed, unfired,
Companioned by a boot-heel and an old cart-wheel,
In thistles attired,

Unfeeling, uncaring; imaginings
Mar not the future; no past sick memory clings,
Yet it seems well to deserve the love we reserve
For animate things.

THE ENGINE HOUSE

It was quiet in there after the crushing
Mill; the only sounds were the clacking belt
And the steady throb of waters rushing
That told of the wild joy those waters felt
In falling. The quiet gave us room to talk:
"How many horse-power is the large turbine?"
"Seventy. The beck is dammed at Greenearth Fork:
Three hundred feet of head. The new pipe-line
Will give another hundred though, at least;
The mill wants power badly." He turned a wheel;
The flapping of the driving-belt increased

And the hum grew shriller. He wiped a steel
Rail with a lump of waste. "And now," he said,
"I'll show you the slimes-house and the vanning shed—
This way." He opened a small wooden door
And the machinery leaped into a roar.

RAIN

This peace can last no longer than the storm
Which started it, this shower wet and warm,
This careless striding through the clinging grass
Perceiving nothing; these will surely pass
When heart and ear-drums are no longer dinned
By shouting air: as surely as the wind
Will bring a lark-song from the clouds, not rain,
Shall I know the meaning of lust again;
Nor sunshine on the weir's dull dreamless roar
Can change me from the thing I was before,
Imperfect body and imperfect mind
Unknowing what it is I seek to find.
I know it: yet for this brief hour or so
I am content, unthinking and aglow,
Made one with horses and with workmen, all
Who seek for shelter by a dripping wall
Or labour in the fields with mist and cloud
And slant rain hiding them as in a shroud.

THE ROOKERY

When we were half asleep we thought it seemed
Stiller than usual; but no one dreamed
That aught was wrong until we came downstairs
And looked, as we had done these many years,
At the huge wall of elms that flanked the lawn
And shouted every time a wind was born.
Someone cried "Look!": we crowded to the pane:
Their tops still glittering from last night's rain,
They swayed a little, and upon their boughs
Swung to and fro each black untidy house

The rooks had made in some past century,
And mended every springtime. But no rook
Showed dark against the early sky, or shook
Down twigs, or cawed; a hungry fledgling's cry,
Waiting a breakfast that would never come,
Was all we heard; the world seemed stricken dumb.
"The rooks have gone, have gone. . . ." We said no word;
But in the silence each one's thought was heard.

Six months later—this was July 1926—Weston came down to stay with me at the seaside. I see him striding towards me, along Yarmouth Pier, a tall figure with loose violent impatient movements, dressed in dirty grey flannels and a black evening bow-tie. On his straw-coloured head was planted a very broad-brimmed black felt hat.

This hat I disliked from the start. It represented, I felt, something self-conscious and sham, something that Oxford had superimposed upon Weston's personality; something which he, in his turn, was trying to impose upon me. He wore it with a certain guilty defiance: he wasn't quite comfortable in it; he wanted me to accept it, with all its implications—and I wouldn't. I will never, as long as I live, accept any of Weston's hats. Since that day, he has tried me with several. There was an opera hat—belonging to the period when he decided that poets ought to dress like bank directors, in morning cut-aways and striped trousers or evening swallow-tails. There was a workman's cap, with a shiny black peak, which he bought while he was living in Berlin, and which had, in the end, to be burnt, because he was sick into it one evening in a cinema. There was, and occasionally still is, a panama with a black ribbon—representing, I think, Weston's conception of himself as a lunatic clergyman; always a favourite role. Also, most insidious of all, there exists, somewhere in the background, a school-master's mortarboard. He has never actually dared to show me this: but I have seen him wearing it in several photographs.

The black hat caused a considerable sensation in the village where I was staying. The village boys and girls, grouped along the inn wall by the bus stop, sniggered loudly as we got out of the bus. Weston was pleased: "Laughter," he announced, "is the first sign of sexual attraction." Throughout the journey, he had entertained our fellow passengers and embarrassed me furiously by holding forth, in resonant Oxonian tones: "Of course, intellect's the only thing that matters at *all*. . . . Apart from Nature, geometry's all there *is*. . . . Geometry belongs to man. Man's got to assert himself against Nature, all the *time*. . . . Of course, I've absolutely no use for colour. Only form. The only really exciting things are volumes and *shapes*. . . . Poetry's got to be made up of images of form. I hate sunsets and flowers. And I loathe the *sea*. The sea is formless . . ."

But however embarrassing such statements might be to me, when uttered in public vehicles, they never for a moment made me feel— as I should have felt if a Poshocrat had been speaking—that Weston himself was a sham. He was merely experimenting aloud; saying over the latest things he had read in books, to hear how they sounded. Also they were a kind of substitute for small talk: for Weston, in his own peculiar way, made strenuous attempts to be the model guest. He really wanted every minute of his visit to be a success—on the highest intellectual plane. I was touched and flattered to discover, bit by bit, that he admired me; looked up to me, indeed, as a sort of literary elder brother. My own vanity and inexperience propelled me into this role easily enough: nowadays I should think twice about assuming such a responsibility—for Weston, who was as lazy as he was prolific, agreed without hesitation to any suggestion I cared to make; never stopping to ask himself whether my judgment was right or wrong. If I wanted an adjective altered, it was altered then and there. But if I suggested that a passage should be rewritten, Weston would say: "Much better scrap the whole thing," and throw the poem, without a murmur, into the waste-paper basket. If, on the other hand, I had praised a line in a poem otherwise condemned, then that line would reappear in a new poem. And if I didn't like this poem, either, but admired a second line, then both the lines would appear in a third poem, and so on— until a poem had been evolved which was a little anthology of my favourite lines, strung together without even an attempt to make connected sense. For this reason, most of Weston's work at that period was extraordinarily obscure.

Over, in any case, were the days of his pastoral simplicity. Since our meetings at Christmas, Weston's literary tastes had undergone a violent revolution. Hardy and Edward Thomas were forgotten. Eliot was now the master. Quotations and misquotations were allowed, together with bits of foreign languages, proper names and private jokes. Weston was peculiarly well equipped for playing the *Waste Land* game. For Eliot's Dante-quotations and classical learning, he substituted oddments of scientific, medical and psycho-analytical jargon: his magpie brain was a hoard of curious and suggestive phrases from Jung, Rivers, Kretschmer and Freud. He peppered his work liberally with such terms as "eutectic," "sigmoid curve," "Arch-Monad," "ligature," "gastropod"; seeking thereby to produce what he himself described as a "clinical" effect. To be "clinically minded" was, he said, the first duty of a poet. Love wasn't exciting or romantic or even disgusting; it was funny. The poet must handle it and similar themes with a wry, bitter smile and a pair of rubber surgical gloves. Poetry must be classic, clinical and austere.

I got very tired of the word "austere" in the course of the next few days: I began to wonder whether it didn't, as a rule, mean simply "pompous" or "priggish." At this time, Weston was a warm admirer of the works of Edwin Arlington Robinson: Robinson, it appeared, was very austere indeed. We nearly had a serious quarrel over:

> *The forehead and the little ears*
> *Have gone where Saturn keeps the years*

a couplet which he particularly liked, but which I thought, and still think, unintentionally very funny.

"Austerity" was also mixed up with Weston's feelings about the heroic Norse literature—his own personal variety of "War"-fixation. Naturally enough, he had been brought up on the Icelandic sagas; for they were the background of his family history. On his recommendation, I now began, for the first time, to read *Grettir* and *Burnt Njal*, which he had with him in his suitcase. These warriors, with their feuds, their practical jokes, their dark threats conveyed in puns and riddles and deliberate understatements ("I think this day will end unluckily for some, but chiefly for those who least expect harm"): they seemed so familiar—where had I met them before? Yes, I recognized them now: they were the boys at our preparatory school. Weston was pleased with the idea: we discussed it a good deal, wondering which of our schoolfellows best corresponded to the saga characters. In time, the school-saga world became for us a kind of Mortmere—a Mortmere founded upon our preparatory-school lives, just as the original Mortmere had been founded upon my life with Chalmers at Cambridge. About a year later, I actually tried the experiment of writing a school story in what was a kind of hybrid language composed of saga phraseology and schoolboy slang. And soon after this, Weston produced a short verse play in which the two worlds are so confused that it is almost impossible to say whether the characters are epic heroes or members of a school O.T.C.

In the intervals of all this talk, we bathed, got mildly drunk at the village pub and sang hymns to the accompaniment of Weston's banging on the piano in our lodgings. Weston, despite the apparent clumsiness of his large pudgy hands, was a competent pianist. He could never resist the sight of a piano, no matter whether it was in the refreshment room of a German railway station or the drawing-room of a strange house: down he would sit, without so much as taking off his hat, and begin to play his beloved hymn tunes, psalms and chants—the last remnants of his Anglican upbringing. When he had finished the keyboard would be littered with ash and tobacco from his huge volcano-like pipe. He smoked enormously, insatiably: "Insufficient weaning," he explained. "I must have something to *suck*." And he drank more cups of tea per day than anybody else I have ever known. It was as if his large, white, apparently bloodless body needed continual reinforcements of warmth. Although this was the height of the summer, he insisted, if the day was cloudy, on having a fire in the sitting-room. At night he slept with two thick blankets, an eiderdown, both our overcoats and all the rugs in his bedroom piled upon his bed.

When he had gone, I sat alone in my seaside lodgings and felt sorry: despite the fact that my most precious books were full of nicotine stains and dirty thumb-prints, that a hole had been burnt in my overcoat with a lighted cigar, and that I could hardly venture to show my face in the pub, since Weston had been practically turned out of it for loudly quoting the most lurid lines of Webster and Tourneur. With or without his hat, Weston was a most stimulating companion; and his short visit had excited and disturbed me profoundly. He had given me a badly needed shaking-up. Inevitably, I compared him with Chalmers. When Chalmers and I were together there were, and had always been, certain reticences between us: parts of our lives were common ground, other parts were not—and these, by mutual consent, we respected and left alone. The same thing was true of my other friends, Philip, the Cheurets, Eric. But Weston left nothing alone and respected nothing: he intruded everywhere; upon my old-maidish tidyness, my intimate little fads, my private ailments, my most secret sexual fears. As mercilessly inquisitive as a child of six, he enquired into the details of my dreams and phantasies, unravelled my complexes and poked, with his blunt finger, the acne on my left shoulder-blade, of which, since the age of eighteen, I had been extravagantly ashamed. I had found myself answering his questions, as one always must answer, when the questioner himself is completely impervious to delicacy or shame. And, after all, when I had finished, the heavens hadn't fallen; and, ah, what a relief to have spoken the words aloud!

Weston's own attitude to sex, in its simplicity and utter lack of inhibition, fairly took my breath away. He was no Don Juan: he didn't run round hunting for his pleasures. But he took what came to him with a matter-of-factness and an appetite as hearty as that which he showed when sitting down to dinner. I don't think that, even in those days, he exaggerated much: certainly, his manner of describing these adventures bore all the marks of truth. I found his shameless prosaic anecdotes only too hard to forget, as I lay restlessly awake at night, listening to the waves, alone in my single bed.

MY GURU
AND HIS DISCIPLE
(1980)

[Isherwood's close relationship with Swami Prabhavananda, head of the Vedanta Society of Southern California, led to his writing a biography, *Ramakrishna and His Disciples*; a translation of *The Bhagavad-Gita*; and, after the Swami's death, *My Guru and His Disciple*. These chapters from the latter show Isherwood's use of his meticulous diaries.]

May 12, 1952. At Trabuco. I've been here since the 4th and plan to stay till the 21st. The Patanjali aphorisms are practically finished.

Now I'm trying to finish part one of my novel before I leave here. I feel very calm and in a way unwilling to leave. But I don't for a moment seriously consider becoming a monk again. I don't consider anything except how to get my novel written. My only worries are financial—how much of my "Camera" royalties should be set aside for income tax?

J., one of the monks, describes this group as "six individualists all going different ways." Yet they are wonderfully harmonious with each other, and all likable. "Too many people around here," says J., "are scared of the Old Man" (meaning Swami) "or they've got him figured all wrong. He's the only person I ever met in my life I like everything about."

I try to fit in unobtrusively and not get in the way of their routine. Am not getting much—or indeed anything, consciously—out of the meditation periods. But I often feel very happy. Hardly any trouble with sex, yet. I think that's mostly middle age. Anyhow, I certainly needed a rest!

I feel sympathy and liking for these boys, but their problems aren't very real to me, because their situation is so utterly different from mine.

They are stuck here. They plod around in their heavy work boots, much of the day, doing outdoor chores. Life here is much more physical than it was at the Hollywood Center. The place demands to be constantly maintained and they are stuck with it, like soldiers with a war. I'm like a correspondent, visiting the front for a few days only.

The chores I do are voluntary and therefore pleasurable—pulling weeds out of the vines or raking the kitchen garden in the blazing sunshine. The hot courtyard with the dark-leaved fruit trees has a sort of secret stillness; one feels hidden away, miles from anywhere. At night we look through the telescope, at Saturn, or at the ranger station on the top of the mountain.

May 19. Shall be going back to Santa Monica the day after tomorrow. I've done wonders of work since I arrived here. Finished Patanjali, finished part one of my novel and made a promising start on part two, worked over some Vedic prayers Swami wanted translated, written lots of letters, and pulled up lots of weeds.

When I typed out the title page of the Patanjali this morning, I wrote "by Swami Prabhavananda and Christopher Isherwood," and Swami said, "Why put <u>and</u>, Chris? It separates us."

It's impossible to convey the sweetness and meaning with which he said this. All day long, he fairly shines with love. It was the same when he was here earlier, at the beginning of my stay, and told us: "If you have a friend and do good things for him for years and years, and then do one bad thing—he'll never forgive you. But if you do bad things to God for years and years, and only one good thing—<u>that</u> He never forgets." What strikes me, again and again, is his complete assurance, and his smiling, almost sly air of having a private source of information.

I asked Swami how it is that he can always end a meditation period so punctually. He said it's like being able to sleep and wake up at a certain time, no matter how deeply you become absorbed. The notion that meditation periods should be of varying length, according to mood, is "romantic," he said.

January 27, 1953. Have been here at Trabuco since January 9. (On the 6th, Caskey and I said goodbye and he left for San Francisco, hoping to get a job on a freighter and ship out to the Orient.)

Today I finished the rough draft of my novel. I am very grateful for this tremendous breakthrough. 88 pages in 18 days, which is about two and a half times my normal writing speed, maintained despite the interruptions of shrine sitting, kitchen chores, ditch digging, and planting trees. I feel as if my whole future as a writer—even my sanity— had been at stake. And yet I daresay I seemed quite cheerful and relaxed, to the others. Such struggles go on deep underground.

This has been the toughest of all my literary experiences. A sheer frontal attack on a laziness block so gross and solid that it seemed sentient and malevolent—the Devil as incarnate tamas, or Goethe's eternally no-saying Mephistopheles. What with having given up smoking, getting no drink and no sex, I was nearly crazy with tension. I actually said to Ramakrishna in the shrine: "If it's your will that I finish this thing, then help me."

The diary version of my prayer to Ramakrishna needs further explanation. I had had, since childhood, an instinctive dislike of petitionary prayer—those church appeals to the Boss God for rain, the good health of the Monarch, victory in war. Swami didn't totally condemn it, but to me there was a sort of impertinence in asking God for the fulfillment of any worldly need. How was I to know what I really needed? I felt this all the more strongly because I didn't doubt that such prayers are quite often answered—or, to put it in another way, that you can sometimes impose your self-will on circumstances which *appear* to be outside your control. When I prayed, it was nearly always for some kind of spiritual reassurance or strength, for faith or devotion.

This prayer to Ramakrishna was therefore a breach of my own rule. What made me break it? I must have been reacting to the pressure which Swami had already begun putting on me, to write a biography of Ramakrishna. He was thus creating a conflict of interest between his project and mine. So I appealed to Ramakrishna to decide the issue. I remember feeling at the time that this was a kind of sophisticated joke—camp about prayer, rather than prayer itself. But camp, according to my definition, must always have a basis of seriousness. Ramakrishna would understand this perfectly.

My prayer could have been better phrased as follows: "Don't let me feel guilty about trying to write this novel. Either convince me that I must drop it altogether, or else take away my writer's block, so I can finish my book quickly and get started on yours."

I have recorded this simply as a psychological experience, not as a proof that Ramakrishna answered my prayer. The unbeliever will maintain that prayer is just oneself talking to oneself, and the Vedantist will partly agree with him, saying that it is the Atman talking to the Atman, since all else is illusion, from an absolute standpoint. Looking back, I can no longer blame Mephistopheles—or whatever one chooses to call the force that blocks an act of creation—even though he did nearly cause me to have a nervous breakdown. Indeed, I feel I ought to be grateful to him. He at least tried to stop me finishing what turned out to be my worst novel: *The World in the Evening*.

That spring, I realized that I had fallen deeply in love with a boy whom I had known for only a short while, Don Bachardy. He was then eighteen years old. The thirty-year difference in our ages shocked some of those who knew us. I myself didn't feel guilty about this, but I did feel awed by the emotional intensity of our relationship, right from its beginning; the strange sense of a fated, mutual discovery. I knew that, this time, I had really committed myself. Don might leave me, but I couldn't possibly leave him, unless he ceased to need me. This sense of a responsibility which was almost fatherly made me anxious but full of joy.

Don's first meeting with Swami was on May 21; Swami came with George to visit us. Don now remembers that "his gestures seemed very precise and delicate, the length of his hands impressed me, they were like long delicate fins; I was able to observe him physically because he didn't try to impress you with his personality, the way most people do."

All I now remember is that Swami made some approving remark about the look in Don's face. Others had noticed this, but their comments merely referred to a vitality, a shining eagerness for experience, which often moves us when we see it in the young. Swami, as I well knew, was able to detect more intrinsic values; he was like a jeweler who can recognize at a glance the water of a diamond. From that moment, I felt that Don, and thus our relationship, was accepted by him.

Gerald, too, accepted and approved of Don. Indeed, he spoke of our relationship as if it were a daring pioneer research project of great scientific importance, urging me to keep a day-to-day record of it. He had now begun to discuss publicly the problems of "the intergrade," meaning the homosexual, and the role which homosexuals might play in social evolution. He had also made what was, for him, a truly revolutionary pronouncement: "One used to believe that tenderness is polar to lust. Now one realizes that that isn't necessarily true."

All this was only part of an astonishing and mysterious transformation. For Gerald's health had greatly improved, and he seemed less dyspeptic, less puritanical, warmer, merrier. He could now be persuaded to accept an occasional glass of sherry and would sometimes even eat meat. One happy result of this transformation was that he and I resumed our old friendship, with Don included in it.

These are two dreams which I had about Swami during 1953:

August 21. I was sharing a bed with Swami in a house which I knew to be a male whorehouse. (I knew this but I don't know how I knew it; there were no other people in the dream, and the room was an ordinary, quite respectable-looking bedroom.) Except that we were sharing a bed, our relations were as they always are. I was full of respect and consideration for him. We were just about to get up and I suggested that he should use the bathroom first. He didn't react to this. But he said, "I've got a new mantram for you, Chris. It is: 'Always dance.' " "What a strange mantram!" I said. Swami laughed: "Yes, it surprised me, too. But I found it in the scriptures."

December 16. This dream was a kind of companion piece to the other, for Swami and I were again in a bedroom. This time, I didn't know that we were in a whorehouse. My vague impression was that this was a hotel and that we were there because we were making a journey together. I was helping Swami get undressed to go to bed. I felt eager

*to attend to all his wants and was very respectful, as before. When I
tried to help him put on his bathrobe, we found that it had somehow
got entangled with mine—the sleeves of my robe were pulled down into
his. Swami said, "Oh, so you have a bathrobe? I was going to give you
mine." And I said, "But I can throw mine away."*

The mood in both these dreams was joyful, but there was more
fun in the first of them and more sentiment in the second. My bringing
Swami into a whorehouse suggests to me a desire to introduce him to
another part of my life, in which he had no share. (Actually, I had
had very little experience of whorehouses myself; and that had been
years earlier.) This dream whorehouse, where no boys are visible,
seems symbolic, anyhow. Sharing a bed with Swami represents a
situation of absolute chastity. Perhaps this was inspired by a memory
of my sensations while using Swami's bedroom, when he was away
from the Center, in 1943.

The dream mantram, "Always dance," makes me think of something which hadn't yet happened at the time of my dream; shortly
before Maria Huxley's death, in 1955, she told a woman friend, "Always wear lipstick." This was a remark which beautifully expressed
Maria's particular kind of courage—taking care to look your best, even
when you are sick and afraid of dying, in order to spare the feelings
of those who love you. "Always dance" could have a similar meaning.
But it also seems to me to refer to Ramakrishna's dancing in ecstasy.
Since this is described throughout *The Gospel of Sri Ramakrishna*,
Swami could truly say that he had "found it in the scriptures."

In the second dream, Swami's bathrobe, with the sleeves of my
bathrobe pulled down into its sleeves, seems an image of the guru's
involvement with his disciple. Hindus believe that it is risky to wear
other people's clothes or use their personal belongings. If you do, you
may to some extent inherit the consequences of the former owner's
thoughts and actions. But your guru is an exception. His cast-off
clothes and belongings cannot bring you anything but good.

The nuns at the Center had enthusiastically adopted this belief.
They would carry off, to keep or distribute, almost anything which
Swami had owned and now didn't want. As the Vedanta Society grew,

and Swami got more and more birthday and other gifts, the turnover became rapid, and devotees treasured mementos of Swami which he had barely had time to use or even touch.

Through the next two years, my diary keeping has many lapses. Here are my only diary entries about Swami in 1955:

March 2. After supper, Swami had a class in the living room. He was asked what it was like to live with an illumined soul—specifically with Brahmananda and Premananda. He answered, "What attracted me was their wonderful common sense." Then he said how few people bothered to come and see Ramakrishna while he was alive, though most of them became ardent devotees after he was dead. I couldn't help thinking that this applies to Swami and myself, nowadays, and I hoped he wasn't thinking the same thing. Later, when we were alone together in his room, he talked about U.

(This was an old lady who had just died, while staying at the Center. In her youth, she had known Vivekananda and some of the other direct disciples.)

Swami recalled how terribly afraid she had been of dying. "And then, when it happened, she didn't feel anything. How very merciful they were to her!"

June 20. On Father's Day, Swami passed on to me a shaving brush he'd just been given but didn't need, because he uses an electric razor. I gave him a bottle of sherry, which had to be hidden from a party of visiting Hindus, who were severely orthodox.

(Swami sometimes drank a glass or two before meals. Alcohol was approved by his doctors as a relaxant, especially in view of the prostate trouble he suffered from in later life. Swami wasn't being hypocritical when he refrained from drinking in the presence of those who would have been shocked by it; he simply tolerated their prejudice, which he anyhow found unimportant.)

. . .

August 25. I called Swami and asked him for his blessing on my birthday tomorrow. He said, "Live many years and I'll watch you from heaven."

September 14. This evening I was up at the Center. Swami looked very well and happy. He said, "I get so bored with philosophy nowadays— even Shankara." Then he told me that this morning, in the shrine room, he had been intensely aware of the presence of Swamiji and Maharaj. "If there hadn't been anyone else there, I'd have bawled."

He says his favorite chapter in the Gita is chapter 12, on the Yoga of Devotion. He says, "I used to want visions and ecstasies—now I don't care. I only pray to love God. I don't care to lecture, now. But when I start talking, I enjoy myself. I enjoy talking about God." (I thought to myself: He's like a young man in love.)

Swami said, "Webster came to me the other day. He said to me, 'Swami, it's your fault that I left the Center. You should have used your power to stop me.' I asked him if he was meditating and making japam. He said, 'No. You must make me do it.' I was very touched. Such devotion!"

(On several other occasions, I had heard Swami rebuke devotees who took Webster's attitude and asked him, so to speak, to do their praying for them. He told them that they were just lazy. So I was all the more impressed by his belief in Webster's sincerity.)

In October 1955, Don and I left for Europe, to visit Italy, Switzerland, Germany, France, and England. We got back to Los Angeles in March 1956.

In my diary, I note that "Swami, with his usual persistence, brought up the question of the Ramakrishna book again." This means that I hadn't kept my part of the bargain made in the Trabuco shrine room three years earlier. Now that my novel was long since published and our traveling was over for the present, I had no more excuses to offer. I knew I must start writing *Ramakrishna and His Disciples* at once. Wanting to do this on an auspicious day, I picked April 1. This year, it was both All Fools' Day and Easter Sunday.

. . .

After our return from Europe, I began to see a good deal of one of the monks at the Hollywood Center. As John Yale, he had become a monastic probationer in 1950. We had met from time to time during the past six years, but not often, because of my various absences from Los Angeles and his journey to India in 1952–53, visiting the Ramakrishna monasteries there—this he later described in his book, *A Yankee and the Swamis*, published in 1961. By 1956, he had taken his first vows (brahmacharya) and been renamed Prema Chaitanya. (*Prema* means "ecstatic love of God." *Chaitanya*, "awakened consciousness," is always added to the other given name of a brahmachari of the Ramakrishna Order.)

Prema was then still in his thirties, slightly built but tough and energetic. He had dark hair and a pale handsome face which sometimes showed great inner suffering but was nevertheless youthful-looking. Before joining the Order, he had been a successful publisher in Chicago. Now he was working to build up the business of the bookshop at the Center, and doing this so efficiently that its mail-order earnings were becoming an important part of the Vedanta Society's assets. He also helped edit our magazine, which would begin printing my Ramakrishna book, chapter by chapter, as it got written. Thus Prema and I found ourselves in constant collaboration.

I often thought that, if Prema and I had arrived at the Center at the same time and begun our monastic life together, we might have been a real support to each other. Certainly we had much in common. We had both revolted against the moral precepts of our upbringing. We both had severe standards of efficiency and were apt to be impatient of the sloppy and the slapdash. We both suffered from self-will and the rage which it engenders. He was more desperate than I, and his desperation might have taught me his courage. I was more diplomatic than he, and might have saved him from offending many people by his outspokenness.

As things turned out, however, our relationship had its frictions. The Chris whom Prema met must have been a disappointment to him. No doubt he had expected a good deal from the part-author of the *Gita* translation which had renewed his religious faith when he had first read it, back in the nineteen-forties. But now I had become a worldling, no longer subject to monastic discipline. My visits to

Swami were like those of a Prodigal Son who returns home again and again, without the least intention of staying, and is always uncritically welcomed by a Father who scolds every other member of the family for the smallest backsliding. I know that Prema was drawn to me, as I was to him, but I must have seemed a creature of self-indulgence and self-advertisement, with the easy modesty of the sufficiently flattered and a religion which was like a hedged bet on both worlds. Prema often envied me and sometimes hated me. He confessed this with touching frankness.

April 14, 1956. With Swami, George, and Prema to a meeting at a women's club, where Swami had to speak for twenty minutes to open a prayer-discussion group. Swami in a gray suit with a pearl-gray tie. He must always seem, at first sight, so much less "religious" than the sort of people who introduce him on these occasions; more like a doctor or even a bank manager than a minister. The stage was hung with blue velvet curtains; on one side, the flag. The audience chiefly composed of women in very small hats, many of them with folded-back veils in which tiny spangles sparkled.

June 15. This afternoon, Swami came to tea, along with George and Prema. Don was pleased because I told him that serving a meal to a swami would probably save him 500 rebirths. After they had left, he drank the remains of Swami's tea as prasad. I think that reading my 1939–44 diary has made him much more interested in everything to do with Vedanta.

June 22. Don and I went to tea at the Center. Swami said to Don, as we were leaving, "Come again—every time Chris comes."

July 15. Swami called today, much worried because Maugham had sent him an essay on the Maharshi, and all the philosophy in it was wrong! Now we have to concoct a tactful reply.

(The Maharshi, a famous holy man, had died only a few years before this. Maugham had met him during a trip to India in 1936. I can't remember what mistakes Maugham made in expounding the Maharshi's philosophy. Our letter, pointing them out, must have been sufficiently tactful, for Maugham replied gratefully and made the suggested alterations in his essay "The Saint." This was published, with four others, in *Points of View*, in 1959.)

October 25. This morning, I went to see Swami. He was in his most loving mood. He seemed entirely relaxed by love, as people are relaxed by a few drinks. He just beamed.

We were talking about the possible number of inhabited worlds. Swami said, "And, only think, the God who made those thousands of worlds comes to earth as a man!" Something about the way he said this—his wonder and his absolute belief, I suppose—made my skin raise goosepimples. I said, "How terrifying!" and that was exactly how I felt. It's quite impossible to convey in words the effect made on you by a situation like this—because what matters isn't what is said but the speaker himself, actually present before you and giving you, in some otherwise quite ordinary sentence, a glimpse of what he is.

He told me that one of his ambitions is to found a boarding school, one half for boys, the other for girls, where "they would be given the ideal"—first on the high-school level, later on the university level. He remarked that boys always seem more restless than girls. They always feel that they ought to do something or get something. Swami would tell them, "You have to be something."

He repeated what he has so often told me, that he feels in all his work responsible to Brahmananda. When he initiates disciples, he hands them over to Brahmananda or to Holy Mother. He would like to stop giving lectures, but if he tries to shirk any duty, he finds that he loses touch with Brahmananda: "I can't find him; then I know he is displeased."

Going to see Swami is like opening a window in my life. I have to keep doing this, or my life gets stuffy. It doesn't matter what we talk about. He said, "Come again soon. I like seeing you, Chris," and I told him I think about him all the time and have conversations with him in my mind. I was moved, as we parted, and felt shy.

. . .

November 8. Went to see Swami—today being the 16th anniversary of my initiation (and the 10th anniversary of my becoming a U.S. citizen!). Swami said that drugs could never change your life or give you the feeling of love and peace which you got from spiritual visions. Drugs only made you marvel—and then later you lost your faith.

In May 1953, having volunteered to be a subject for the psychiatric researches of Dr. Humphry Osmond, Aldous Huxley had taken four tenths of a gram of mescaline. Early the next year, he had published *The Doors of Perception*, an account of his experiences under the drug. Since then, Aldous and Gerald had been meeting occasionally with a few friends, either to take mescaline or lysergic acid or to talk about the insights they had obtained from them. It should be emphasized that the talking was far in excess of the taking; these were all prudent people of high intellectual seriousness, not thrill seekers on a spree.

At the height of the psychedelic-drug craze in the nineteen-sixties, it wasn't unusual to hear a taker claim casually that he or she had been in samadhi. It was generally accepted that all spiritual states could be drug-induced. To Swami, this was a deadly heresy, and he regarded Aldous and Gerald as its originators. Actually, their statements on the question varied slightly from time to time and left their hearers or readers with differing impressions.

Swami himself had had only one experience with any kind of hallucinogen; while he was still a young monk in India, he had been given by his fellow monks, as a practical joke, a liquid prepared from hemp. Not knowing what this was, Swami had drunk a lot of it and had had disagreeable psychic visions followed by a long period of spiritual dryness, during which he had lost his faith altogether. My diary account of his story continues:

I asked him, hadn't he considered leaving the monastery at that time? "NO!"—Swami can say that word with more emphasis than anyone I have ever known—"Why should I do that? Because I had stopped believing in God, that did not mean that I believed in the world."

But I wasn't ready to accept Swami's condemnation without experimenting for myself. I had asked both Aldous and Gerald to let me join in a drug session and had got evasive answers. Then I was told, by a third party, that they had agreed I was too unstable emotionally to be a suitable subject. I was indignant, and at once decided to try mescaline on my own. In 1955, it was still legal. I had bought some tablets while Don and I were in New York, about to sail for Europe.

On our way there, while stopping off in Tangier, we had had an unexpected opportunity to try hashish. Puffing at kif cigarettes and gobbling majoun with the overeagerness of beginners, we launched ourselves into a nightmare adventure. Don became paranoid; I discovered claustrophobia. Looking back, twenty-four hours later, I had felt that this had brought Don and me even closer together; it was like a shared physical danger. I had reacted to it by making japam. But I might equally well have done that if we had been on a small boat in a storm. The adventure itself couldn't be described as spiritual.

About four months after this, in London, I took one of the mescaline tablets, alone; we had agreed that Don should remain an objective observer of my behavior. In general, the effects were very much as I had heard them described. I felt exhilarated. My senses, particularly my sight, seemed extraordinarily keen. Certain patches of color were almost scandalously vivid. Faces on the street looked like caricatures of themselves, each one boldly displaying its owner's dominant characteristic—anxiety, vanity, aggression, laziness, extravagance, love.

I told Don that we must take a taxi to the Catholic cathedral in Westminster, "to see if God is there." God wasn't. His absence was so utter that it made me laugh. So we went on to Westminster Abbey. Here the situation appeared even more comic to me. I had to go into a dark corner and stay there until I could control my giggles.

The Abbey's old rock-ribbed carcass was greatly shrunken; I felt I was inside a dead dried-up whale. And it was full of ridiculous statues— the one of Sir Cloudesley Shovell was especially pleasing. No God there. Nothing alive at all. Even the poppies around the tomb of the Unknown Soldier were artificial.

I had taken mescaline twice more after this, later in 1956, with almost exactly the same effects. I still didn't feel sure enough of the nature of the experience to be able to agree wholeheartedly either with

Swami or with Aldous and Gerald. I therefore said as little as possible whenever the subject was being discussed by either party.

During November 1956, a young man whom Swami and I both knew was arrested and charged with sexual solicitation in a men's washroom. Swami's reaction was: "Oh, Chris, if only he hadn't got caught! Why didn't he go to some bar?"

This was one of the times when Swami's unworldly worldliness made me laugh out loud.

November 22. Have just returned from seeing Swami. He talked about grace—how Maharaj had told them that there are some people who just get it. "God can't be bought." Even if you do all the japam and spiritual disciplines, you still can't command enlightenment. It's always given by grace.

Swami's younger brother went into samadhi while being initiated by Swami Saradananda. Then, as he grew older, he became an extremely avaricious lawyer. But, no matter what he does, he is liberated. On his deathbed, he'll "remember."

January 23, 1957. Swami took us to the little house in South Pasadena (309 Monterey Road) where Vivekananda stayed for a few weeks in 1900. Went upstairs to his bedroom, which has been made into a shrine since the Vedanta Society took the house over. Sat there with Swami, while the other guests chattered loudly downstairs. Swami meditated and I tried to concentrate on his meditation. What a privilege—to be with him in Vivekananda's presence! Felt a keen elation. I was so safe with him. I tried to hold this feeling. I want some of it for when I'm dying. How could I be afraid then, if I felt he was with me?

On February 12, I discovered a small tumor on the side of my lower abdomen. It hadn't been there the previous night when I went to bed. Even on first examining it, the doctor didn't think it was malignant, though he said it must be removed at once, to make sure. So I went through three days of dread, this being my first cancer scare. What really shocked me was how suddenly such a growth can appear.

During the waiting period, I saw Swami. Without telling him about the tumor, I got him talking on the subject of death.

He said he now isn't afraid of dying at all—though of course he would prefer to avoid pain. This life seems to him "all shadows." He was very convincing, and I believed in his belief. But there is one problem which he doesn't have—the extra pain I would feel in parting from Don, knowing that he isn't a devotee. I certainly don't want to go to the plane of existence, the loka, where the devotees of Ramakrishna are said to go, unless I could believe he'd be following me there.

(The tumor did prove to be non-malignant.)

February 21. I feel a new or renewed relationship to Swami. This has been growing for months. It's as if he were exposing me to stronger and stronger waves of his love—yet, all the while, making almost no personal demands on me. I saw him last night—still, as he said, "floating a little," after an operation he had had on a cyst. He was like a small adorable animal with ruffled fur as he sat on his bed telling us about the early days in the monastery in India. I don't feel he is altogether a person any longer.

March 3. This evening, we drove up to the Center in time to catch the end of the vespers of the Ramakrishna puja and be touched by Swami with the tray of relics. It was Don's own idea that he should come with me and do this and I was very happy that he suggested it. (When we went to vespers at the Brahmananda puja on February 1, he didn't come forward to be touched—because, I suppose, he didn't want to commit himself and perhaps get in too deep.)

April 10. I've just been up to the Center. Swami told me that he dreamt he was handing out copies of my book on Ramakrishna to crowds of people, and he was saying, "Chris's book!" I was there, too, in his dream.

Swami is very excited about the book and wildly overoptimistic. He says it will be "a turning point in the growth of the Society."

And now for the first time I dimly get a new conception of the book. I want to introduce some autobiographical material, telling how I myself got to know about Ramakrishna. I mentioned this to Swami this evening. He said, "However you write it will be all right."

. . .

June 12. To see Swami. When I put out my hand to shake his, he first made me bend down and gave me his blessing. He seldom does this. He told me, "Whenever you think of God, He thinks of you."

August 23. Swami told me that George is going to India to take the vows of sannyas sometime next spring. That got us talking about him. How, from being a comic figure, he has developed during these past fifteen years. He's still cantankerous and obstinate, but he's so devoted and so full of love that Swami feels he is turning into "a great soul."

September 13. Not to be sly—this is the essence of a revelation Prema feels he's had, as the result of cooking for Swami at a cabin camp up in the Sierras. Prema says he used to be ashamed of Swami because he sounded off and yelled at people and banged the table; but now he sees that it's wonderful not to be afraid to show one's feelings. "We must be bold," Prema said. "We mustn't be conservative."

He told me that Swami spent most of his time shut up in his cabin, and that his mood seemed continuously indrawn.

September 18. Saw Swami for the first time since he got back from the Sierras. I remarked that Prema had told me he had spent most of his time in his cabin, and he said, "Yes, I was having such a wonderful time with the Lord."

It is a measure of my psychological double vision that I can both accept this statement as literally true and marvel that such a statement, made by anybody, could ever be literally true.

I realize, more and more, that Swami is my only link with spiritual life. But that's like a San Franciscan saying that the Golden Gate Bridge is his only link with Marin County. What more could I ask for?

I was very much moved as we sat together and Swami told me that he wants to have this joy not only occasionally but always. "Then I can pass it on to you all."

"It's all Maharaj," he said. "Everything he told me is coming true. I didn't understand him at the time. Now I begin to know what he was talking about."

Swami keeps repeating that Maharaj matters most to him—more than Ramakrishna, because Swami actually knew Maharaj. "And that's how I feel about you," I said. "Ah, but, Chris, I am like a little pebble against the Himalayas." "I have absolute confidence in you, Swami," I said, with tears in my eyes but still aware how funny it sounded.

September 25. Swami told me about Swami Sankarananda, who is now president of the Ramakrishna Order. He used to be Brahmananda's secretary. Sankarananda became officious in the performance of his duties and took it upon himself to decide which visitors should be allowed to meet Brahmananda and which should not. When Brahmananda found out what was happening, he got very angry. He sent Sankarananda away to live in another monastery and refused to see him for years. In fact, Brahmananda waited until he himself was dying before he allowed Sankarananda to come back, and forgave him.

I have accepted the idea that Brahmananda's scoldings, even when they were unjustified, could be spiritually beneficial. But his behavior, in this instance, really puzzles me. Swami defends it by saying that it gave Sankarananda an opportunity to show his greatness of character by remaining in the Order and not bearing Brahmananda any ill will. He also says that Brahmananda lent people strength to endure his displeasure. However, Swami does admit that he was shocked, at that time, and even protested to Brahmananda against his seeming cruelty. So this is maybe one of the things Swami was referring to the other day—the things he has only come to understand lately, about Maharaj.

On October 8, Don and I began a journey which would take us right around the world. We flew to Japan, spending two weeks there, then on to Hong Kong, from which we took a boat to Singapore and Bali and back to Singapore. Then we flew to Bangkok, with a side trip to Angkor. Then, on November 30, we flew from Bangkok to Calcutta.

Visiting Calcutta and its neighborhood was the reason for our whole journey, from Swami's point of view. I had told him that, before I wrote the final draft of my biography, I wanted to see the places associated with Ramakrishna. There are not many of them—the villages of Kamarpukur (his birthplace) and Jayrambati (the birthplace of Holy Mother), which are about three miles apart from each other and seventy from the city, and also a few buildings within the Calcutta area, notably the temple at Dakshineswar, where Ramakrishna spent nearly all of his adult life.

I arrived in Calcutta suffering from the ill effects of some bug picked up in Bangkok. This made the necessary sightseeing depressing for both of us, although it was well organized by some of the swamis of the Order, chiefly Vitashokananda. After four days we were invited by them to leave our grand but dirty hotel and move into the simple clean guesthouse of the Belur Math. While we were there, we briefly met Sankarananda, now a massive stately courteous old man whose health was failing.

On December 9, we flew from Calcutta to London, and on January 12, 1958, from London to New York. We got back to Los Angeles on January 30.

On December 11, 1957, while we were staying in London, I had had a dream about Brahmananda.

The first part of my dream had no particular location. I was somewhere talking to someone in monastic robes whom I knew to be Brahmananda. I say "knew" rather than "recognized," because I had no clear image of his physical features—although they were so familiar to me when I was awake, because of all the photographs I had seen.

Brahmananda said to me that he couldn't understand why Ramakrishna had traveled from one place to another, since he was able to see God anywhere. I went away and thought this remark over. Then I decided to go back and ask Brahmananda why *he* had traveled around so much—far more, actually, than Ramakrishna had.

When I returned to put my question, Brahmananda was seated on a platform; this was about six feet high, with trees growing behind it. Both the platform and the trees were somewhat Japanese in appearance. (Remembering them after waking, I thought that I might have borrowed them from the scenery of the Kyoto temples, which Don and I had recently visited.)

As I approached the platform, Brahmananda prostrated before me. And I prostrated before him, shedding tears and thinking of my unworthiness but also feeling a tremendous joy. Although my forehead was bowed down to the ground below the platform and the platform was so high, I felt Brahmananda's hands touching the back of my head in blessing—which would have been physically impossible for him. (This may have signified that the power of a blessing cannot be limited by distance.)

I suppose that the astonishment and joy caused by Brahmananda's prostration and blessing made me forget about my question. Anyhow, I didn't ask it. As I got up and walked away from the platform, there were suddenly other people around me. One of them asked, "Did Maharaj tell you anything you may tell *us?*" This was said with deep respect. I knew that Brahmananda's behavior toward me had made them regard me as someone of importance. I shook my head, still shedding tears but now beginning to feel vain and take credit to myself for the grace which had been shown me. Then I woke up.

During my dream, it had seemed to me that I understood why Brahmananda prostrated before me. I had interpreted his action by relating it to a scene in Dostoevsky's *The Brothers Karamazov*, in which the saintly Father Zosima bows down at Dmitri Karamazov's feet. Zosima later explains that he had bowed down to the great suffering which he saw was in store for Dmitri.

However, when I was awake again and was considering the dream, I realized that this interpretation couldn't be correct. Zosima's reaction, produced by Dostoevsky's own obsession with suffering and guilt, would be quite foreign to Brahmananda's way of thinking as a Vedantist. Even if my karma was as bad as Dmitri's, Brahmananda would still regard me as an embodiment of the Atman, not as a *jiva*, an individual soul living in ignorance of its divine nature. I now interpreted Brahmananda's prostration as a reminder—the Atman in himself was bowing down to the Atman in me in order to remind me of what I truly was. Brahmananda, unlike Zosima, had not only bowed down but also blessed me as an individual soul, thus reassuring me that he loved and accepted me even with all my present imperfections.

Although my dream had had a dreamlike setting, my change of attitude in it, from humble thankfulness to smug self-congratulation, had been psychologically life-like. I had been very much my ordinary self throughout it, despite its extraordinary happenings. Thus it had had some of the quality of a normal experience.

I now realized that I had never, before this, felt strongly drawn to Maharaj. That was because I had misunderstood his nature, finding him awesome and remote. Vivekananda's humorous, aggressive, sparkling personality attracted me much more because he seemed more human—that is, more of an individual. But what my dream experience had given me was a moment's awareness of a love which was larger than human. For the first time, I began to understand what Swami meant when he said that Maharaj had *become* love. That, perhaps, was why I had been conscious of him in my dream as a presence, rather than as an outwardly recognizable person.

When I described all this to Swami, he assured me that my dream had actually been a vision. He was speaking from his own experience in stating that you could have a vision either when awake or when asleep; both kinds were equally valid.

"It was a great grace," he told me solemnly. On another occasion, speaking to Prema, he interpreted this vision as having been a sign from Maharaj that I was the proper person to write the Ramakrishna biography. How like Swami that was! When he had set his heart on something, it *had* to have the Lord's blessing.

March 13, 1958. Swami told me that the people at Belur Math had written that George had been utterly transformed by sannyas in a single day—but they didn't say how. George himself had written: "Three days ago, I became a Brahmin. Two days ago, I became a ghost—one always becomes what one fears! Yesterday I became Krishnananda." There is a majestic note of impersonality in this last sentence. It's like when you say, in the ritual worship, "I am He."

(George was referring to different stages of his preparation to take the vows of sannyas. The sannyasin has to renounce all caste distinctions. Since you can't renounce what you haven't got, George had first to be admitted into the highest caste, that of the Brahmins. Taking sannyas is regarded as a spiritual rebirth. Since you can't be reborn as long as you are still alive, George had first to think of himself as having died and become a ghost.)

March 28. Swami said he has only recently discovered that God's grace is actually in the mantram. Maharaj had told him that this was so.

. . .

April 24. Swami says that visions don't matter—only devotion matters. He told me to "remember the Lord."

May 9. Swami said that enlightenment is not loss of individuality but enlargement of individuality, because you realize that you're everything.

June 26. Swami told me that he feels the presence of the Lord almost continuously; he no longer has to make much of an effort. When he wakes up in the night—which he has to do, two or three times, to go to the toilet, because of his prostate trouble—he feels the presence. Sometimes it is Ramakrishna, sometimes Holy Mother, Maharaj, or Swamiji. I asked if it made any difference that he had known Maharaj and seen Holy Mother during their lifetimes, but not the others. No, he said, they were all equally real.

He says he never prays directly for problems to be solved. He only asks for more devotion to the Lord.

August 22. Unwillingly, I have to admit to myself that the whole introductory section of Ramakrishna and His Disciples—telling how I personally came to know about him—is irrelevant. I've written seventy pages and it's not that they're bad; they just don't belong in this book. I can probably use them, one of these days, somewhere else.

(The Vedanta Society's press published a revised version of this material in 1963, as a pamphlet called *An Approach to Vedanta*.)

August 31. Swami told me on the phone that a well-known actress came to him and asked if she should go to India. Swami said, "Why? You won't get anything out of India unless you have reached something inside yourself." He then asked her if she had been meditating according to his instructions. When she told him no, he "got all excited" and told her not to come back until she had done so for a month. So then she got out of her chair and sat on the floor at Swami's feet and said, "Teach me once again." So he did, and she went away—on probation!

. . .

November 19. Tonight I went up to the Center. Suddenly I was so glad to be sitting on the floor beside Swami's chair—like his dog, without saying a word. After supper, I read them the revised first chapter of the Ramakrishna book.

December 11. Swami told me that he'd had "a terrible time" that morning, in the shrine room: "I mean, a good terrible time." He had been overpowered by the knowledge that "there is abundant grace." He had cried so much that he had had to leave the temple. He said, what was the use of reasoning and philosophy, when all that mattered was love of God.

Early in January 1959, while I was having supper with Swami, he mentioned the apartment house which the Vedanta Society was about to have built, as an income property. Several devotees were planning to move into it. He urged me and Don to take one of the apartments.

To have done this would have been almost the same as moving into the Center itself, right across the street. We should have become involved in all its activities, to the gradual exclusion of our own. No doubt, Swami would soon have got into the habit of sending for me at all hours, just as he would send for one of the monks or nuns, whenever he was troubled by an anxiety or inspired by a new project . . . No, the apartment house was out of the question for us, and I never considered it seriously, though I had to pretend to him for a while that I was doing so.

Swami's suggestion was obviously his first move in another back-to-the-monastery campaign. This time, my relationship with Don was under attack. When monk- or nun-making was possible, one had to accept the fact that Swami, being Swami, would do his best to break up any worldly relationship, however fond he might be of the individuals involved in it.

Though I knew better than to try to persuade Don, I did, of course, hope that he might eventually become Swami's disciple. I longed to share that part of my life with him. But, in that case, Swami would have to accept us as a pair of householder devotees. I couldn't imagine myself becoming a monk again under any circumstances, as long as I had Don. If Don were to decide to become a monk, I suppose I might have followed him back into the Order—even though I knew that this would be a separation; a more painful one, perhaps, than death or desertion. Swami would keep us living apart from each other in different centers. He had already "put asunder" several married couples who wished to become monastics, sending the wife to Montecito and the husband to Trabuco. The old permissive days of the single Hollywood household were long since over.

April 29, 1959. Swami told us he believes that he, as an old man during his last incarnation, met Brahmananda as a young man. This was during the eighteen-eighties, on the bank of the river Narmada, where they were both practicing austerities.

I don't think I had ever heard Swami say this before—as he grew older, he revealed more and more of his past life. If I had heard this earlier, I should have remembered it as a possible explanation of Maharaj's otherwise mysterious question, when he and Abanindra first met: "Haven't I seen you before?"

Swami's statement also relates to a story which is printed in his book about Brahmananda, *The Eternal Companion*:

I was sitting cross-legged in front of Maharaj with his feet resting on my knees. This was the position in which I often used to massage his feet. Then something happened to me which I cannot explain, though I feel certain that it was Maharaj's doing. I found myself in a condition in which I was talking and talking, forgetting my usual restraint; it seemed to me that I spoke freely and even eloquently for a long time, but I do not remember what I said. Maharaj listened and said nothing.

Suddenly I returned to normal consciousness and became aware of Maharaj leaning toward me and asking with an amused smile, "What did you say?" I then realized that I had addressed him as "tumi" (the familiar form of "you," which is used in speaking to equals and friends). I hastened to correct myself, repeating the sentence—I have forgotten what it was—but using "apani" (the respectful form of "you," by which we addressed him). At this, he seemed to lose all interest in the conversation and sat upright again.

I can only assume that Maharaj wanted to corroborate his own intuitive knowledge of my past lives and that he therefore put me into this unusual state of consciousness in which I was able to tell him what he wanted to know.

(The Hindus believe that memory of our past lives is stored in the mind and can be evoked by oneself or by another person. If Swami had been an old man at the time of this previous meeting with Brahmananda, it would have been natural for him to address the young Brahmananda familiarly.)

In the middle of that summer, one of the monks at Trabuco decided that he wanted to leave the Order and marry a woman he had met. He had been in the monastery for years and the monastic life had seemed to be his true and contentedly accepted vocation.

Swami had been known to get violently upset in such situations, shedding tears and lying awake for nights on end. On first hearing about the woman, he had exclaimed, "I'd like to poison her!" Later, however, he became calm and seemed almost indifferent—which rather hurt the monk's feelings. This intrigued me. When I questioned Swami, he showed a curious objectivity, as he often did when discussing his own reactions. "I couldn't pray for him, Chris. I don't know why. I only said that the Lord must do his will. I prayed three whole nights for ———," naming another monastic who had left the Order.

Swami's view was: Why did the monk have to marry this woman right away? Why didn't he go off with her somewhere and have an affair? Then he would probably get tired of her and want to come back to the Order. Swami was quite ready to take the monk back, as long as he wasn't married; but if he did rejoin the Order, Swami said, he would be sent to one of the Ramakrishna monasteries in India for a while, before returning to Trabuco. The monk finally got married, however.

Lest readers think that Swami's attitude to the woman betrayed male chauvinism, I should mention that on another occasion, when one of the nuns wanted to marry a man, Swami's attitude to him was equally ruthless.

. . .

On September 22, 1959, Swami left for India with five nuns who had just taken their final vows, thus becoming our first *pravrajikas*, female swamis. Swami returned three months later.

During 1960, my diary records almost nothing of interest about Swami or the Vedanta centers.

On September 17, I had a visit from one of the newer monks at Trabuco. He was obviously uncertain whether he wanted to go on living there or not and hoped to get some reassurance from me. Could I give it to him? *Should* I give it to him? I had been in this situation several times before, and it was always tricky.

He asked me about my time up at the Center in the nineteen-forties, why I joined and why I left. I tried to avoid presenting myself to him as a model he could identify with—pointing out that I didn't start off by deciding to become a monk, that I was drawn into the Center because of Swami's desire to have me as a collaborator on his Gita translation, that when I decided to leave there was no dramatic break, that I have continued to see Swami and be his collaborator ever since.

"So really," he asked, "it's much the same now as if you'd stayed on there being a monk?" But I couldn't let him think that. So I owned that there had been a "jazzy" (the words I sometimes pick!) period in my life after I'd left, and that, indeed, people had come to Swami and told him I was going to the dogs—and that Swami had charmingly shut them up . . . So then I got the conversation off onto Swami and how marvelously he has changed since I've known him—proving that the spiritual life does bring its reward . . . I hope he was satisfied.

(Apparently he wasn't, since he left the Order not long after this.)

December 26. Swami's birthday lunch. Swami radiant, all in white. "You don't have to tell me that you love me," he said to us, after the girls had sung the gooey second verse of the Happy Birthday song.

February 17, 1961. Today was the Ramakrishna puja, so I went to vespers. There were lots of people, and Swami unwisely decided to save time—he thought it would take too long for each one of us to come up into the shrine room, be touched by the relics, offer a flower, and leave again. So, instead, he came down out of the shrine room with the tray of relics and moved around among us, touching us with it as we sat on the floor of the temple. This arrangement would have worked if each person had got up and left the temple after being touched. Only, a lot of them didn't. Prema said he believed that one individual was dead drunk, but I think it was sheer affectation; some like to pretend to themselves that the touch of the relics has put them into a trance. Thus an absurd traffic jam was created and Swami became confused. So several were touched twice and others not at all.

March 2. Yesterday I called the Center and told them that I wouldn't be coming there for supper, as I usually do on Wednesdays—this was because I wanted to get on with my work. A bit later, Swami called me and said, "I'm lonely for you, Chris." It wasn't that he was nagging at me to come. He just felt like saying this, so he picked up the phone and said it. There are no strings attached to his love, therefore it is never embarrassed. The ordinary so-called lover is out to get something from his beloved, therefore he is afraid of going too far and becoming tiresome.

Don spent nearly all of that year in London, studying art at the Slade School. In April, I went over there to be with him. I returned in October.

In November, I went to stay at Trabuco with Swami and with Swami Ritajananda, who was leaving soon to take charge of the Vedanta Society at Gretz, just outside Paris.

As we sat in the cloister, with that marvelous still-empty prospect of lion-golden hills opening away to the line of the sea, I said to Swami: "You're really certain that God exists?"

He laughed: "Of course! If he doesn't exist, then I don't exist."

"And do you feel he gives you strength to bear misfortune?"

"I don't think of it like that. I just know he will take care of me. It's rather hard to explain. Whatever happens, it will be all right."

I asked him when he began to feel certain that God existed.

"When I met Maharaj. Then I knew that one could know God. He even made it seem easy . . . And now I feel God's presence every day. But it's only very seldom that I see him."

Later, after Ritajananda had joined us, Swami said, "Stay here, Chris, and I'll give you sannyas. You shall have a special dispensation from the Pope." He said this laughingly, but I had a feeling that he really meant it—otherwise, he surely wouldn't have said it in Ritajananda's presence.

I said, "Swami, that would be a mistake worthy of Vivekananda himself."

(This was an allusion to the fact that Vivekananda had sometimes given sannyas to Western disciples who were—judging from their subsequent behavior—quite unworthy of it.)

Swami says that the Hindu astrologers predict the world will come to an end next February 2nd. However, the astrologers themselves are praying that it shan't happen. I objected—rather cleverly, I thought— that Ramakrishna has predicted another incarnation for himself on earth, and that this contradicts any such prophecy. Swami agreed.

November 8. Yesterday evening, I got back from Trabuco and went up to the Hollywood Center to attend the Kali puja, just to please Swami. I never feel I have any personal part in it. It belongs, quite naturally, to the women, and how they dress up for it, in their saris! One of them had let her hair down, falling loose over her shoulders but, oh, so elegantly arranged. Well, it's their party . . . Meanwhile, I sat outside the shrine room in a corner and gossiped cozily in whispers with one of the monks from Trabuco, as we waited for Swami to asperse us with Ganges water. This he did vigorously, as if he were ridding a room of flies with DDT.

(This reminds me of another, earlier occasion, at a puja also being held at night, when Swami was about to asperse the assembled devotees. Suddenly he burst out laughing and exclaimed, "You look so funny, sitting there!" His laughter—in which, after a moment's shock, we all joined—shattered the gravity of this ancient ritual, making it now and new.)

A SINGLE MAN

(1964)

[A *Single Man*, Isherwood's personal favorite of his novels,
describes one day in the life of George, an Englishman who
teaches at a Los Angeles college.]

WAKING UP BEGINS with saying *am* and *now*. That which has awoken then lies for a while staring up at the ceiling and down into itself until it has recognized *I*, and therefrom deduced *I am, I am now*. *Here* comes next, and is at least negatively reassuring; because *here*, this morning, is where it has expected to find itself: what's called *at home*.

But *now* isn't simply now. *Now* is also a cold reminder: one whole day later than yesterday, one year later than last year. Every *now* is labeled with its date, rendering all past *nows* obsolete, until—later or sooner—perhaps—no, not perhaps—quite certainly: it will come.

Fear tweaks the vagus nerve. A sickish shrinking from what waits, somewhere out there, dead ahead.

But meanwhile the cortex, that grim disciplinarian, has taken its place at the central controls and has been testing them, one after another: the legs stretch, the lower back is arched, the fingers clench and relax. And now, over the entire intercommunication system, is issued the first general order of the day: UP.

Obediently the body levers itself out of bed—wincing from twinges in the arthritic thumbs and the left knee, mildly nauseated by the pylorus in a state of spasm—and shambles naked into the bathroom, where its bladder is emptied and it is weighed: still a bit over 150 pounds, in spite of all that toiling at the gym! Then to the mirror.

What it sees there isn't so much a face as the expression of a predicament. Here's what it has done to itself, here's the mess it has somehow managed to get itself into during its fifty-eight years; expressed in terms of a dull, harassed stare, a coarsened nose, a mouth dragged down by the corners into a grimace as if at the sourness of its own toxins, cheeks sagging from their anchors of muscle, a throat hanging limp in tiny wrinkled folds. The harassed look is that of a desperately tired swimmer or runner; yet there is no question of stopping. The creature we are watching will struggle on and on until it drops. Not because it is heroic. It can imagine no alternative.

Staring and staring into the mirror, it sees many faces within its face—the face of the child, the boy, the young man, the not-so-young man—all present still, preserved like fossils on superimposed layers, and, like fossils, dead. Their message to this live dying creature is: Look at us—we have died—what is there to be afraid of?

It answers them: But that happened so gradually, so easily. *I'm afraid of being rushed.*

It stares and stares. Its lips part. It starts to breathe through its mouth. Until the cortex orders it impatiently to wash, to shave, to brush its hair. Its nakedness has to be covered. It must be dressed up in clothes because it is going outside, into the world of the other people; and these others must be able to identify it. Its behavior must be acceptable to them.

Obediently, it washes, shaves, brushes its hair, for it accepts its responsibilities to the others. It is even glad that it has its place among them. It knows what is expected of it.

It knows its name. It is called George.

By the time it has gotten dressed, it has become *he*; has become already more or less George—though still not the whole George they demand and are prepared to recognize. Those who call him on the phone at this hour of the morning would be bewildered, maybe even scared, if they could realize what this three-quarters-human thing is that they are talking to. But, of course, they never could—its voice's mimicry of their George is nearly perfect. Even Charlotte is taken in by it. Only two or three times has she sensed something uncanny and asked, "Geo—are you *all right?*"

He crosses the front room, which he calls his study, and comes down the staircase. The stairs turn a corner; they are narrow and steep. You can touch both handrails with your elbows, and you have to bend your head, even if, like George, you are only five eight. This is a tightly planned little house. He often feels protected by its smallness; there is hardly room enough here to feel lonely.

Nevertheless . . .

Think of two people, living together day after day, year after year, in this small space, standing elbow to elbow cooking at the same small stove, squeezing past each other on the narrow stairs, shaving in front of the same small bathroom mirror, constantly jogging, jostling, bumping against each other's bodies by mistake or on purpose, sensually, aggressively, awkwardly, impatiently, in rage or in love—think what deep though invisible tracks they must leave, everywhere, behind them! The doorway into the kitchen has been built too narrow. Two people in a hurry, with plates of food in their hands, are apt to keep colliding here. And it is here, nearly every morning, that George, having reached the bottom of the stairs, has this sensation of suddenly finding himself on an abrupt, brutally broken off, jagged edge—as though the track had disappeared down a landslide. It is here that he stops short and knows, with a sick newness, almost as though it were for the first time: Jim is dead. Is dead.

He stands quite still, silent, or at most uttering a brief animal grunt, as he waits for the spasm to pass. Then he walks into the kitchen. These morning spasms are too painful to be treated sentimentally. After them, he feels relief, merely. It is like getting over a bad attack of cramp.

Today, there are more ants, winding in column across the floor, climbing up over the sink and threatening the closet where he keeps the jams and the honey. Doggedly he destroys them with a Flit gun and has a sudden glimpse of himself doing this: an obstinate, malevolent old thing imposing his will upon these instructive and admirable insects. Life destroying life before an audience of objects—pots and pans, knives and forks, cans and bottles—that have no part in the kingdom of evolution. Why? Why? Is it some cosmic enemy, some arch-tyrant who tries to blind us to his very existence by setting us against our natural allies, the fellow victims of his tyranny? But, alas, by the time George has thought all this, the ants are already dead and mopped up on a wet cloth and rinsed down the sink.

He fixes himself a plate of poached eggs, with bacon and toast and coffee, and sits down to eat them at the kitchen table. And meanwhile, around and around in his head goes the nursery jingle his nanny taught him when he was a child in England, all those years ago:

Poached eggs on toast are very nice—

(He sees her so plainly still, gray-haired with mouse-bright eyes, a plump little body carrying in the nursery breakfast tray, short of breath from climbing all those stairs. She used to grumble at their steepness and call them "The Wooden Mountains"—one of the magic phrases of his childhood.)

Poached eggs on toast are very nice,
If you try them once you'll want them twice!

Ah, the heartbreakingly insecure snugness of those nursery pleasures! Master George enjoying his eggs; Nanny watching him and smiling reassurance that all is safe in their dear tiny doomed world!

Breakfast with Jim used to be one of the best times of their day. It was then, while they were drinking their second and third cups of coffee, that they had their best talks. They talked about everything that came into their heads—including death, of course, and is there survival, and, if so, what exactly is it that survives. They even discussed the relative advantages and disadvantages of getting killed instantly and of knowing you're about to die. But now George can't for the life of him remember what Jim's views were on this. Such questions are hard to take seriously. They seem so academic.

Just suppose that the dead do revisit the living. That something approximately to be described as Jim can return to see how George is making out. Would this be at all satisfactory? Would it even be worth-while? At best, surely, it would be like the brief visit of an observer from another country who is permitted to peep in for a moment from the vast outdoors of his freedom and see, at a distance, through glass, this figure who sits solitary at the small table in the narrow room, eating his poached eggs humbly and dully, a prisoner for life.

The living room is dark and low-ceilinged, with bookshelves all along the wall opposite the windows. These books have not made George nobler or better or more truly wise. It is just that he likes listening to their voices, the one or the other, according to his mood. He misuses them quite ruthlessly—despite the respectful way he has to talk about them in public—to put him to sleep, to take his mind off the hands of the clock, to relax the nagging of his pyloric spasm, to gossip him out of his melancholy, to trigger the conditioned reflexes of his colon.

He takes one of them down now, and Ruskin says to him:

. . . you liked pop-guns when you were schoolboys, and rifles and Armstrongs are only the same things better made: but then the worst of it is, that what was play to you when boys, was not play to the sparrows; and what is play to you now, is not play to the small birds of State neither; and for the black eagles, you are somewhat shy of taking shots at them, if I mistake not.

Intolerable old Ruskin, always absolutely in the right, and crazy, and so cross, with his whiskers, scolding the English—he is today's perfect companion for five minutes on the toilet. George feels a bowel movement coming on with agreeable urgency and climbs the stairs briskly to the bathroom, book in hand.

Sitting on the john, he can look out of the window. (They can see his head and shoulders from across the street, but not what he is doing.) It is a gray lukewarm California winter morning; the sky is low and soft with Pacific fog. Down at the shore, ocean and sky will be one soft, sad gray. The palms stand unstirred and the oleander bushes drip moisture from their leaves.

This street is called Camphor Tree Lane. Maybe camphor trees grew here once; there are none now. More probably the name was chosen for its picturesqueness by the pioneer escapists from dingy downtown Los Angeles and stuffy-snobbish Pasadena who came out here and founded this colony back in the early twenties. They referred to their stucco bungalows and clapboard shacks as cottages, giving them cute names like "The Fo'c'sle" and "Hi Nuff." They called their streets lanes, ways or trails, to go with the woodsy atmosphere they wanted to create. Their utopian dream was of a subtropical English village with Montmartre manners: a Little Good Place where you could paint a bit, write a bit, and drink lots. They saw themselves as rear-guard individualists, making a last-ditch stand against the twentieth century. They gave thanks loudly from morn till eve that they had escaped the soul-destroying commercialism of the city. They were tacky and cheerful and defiantly bohemian, tirelessly inquisitive about each other's doings, and boundlessly tolerant. When they fought, at least it was with fists and bottles and furniture, not lawyers. Most of them were lucky enough to have died off before the Great Change.

The Change began in the late forties, when the World War Two vets came swarming out of the East with their just-married wives, in search of new and better breeding grounds in the sunny Southland, which had been their last nostalgic glimpse of home before they shipped out to the Pacific. And what better breeding ground than a hillside neighborhood like this one, only five minutes' walk from the beach and with no through traffic to decimate the future tots? So, one by one, the cottages which used to reek of bathtub gin and reverberate with the poetry of Hart Crane have fallen to the occupying army of Coke-drinking television watchers.

The vets themselves, no doubt, would have adjusted pretty well to the original bohemian utopia; maybe some of them would even have taken to painting or writing between hangovers. But their wives explained to them, right from the start and in the very clearest language, that breeding and bohemianism do not mix. For breeding you need a steady job, you need a mortgage, you need credit, you need insurance. And don't you dare die, either, until the family's future is provided for.

So the tots appeared, litter after litter after litter. And the small old schoolhouse became a group of big new airy buildings. And the shabby market on the ocean front was enlarged into a super. And on Camphor Tree Lane two signs were posted. One of them told you not to eat the watercress which grew along the bed of the creek, because the water was polluted. (The original colonists had been eating it for years; and George and Jim tried some and it tasted delicious and nothing happened.) The other sign—those sinister black silhouettes on a yellow ground—said CHILDREN AT PLAY.

George and Jim saw the yellow sign, of course, the first time they came down here, house-hunting. But they ignored it, for they had already fallen in love with the house. They loved it because you could only get to it by the bridge across the creek; the surrounding trees and the steep bushy cliff behind shut it in like a house in a forest clearing. "As good as being on our own island," George said. They waded ankle-deep in dead leaves from the sycamore (a chronic nuisance); determined, now, to like everything. Peering into the low damp dark living room, they agreed how cozy it would be at night with a fire. The garage was covered with a vast humped growth of ivy, half dead, half alive, which made it twice as big as itself; inside it was tiny, having been built in the days of the Model T Ford. Jim thought it would be useful for keeping some of the animals in. Their cars were both too big for it, anyway, but they could be parked on the bridge. The bridge was beginning to sag a little, they noticed. "Oh well, I expect it'll last our time," said Jim.

No doubt the neighborhood children see the house very much as George and Jim saw it that first afternoon. Shaggy with ivy and dark and secret-looking, it is just the lair you'd choose for a mean old storybook monster. This is the role George has found himself playing, with increasing violence, since he started to live alone. It releases a part of his nature which he hated to let Jim see. What would Jim say if he could see George waving his arms and roaring like a madman from the window, as Mrs. Strunk's Benny and Mrs. Garfein's Joe dash back and forth across the bridge on a dare? (Jim always got along with them so easily. He would let them pet the skunks and the raccoon and talk to the myna bird; and yet they never crossed the bridge without being invited.)

Mrs. Strunk, who lives opposite, dutifully scolds her children from time to time, telling them to leave him alone, explaining that he's a professor and has to work so hard. But Mrs. Strunk, sweet-natured though she is—grown wearily gentle from toiling around the house at her chores, gently melancholy from regretting her singing days on radio; all given up in order to bear Mr. Strunk five boys and two girls—even she can't refrain from telling George, with a smile of motherly indulgence and just the faintest hint of approval, that Benny (her youngest) now refers to him as "That Man," since George ran Benny clear out of the yard, across the bridge and down the street; he had been beating on the door of the house with a hammer.

George is ashamed of his roarings because they aren't play-acting. He does genuinely lose his temper and feels humiliated and sick to his stomach later. At the same time, he is quite well aware that the children want him to behave in this way. They are actually willing him to do it. If he should suddenly refuse to play the monster, and they could no longer provoke him, they would have to look around for a substitute. The question Is this playacting or does he really hate us? never occurs to them. They are utterly indifferent to him except as a character in their myths. It is only George who cares. Therefore he is all the more ashamed of his moment of weakness about a month ago, when he bought some candy and offered it to a bunch of them on the street. They took it without thanks, looking at him curiously and uneasily; learning from him maybe at that moment their first lesson in contempt.

Meanwhile, Ruskin has completely lost his wig. "Taste is the O N L Y morality!" he yells, wagging his finger at George. He is getting tiresome, so George cuts him off in midsentence by closing the book. Still sitting on the john, George looks out of the window.

The morning is quiet. Nearly all the kids are in school; the Christmas vacation is still a couple of weeks away. (At the thought of Christmas, George feels a chill of desperation. Maybe he'll do something drastic, take a plane to Mexico City and be drunk for a week and run wild around the bars. *You won't, and you never will*, a voice says, coldly bored with him.)

Ah, here's Benny, hammer in hand. He hunts among the trash

cans set out ready for collection on the sidewalk and drags out a broken bathroom scale. As George watches, Benny begins smashing it with his hammer, uttering cries as he does so; he is making believe that the machine is screaming with pain. And to think that Mrs. Strunk, the proud mother of this creature, used to ask Jim, with shudders of disgust, how he could bear to touch those harmless baby king snakes!

And now out comes Mrs. Strunk onto her porch, just as Benny completes the murder of the scale and stands looking down at its scattered insides. "Put them back!" she tells him. "Back in the can! Put them back, now! Back! Put them back! Back in the can!" Her voice rises, falls, in a consciously sweet singsong. She never yells at her children. She has read all the psychology books. She knows that Benny is passing through his Aggressive Phase, right on schedule; it just couldn't be more normal and healthy. She is well aware that she can be heard clear down the street. It is her right to be heard, for this is the Mothers' Hour. When Benny finally drops some of the broken parts back into the trash can, she singsongs "Attaboy!" and goes back smiling into the house.

So Benny wanders off to interfere with three much smaller tots, two boys and a girl, who are trying to dig a hole on the vacant lot between the Strunks and the Garfeins. (Their two houses face the street frontally, wide-openly, in apt contrast to the sidewise privacy of George's lair.)

On the vacant lot, under the huge old eucalyptus tree, Benny has taken over the digging. He strips off his windbreaker and tosses it to the little girl to hold; then he spits on his hands and picks up the spade. He is someone or other on TV, hunting for buried treasure. These tot-lives are nothing but a medley of such imitations. And soon as they can speak, they start trying to chant the singing commercials.

But now one of the boys—perhaps because Benny's digging bores him in the same way that Mr. Strunk's scoutmasterish projects bore Benny—strolls off by himself, firing a carbide cannon. George has been over to see Mrs. Strunk about this cannon, pleading with her to please explain to the boy's mother that it is driving him slowly crazy. But Mrs. Strunk has no intention of interfering with the anarchy of nature. Smiling evasively, she tells George, "I never hear the noise children make—just as long as it's a *happy* noise."

Mrs. Strunk's hour and the power of motherhood will last until midafternoon, when the big boys and girls return from school. They arrive in mixed groups—from which nearly all of the boys break away at once, however, to take part in the masculine hour of the ball-playing. They shout loudly and harshly to each other, and kick and leap and catch with arrogant grace. When the ball lands in a yard, they trample flowers, scramble over rock gardens, burst into patios without even a thought of apology. If a car ventures along the street, it must stop and wait until they are ready to let it through; they know their rights. And now the mothers must keep their tots indoors out of harm's way. The girls sit out on the porches, giggling together. Their eyes are always on the boys, and they will do the weirdest things to attract their attention: for example, the Cody daughters keep fanning their ancient black poodle as though it were Cleopatra on the Nile. They are disregarded, nevertheless, even by their own boy friends; for this is not their hour. The only boys who will talk to them now are soft-spoken and gentle, like the doctor's pretty sissy son, who ties ribbons to the poodle's curls.

And then, at length, the men will come home from their jobs. And it is their hour; and the ball-playing must stop. For Mr. Strunk's nerves have not been improved by trying all day long to sell that piece of real estate to a butterfly-brained rich widow, and Mr. Garfein's temper is uncertain after the tensions of his swimming-pool installation company. They and their fellow fathers can bear no more noise. (On Sundays Mr. Strunk will play ball with his sons, but this is just another of his physical education projects, polite and serious and no real fun.)

Every weekend there are parties. The teen-agers are encouraged to go off and dance and pet with each other, even if they haven't finished their homework; for the grownups need desperately to relax, unobserved. And now Mrs. Strunk prepares salads with Mrs. Garfein in the kitchen, and Mr. Strunk gets the barbecue going on the patio, and Mr. Garfein, crossing the vacant lot with a tray of bottles and a shaker, announces joyfully, in Marine Corps tones, "Martoonies coming up!"

And two, three hours later, after the cocktails and the guffaws, the quite astonishingly dirty stories, the more or less concealed pinching of other wives' fannies, the steaks and the pie, while The Girls—

as Mrs. Strunk and the rest will continue to call themselves and each other if they live to be ninety—are washing up, you will hear Mr. Strunk and his fellow husbands laughing and talking on the porch, drinks in hand, with thickened speech. Their business problems are forgotten now. And they are proud and glad. For even the least among them is a co-owner of the American utopia, the kingdom of the good life upon earth—crudely aped by the Russians, hated by the Chinese— who are nonetheless ready to purge and starve themselves for generations, in the hopeless hope of inheriting it. Oh yes indeed, Mr. Strunk and Mr. Garfein are proud of their kingdom. But why, then, are their voices like the voices of boys calling to each other as they explore a dark unknown cave, growing ever louder and louder, bolder and bolder? Do they know that they are afraid? No. But they are very afraid.

What are they afraid of?

They are afraid of what they know is somewhere in the darkness around them, of what may at any moment emerge into the undeniable light of their flashlamps, nevermore to be ignored, explained away. The fiend that won't fit into their statistics, the Gorgon that refuses their plastic surgery, the vampire drinking blood with tactless uncultured slurps, the bad-smelling beast that doesn't use their deodorants, the unspeakable that insists, despite all their shushing, on speaking its name.

Among many other kinds of monster, George says, they are afraid of little me.

Mr. Strunk, George supposes, tries to nail him down with a word. *Queer*, he doubtless growls. But, since this is after all the year 1962, even he may be expected to add, I don't give a damn what he does just as long as he stays away from me. Even psychologists disagree as to the conclusions which may be reached about the Mr. Strunks of this world, on the basis of such a remark. The fact remains that Mr. Strunk himself, to judge from a photograph of him taken in football uniform at college, used to be what many would call a living doll.

But Mrs. Strunk, George feels sure, takes leave to differ gently from her husband; for she is trained in the new tolerance, the technique of annihilation by blandness. Out comes her psychology book—bell and candle are no longer necessary. Reading from it in sweet singsong she proceeds to exorcise the unspeakable out of George. No reason for disgust, she intones, no cause for condemnation. Nothing here that is willfully vicious. All is due to heredity, early environment (Shame on those possessive mothers, those sex-segregated British schools!), arrested development at puberty, and-or glands. Here we have a misfit, debarred forever from the best things of life, to be pitied, not blamed. Some cases, caught young enough, *may* respond to therapy. As for the rest—ah, it's so sad; especially when it happens, as let's face it it does, to truly worthwhile people, people who might have had so much to offer. (Even when they are geniuses in spite of it, their masterpieces are invariably *warped*.) So let us be understanding, shall we, and remember that, after all, there *were* the Greeks (though that was a bit different, because they were pagans rather than neurotics). Let us even go so far as to say that this kind of relationship can sometimes be almost beautiful—particularly if one of the parties is already dead, or, better yet, both.

How dearly Mrs. Strunk would enjoy being sad about Jim! But, aha, she doesn't know; none of them know. It happened in Ohio, and the L.A. papers didn't carry the story. George has simply spread it around that Jim's folks, who are getting along in years, have been trying to persuade him to come back home and live with them; and that now, as the result of his recent visit to them, he will be remaining in the East indefinitely. Which is the gospel truth. As for the animals, those devilish reminders, George had to get them out of his sight immediately; he couldn't even bear to think of them being anywhere in the neighborhood. So, when Mrs. Garfein wanted to know if he would sell the myna bird, he answered that he'd shipped them all back to Jim. A dealer from San Diego took them away.

And now, in reply to the questions of Mrs. Strunk and the others, George answers that, yes indeed, he has just heard from Jim and that Jim is fine. They ask him less and less often. They are inquisitive but quite incurious, really.

But your book is wrong, Mrs. Strunk, says George, when it tells you that Jim is the substitute I found for a real son, a real kid brother, a real husband, a real wife. Jim wasn't a substitute for anything. And there is no substitute for Jim, if you'll forgive my saying so, anywhere.

Your exorcism has failed, dear Mrs. Strunk, says George, squatting on the toilet and peeping forth from his lair to watch her emptying the dustbag of her vacuum cleaner into the trash can. The unspeakable is still here—right in your very midst.

Damnation. The phone.

Even with the longest cord the phone company will give you, it won't reach into the bathroom. George gets himself off the seat and shuffles into the study, like a man in a sack race.

"Hello."

"Hello—is that—it *is* you, Geo?"

"Hello, Charley."

"I say, I didn't call too early, did I?"

"No." (Oh dear, she has managed to get him irritated already! Yet how can he reasonably blame her for the discomfort of standing nastily unwiped, with his pants around his ankles? One must admit, though, that Charlotte has a positively clairvoyant knack of picking the wrong moment to call.)

"You're sure?"

"Of course I'm sure. I've already had breakfast."

"I was afraid if I waited any longer you'd have gone off to the college. . . . My goodness, I hadn't noticed it was *so* late! Oughtn't you to have started already?"

"This is the day I have only one class. It doesn't begin until eleven thirty. My early days are Mondays and Wednesdays." (All this is explained in a tone of slightly emphasized patience.)

"Oh yes—yes, of course! How stupid of me! I *always* forget."

(A silence. George knows she wants to ask him something. But he won't help her. He is rubbed the wrong way by her blunderings. *Why* does she imply that she *ought* to know his college schedule? Just more of her possessiveness. Then why, if she really thinks she ought to know it, does she get it all mixed up?)

"Geo—" (very humbly) "would you *possibly* be free tonight?"

"Afraid not. No." (One second before speaking he couldn't have told you what he was going to answer. It's the desperation in Charlotte's voice that decides him. He isn't in the mood for one of her crises.)

"Oh—I see. . . . I was afraid you wouldn't be. It *is* short notice, I know." (She sounds half stunned, very quiet, hopeless. He stands there listening for a sob. None can be heard. His face is puckered into a grimace of guilt and discomfort—the latter caused by his increasing awareness of stickiness and trussed ankles.)

"I suppose you couldn't—I mean—I suppose it's something important?"

"I'm afraid it is." (The grimace of guilt relaxes. He is mad at her now. He won't be nagged at.)

"I see. . . . Oh well, never mind." (She's brave, now.) "I'll try you again, may I, in a few days?"

"Of course." (Oh—why not be a little nicer, now she's been put in her place?) "Or I'll call you."

(A pause.)

"Well—goodbye, Geo."

"Goodbye, Charley."

Twenty minutes later, Mrs. Strunk, out on her porch watering the hibiscus bushes, watches him back his car out across the bridge. (It is sagging badly nowadays. She hopes he will have it fixed; one of the children might get hurt.) As he makes the half-turn onto the street, she waves to him. He waves to her.

Poor man, she thinks, living there all alone. He has a kind face.

It is one of the marvels and blessings of the Los Angeles freeway system that you can now get from the beach to San Tomas State College in fifty minutes, give or take five, instead of the nearly two hours you would have spent, in the slow old days, crawling from stop light to stop light clear across the downtown area and out into the suburbs beyond.

George feels a kind of patriotism for the freeways. He is proud that they are so fast, that people get lost on them and even sometimes panic and have to bolt for safety down the nearest cutoff. George loves the freeways because he can still cope with them; because the fact that he can cope proves his claim to be a functioning member of society. He can still *get by*.

(Like everyone with an acute criminal complex, George is hyperconscious of all bylaws, city ordinances, rules and petty regulations. Think of how many Public Enemies have been caught just because they neglected to pay a parking ticket! Never once has he seen his passport stamped at a frontier, his driver's license accepted by a post-office clerk as evidence of identity, without whispering gleefully to himself, *Idiots—fooled them again!*)

He will fool them again this morning, in there, in the midst of the mad metropolitan chariot race—Ben-Hur would certainly chicken out—jockeying from lane to lane with the best of them, never dropping below eighty in the fast left lane, never getting rattled when a crazy teen-ager hangs on to his tail or a woman (it all comes of letting them go first through doorways) cuts in sharply ahead of him. The cops on their motorcycles will detect nothing, yet, to warn them to roar in pursuit flashing their red lights, to signal him off to the side, out of the running, and thence to escort him kindly but ever so firmly to some beautifully ordered nursery-community where Senior Citizens ("old," in our country of the bland, has become nearly as dirty a word as "kike" or "nigger") are eased into senility, retaught their childhood games but with a difference: it's known as "passive recreation" now. Oh, by all means let them screw, if they can still cut the mustard; and, if they can't, let them indulge without inhibitions in babylike erotic play. Let them get married, even—at eighty, at ninety, at a hundred—who cares? Anything to keep them busy and stop them wandering around blocking the traffic.

There's always a slightly unpleasant moment when you drive up the ramp which leads onto the freeway and become what's called "merging traffic." George has that nerve-crawling sensation which can't be removed by simply checking the rearview mirror: that, inexplicably, invisibly, he's about to be hit in the back. And then, next moment, he has merged and is away, out in the clear, climbing the long, easy gradient toward the top of the pass and the Valley beyond.

And now, as he drives, it is as if some kind of auto-hypnosis exerts itself. We see the face relax, the shoulders unhunch themselves, the body ease itself back into the seat. The reflexes are taking over; the left foot comes down with firm, even pressure on the clutch pedal, while the right prudently feeds in gas. The left hand is light on the wheel; the right slips the gearshift with precision into high. The eyes, moving unhurriedly from road to mirror, mirror to road, calmly measure the distances ahead, behind, to the nearest car. . . . After all, this is no mad chariot race—that's only how it seems to onlookers or nervous novices—it is a river, sweeping in full flood toward its outlet with a soothing power. There is nothing to fear, as long as you let yourself go with it; indeed, you discover, in the midst of its stream-speed, a sense of indolence and ease.

And now something new starts happening to George. The face is becoming tense again, the muscles bulge slightly at the jaw, the mouth tightens and twitches, the lips are pressed together in a grim line, there is a nervous contraction between the eyebrows. And yet, while all this is going on, the rest of the body remains in a posture of perfect relaxation. More and more it appears to separate itself, to become a separate entity: an impassive anonymous chauffeur-figure with little will or individuality of its own, the very embodiment of muscular co-ordination, lack of anxiety, tactful silence, driving its master to work.

And George, like a master who has entrusted the driving of his car to a servant, is now free to direct his attention elsewhere. As they sweep over the crest of the pass, he is becoming less and less aware of externals—the cars all around, the dip of the freeway ahead, the Valley with its homes and gardens opening below, under a long brown smear of smog, beyond and above which the big barren mountains rise. He has gone deep down inside himself.

What is he up to?

On the edge of the beach, a huge, insolent high-rise building which will contain one hundred apartments is growing up within its girders; it will block the view along the coast from the park on the cliffs above. A spokesman for this project says, in answer to objections, Well, that's progress. And anyhow, he implies, if there are people who are prepared to pay $450 a month for this view by renting our apartments, why should you park-users (and that includes George) get it for free?

A local newspaper editor has started a campaign against sex deviates (by which he means people like George). They are everywhere, he says; you can't go into a bar any more, or a men's room, or a public library, without seeing hideous sights. And they all, without exception, have syphilis. The existing laws against them, he says, are far too lenient.

A senator has recently made a speech, declaring that we should attack Cuba right now, with everything we've got, lest the Monroe Doctrine be held cheap and of no account. The senator does not deny that this will probably mean rocket war. We must face this fact; the alternative is dishonor. We must be prepared to sacrifice three quarters of our population (including George).

It would be amusing, George thinks, to sneak into that apartment building at night, just before the tenants moved in, and spray all the walls of all the rooms with a specially prepared odorant which would be scarcely noticeable at first but which would gradually grow in strength until it reeked like rotting corpses. They would try to get rid of it with every deodorant known to science, but in vain; and when they had finally, in desperation, ripped out the plaster and woodwork, they would find that the girders themselves were stinking. They would abandon the place as the Khmers did Angkor; but its stink would grow and grow until you could smell it clear up the coast to Malibu. So at last the entire structure would have to be taken apart by workers in gas masks and ground to powder and dumped far out in the ocean. . . . Or perhaps it would be more practical to discover a kind of virus which would eat away whatever it is that makes metal hard. The advantage that this would have over the odorant would be that only a single injection in one spot would be necessary, for the virus would then eat through all the metal in the building. And then, when everybody had moved in and while a big housewarming party was in progress, the whole thing would sag and subside into a limp tangled heap, like spaghetti.

Then, that newspaper editor, George thinks, how funny to kidnap him and the staff-writers responsible for the sex-deviate articles—and maybe also the police chief, and the head of the vice squad, and those ministers who endorsed the campaign from their pulpits—and take them all to a secret underground movie studio where, after a little persuasion—no doubt just showing them the red-hot pokers and pincers would be quite sufficient—they would perform every possible sexual act, in pairs and in groups, with a display of the utmost enjoyment. The film would then be developed and prints of it would be rushed to all the movie theaters. George's assistants would chloroform the ushers so the lights couldn't be turned up, lock the exits, overpower the projectionists, and proceed to run the film under the heading of Coming Attractions.

And as for that senator, wouldn't it be rather amusing to . . .

No.

(At this point, we see the eyebrows contract in a more than usually violent spasm, the mouth thin to knife-blade grimness.)

No. Amusing is *not* the word. These people are not amusing. They should never be dealt with amusingly. They understand only one language: brute force.

Therefore we must launch a campaign of systematic terror. In order to be effective, this will require an organization of at least five hundred highly skilled killers and torturers, all dedicated individuals. The head of the organization will draw up a list of clearly defined, simple objectives, such as the removal of that apartment building, the suppression of that newspaper, the retirement of that senator. They will then be dealt with in order, regardless of the time taken or the number of casualties. In each case, the principal criminal will first receive a polite note, signed "Uncle George," explaining exactly what he must do before a certain deadline if he wants to stay alive. It will also be explained to him that Uncle George operates on the theory of guilt by association.

One minute after the deadline, the killing will begin. The execution of the principal criminal will be delayed for some weeks or months, to give him opportunity for reflection. Meanwhile, there will be daily reminders. His wife may be kidnapped, garroted, embalmed and seated in the living room to await his return from the office. His children's heads may arrive in cartons by mail, or tapes of the screams his relatives utter as they are tortured to death. His friends' homes may be blown up in the night. Anyone who has ever known him will be in mortal danger.

When the organization's 100 per cent efficiency has been demonstrated a sufficient number of times, the population will slowly begin to learn that Uncle George's will must be obeyed instantly and without question.

But does Uncle George *want* to be obeyed? Doesn't he prefer to be defied so he can go on killing and killing—since all these people are just vermin and the more of them that die the better? All are, in the last analysis, responsible for Jim's death; their words, their thoughts, their whole way of life willed it, even though they never knew he existed. But, when George gets in as deep as this, Jim hardly matters any more. Jim is nothing now but an excuse for hating three quarters of the population of America. . . . George's jaws work, his teeth grind, as he chews and chews the cud of his hate.

But does George really hate all these people? Aren't they themselves merely an excuse for hating? What *is* George's hate, then? A stimulant, nothing more; though very bad for him, no doubt. Rage, resentment, spleen—of such is the vitality of middle age. If we say that he is quite crazy at this particular moment, then so, probably, are at least half a dozen others in these many cars around him, all slowing now as the traffic thickens, going downhill, under the bridge, up again past the Union Depot. . . . God! Here we are, downtown already! George comes up dazed to the surface, realizing with a shock that the chauffeur-figure has broken a record: never before has it managed to get them this far entirely on its own. And this raises a disturbing question: Is the chauffeur steadily becoming more and more of an individual? Is it getting ready to take over much larger areas of George's life?

No time to worry about that now. In ten minutes they will have arrived on campus. In ten minutes, George will have to be George— the George they have named and will recognize. So now he consciously applies himself to thinking their thoughts, getting into their mood. With the skill of a veteran he rapidly puts on the psychological make-up for this role he must play.

No sooner have you turned off the freeway onto San Tomas Avenue than you are back in the tacky sleepy slowpoke Los Angeles of the thirties, still convalescent from the Depression, with no money to spare for fresh coats of paint. And how charming it is! An up-and-down terrain of steep little hills with white houses of cracked stucco perched insecurely on their sides and tops, it is made to look quaint rather than ugly by the mad, hopelessly intertwisted cat's cradle of wires and telephone poles. Mexicans live here, so there are lots of flowers. Negroes live here, so it is cheerful. George would not care to live here, because they all blast all day long with their radios and television sets. But he would never find himself yelling at their children, because these people are not The Enemy. If they would ever accept George, they might even be allies. They never figure in the Uncle George fantasies.

The San Tomas State College campus is back on the other side of the freeway. You cross over to it by a bridge, back into the nowadays of destruction-reconstruction-destruction. Here the little hills have been trucked away bodily or had their tops sliced off by bulldozers, and the landscape is gashed with raw terraces. Tract upon tract of low-roofed dormitory-dwellings (invariably called "homes" and described as "a new concept in living") are being opened up as fast as they can be connected with the sewers and the power lines. It is a slander to say that they are identical; some have brown roofs, some green, and the tiles in their bathrooms come in several different colors. The tracts have their individuality, too. Each one has a different name, of the kind that realtors can always be relied on to invent: Sky Acres, Vista Grande, Grovenor Heights.

The storm center of all this grading, shoveling, hauling and hammering is the college campus itself. A clean modern factory, brick and glass and big windows, already three-quarters built, is being finished in a hysterical hurry. (The construction noises are such that in some classrooms the professors can hardly be heard.) When the factory is fully operational, it will be able to process twenty thousand graduates. But, in less than ten years, it will have to cope with forty or fifty thousand. So then everything will be torn down again and built up twice as tall.

However, it is arguable that by that time the campus will be cut off from the outside world by its own parking lots, which will then form an impenetrable forest of cars abandoned in despair by the students during the week-long traffic jams of the near future. Even now, the lots are half as big as the campus itself and so full that you have to drive around from one to another in search of a last little space. Today George is lucky. There is room for him on the lot nearest his classroom. George slips his parking card into the slot (thereby offering a piece of circumstantial evidence that he *is* George); the barrier rises in spastic, mechanical jerks, and he drives in.

George has been trying to train himself, lately, to recognize his

students' cars. (He is continually starting these self-improvement projects: sometimes it's memory training, sometimes a new diet, sometimes
just a vow to read some unreadable Hundredth Best Book. He seldom
perseveres in any of them for long.) Today he is pleased to be able to
spot three cars—not counting the auto scooter which the Italian exchange student, with a courage or provincialism bordering on insanity,
rides up and down the freeway as though he were on the Via Veneto.
There's the beat-up, not-so-white Ford coupe belonging to Tom Kugelman, on the back of which he has printed SLOW WHITE. There's
the Chinese-Hawaiian boy's grime-gray Pontiac, with one of those
joke-stickers in the rear window: THE ONLY ISM I BELIEVE IN
IS ABSTRACT EXPRESSIONISM. The joke isn't a joke in his
particular case, because he really is an abstract painter. (Or is this
some supersubtlety?) At all events, it seems incongruous that anyone
with such a sweet Chessy-cat smile and cream-smooth skin and cat-
clean neatness could produce such gloomy muddy canvases or own
such a filthy car. He has the beautiful name of Alexander Mong. And
there's the well-waxed, spotless scarlet MG driven by Buddy Sorensen,
the wild watery-eyed albino who is a basketball star and wears a "Ban
the Bomb" button. George has caught glimpses of Buddy streaking
past on the freeway, laughing to himself as if the absurd little sitzbath
of a thing had run away with him and he didn't care.

So now George has arrived. He is not nervous in the least. As
he gets out of his car, he feels an upsurge of energy, of eagerness for
the play to begin. And he walks eagerly, with a springy step, along the
gravel path past the Music Building toward the Department office. He
is all actor now—an actor on his way up from the dressing room,
hastening through the backstage world of props and lamps and stagehands to make his entrance. A veteran, calm and assured, he pauses
for a well-measured moment in the doorway of the office and then,
boldly, clearly, with the subtly modulated British intonation which
his public demands of him, speaks his opening line: "Good morning!"

And the three secretaries—each one of them a charming and
accomplished actress in her own chosen style—recognize him instantly, without even a flicker of doubt, and reply "Good morning!"
to him. (There is something religious here, like responses in church—
a reaffirmation of faith in the basic American dogma that it is, always,

a *good* morning. Good, despite the Russians and their rockets, and all the ills and worries of the flesh. For of course we know, don't we, that the Russians and the worries are not really real? They can be un-thought and made to vanish. And therefore the morning can be made to be good. Very well then, it *is* good.)

Every teacher in the English Department has his or her pigeon-hole in this office, and all of them are stuffed with papers. What a mania for communication! A notice of the least important committee meeting on the most trivial of subjects will be run off and distributed in hundreds of copies. Everybody is informed of everything. George glances through all his papers and then tosses the lot into the waste-basket, with one exception: an oblong card slotted and slitted and ciphered by an IBM machine, expressing some poor bastard of a stu-dent's academic identity. Indeed, this card *is* his identity. Suppose, instead of signing it as requested and returning it to the Personnel office, George were to tear it up? Instantly, that student would cease to exist, as far as San Tomas State was concerned. He would become academically invisible and only reappear with the very greatest diffi-culty, after performing the most elaborate propitiation ceremonies: countless offerings of forms filled out in triplicate and notarized affi-davits to the gods of the IBM.

George signs the card, holding it steady with two fingertips. He dislikes even to touch these things, for they are the runes of an idiotic but nevertheless potent and evil magic: the magic of the think-machine gods, whose cult has one dogma, *We cannot make a mistake.* Their magic consists in this: that whenever they do make a mistake, which is quite often, it is perpetuated and thereby becomes a non-mistake. . . . Carrying the card by its extreme corner, George brings it over to one of the secretaries, who will see that it gets back to Personnel. The secretary has a nail file on her desk. George picks it up, saying, "Let's see if that old robot'll know the difference," and pretends to be about to punch another slit in the card. The girl laughs, but only after a split-second look of sheer terror; and the laugh itself is forced. George has uttered blasphemy.

Feeling rather pleased with himself, he leaves the Department building, headed for the cafeteria.

He starts across the largish open space which is the midst of the campus, surrounded by the Art Building, the gymnasium, the Science Building and the Administration Building, and newly planted with grass and some hopeful little trees which should make it leafy and shadowy and pleasant within a few years: that is to say, about the time when they start tearing the whole place apart again. The air has a tang of smog—called "eye irritation" in blandese. The mountains of the San Gabriel Range—which still give San Tomas State something of the glamour of a college high on a plateau of the Andes, on the few days you can see them properly—are hidden today as usual in the sick yellow fumes which arise from the metropolitan mess below.

And now, all around George, approaching him, crossing his path from every direction, is the male and female raw material which is fed daily into this factory, along the conveyer belts of the freeways, to be processed, packaged and placed on the market: Negroes, Mexicans, Jews, Japanese, Chinese, Latins, Slavs, Nordics, the dark heads far predominating over the blond. Hurrying in pursuit of their schedules, loitering in flirty talk, strolling in earnest argument, muttering some lesson to themselves alone—all book-burdened, all harassed.

What do they think they're up to, here? Well, there is the official answer: preparing themselves for life which means a job and security in which to raise children to prepare themselves for life which means a job and security in which. But, despite all the vocational advisers, the pamphlets pointing out to them what good money you can earn if you invest in some solid technical training—pharmacology, let's say, or accountancy, or the varied opportunities offered by the vast field of electronics—there are still, incredibly enough, quite a few of them who persist in writing poems, novels, plays! Goofy from lack of sleep, they scribble in snatched moments between classes, part-time employment and their married lives. Their brains are dizzy with words as they mop out an operating room, sort mail at a post office, fix baby's bottle, fry hamburgers. And somewhere, in the midst of their servitude to the must-be, the mad might-be whispers to them to live, know, experience—what? *Marvels!* The Season in Hell, the Journey to the End of the Night, the Seven Pillars of Wisdom, the Clear Light of the Void. . . . Will any of them make it? Oh, sure. One, at least. Two or three at most—in all these searching thousands.

Here, in their midst, George feels a sort of vertigo. Oh God, what will become of them all? What chance have they? Ought I to yell out to them, right now, here, that it's hopeless?

But George knows he can't do that. Because, absurdly, inadequately, in spite of himself, almost, he is a representative of the hope. And the hope is not false. No. It's just that George is like a man trying to sell a real diamond for a nickel, on the street. The diamond is protected from all but the tiniest few, because the great hurrying majority can never stop to dare to believe that it could conceivably be real.

Outside the cafeteria are announcements of the current student activities: Squaws' Night, Golden Fleece Picnic, Fogcutters' Ball, Civic Society Meeting and the big game against LPSC. These advertised rituals of the San Tomas Tribe aren't quite convincing; they are promoted only by a minority of eager beavers. The rest of these boys and girls do not really think of themselves as a tribe, although they are willing to pretend that they do on special occasions. All that they actually have in common is their urgency: the need to get with it, to finish that assignment which should have been handed in three days ago. When George eavesdrops on their conversation, it is nearly always about what they have failed to do, what they fear the professor will make them do, what they have risked not doing and gotten away with.

The cafeteria is crammed. George stands at the door, looking around. Now that he is a public utility, the property of STSC, he is impatient to be used. He hates to see even one minute of himself being wasted. He starts to walk among the tables with a tentative smile, a forty-watt smile ready to be switched up to a hundred and fifty watts just as soon as anyone asks for it.

Now, to his relief, he sees Russ Dreyer, and Dreyer rises from his table to greet him. He has no doubt been on the lookout for George. Dreyer has gradually become George's personal attendant, executive officer, bodyguard. He is an angular, thin-faced young man with a flat-top haircut and rimless glasses. He wears a somewhat sporty Hawaiian shirt which, on him, seems like a prim shy concession to the sportiness of the clothes around him. His undershirt, appearing in the open V of his unbuttoned collar, looks surgically clean, as always. Dreyer is a grade A scholar, and his European counterpart would probably be a rather dry and brittle stick. But Dreyer is neither dry nor brittle. He has discreet humor and, as an ex-Marine, considerable toughness. He once described to George a typical evening he and his wife, Marinette, spent with his buddy Tom Kugelman and Tom's wife. "Tom and I got into an argument about *Finnegans Wake*. It went on all through supper. So then the girls said they were sick of listening to us, so they went out to a movie. Tom and I did the dishes and it got to be ten o'clock and we were still arguing and we hadn't convinced each other. So we got some beer out of the icebox and went out in the yard. Tom's building a shed there, but he hasn't got the roof on yet. So then he challenged me to a chinning match, and we started chinning ourselves on the crossbeam over the door, and I whipped him thirteen to eleven."

George is charmed by this story. Somehow, it's like classical Greece.

"Good morning, Russ."

"Good morning, sir." It isn't the age difference which makes Dreyer call George "sir." As soon as they come to the end of this quasi-military relationship, he will start saying "George," or even "Geo," without hesitation.

Together they go over to the coffee machine, fill mugs, select doughnuts from the counter. As they turn toward the cash desk, Dreyer slips ahead of George with the change ready. "No—let me, sir."

"You're always paying."

Dreyer grins. "We're in the chips, since I put Marinette to work."

"She got that teaching job?"

"It just came through. Of course, it's only temporary. The only snag is, she has to get up an hour earlier."

"So you're fixing your own breakfast?"

"Oh, I can manage. Till she gets a job nearer in. Or I get her pregnant." He visibly enjoys this man-to-man stuff with George. (Does he know about me? George wonders; do any of them? Oh yes, probably. It wouldn't interest them. They don't want to know about my feelings or my glands or anything below my neck. I could just as well be a severed head carried into the classroom to lecture to them from a dish.)

"Say, that reminds me," Dreyer is saying, "Marinette wanted me to ask you, sir—we were wondering if you could manage to get out to us again before too long? We could cook up some spaghetti. And maybe Tom could bring over that tape I was telling you about—the one he got from the audio-visual up at Berkeley, of Katherine Anne Porter reading her stuff—"

"That'd be fine," says George vaguely, with enthusiasm. He glances up at the clock. "I say, we ought to be going."

Dreyer isn't in the least damped by his vagueness. Probably he does not want George to come to supper any more than George wants to go. It is all, all symbolic. Marinette has told him to ask, and he has asked, and now it is on record that George has accepted, for the second time, an invitation to their home. And this means that George is an intimate and can be referred to in after years as part of their circle in the old days. Oh yes, the Dreyers will loyally do their part to make George's place secure among the grand old bores of yesteryear. George can just picture one of those evenings in the 1990s, when Russ is dean of an English department in the Middle West and Marinette is the mother of grown-up sons and daughters. An audience of young instructors and their wives, symbolically entertaining Dr. and Mrs. Dreyer, will be symbolically thrilled to catch the Dean in an anecdotal mood, mooning and mumbling with a fuddled smile through a maze of wowless sagas, into which George and many many others will enter, uttering misquotes. And Marinette, permanently smiling, will sit listening with the third ear—the one that has heard it all before—and praying for eleven o'clock to come. And it will come. And all will agree that this has been a memorable evening indeed.

As they walk toward the classroom, Dreyer asks George what he thinks about what Dr. Leavis said about Sir Charles Snow. (These far-off unhappy Old Things and their long-ago battles are still hot news out here in Sleepy Hollow State.) "Well, first of all—" George begins.

They are passing the tennis courts at this moment. Only one court is occupied, by two young men playing singles. The sun has come out with sudden fierce heat through the smog-haze, and the two are stripped nearly naked. They have nothing on their bodies but gym shoes and thick sweatsocks and knit shorts of the kind cyclists wear, very short and close-fitting, molding themselves to the buttocks and the loins. They are absolutely unaware of the passers-by, isolated in the intentness of their game. You would think there was no net between them. Their nakedness makes them seem close to each other and directly opposed, body to body, like fighters. If this were a fight, though, it would be one-sided, for the boy on the left is much the smaller. He is Mexican, maybe, black-haired, handsome, catlike, cruel, compact, lithe, muscular, quick and graceful on his feet. His body is a natural dark gold-brown; there is a fuzz of curly black hair on his chest and belly and thighs. He plays hard and fast, with cruel mastery, baring his white teeth, unsmiling, as he slams back the ball. He is going to win. His opponent, the big blond boy, already knows this; there is a touching gallantry in his defense. He is so sweet-naturedly beautiful, so nobly made; and yet his classical cream-marble body seems a handicap to him. The rules of the game inhibit it from functioning. He is fighting at a hopeless disadvantage. He should throw away his useless racket, vault over the net, and force the cruel little gold cat to submit to his marble strength. No, on the contrary, the blond boy accepts the rules, binds himself by them, will suffer defeat and humiliation rather than break them. His helpless bigness and blondness give him an air of unmodern chivalry. He will fight clean, a perfect sportsman, until he has lost the last game. And won't this keep happening to him all through his life? Won't he keep getting himself involved in the wrong kind of game, the kind of game he was never born to play, against an opponent who is quick and clever and merciless?

This game is cruel; but its cruelty is sensual and stirs George into hot excitement. He feels a thrill of pleasure to find the senses so eager in their response; too often, now, they seem sadly jaded. From his heart, he thanks these young animals for their beauty. And they will never know what they have done to make this moment marvelous to him, and life itself less hateful. . . .

Dreyer is saying, "Sorry, sir—I lost you for a minute, there. I understand about the two cultures, of course—but do you mean you *agree* with Dr. Leavis?" Far from taking the faintest interest in the tennis players, Dreyer walks with his body half turned away from them, his whole concentration fixed upon George's talking head.

For it obviously *has* been talking. George realizes this with the same discomfiture he felt on the freeway, when the chauffeur-figure got them clear downtown. Oh yes, he knows from experience what the talking head can do, late in the evening, when he is bored and tired and drunk, to help him through a dull party. It can play back all of George's favorite theories—just as long as it isn't argued with; then it may become confused. It knows at least three dozen of his best anecdotes. But *here*, in broad daylight, during campus hours, when George should be on-stage every second, in full control of his performance! Can it be that talking head and the chauffeur are in league? *Are they maybe planning a merger?*

"We really haven't time to go into all this right now," he tells Dreyer smoothly. "And anyhow, I'd like to check up on the Leavis lecture again. I've still got that issue of *The Spectator* somewhere at home, I think. . . . Oh, by the way, did you ever get to read that piece on Mailer, about a month ago—in *Esquire*, wasn't it? It's one of the best things I've seen in a long time. . . ."

George's classroom has two doors in its long side wall, one up front, the other at the back of the room. Most of the students enter from the back because, with an infuriating sheep-obstinacy, they love to huddle together, confronting their teachers from behind a barricade of empty seats. But this semester the class is only a trifle smaller than the capacity of the room. Late-comers are forced to sit farther and farther forward, to George's sly satisfaction; finally, they have to take the second row. As for the front row, which most of them shun so doggedly, George can fill that up with his regulars: Russ Dreyer, Tom Kugelman, Sister Maria, Mr. Stoessel, Mrs. Netta Torres, Kenny Potter, Lois Yamaguchi.

George never enters the classroom with Dreyer, or any other student. A deeply rooted dramatic instinct forbids him to do so. This is really all that he uses his office for—as a place to withdraw into before class, simply in order to re-emerge from it and make his entrance. He doesn't interview students in it, because these offices are shared by at least two faculty members, and Dr. Gottlieb, who teaches the Metaphysical Poets, is nearly always there. George cannot talk to another human being as if the two of them were alone when, in fact, they aren't. Even such a harmless question as "What do you *honestly* think of Emerson?" sounds indecently intimate, and such a mild criticism as "What you've written is a mixed metaphor and it doesn't mean anything" sounds unnecessarily cruel, when Dr. Gottlieb is right there at the other desk listening or, what's worse, pretending not to listen.

But Gottlieb obviously doesn't feel this way. Perhaps it is a peculiarly British scruple.

So now, leaving Dreyer, George goes into the office. It is right across the hallway. Gottlieb isn't there, for a wonder. George peeps out of the window between the slats of the Venetian blinds and sees, in the far distance, the two tennis players still at their game. He coughs, fingers the telephone directory without looking at it, closes the empty drawer in his desk, which has been pulled open a little. Then, abruptly, he turns, takes his briefcase out of the closet, leaves the office and crosses to the front classroom door.

His entrance is quite undramatic according to conventional standards. Nevertheless, this is a subtly contrived, outrageously theatrical effect. No hush falls as George walks in. Most of the students go right on talking. But they are all watching him, waiting for him to give some sign, no matter how slight, that the class is to begin. The effect is a subtle but gradually increasing tension, caused by George's teasing refusal to give this sign and the students' counterdetermination not to stop talking until he gives it.

Meanwhile, he stands there. Slowly, deliberately, like a magician, he takes a single book out of his briefcase and places it on the reading desk. As he does this, his eyes move over the faces of the class. His lips curve in a faint but bold smile. Some of them smile back at him. George finds this frank confrontation extraordinarily exhilarating. He draws strength from these smiles, these bright young eyes. For him, this is one of the peak moments of the day. He feels brilliant, vital, challenging, slightly mysterious and, above all, *foreign*. His neat dark clothes, his white dress shirt and tie (the only tie in the room) are uncompromisingly alien from the aggressively virile informality of the young male students. Most of these wear sneakers and garterless white wool socks, jeans in cold weather, and in warm weather shorts (the thigh-clinging Bermuda type—the more becoming short ones aren't considered quite decent). If it is really warm, they'll roll up their sleeves and sometimes leave their shirts provocatively unbuttoned to show curly chest hair and a St. Christopher medal. They look as if they were ready at any minute to switch from studying to ditchdigging or gang fighting. They seem like mere clumsy kids in contrast with the girls, for these have all outgrown their teen-age phase of Capri pants, sloppy shirts and giant heads of teased-up hair. They are mature women, and they come to class dressed as if for a highly respectable party.

This morning George notes that all of his front-row regulars are present. Dreyer and Kugelman are the only ones he has actually asked to help fill the gap by sitting there; the rest of them have their individual reasons for doing so. While George is teaching, Dreyer watches him with an encouraging alertness; but George knows that Dreyer isn't really impressed by him. To Dreyer, George will always remain an academic amateur; his degrees and background are British and there-fore dubious. Still, George is the Skipper, the Old Man; and Dreyer, by supporting his authority, supports the structure of values up which he himself proposes to climb. So he wills George to be brilliant and impress the outsiders—that is to say, everyone else in the class. The funny thing is that Dreyer, with the clear conscience of absolute loy-alty, feels free to whisper to Kugelman, *his* lieutenant, as often as he wants to. Whenever this happens, George longs to stop talking and listen to what they are saying about him. Instinctively, George is sure that Dreyer would never dream of talking about anyone else during class: *that* would be bad manners.

Sister Maria belongs to a teaching order. Soon she'll get her credential and become a teacher herself. She is, no doubt, a fairly normal, unimaginative, hardworking good young woman; and no doubt she sits up front because it helps her concentrate, maybe even because the boys still interest her a little and she wants to avoid looking at them. But we, most of us, lose our sense of proportion in the presence of a nun; and George, thus exposed at short range to this bride of Christ in her uncompromising medieval habit, finds himself becoming flustered, defensive. An unwilling conscript in Hell's legions, he faces the soldier of Heaven across the front line of an exceedingly polite cold war. In every sentence he addresses to her, he calls her "Sister"; which is probably just what she doesn't want.

Mr. Stoessel sits in the front row because he is deaf and middle-aged and only lately arrived from Europe, and his English is terrible.

Mrs. Netta Torres is also middle-aged. She seems to be taking this course out of mere curiosity or to fill in idle hours. She has the look of a divorcee. She sits up front because her interest is centered frankly and brutally on George as George. She watches rather than listens to him. She even seems to be "reading" his words indirectly, through a sort of Braille made up of his gestures, inflections, mannerisms. And this almost tactile scrutiny is accompanied by a motherly smile, for, to Mrs. Torres, George is just a small boy, really, and so cute. George would love to catch her out and discourage her from attending his class by giving her low grades. But, alas, he can't. Mrs. Torres is listening as well as watching; she can repeat what he has been saying, word for word.

Kenny Potter sits in the front row because he's what's nowadays called crazy, meaning only that he tends to do the opposite of what most people do; not on principle, however, and certainly not out of aggressiveness. Probably he's too vague to notice the manners and customs of the tribe, and too lazy to follow them, anyway. He is a tall skinny boy with very broad stooped shoulders, gold-red hair, a small head, small bright-blue eyes. He would be conventionally handsome if he didn't have a beaky nose; but it is a nice one, a large, humorous organ.

George finds himself almost continuously aware of Kenny's presence in the room, but this doesn't mean that he regards Kenny as an ally. Oh, no—he can never venture to take Kenny for granted. Sometimes when George makes a joke and Kenny laughs his deep, rather wild, laugh, George feels he is being laughed with. At other times, when the laugh comes a fraction of a moment late, George gets a spooky impression that Kenny is laughing not at the joke but at the whole situation: the educational system of this country, and all the economic and political and psychological forces which have brought them into this classroom together. At such times, George suspects Kenny of understanding the innermost meaning of life—of being, in fact, some sort of a genius (though you would certainly never guess this from his term papers). And then again, maybe Kenny is just very young for his age, and misleadingly charming, and silly.

Lois Yamaguchi sits beside Kenny because she is his girl friend; at least, they are nearly always together. She smiles at George in a way that makes him wonder if she and Kenny have private jokes about him—but who can be sure of anything with these enigmatic Asians? Alexander Mong smiles enigmatically, too, though his beautiful head almost certainly contains nothing but clotted oil paint. Lois and Alexander are by far the most beautiful creatures in the class; their beauty is like the beauty of plants, seemingly untroubled by vanity, anxiety or effort.

All this while, the tension has been mounting. George has continued to smile at the talkers and to preserve his wonderful provocative melodramatic silence. And now, at last, after nearly four whole minutes, his silence has conquered them. The talking dies down. Those who have already stopped talking shush the others. George has triumphed. But his triumph lasts only for a moment. For now he must break his own spell. Now he must cast off his mysteriousness and stand revealed as that dime-a-dozen thing, a teacher, to whom the class has got to listen, no matter whether he drools or stammers or speaks with the tongue of an angel—that's neither here nor there. The class has got to listen to George because, by virtue of the powers vested in him by the State of California, he can make them submit to and study even his crassest prejudices, his most irresponsible caprices, as so many valuable clues to the problem: How can I impress, flatter or otherwise con this cantankerous old thing into giving me a good grade?

Yes, alas, now he must spoil everything. Now he must speak.

"After many a summer *dies* the swan." George rolls the words off his tongue with such hammy harmonics, such shameless relish, that this sounds like a parody of W. B. Yeats reciting. (He comes down on "dies" with a great thump to compensate for the "And" which Aldous Huxley has chopped off from the beginning of the original line.) Then, having managed to startle or embarrass at least a few of them, he looks around the room with an ironical grin and says quietly, schoolmasterishly, "I take it you've all read the Huxley novel by this time, seeing that I asked you to more than three weeks ago?"

Out of the corner of his eye, he notices Buddy Sorensen's evident dismay, which is not unexpected, and Estelle Oxford's indignant *now-they-tell-me* shrug of the shoulders, which is more serious. Estelle is one of his brightest students. Just because she is bright, she is more conscious of being a Negro, apparently, than the other colored students in the class are; in fact, she is hypersensitive. George suspects her of suspecting him of all kinds of subtle discrimination. Probably she wasn't in the room when he told them to read the novel. Damn, he should have noticed that and told her later. He is a bit intimidated by her. Also he likes her and is sorry. Also he resents the way she makes him feel.

"Oh well," he says, as nicely as he can, "if any of you haven't read it yet, that's not too important. Just listen to what's said this morning, and then you can read it and see if you agree or disagree."

He looks at Estelle and smiles. She smiles back. So, this time, it's going to be all right.

"The title is, of course, a quotation from Tennyson's poem 'Tithonus.' And, by the way, while we're on the subject—who *was* Tithonus?"

Silence. He looks from face to face. Nobody knows. Even Dreyer doesn't know. And, Christ, how typical this is! Tithonus doesn't concern them because he's at two removes from their subject. Huxley, Tennyson, Tithonus. They're prepared to go as far as Tennyson, but not one step farther. There their curiosity ends. Because, basically, *they don't give a shit.* . . .

"You *seriously* mean to tell me that none of you know who Tithonus was? That none of you could be bothered to find out? Well then, I advise you *all* to spend part of your weekend reading Graves' *Greek Myths, and* the poem itself. I must say, I don't see how anyone can pretend to be interested in a novel when he doesn't even stop to ask himself what its title means."

This spurt of ill temper dismays George as soon as he has discharged it. Oh dear, he *is* getting nasty! And the worst is, he never knows when he's going to behave like this. He has no time to check himself. Shamefaced now, and avoiding all their eyes—Kenny Potter's particularly—he fastens his gaze high up on the wall opposite.

"Well, to begin at the beginning, Aphrodite once caught her lover Ares in bed with Eos, the goddess of the Dawn. (You'd better look them *all* up, while you're about it.) Aphrodite was furious, of course, so she cursed Eos with a craze for handsome mortal boys—to teach her to leave other people's gods alone." (George gets a giggle on this line from someone and is relieved; he has feared they would be offended by their scolding and would sulk.) Not lowering his eyes yet, he continues, with a grin sounding in his voice, "Eos was terribly embarrassed, but she found she just couldn't control herself, so she started kidnapping and seducing boys from the earth. Tithonus was one of them. As a matter of fact, she took his brother Ganymede along, too—for company—" (Louder giggles, from several parts of the room, this time.) "Unfortunately, Zeus saw Ganymede and fell madly in love with him." (If Sister Maria is shocked, that's too bad. George doesn't look at her, however, but at Wally Bryant—about whom he couldn't be more certain—and, sure enough, Wally is wriggling with delight.) "So, knowing that she'd have to give up Ganymede anyway, Eos asked Zeus, wouldn't he, in exchange, make Tithonus immortal? So Zeus said, of course, why not? And he did it. But Eos was so stupid, she forgot to ask him to give Tithonus eternal youth as well. Incidentally, that could quite easily have been arranged; Selene, the Moon goddess, fixed it up for her boy friend Endymion. The only trouble there was that Selene didn't care to do anything but kiss, whereas Endymion had other ideas; so she put him into an eternal sleep to keep him quiet. And it's not much fun being beautiful forever and ever, when you can't even wake up and look at yourself in a mirror." (Nearly everybody is smiling, now—yes, even Sister Maria. George beams at them. He does so hate unpleasantness.) "Where was I? Oh yes—so poor Tithonus gradually became a repulsively immortal old man—" (Loud laughter.) "And Eos, with the characteristic heartlessness of a goddess, got bored with him and locked him up. And he got more and more gaga, and his voice got shriller and shriller, until suddenly one day he turned into a cicada."

This is a miserably weak payoff. George hasn't expected it to work, and it doesn't. Mr. Stoessel is quite frantic with incomprehension and appeals to Dreyer in desperate whispers. Dreyer whispers back explanations, which cause further misunderstandings. Mr. Stoessel gets it at last and exclaims, "Ach so—*eine Zikade!*" in a reproachful tone which implies that it's George and the entire Anglo-American world who have been mispronouncing the word. But by now George has started up again—and with a change of attitude. He's no longer wooing them, entertaining them; he's telling them, briskly, authoritatively. It is the voice of a judge, summing up and charging the jury.

"Huxley's general reason for choosing this title is obvious. However, you will have to ask yourselves how far it will bear application in detail to the circumstances of the story. For example, the fifth Earl of Gonister can be accepted as a counterpart of Tithonus, and he ends by turning into a monkey, just as Tithonus turned into an insect. But what about Jo Stoyte? And Dr. Obispo? He's far more like Goethe's Mephistopheles than like Zeus. And who is Eos? Not Virginia Maunciple, surely. For one thing, I feel sure she doesn't get up early enough." Nobody sees this joke. George still sometimes throws one away, despite all his experience, by muttering it, English style. A bit piqued by their failure to applaud, he continues, in an almost bullying tone, "But, before we can go any further, you've got to make up your minds what this novel actually *is* about."

They spend the rest of the hour making up their minds.

At first, as always, there is blank silence. The class sits staring, as it were, at the semantically prodigious word. *About. What is it about?* Well, what does George want them to say it's about? They'll say it's about anything he likes, anything at all. For nearly all of them, despite their academic training, deep, deep down still regard this *about* business as a tiresomely sophisticated game. As for the minority who have cultivated the *about* approach until it has become second nature, who dream of writing an *about* book of their own one day, on Faulkner, James or Conrad, proving definitively that all previous *about* books on that subject are about nothing—they aren't going to say anything yet awhile. They are waiting for the moment when they can come forward like star detectives with the solution to Huxley's crime. Meanwhile, let the little ones flounder. Let the mud be stirred up, first.

The mud is obligingly stirred up by Alexander Mong. He knows what he's doing, of course. He isn't dumb. Maybe it's even part of his philosophy as an abstract painter to regard anything figurative as merely childish. A Caucasian would get aggressive about this, but not Alexander. With that beautiful Chinese smile, he says, "It's about this rich guy who's jealous because he's afraid he's too old for this girl of his, and he thinks this young guy is on the make for her, only he isn't, and he doesn't have a hope, because she and the doctor already made the scene. So the rich guy shoots the young guy by mistake, and the doctor like covers up for them and then they all go to England to find this Earl character who's monkeying around with a chick in a cellar—"

A roar of joy at this. George smiles good-sportingly and says, "You left out Mr. Pordage and Mr. Propter—what do they do?"

"Pordage? Oh yes—he's the one that finds out about the Earl eating those crazy fish—"

"Carp."

"That's right. And Propter"—Alexander grins and scratches his head, clowning it up a bit—"I'm sorry, sir. You'll just have to excuse me. I mean, I didn't hit the sack till like half past two this morning, trying to figure that cat out. Wow! I don't dig that jazz."

More laughter. Alexander has fulfilled his function. He has put the case, charmingly, for the philistines. Now tongues are loosened and the inquest can proceed.

Here are some of its findings:

Mr. Propter shouldn't have said the ego is unreal; this proves that he has no faith in human nature.

This novel is arid and abstract mysticism. What do we need eternity for, anyway?

This novel is clever but cynical. Huxley should dwell more on the warm human emotions.

This novel is a wonderful spiritual sermon. It teaches us that we aren't meant to pry into the mysteries of life. We mustn't tamper with eternity.

Huxley is marvelously zany. He wants to get rid of people and make the world safe for animals and spirits.

To say time is evil because evil happens in time is like saying the ocean is a fish because fish happen in the ocean.

Mr. Propter has no sex life. This makes him unconvincing as a character.

Mr. Pordage's sex life is unconvincing.

Mr. Propter is a Jeffersonian democrat, an anarchist, a bolshevik, a proto-John-Bircher.

Mr. Propter is an escapist. This is illustrated by the conversation with Pete about the Civil War in Spain. Pete was a good guy until Mr. Propter brainwashed him and he had a failure of nerve and started to believe in God.

Huxley really understands women. Giving Virginia a rose-colored motor scooter was a perfect touch.

And so on and so forth. . . .

George stands there smiling, saying very little, letting them enjoy themselves. He presides over the novel like an attendant at a carnival booth, encouraging the crowd to throw and smash their targets; it's all good clean fun. However, there are certain ground rules which must be upheld. When someone starts in about mescaline and lysergic acid, implying that Mr. Huxley is next door to being a dope addict, George curtly contradicts him. When someone else coyly tries to turn the *clef* in the *roman*—Is there, couldn't there be some connection between a certain notorious lady and Jo Stoyte's shooting of Pete?—George tells him absolutely not; *that* fairytale was exploded back in the thirties.

And now comes a question George has been expecting. It is asked, of course, by Myron Hirsch, that indefatigable heckler of the *goyim*. "Sir, here on page seventy-nine, Mr. Propter says the stupidest text in the Bible is '*they hated me without a cause.*' Does he mean by that the Nazis were right to hate the Jews? Is Huxley antisemitic?"

George draws a long breath. "No," he answers mildly.

And then, after a pause of expectant silence—the class is rather thrilled by Myron's bluntness—he repeats, loudly and severely, "No —Mr. Huxley is *not* antisemitic. The Nazis were *not* right to hate the Jews. But their hating the Jews was *not* without a cause. No one *ever* hates without a cause. . . .

"Look—let's leave the Jews out of this, shall we? Whatever attitude you take, it's impossible to discuss Jews objectively nowadays. It probably won't be possible for the next twenty years. So let's think about this in terms of some other minority, any one you like, but a small one—one that isn't organized and doesn't have any committees to defend it. . . ."

George looks at Wally Bryant with a deep shining look that says, I am with you, little minority-sister. Wally is plump and sallow-faced, and the care he takes to comb his wavy hair and keep his nails filed and polished and his eyebrows discreetly plucked only makes him that much less appetizing. Obviously he has understood George's look. He is embarrassed. Never mind! George is going to teach him a lesson now that he'll never forget. Is going to turn Wally's eyes into his timid soul. Is going to give him courage to throw away his nail file and face the truth of his life. . . .

"Now, for example, people with freckles aren't thought of as a minority by the non-freckled. They *aren't* a minority in the sense we're talking about. And why aren't they? Because a minority is only thought of as a minority when it constitutes some kind of a threat to the majority, real or imaginary. And no threat is ever *quite* imaginary. Anyone here disagree with that? If you do, just ask yourself, What would this particular minority do if it suddenly became the majority overnight? You see what I mean? Well, if you don't—think it over!

"All right. Now along come the liberals—including everybody in this room, I trust—and they say, 'Minorities are just people, like us.' Sure, minorities are people—*people*, not angels. Sure, they're like us— but not *exactly* like us; that's the all-too-familiar state of liberal hysteria in which you begin to kid yourself you honestly cannot see any difference between a Negro and a Swede. . . ." (Why, oh why daren't George say "between Estelle Oxford and Buddy Sorensen"? Maybe, if he did dare, there would be a great atomic blast of laughter, and everybody would embrace, and the kingdom of heaven would begin, right here in classroom 278. But then again, maybe it wouldn't.)

"So, let's face it, minorities are people who probably look and act and think differently from us and have faults we don't have. We may dislike the way they look and act, and we may hate their faults. And it's *better* if we admit to disliking and hating them than if we try to smear our feelings over with pseudo-liberal sentimentality. If we're frank about our feelings, we have a safety valve; and if we have a safety valve, we're actually less likely to start persecuting. I know that theory is unfashionable nowadays. We all keep trying to believe that if we ignore something long enough it'll just vanish. . . .

"Where was I? Oh yes. Well, now, suppose this minority does get persecuted, never mind why—political, economic, psychological reasons. There always *is* a reason, no matter how wrong it is—that's my point. And, of course, persecution itself is always wrong; I'm sure we all agree there. But the worst of it is, we now run into another liberal heresy. *Because* the persecuting majority is vile, says the liberal, *therefore* the persecuted minority must be stainlessly pure. Can't you see what nonsense that is? What's to prevent the bad from being persecuted by the worse? Did all the Christian victims in the arena have to be saints?

"And I'll tell you something else. A minority has its own kind of aggression. It absolutely dares the majority to attack it. It hates the majority—not without a cause, I grant you. It even hates the other minorities, because all minorities are in competition: each one proclaims that its sufferings are the worst and its wrongs are the blackest. And the more they all hate, and the more they're all persecuted, the nastier they become! Do you think it makes people nasty to be loved? You know it doesn't! Then why should it make them nice to be loathed? While you're being persecuted, you hate what's happening to you, you hate the people who are making it happen; you're in a world of hate. Why, you wouldn't recognize love if you met it! You'd suspect love! You'd think there was something behind it—some motive—some trick. . . ."

By this time, George no longer knows what he has proved or disproved, whose side, if any, he is arguing on, or indeed just exactly what he is talking about. And yet these sentences have blurted themselves out of his mouth with genuine passion. He has meant every one of them, be they sense or nonsense. He has administered them like strokes of a lash, to whip Wally awake, and Estelle too, and Myron, and all of them. He who has ears to hear, let him hear. . . .

Wally continues to look embarrassed—but, no, neither whipped nor awakened. And now George becomes aware that Wally's eyes are no longer on his face; they are raised and focused on a point somewhere behind him, on the wall above his head. And now, as he glances rapidly across the room, faltering, losing momentum, George sees all the other pairs of eyes raised also—focused on that damned clock. He doesn't need to turn and look for himself; he knows he must be running overtime. Brusquely he breaks off, telling them, "We'll go on with this on Monday." And they all rise instantly to their feet, collecting their books, breaking into chatter.

Well, after all, what else can you expect? They have to hurry, most of them, to get someplace else within the next ten minutes. Nevertheless, George's feathers are ruffled. It's been a long time since last he forgot and let himself get up steam like this, right at the end of a period. How humiliating! The silly enthusiastic old prof, rambling on, disregarding the clock, and the class sighing to itself, He's off again! Just for a moment, George hates them, hates their brute basic indifference, as they drain quickly out of the room. Once again, the diamond has been offered publicly for a nickel, and they have turned from it with a shrug and a grin, thinking the old peddler crazy.

So he smiles with an extra benevolence on the three who have lingered behind to ask him questions. But Sister Maria merely wants to know if George, when he sets the final examination, will require them to have read all of those books which Mr. Huxley mentions in this novel. George thinks, How amusing to tell her yes, including *The 120 Days of Sodom*. But he doesn't, of course. He reassures her and she goes away happy, her academic load that much lighter.

And then Buddy Sorensen merely wants to excuse himself. "I'm sorry, sir. I didn't read the Huxley because I thought you'd be going through it with us first." Is this sheer idiocy or slyness? George can't be bothered to find out. "Ban the Bomb!" he says, looking at Buddy's button; and Buddy, to whom he has said this before, grins happily. "Yes, sir, you bet!"

Mrs. Netta Torres wants to know if Mr. Huxley had an actual English village in mind as the original of his Gonister. George is unable to answer this. He can only tell Mrs. Torres that, in the last chapter, when Obispo and Stoyte and Virginia are in search of the fifth Earl, they appear to be driving out of London in a southwesterly direction. So, most likely, Gonister is supposed to be somewhere in Hampshire or Sussex. . . . But now it becomes clear that Mrs. Torres' question has been a pretext, merely. She has brought up the subject of England in order to tell him that she spent three unforgettable weeks there, ten years ago. Only most of it was in Scotland, and the rest all in London. "Whenever you're speaking to us," she tells George, as her eyes fervently probe his face, "I keep remembering that beautiful accent. It's like music." (George is strongly tempted to ask her just which accent she has in mind. Can it be Cockney or Gorbals?) And now Mrs. Torres wants to know the name of his birthplace, and he tells her, and she has never heard of it. He takes advantage of her momentary frustration to break off their *tête-à-tête*.

·   ·   ·

Again George's office comes in useful; he goes into it to escape from Mrs. Torres. He finds Dr. Gottlieb there.

Gottlieb is all excited because he has just received from England a new book about Francis Quarles, written by an Oxford don. Gottlieb probably knows every bit as much about Quarles as the don does. But Oxford, towering up in all its majesty behind this don, its child, utterly overawes poor little Gottlieb, who was born in one of the wrong parts of Chicago. "It makes you realize," he says, "the background you need, to do a job like this." And George feels saddened and depressed, because Gottlieb obviously wishes, above all else in life, that he could turn himself into that miserable don and learn to write his spiteful-playful, tight-assed vinegar prose.

Having held the book in his hands for a moment and turned its pages with appropriate respect, George decides that he needs something to eat. As he steps out of the building, the first people he recognizes are Kenny Potter and Lois Yamaguchi. They are sitting on the grass under one of the newly planted trees. Their tree is even smaller than the others. It has barely a dozen leaves on it. To sit under it at all seems ridiculous; perhaps this is just why Kenny chose it. He and Lois look as though they were children playing at being stranded on a South Pacific atoll. Thinking this, George smiles at them. They smile back, and then Lois starts to laugh, in her dainty-shamefaced Japanese way. George passes quite close by their atoll as a steamship might, without stopping. Lois seems to know what he is, for she waves gaily to him exactly as one waves to a steamship, with an enchantingly delicate gesture of her tiny wrist and hand. Kenny waves also, but it is doubtful if *he* knows; he is only following Lois's example. Anyhow, their waving charms George's heart. He waves back to them. The old steamship and the young castaways have exchanged signals—but not signals for help. They respect each other's privacy. They have no desire for involvement. They simply wish each other well. Again, as by the tennis players, George feels that his day has been brightened; but, this time, the emotion isn't in the least disturbing. It is peaceful, radiant. George steams on toward the cafeteria, smiling to himself, not even wanting to look back.

But then he hears "Sir!" right behind him, and he turns and it's Kenny. Kenny has come running up silently in his sneakers. George supposes he will ask some specific question such as what book are they going to read next in class, and then leave again. But no, Kenny drops into step beside him, remarking in a matter-of-fact voice, "I have to go down to the bookshop." He doesn't ask if George is going to the bookshop and George doesn't tell him that he hasn't been planning to.

"Did you ever take mescaline, sir?"

"Yes, once. In New York. That was about eight years ago. There weren't any regulations against selling it then. I just went into a drugstore and ordered some. They'd never heard of it, but they got it for me in a few days."

"And did it make you see things—like mystical visions and stuff?"

"No. Not what you could call visions. At first I felt seasick. Not badly. And scared a bit, of course. Like Dr. Jekyll might have felt after he'd taken his drug for the first time. And then certain colors began to get very bright and stand out. You couldn't think why everybody didn't notice them. I remember a woman's red purse lying on a table in a restaurant—it was like a public scandal! And people's faces turn into caricatures; I mean, you seem to see what each one is about, and it's very crude and simplified. One's absurdly vain, and another is literally worrying himself sick, and another is longing to pick a fight. And then you see a very few who are simply beautiful, just cause they aren't anxious or aggressive about anything; they're taking life as it comes. . . . Oh, and everything becomes more and more three-dimensional: Curtains get heavy and sculptured-looking, and wood is very grainy. And flowers and plants are quite obviously alive. I remember a pot of violets—they weren't moving, but you knew they could move. Each one was like a snake reared up motionless on its coils. . . . And then, while the thing is working full strength, it's as if the walls of the room and everything around you are breathing, and the grain in woodwork begins to flow, as though it were a liquid. . . . And then it all slowly dies down again, back to normal. You don't have any hangover. Afterwards I felt fine. I ate a huge supper."

"You didn't take it again after that?"

"No. I found I didn't want to, particularly. It was just an experience I'd had. I gave the rest of the capsules to friends. One of them

saw pretty much what I saw, and another didn't see anything. And
one told me she'd never been so scared in her whole life. But I suspect
she was only being polite. Like thanking for a party—"

"You don't have any of those capsules left now, do you, sir?"

"No, Kenny, I do not! And even if I had, I wouldn't distribute
them among the student body. I can think of much more amusing
ways to get myself thrown out of this place."

Kenny grins. "Sorry, sir. I was only wondering. . . . I guess, if I
really wanted the stuff, I could get it all right. You can get most
anything of that kind, right here on campus. This friend of Lois's got
it here. *He* claims, when he took it, he saw God."

"Well, maybe he did. Maybe I just didn't take enough."

Kenny looks down at George. He seems amused. "You know
something, sir? I bet, even if you *had* seen God, you wouldn't tell
us."

"What makes you say that?"

"It's what Lois says. She thinks you're—well, kind of cagey. Like
this morning, when you were listening to all that crap we were talking
about Huxley—"

"I didn't notice *you* doing much talking. I don't think you opened
your mouth once."

"I was watching you. No kidding, I think Lois is right! You let
us ramble on, and then you straighten us out, and I'm not saying you
don't teach us a lot of interesting stuff—you do—but you never tell
us *all* you know about something. . . ."

George feels flattered and excited. Kenny has never talked to him
like this before. He can't resist slipping into the role Kenny so tempt-
ingly offers him.

"Well—maybe that's true, up to a point. You see, Kenny, there
are some things you don't even *know* you know, until you're asked."

They have reached the tennis courts. The courts are all in use
now, dotted with moving figures. But George, with the lizard-quick
glance of a veteran addict, has already noted that the morning's pair
has left, and that none of these players are physically attractive. On
the nearest court, a fat, middle-aged faculty member is playing to work
up a sweat, against a girl with hair on her legs.

"Someone has to ask you a question," George continues mean-ingly, "before you can answer it. But it's so seldom you find anyone who'll ask the right questions. Most people aren't that much interested. . . ."

Kenny is silent. Is he thinking this over? Is he going to ask George something right now? George's pulse quickens with anticipation.

"It's not that I *want* to be cagey," he says, keeping his eyes on the ground and making this as impersonal as he can. "You know, Kenny, so often I feel I want to *tell* things, *discuss* things, absolutely frankly. I don't mean in class, of course—that wouldn't work. Someone would be sure to misunderstand. . . ."

Silence. George glances quickly up at Kenny and sees that he's looking, though without any apparent interest, at the hirsute girl. Perhaps he hasn't even been listening. It's impossible to tell.

"Maybe this friend of Lois's didn't see God, after all," says Kenny abruptly. "I mean, he might have been kidding himself. I mean, not too long after he took the stuff, he had a breakdown. He was locked up for three months in an institution. He told Lois that while he was having this breakdown he turned into a devil and he could put out stars. I'm not kidding! He said he could put out seven of them at a time. He was scared of the police, though. He said the police had a machine for catching devils and liquidating them. It was called a *Mo*-machine. *Mo*, that's *Om*—you know, sir, that Indian word for God—spelled backwards."

"If the police liquidated devils, that would mean they were angels, wouldn't it? Well, that certainly makes sense. A place where the police are angels has to be an insane asylum."

Kenny is still laughing loudly at this when they reach the bookshop. He wants to buy a pencil sharpener. They have them in plastic covers, red or green or blue or yellow. Kenny takes a red one.

"What was it you wanted to get, sir?"

"Well, nothing, actually."

"You mean, you walked all the way down here just to keep me company?"

"Sure. Why not?"

Kenny seems sincerely surprised and pleased. "Well, I think you deserve something for that! Here, sir, take one of these. It's on me."

"Oh, but—well, thank you!" George is actually blushing a little.

It's as if he has been offered a rose. He chooses a yellow sharpener.

Kenny grins. "I kind of expected you'd pick blue."

"Why?"

"Isn't blue supposed to be spiritual?"

"What makes you think I want to be spiritual? And how come you picked red?"

"What's red stand for?"

"Rage and lust."

"No kidding?"

They remain silent, grinning almost intimately. George feels that, even if all this doubletalk hasn't brought them any closer to understanding each other, the not-understanding, the readiness to remain at cross-purposes, is in itself a kind of intimacy. Then Kenny pays for the pencil sharpeners and waves his hand with a gesture which implies casual, undeferential dismissal. "I'll see you around."

He strolls away. George lingers on in the bookshop for a few minutes, lest he should seem to be following him.

If eating is regarded as a sacrament, then the faculty dining room must be compared to the bleakest and barest of Quaker meetinghouses. No concession here to the ritualism of food served snugly and appetizingly in togetherness. This room is an anti-restaurant. It is much too clean, with its chromium-and-plastic tables; much too tidy, with its brown metal wastebaskets for soiled paper napkins and used paper cups; and, in contrast to the vast human rattle of the students' dining room, much too quiet. Its quietness is listless, embarrassed, self-conscious. And the room isn't even made venerable or at least formidable, like an Oxford or Cambridge high table, by the age of its occupants. Most of these people are relatively young; George is one of the eldest.

Christ, it is sad, sad to see on quite a few of these faces—young ones particularly—a glum, defeated look. Why do they feel this way about their lives? Sure, they are underpaid. Sure, they have no great prospects, in the commercial sense. Sure, they can't enjoy the bliss of mingling with corporation executives. But isn't it any consolation to be with students who are still three-quarters alive? Isn't it some tiny satisfaction to be *of use*, instead of helping to turn out useless consumer goods? Isn't it something to know that you belong to one of the few professions in this country which isn't hopelessly corrupt?

For these glum ones, apparently not. They would like out, if they dared try. But they have prepared themselves for this job, and now they have got to go through with it. They have wasted the time in which they should have been learning to cheat and grab and lie. They have cut themselves off from the majority—the middlemen, the hucksters, the promoters—by laboriously acquiring all this dry, discredited knowledge—discredited, that is to say, by the middleman, because he can get along without it. All the middleman wants are its products, its practical applications. These professors are suckers, he says. What's the use of knowing something if you don't make money out of it? And the glum ones more than half agree with him and feel privately ashamed of not being smart and crooked.

George goes through into the serving room. On the counter are steaming casseroles from which the waitresses dish you out stew, vegetables or soup. Or you can have salad or fruit pie or a strange deadly-looking jelly which is semitransparent, with veins of brilliant green. Gazing at one of these jellies with a kind of unwilling fascination, as though it were something behind glass in a reptile house, is Grant Lefanu, the young physics professor who writes poetry. Grant is the very opposite of glum, and he couldn't be less defeated; George rather loves him. He is small and thin, and has glasses and large teeth and the maddish smile of genuine intellectual passion. You can easily imagine him as one of the terrorists back in Czarist Russia a hundred years ago. Given the opportunity, he would be that kind of fanatic hero who follows an idea, without the least hesitation and as a matter of course, straight through to its expression in action. The talk of pale, burning-eyed students, anarchists and utopians all, over tea and cigarettes in a locked room long past midnight, is next morning translated, with the literalness of utter innocence, into the throwing of the bomb, the shouting of the proud slogan, the dragging away of the young dreamer-doer, still smiling, to the dungeon and the firing squad. On Grant's face you often see such a smile—of embarrassment, almost, at having had to express his meaning so crudely. He is like a shy mumbler who suddenly in desperation speaks much too loud.

As a matter of fact, Grant has recently performed at least one act of minor heroism. He has appeared in court as a defense witness for a bookseller caught peddling some grand old sex classic of the twenties; it used to be obtainable only in the lands of the Latins, but now, through a series of test cases, it is fighting for its right to be devoured by American youth. (George can't be absolutely sure if this is the same book he himself read as a young man, during a trip to Paris. At all events, he remembers throwing this, or some other book just like it, into the wastebasket, in the middle of the big screwing scene. Not that one isn't broad-minded, of course; let them write about heterosexuality if they must, and let everyone read it who cares to. Just the same, it is a deadly bore and, to be frank, a wee bit distasteful. Why can't these modern writers stick to the old simple wholesome themes—such as, for example, boys?)

Grant Lefanu's heroism on this occasion consisted in his defense of the book at the risk of his academic neck. For a very important and senior member of the STSC faculty had previously appeared as a witness for the prosecution and had guaranteed the book dirty, degenerate and dangerous. When Grant was called to the stand and cross-examined by the prosecuting attorney, he begged, with his shy smile, to differ from his colleague. At length, after some needling and after having been cautioned three times to speak up, he blurted out a statement to the effect that it wasn't the book, but its attackers, who deserved the three adjectives. To make matters worse, one of the local liberal columnists gleefully reported all of this, casting the senior faculty member as a reactionary old ass and Grant as a bright young upholder of civil liberty, and twisting his testimony into a personal insult. So now the question is, Will Grant get his tenure prolonged at the end of the academic year?

Grant treats George as a fellow subverter, a compliment which George hardly deserves, since, with his seniority, his license to play the British eccentric, and, in the last resort, his little private income, he can afford to say pretty much anything he likes on campus. Whereas poor Grant has no private income, a wife and three imprudently begotten children.

"What's new?" George asks him, implying, What has the Enemy been up to?

"You know those courses for police students? Today a special man from Washington is addressing them on twenty ways to spot a Commie."

"You're kidding!"

"Want to go? We might ask him some awkward questions."

"What time is it?"

"Four-thirty."

"Can't. I've got to be downtown in an hour."

"Too bad."

"Too bad," George agrees, relieved. He isn't absolutely sure if this was a bona fide dare or not, however. Various other times, in the same half-serious tone, Grant has suggested that they go and heckle a John Birch Society meeting, smoke pot in Watts with the best unknown poet in America, meet someone high up in the Black Muslim movement. George doesn't seriously suspect Grant of trying to test him. No doubt Grant really does do such things now and then, and it simply does not occur to him that George might be scared. He probably thinks George excuses himself from these outings for fear of being bored.

As they move down the counter, ending up with only coffee and salad—George watches his weight and Grant has an appetite as slender as his build—Grant tells about a man he knows who has been talking to some experts at a big firm which makes computers. These experts say that it doesn't really matter if there's a war, because enough people will survive to run the country with. Of course, the people who survive will tend to be those with money and influence, because they'll have the better type of shelter, not the leaky death traps which a lot of crooks have been offering at bargain prices. When you get your shelter built, say the experts, you should go to at least three different contractors, so nobody will know what it is you're building; because if the word gets around that you have a better type shelter, you'll be mobbed at the first emergency. For the same reason, you ought to be realistic and buy a submachine gun. This is no time for false sentiment.

George laughs in an appropriately sardonic manner, since this is what Grant expects of him. But this gallows humor sickens his heart. In all those old crises of the twenties, the thirties, the war—each one of them has left its traces upon George, like an illness—what was terrible was the fear of annihilation. Now we have with us a far more terrible fear, the fear of survival. Survival into a Rubble Age, in which it will be quite natural for Mr. Strunk to gun down Grant and his wife and three children, because Grant has neglected to lay in sufficient stores of food and they are starving and may therefore possibly become dangerous and this is no time for sentiment.

"There's Cynthia," Grant says, as they re-enter the dining room. "Want to join her?"

"Do we have to?"

"I guess so." Grant giggles nervously. "She's seen us."

And, indeed, Cynthia Leach is waving to them. She is a handsome young New Yorker, Sarah Lawrence–trained, the daughter of a rich family. Maybe it was partly to annoy them that she recently married Leach, who teaches history here. But their marriage seems to work quite well. Though Andy is slim and white-skinned, he is no weakling; his dark eyes sparkle sexily and he has the unaggressive litheness of one who takes a great deal of exercise in bed. He is somewhat out of his league socially, but no doubt he enjoys the extra effort required to keep up with Cynthia. They give parties to which everyone comes because the food and drink are lavish, thanks to Cynthia's money, and Andy is popular anyhow, and Cynthia isn't that bad. Her only trouble is that she thinks of herself as an Eastern aristocrat slumming; she tries to be patrician and is merely patronizing.

"Andy stood me up," Cynthia tells them. "Talk to me." Then, as they sit down at her table, she turns to Grant. "Your wife's never going to forgive me."

"Oh?" Grant laughs with quite extraordinary violence.

"She didn't tell you about it?"

"Not a word!"

"She didn't?" Cynthia is disappointed. Then she brightens. "Oh, but she *must* be mad at me! I was telling her how hideously they dress the children here."

"But she agreed with you, I'm sure. She's always talking about it."

"They're being cheated out of their childhood," Cynthia says, ignoring this. "They're being turned into *junior consumers*! All those dreadful dainty little creatures, wearing lipstick! I was down in Mexico last month. It was like a breath of fresh air. Oh, I can't tell you! Their children are so real. No anxiety. No other-direction. They just bloom."

"The only question is—" Grant begins. Obviously he is starting not to agree with Cynthia. For this very reason, he mumbles, he can barely be heard. Cynthia chooses not to hear him.

"And then that night we came back across the border! Shall I ever forget it? I said to myself, Either these people are insane or I am. They all seemed to be *running*, the way they do in the old silent newsreels. And the *hostess* in the restaurant—it had never struck me before how truly sinister it is to call them that. The way she *smiled* at us! And those enormous menus, with nothing on them that was really edible. And those weird zombie busboys, bringing nothing but glasses of *water* and simply refusing to speak to you! I just could not believe my own eyes. Oh, and then we stayed the night at one of these ghastly new motels. I had the feeling that it had only just been brought from someplace else, some factory, and set up exactly one minute before we arrived. It didn't belong *anywhere*. I mean—after all those marvelous old hotels in Mexico—each one of them is really a *place*—but this was just utterly unreal—"

Again, Grant seems about to attempt some kind of a protest. But this time his mumbling is still lower. Even George can't understand him. George takes a big drink of his coffee, feels the kick of it in his nearly empty stomach, and finds himself suddenly high. "Really, Cynthia, my dear!" he hears himself exclaim. "How can you talk such incredible nonsense?"

Grant giggles with astonishment. Cynthia looks surprised but rather pleased. She is the kind of bully who likes being challenged; it soothes the itch of her aggression.

"Honestly! Are you out of your mind?" George feels himself racing down the runway, becoming smoothly, exhilaratingly airborne. "My God, you sound like some dreary French intellectual who's just set foot in New York for the first time! That's exactly the way they talk! *Unreal!* American motels are unreal! My good girl—you know and I know that our motels are deliberately designed to be unreal, if you must use that idiotic jargon, for the very simple reason that an American motel room isn't *a* room in *an* hotel, it's *the* room, definitively, period. There is only one: *The Room*. And it's a symbol—an advertisement in three dimensions, if you like—for our way of life. And what's our way of life? A building code which demands certain measurements, certain utilities and the use of certain apt materials; no more and no less. Everything else you've got to supply for yourself. But just try telling that to the Europeans! It scares them to death. The truth is, our way of life is far too austere for them. We've reduced the things of the material plane to mere symbolic conveniences. And why? Because that's the essential first step. Until the material plane has been defined and relegated to its proper place, the mind can't ever be truly free. One would think that was obvious. The stupidest American seems to understand it intuitively. But the Europeans call us inhuman—or they prefer to say immature, which sounds ruder—because we've renounced their world of individual differences and romantic inefficiency and objects-for-the-sake-of-objects. All that dead old cult of cathedrals and first editions and Paris models and vintage wines. Naturally, they never give up, they keep trying to subvert us, every moment, with their loathsome cult-propaganda. If they ever succeed, we'll be done for. *That's* the kind of subversion the Un-American Activities Committee *ought* to be investigating. The Europeans hate us because we've retired to live inside our advertisements, like hermits going into caves to contemplate. We sleep in symbolic bedrooms, eat symbolic meals, are symbolically entertained—and that terrifies them, that fills them with fury and loathing because they can never understand it. They keep yelling out, 'These people are zombies!' They've got to make themselves believe that, because the alternative is to break down and admit that Americans are able to live like this because, actually, they're a far, far more advanced culture—five hundred, maybe a thousand years ahead of Europe, or anyone else on earth, for that matter. Essentially we're creatures of spirit. Our life is all in the mind. That's why we're completely at home with symbols like the American motel room. Whereas the European has a horror of symbols because he's such a groveling little materialist. . . ."

Some moments before the end of this wild word-flight, George has seen, as it were from a great altitude, Andy Leach enter the dining room. Which is indeed a lucky deliverance, for already George has felt his engines cut out, felt himself losing thrust. So now, with the skill of a veteran pilot, he swoops down to a perfect landing. And the beauty of it is, he appears to stop talking out of mere politeness, because Andy has reached their table.

"Did I miss something?" Andy asks, grinning.

A performer at the circus has no theater curtain to come down and hide him and thus preserve the magic spell of his act unbroken. Poised high on the trapeze under the blazing arcs, he has flashed and pulsed like a star indeed. But now, grounded, unsparkling, unfollowed by spotlights, yet plainly visible to anyone who cares to look at him— they are all watching the clowns—he hurries past the tiers of seats toward the exit. Nobody applauds him any more. Very few spare him a single glance.

Together with this anonymity, George feels a fatigue come over him which is not disagreeable. The tide of his vitality is ebbing fast, and he ebbs with it, content. This is a way of resting. All of a sudden he is much, much older. On his way out to the parking lot he walks differently, with less elasticity, moving his arms and his shoulders stiffly. He slows down. Now and then his steps actually shuffle. His head is bowed. His mouth loosens and the muscles of his cheeks sag. His face takes on a dull dreamy placid look. He hums queerly to himself, with a sound like bees around a hive. From time to time, as he walks, he emits quite loud, prolonged farts.

The hospital stands tall on a sleepy by-passed hill, rising from steep lawns and flowering bushes, within sight of the freeway itself. A tall reminder to the passing motorists—*this is the end of the road, folks*—it has a pleasant aspect, nevertheless. It stands open to all the breezes, and there must be many of its windows from which you can see the ocean and the Palos Verdes headland and even Catalina Island, in the clear winter weather.

The nurses at the reception desk are pleasant, too. They don't fuss you with a lot of questions. If you know the number of the room you want to visit, you don't even have to ask for their permission; you can go right up.

George works the elevator himself. At the second floor it is stopped, and a colored male nurse wheels in a prone patient. She is for surgery, he tells George, so they must descend again to the ground floor, where the operating rooms are. George offers respectfully to get off the elevator but the young nurse (who has very sexy muscular arms) says, "You don't have to"; so there he stands, like a spectator at the funeral of a stranger, furtively peeking at the patient. She appears to be fully conscious, but it would be a kind of sacrilege to speak to her, for already she is the dedicated, the ritually prepared victim. She seems to know this and consent to it; to be entirely relaxed in her consent. Her gray hair looks so pretty; it must have been recently waved.

This is the gate, George says to himself.

Must I pass through here, too?

Ah, how the poor body recoils with its every nerve from the sight, the smell, the feel of this place! Blindly it shies, rears, struggles to escape. That it should ever be brought here—stupefied by their drugs, pricked by their needles, cut by their little knives—what an unthinkable outrage to the flesh! Even if they were to cure it and release it, it could never forget, never forgive. Nothing would be the same any more. It would have lost all faith in itself.

Jim used to moan and complain and raise hell over a head cold, a cut finger, a pile. But Jim was lucky at the end—the only time when luck really counts. The truck hit his car just right; he never felt it. And they never got him into a place like this one. His smashed leavings were of no use to them for their rituals.

Doris' room is on the top floor. The hallway is deserted, for the moment, and the door stands open with a screen hiding the bed. George peeps over the top of the screen before going in. Doris is lying with her face toward the window.

George has gotten quite accustomed by now to the way she looks. It isn't even horrible to him any more, because he has lost his sense of a transformation. Doris no longer seems changed. She is a different creature altogether—this yellow shriveled mannequin with its sticks of arms and legs, withered flesh and hollow belly, making angular outlines under the sheet. What has it to do with that big arrogant animal of a girl? With that body which sprawled stark naked, gaping wide in shameless demand, underneath Jim's naked body? Gross insucking vulva, sly ruthless greedy flesh, in all the bloom and gloss and arrogant resilience of youth, demanding that George shall step aside, bow down

and yield to the female prerogative, hide his unnatural head in shame.
I am Doris. I am Woman. I am Bitch–Mother Nature. The Church
and the Law and the State exist to support me. I claim my biological
rights. I demand Jim.

George has sometimes asked himself, Would I ever, even in those
days, have wished this on her?

The answer is No. Not because George would be incapable of
such fiendishness; but because Doris, then, was infinitely more than
Doris, was Woman the Enemy, claiming Jim for herself. No use
destroying Doris, or ten thousand Dorises, as long as Woman triumphs.
Woman could only be fought by yielding, by letting Jim go away with
her on that trip to Mexico. By urging him to satisfy all his curiosity
and flattered vanity and lust (vanity, mostly) on the gamble that he
would return (as he did) saying, *She's disgusting*, saying, *Never again*.

And wouldn't you be twice as disgusted, Jim, if you could see
her now? Wouldn't you feel a crawling horror to think that maybe,
even then, her body you fondled and kissed hungrily and entered with
your aroused flesh already held seeds of this rottenness? You used to
bathe the sores on cats so gently and you never minded the stink of
old diseased dogs; yet you had a horror, in spite of yourself, of human
sickness and people who were crippled. I know something, Jim. I feel
certain of it. You'd refuse absolutely to visit her here. You wouldn't
be able to force yourself to do it.

George walks around the screen and into the room, making just
the necessary amount of noise. Doris turns her head and sees him,
seemingly without surprise. Probably, for her, the line between reality
and hallucination is getting very thin. Figures keep appearing, dis-
appearing. If one of them sticks you with a needle, then you can be
sure it actually *is* a nurse. George may be George or, again, he may
not. For convenience she will treat him as George. Why not? What
does it matter either way?

"Hello," she says. Her eyes are a wild brilliant blue in her sick
yellow face.

"Hello, Doris."

A good while since, George has stopped bringing her flowers or
other gifts. There is nothing of any significance he can bring into this
room from the outside now; not even himself. Everything that matters

to her is now right here in this room, where she is absorbed in the business of dying. Her preoccupation doesn't seem egotistic, however; it does not exclude George or anyone else who cares to share in it. This preoccupation is with death, and we can all share in that, at any time, at any age, well or ill.

George sits down beside her now and takes her hand. If he had done this even two months ago, it would have been loathsomely false. (One of his most bitterly shameful memories is of a time he kissed her cheek—Was it aggression, masochism? Oh, damn all such words!— right after he found out she'd been to bed with Jim. Jim was there when it happened. When George moved toward her to kiss her, Jim's eyes looked startled and scared, as if he feared George was about to bite her like a snake.) But now taking Doris' hand isn't false, isn't even an act of compassion. It is necessary—he has discovered this on previous visits—in order to establish even partial contact. And holding her hand he feels less embarrassed by her sickness; for the gesture means, *We are on the same road, I shall follow you soon.* He is thus excused from having to ask those ghastly sickroom questions, How are you, how's it going, how do you feel?

Doris smiles faintly. Is it because she's pleased that he has come?

No. She is smiling with amusement, it seems. Speaking low but very distinctly, she says, "I made such a noise, yesterday."

George smiles too, waiting for the joke.

"Was it yesterday?" This is in the same tone, but addressed to herself. Her eyes no longer see him; they look bewildered and a bit scared. Time must have become a very odd kind of mirror-maze for her now; and mazes can change at any instant from being funny to being frightening.

But now the eyes are aware of him again; the bewilderment has passed. "I was screaming. They heard me clear down the hall. They had to fetch the doctor." Doris smiles. This, apparently, is the joke.

"Was it your back?" George asks. The effort to keep sympathy out of his voice makes him speak primly, like someone who is trying to suppress an ungentlemanly native accent. But Doris disregards the question. She is off in some new direction of her own, frowning a little. She asks abruptly, "What time is it?"

"Nearly three."

There is a long silence. George feels a terrible need to say something, anything.

"I was out on the pier the other day. I hadn't been there in ages. And, do you know, they've torn down the old roller-skating rink? Isn't that a shame? It seems as if they can't bear to leave anything the way it used to be. Do you remember that booth where the woman used to read your character from your handwriting? That's gone too—"

He stops short, dismayed.

Can memory really get away with such a crude trick? Seemingly it can. For he has picked the pier from it as casually as you pick a card at random from a magician's deck—and behold, the card has been forced! It was while George and Jim were roller-skating that they first met Doris. (She was with a boy named Norman whom she quickly ditched.) And later they all went to have their handwriting read. And the woman told Jim that he had latent musical talent, and Doris that she had a great capacity for bringing out the best in other people—

Does she remember? Of course she must! George glances at her anxiously. She lies staring at the ceiling, frowning harder.

"What did you say the time was?"

"Nearly three. Four minutes of."

"Look outside in the hall, will you? See if anyone's there."

He gets up, goes to the door, looks out. But before he has even reached it, she has asked with harsh impatience, "Well?"

"There's no one."

"Where's that fucking nurse?" It comes out of her so harshly, so nakedly desperate.

"Shall I go look for her?"

"She knows I get a shot at three. The doctor told her. She doesn't give a shit."

"I'll find her."

"That bitch won't come till she's good and ready."

"I'm sure I can find her."

"No! Stay here."

"Okay."

"Sit down again."

"Sure." He sits down. He knows she wants his hand. He gives it to her. She grips it with astonishing strength.

"George—"

"Yes?"

"You'll stay here till she comes?"

"Of course I will."

Her grip tightens. There is no affection in it, no communication. She isn't gripping a fellow creature. His hand is just something to grip. He dare not ask her about the pain. He is afraid of releasing some obscene horror, something visible and tangible and stinking, right here between them in the room.

Yet he is curious, too. Last time, the nurse told him that Doris has been seeing a priest. (She was raised a Catholic.) And, sure enough, here on the table beside the bed is a little paper book, gaudy and cute as a Christmas card: The Stations of the Cross. . . . Ah, but when the road narrows to the width of this bed, when there is nothing in front of you that is known, dare you disdain any guide? Perhaps Doris has learned something already about the journey ahead of her. But, even supposing that she has and that George could bring himself to ask her, she could never tell him what she knows. For that could only be expressed in the language of the place to which she is going. And that language—though some of us gabble it so glibly—has no real meaning in our world. In our mouths, it is just a lot of words.

Here's the nurse, smiling, in the doorway. "I'm punctual today, you see!" She has a tray with the hypodermic and the ampoules.

"I'll be going," George says, rising at once.

"Oh, you don't have to do that," says the nurse. "If you'll just step outside for a moment. This won't take any time at all."

"I have to go anyway," George says, feeling guilty as one always does about leaving any sickroom. Not that Doris herself makes him feel guilty. She seems to have lost all interest in him. Her eyes are fixed on the needle in the nurse's hand.

"She's been a bad girl," the nurse says. "We can't get her to eat her lunch, can we?"

"Well, so long, Doris. See you again in a couple of days."

"Goodbye, George." Doris doesn't even glance at him, and her tone is utterly indifferent. He is leaving her world and thereby ceasing to exist. He takes her hand and presses it. She doesn't respond. She watches the bright needle as it moves toward her.

Did she *mean* goodbye? This could be, soon will be. As George leaves the room, he looks at her once again over the top of the screen, trying to catch and fix some memory in his mind, to be aware of the occasion or at least of its possibility: the last time I saw her alive.

Nothing. It means nothing. He feels nothing.

As George pressed Doris' hand just now, he knew something: that the very last traces of the Doris who tried to take Jim from him have vanished from this shriveled mannequin, and, with them, the last of his hate. As long as one tiny precious drop of hate remained, George could still find something left in her of Jim. For he hated Jim too, nearly as much as her, while they were away together in Mexico. That has been the bond between him and Doris. And now it is broken. And one more bit of Jim is lost to him forever.

As George drives down the boulevard, the big unwieldy Christmas decorations—reindeer and jingle bells slung across the street on cables secured to metal Christmas trees—are swinging in a chill wind. But they are merely advertisements for Christmas, paid for by the local merchants. Shoppers crowd the stores and the sidewalks, their faces somewhat bewildered, their eyes reflecting, like polished buttons, the cynical sparkle of the Yuletide. Hardly more than a month ago, before Khrushchev agreed to pull his rockets out of Cuba, they were cramming the markets, buying the shelves bare of beans, rice and other foodstuffs, utterly useless, most of them, for air-raid-shelter cookery, because they can't be prepared without pints of water. Well, the shoppers were spared—this time. Do they rejoice? They are too dull for that, poor dears; they never knew what didn't hit them. No doubt because of that panic buying, they have less money now for gifts. But they have enough. It will be quite a good Christmas, the merchants predict. Everyone can afford to spend at least something, except, maybe, some of the young hustlers (recognizable at once to experienced eyes like George's) who stand scowling on the street corners or staring into shops with the maximum of peripheral vision.

George is very far, right now, from sneering at any of these fellow creatures. They may be crude and mercenary and dull and low, but he is proud, is glad, is almost indecently gleeful to be able to stand up and be counted in their ranks—the ranks of that marvelous minority, The Living. They don't know their luck, these people on the sidewalk, but George knows his—for a little while at least—because he is freshly returned from the icy presence of The Majority, which Doris is about to join.

I am alive, he says to himself, *I am alive!* And life-energy surges hotly through him, and delight, and appetite. How good to be in a body—even this old beat-up carcass—that still has warm blood and live semen and rich marrow and wholesome flesh! The scowling youths on the corners see him as a dodderer, no doubt, or at best as a potential score. Yet he still claims a distant kinship with the strength of their young arms and shoulders and loins. For a few bucks he could get any one of them to climb into the car, ride back with him to his house, strip off butch leather jacket, skin-tight levis, shirt and cowboy boots and take part, a naked, sullen young athlete, in the wrestling bout of his pleasure. But George doesn't want the bought unwilling bodies of these boys. He wants to rejoice in his own body—the tough triumphant old body of a survivor. The body that has outlived Jim and is going to outlive Doris.

He decides to stop by the gym—although this isn't one of his regular days—on his way home.

In the locker room, George takes off his clothes, gets into his sweatsocks, jockstrap and shorts. Shall he put on a tee shirt? He looks at himself in the long mirror. Not too bad. The bulges of flesh over the belt of the shorts are not so noticeable today. The legs are quite good. The chest muscles, when properly flexed, don't sag. And, as long as he doesn't have his spectacles on, he can't see the little wrinkles inside the elbows, above the kneecaps and around the hollow of the sucked-in belly. The neck is loose and scraggy under all circumstances, in all lights, and would look gruesome even if he were half-blind. He has abandoned the neck altogether, like an untenable military position.

Yet he looks—and doesn't he know it!—better than nearly all of his age-mates at this gym. Not because they're in such bad shape—they are healthy enough specimens. What's wrong with them is their fatalistic acceptance of middle age, their ignoble resignation to grandfatherhood, impending retirement and golf. George is different from them because, in some sense which can't quite be defined but which

is immediately apparent when you see him naked, *he hasn't given up.*
He is still a contender, and they aren't. Maybe it's nothing more
mysterious than vanity which gives him this air of a withered boy?
Yes, despite his wrinkles, his slipped flesh, his graying hair, his grim-
lipped, strutting spryness, you catch occasional glimpses of a ghostly
someone else, soft-faced, boyish, pretty. The combination is bizarre,
it is older than middle age itself, but it is there.

Looking grimly into the mirror, with distaste and humor, George
says to himself, You old ass, who are you trying to seduce? And he
puts on his tee shirt.

In the gym there are only three people. It's still too early for the
office workers. A big heavy man named Buck—all that remains at fifty
of a football player—is talking to a curly-haired young man named
Rick, who aspires to television. Buck is nearly nude; his rolling belly
bulges indecently over a kind of bikini, pushing it clear down to the
bush line. He seems quite without shame. Whereas Rick, who has a
very well-made muscular body, wears a gray wool sweatshirt and pants,
covering all of it from the neck to the wrists and ankles. "Hi, George"
they both say, nodding casually at him; and this, George feels, is the
most genuinely friendly greeting he has received all day.

Buck knows all about the history of sport; he is an encyclopedia
of batting averages, handicaps, records and scores. He is in the midst
of telling how someone took someone else in the seventh round. He
mimes the knockout: *"Pow! Pow!* And, boy, he'd *had* it!" Rick listens,
seated astride a bench. There is always an atmosphere of leisureliness
in this place. A boy like Rick will take three or four hours to work
out, and spend most of the time just yakking about show biz, about
sport cars, about football and boxing—very seldom, oddly enough,
about sex. Perhaps this is partly out of consideration for the morals of
the various young kids and early teen-agers who are usually around.
When Rick talks to grownups, he is apt to be smart-alecky or actor-
sincere; but with the kids he is as unaffected as a village idiot. He
clowns for them and does magic tricks and tells them stories, deadpan,
about a store in Long Beach (he gives its exact address) where once in
a great while, suddenly and without any previous announcement, they
declare a Bargain Day. On such days, every customer who spends
more than a dollar gets a Jag or a Porsche or an MG for free. (The

rest of the time, the place is an ordinary antique shop.) When Rick is challenged to show the car *he* got, he takes the kids outside and points to a suitable one on the street. When they look at its registration slip and find that it belongs to someone else, Rick swears that that's his real name; he changed it when he started acting. The kids don't absolutely disbelieve him, but they yell that he's a liar and crazy and they beat on him with their fists. While they do this, Rick capers grinning around the gym on all fours, like a dog.

George lies down on one of the inclined boards in order to do sit-ups. This is always something you have to think yourself into; the body dislikes them more than any other exercise. While he is getting into the mood, Webster comes over and lies down on the board next to his. Webster is maybe twelve or thirteen, slender and graceful and tall for his age, with long smooth golden boy-legs. He is gentle and shy, and he moves about the gym in a kind of dream; but he keeps steadily on with his workout. No doubt he thinks he looks scrawny and has vowed to become a huge wide awkward overloaded muscle man. George says, "Hi, Web," and Webster answers, "Hi, George," in a shy, secretive whisper.

Now Webster begins doing his sit-ups, and George, peeling off his tee shirt on a sudden impulse, follows his example. As they continue, George feels an empathy growing between them. They are not competing with each other; but Webster's youth and litheness seem to possess George, and this borrowed energy is terrific. Withdrawing his attention from his own protesting muscles and concentrating it upon Webster's flexing and relaxing body, George draws the strength from it to go on beyond his normal forty sit-ups, to fifty, to sixty, to seventy, to eighty. Shall he try for a hundred? Then, all at once, he is aware that Webster has stopped. The strength leaves him instantly. He stops too, panting hard—though not any harder than Webster himself. They lie there panting, side by side. Webster turns his head and looks at George, obviously rather impressed.

"How many do you do?" he asks.

"Oh—it depends."

"These things just kill me. Man!"

How delightful it is to be here. If only one could spend one's entire life in this state of easygoing physical democracy. Nobody is bitchy here, or ill-tempered, or inquisitive. Vanity, including the most outrageous posings in front of the mirrors, is taken for granted. The godlike young baseball player confides to all his anxiety about the smallness of his ankles. The plump banker, rubbing his face with skin cream, says simply, "I can't afford to get old." No one is perfect and no one pretends to be. Even the half-dozen quite well-known actors put on no airs. The youngest kids sit innocently naked beside sixty- and seventy-year-olds in the steam room, and they call each other by their first names. Nobody is too hideous or too handsome to be accepted as an equal. Surely everyone is nicer in this place than he is outside it?

Today George feels more than usually unwilling to leave the gym. He does his exercises twice as many times as he is supposed to; he spends a long while in the steam room; he washes his hair.

When he comes out onto the street again, it is already getting toward sunset. And now he makes another impulsive decision: instead of driving directly back to the beach, he will take a long detour through the hills.

Why? Partly because he wants to enjoy the uncomplicated relaxed happy mood which is nearly always produced by a workout at the gym. It is so good to feel the body's satisfaction and gratitude; no matter how much it may protest, it likes being forced to perform these tasks. Now, for a while at least, the vagus nerve won't twitch, the pylorus will be quiet, the arthritic thumbs and knee won't assert themselves. And how restful, now that there's no need for stimulants, not to have to hate anyone at all! George hopes to be able to stay in this mood as long as he keeps on driving.

Also, he wants to take a look at the hills again; he hasn't been up there in a long time. Years ago, before Jim even, when George first came to California, he used to go into the hills often. It was the wildness of this range, largely uninhabited yet rising right up out of the city, that fascinated him. He felt the thrill of being a foreigner, a trespasser there, of venturing into the midst of a primitive, alien nature. He would drive up at sunset or very early in the morning, park his car, and wander off along the firebreak trails, catching glimpses of deer moving deep in the chaparral of a canyon, stopping to watch a hawk circling overhead, stepping carefully among hairy tarantulas crawling across his path, following twisty tracks in the sand until he came upon a coiled dozing rattler. Sometimes, in the half-light of dawn, he would meet a pack of coyotes trotting toward him, tails down, in single file. The first time this happened he took them for dogs; and then, suddenly, without uttering a sound, they broke formation and went bounding away downhill, with great uncanny jumps.

But this afternoon George can feel nothing of that long-ago excitement and awe; something is wrong from the start. The steep, winding road, which used to seem romantic, is merely awkward now, and dangerous. He keeps meeting other cars on blind corners and having to swerve sharply. By the time he has reached the top, he has lost all sense of relaxation. Even up here they are building dozens of new houses. The area is getting suburban. True, there are still a few uninhabited canyons, but George can't rejoice in them; he is oppressed by awareness of the city below. On both sides of the hills, to the north and to the south, it has spawned and spread itself over the entire plain. It has eaten up the wide pastures and ranchlands and the last stretches of orange grove; it has sucked out the surrounding lakes and sapped the forests of the high mountains. Soon it will be drinking converted sea water. And yet it will die. No need for rockets to wreck it, or another ice age to freeze it, or a huge earthquake to crack it off and dump it in the Pacific. It will die of overextension. It will die because its taproots have dried up—the brashness and greed which have been its only strength. And the desert, which is the natural condition of this country, will return.

Alas, how sadly, how certainly George knows this! He stops the car and stands at the road's rough yellow dirt edge, beside a manzanita bush, and looks out over Los Angeles like a sad Jewish prophet of doom, as he takes a leak. *Babylon is fallen, is fallen, that great city.* But this city is not great, was never great, and has nearly no distance to fall.

Now he zips up his pants and gets into the car and drives on, thoroughly depressed. The clouds close in low upon the hills, making them seem northern and sad like Wales; and the day wanes, and the lights snap on in their sham jewel colors all over the plain, as the road winds down again on to Sunset Boulevard and he nears the ocean.

The supermarket is still open; it won't close till midnight. It is brilliantly bright. Its brightness offers sanctuary from loneliness and the dark. You could spend hours of your life here, in a state of suspended insecurity, meditating on the multiplicity of things to eat. Oh dear, there is so much! So many brands in shiny boxes, all of them promising you good appetite. Every article on the shelves cries out to you, Take me, take me; and the mere competition of their appeals can make you imagine yourself wanted, even loved. But beware— when you get back to your empty room, you'll find that the false flattering elf of the advertisement has eluded you; what remains is only cardboard, cellophane and food. And you have lost the heart to be hungry.

This bright place isn't really a sanctuary. For, ambushed among its bottles and cartons and cans, are shockingly vivid memories of meals shopped for, cooked, eaten with Jim. They stab out at George as he passes, pushing his shopping cart. Should we ever feel truly lonely if we never ate alone?

But to say, I won't eat alone tonight—isn't that deadly dangerous? Isn't it the start of a long landslide—from eating at counters and drinking at bars to drinking at home without eating, to despair and sleeping pills and the inevitable final overdose? But who says I have to be brave? George asks. Who depends on me now? Who cares?

We're getting maudlin, he says, trying to make his will choose between halibut, sea bass, chopped sirloin, steaks. He feels a nausea of distaste for them all; then sudden rage. Damn all food. Damn all life. He would like to abandon his shopping cart, although it's already full of provisions. But that would make extra work for the clerks, and one of them is cute. The alternative, to put the whole lot back in the proper places himself, seems like a labor of Hercules; for the overpowering sloth of sadness is upon him. The sloth that ends in going to bed and staying there until you develop some disease.

So he wheels the cart to the cash desk, pays, stops on the way out to the car lot, enters the phone booth, dials.

"Hello."

"Hello, Charley."

"*Geo!*"

"Look—is it too late to change my mind? About tonight? You see—when you called this morning—I thought I had this date—But I just heard from them that—"

"*Of course* it isn't too late!" She doesn't even bother to listen to his lying excuses. Her gladness flashes its instantaneous way to him, even faster than her words, across the zigzag of the wires. And at once Geo and Charley are linked, are yet another of this evening's lucky pairs, amidst all of its lonely wanderers. If any of the clerks were watching, they would see his face inside the glass box brighten, flush with joy like a lover's.

"Can I bring you anything? I'm at the market—"

"Oh no—no thank you, Geo dear! I have loads of food. I always seem to get too much nowadays. I suppose it's because . . ."

"I'll be over in a little while then. Have to stop by the house, first. So long."

"Oh, Geo—this *is* nice! Au revoir!"

But he is so utterly perverse that his mood begins to change again before he has even finished unloading his purchases into the car. Do I really want to see her? he asks himself, and then, What in the world made me do that? He pictures the evening he might have spent, snugly at home, fixing the food he has bought, then lying down on the couch beside the bookcase and reading himself slowly sleepy. At first glance this is an absolutely convincing and charming scene of domestic contentment. Only after a few instants does George notice the omission that makes it meaningless. What is left out of the picture is Jim, lying opposite him at the other end of the couch, also reading; the two of them absorbed in their books yet so completely aware of each other's presence.

Back at home, he changes out of his suit into an army-surplus-store khaki shirt, faded blue denims, moccasins, a sweater. (He has had doubts from time to time about this kind of costume: Doesn't it give the impression that he's trying to dress young? But Jim used to tell him, No, it was just right for him—it made him look like Rommel in civilian clothes. George loved that.)

Just when he's ready to leave the house again, there is a ring at his doorbell. Who can it be at this hour?

Mrs. Strunk!

(What have I done that she can have come to complain about?)

"Oh, good evening—" (Obviously she's nervous, self-conscious; very much aware, no doubt, of having crossed the frontier-bridge and being on enemy territory.) "I know this is terribly short notice. I— we've meant to ask you so many times—I know how busy you are— but we haven't gotten together in such a long while—and we were wondering—would you possibly have time to come over for a drink?"

"You mean, right now?"

"Why, yes. There's just the two of us at home."

"I'm most terribly sorry. I'm afraid I have to go out, right away."

"Oh. Well. I was afraid you wouldn't have time. But—"

"No, listen," says George, and he means it; he is extremely surprised and pleased and touched. "I really *would* like to. Very much indeed. Do you suppose I could take a rain check?"

"Well, yes, of course." But Mrs. Strunk doesn't believe him. She smiles sadly. Suddenly it seems all-important to George to convince her.

"I would *love* to come. How about tomorrow?"

Her face falls. "Oh well, tomorrow. Tomorrow wouldn't be so good, I'm afraid. You see, tomorrow we have some friends coming over from the Valley, and . . ."

And they might notice something queer about me, and you'd feel ashamed, George thinks, okay, okay.

"I understand, of course," he says. "But let's make it very soon, shall we?"

"Oh *yes*," she agrees fervently, "*very* soon. . . ."

Charlotte lives on Soledad Way, a narrow uphill street which at night is packed so tight with cars parked on both sides of it that two drivers can scarcely squeeze past each other. If you arrive after its residents have returned home from their jobs, you will probably have to leave your car several blocks away, at the bottom of the hill. But this is no problem for George, because he can walk over to Charley's from his house in less than five minutes.

Her house is high up on the hillside, at the top of three flights
of lopsided rustic wooden steps, seventy-five of them in all. Down on
the street level there is a tumbledown shack intended for a garage. She
keeps it crammed to the ceiling with battered trunks and crates full of
unwanted junk. Jim used to say that she kept the garage blocked in
order not to be able to own a car. In any case, she absolutely refuses
to learn to drive. If she needs to go someplace and no one offers to
give her a ride, well then, that's too bad, she can't go. But the neighbors
nearly always do help her; she has them utterly intimidated and be-
witched by this Britishness which George himself knows so well how
to employ, though with a different approach.

The house next to Charlotte's is on the street level. As you begin
to climb her steps, you get an intimate glimpse of domestic squalor
through its bathroom window (it must be frankly admitted that Soledad
is one whole degree socially inferior to Camphor Tree Lane): a tub
hung with panties and diapers, a douche bag slung over the shower
pipe, a plumber's snake on the floor. None of the neighbors' kids are
visible now, but you can see how the hillside above their home has
been trampled into a brick-hard slippery surface with nothing alive on
it but some cactus. At the top of the slope there is a contraption like
a gallows, with a net for basketball attached to it.

Charlotte's slice of the hill can still just be described as a garden.
It is terraced, and a few of the roses on it are in bloom. But they have
been sadly neglected; when Charley is in one of her depressive moods,
even the poor plants must suffer for it. They have been allowed to
grow out into a tangle of long thorny shoots, with the weeds thick
between them.

George climbs slowly, taking it easy. (Only the very young are
not ashamed to arrive panting.) These outdoor staircases are a feature
of the neighborhood. A few of them have the original signs on their
steps which were painted by the bohemian colonists and addressed,
apparently, to guests who were clambering upstairs on their hands and
knees, drunk: Upward and onward. Never weaken. You're in bad
shape, sport. Hey—you can't die *here*! Ain't this *heaven*?

The staircases have become, as it were, the instruments of the
colonists' posthumous vengeance on their supplanters, the modern
housewives; for they defy all labor-saving devices. Short of bringing in

a giant crane, there is absolutely no way of getting anything up them except by hand. The icebox, the stove, the bathtub and all of the furniture have had to be pushed and dragged up to Charley's by strong, savagely cursing men. Who then clapped on huge extra charges and expected triple tips.

Charley comes out of the house as he nears the top. She has been watching for him, as usual, and no doubt fearing some last-moment change in his plans. They meet on the tiny unsafe wooden porch outside the front door, and hug. George feels her soft bulky body pressed against his. Then, abruptly, she releases him with a smart pat on the back, as much as to show him that she isn't going to overdo the affection; she knows when enough is enough.

"Come along in with you," she says.

Before following her indoors, George casts a glance out over the little valley to the line of boardwalk lamps where the beach begins and the dark unseen ocean. This is a mild windless night, with streaks of sea fog dimming the lights in the houses below. From this porch, when the fog is really thick, you can't see the houses at all and the lights are just blurs, and Charlotte's nest seems marvelously remote from everywhere else in the world.

It is a simple rectangular box, one of those prefabs which were put up right after the war. Newspapers enthused over them, they were acclaimed as the homes of the future; but they didn't catch on. The living room is floored with tatami, and more than somewhat Oriental-gift-shop in decor. A teahouse lantern by the door, wind bells at the windows, a huge red paper fish-kite pinned to the wall. Two picture scrolls: a madly Japanese tiger snarling at a swooping (American?) eagle; an immortal sitting under a tree, with half a dozen twenty-foot hairs growing out of his chin. Three low couches littered with gay silk cushions, too tiny for any useful purpose but perfect for throwing at people.

"I say, I've just realized that there's a most ghastly smell of cooking in here!" Charlotte exclaims. There certainly is. George answers politely that it's a delicious smell and that it makes him hungry.

"I'm trying a new kind of stew, as a matter of fact. I got the idea from a marvelous travel book Myrna Custer just brought me—about Borneo. Only the author gets slightly vague, so I've had to improvise a bit. I mean, he doesn't come right out and say so, but I have a suspicion that one's *supposed* to make it with human flesh. Actually, I've used leftovers from a joint . . ."

She is a lot younger than George—forty-five next birthday—but, already, like him, she is a survivor. She has the survivor's typical battered doggedness. To judge from photographs, she was adequately pretty as long as her big gray eyes were combined with soft youthful coloring. Her poor cheeks are swollen and inflamed now, and her hair, which must once have made a charming blur around her face, is merely untidy. Nevertheless, she hasn't given up. Her dress shows a grotesque kind of gallantry, ill-advised but endearing: an embroidered peasant blouse in bold colors, red, yellow and violet, with the sleeves rolled up to the elbows; a gypsyish Mexican skirt which looks as if she had girded it on like a blanket, with a silver-studded cowboy belt—it only emphasizes her lack of shape. Oh, and if she must wear sandals with bare feet, why won't she make up her toenails? (Maybe a lingering middle-class Midlands puritanism is in operation here.) Jim once said to her kiddingly about a similar outfit, "I see you've adopted our native costume, Charley." She laughed, not at all offended, but she didn't get the point. She hasn't gotten it yet. This *is* her idea of informal Californian playwear, and she honestly cannot see that she dresses any differently from Mrs. Peabody next door.

"Have I told you, Geo? No, I'm sure I haven't. I've already made two New Year's resolutions—only they're effective immediately. The first is, I'm going to admit that I loathe bourbon." (She pronounces it like the dynasty, not the drink.) "I've been pretending not to, ever since I came to this country—all because Buddy drank it. But, let's face it, who do I think I'm kidding *now?*" She smiles at George very bravely and brightly, reassuring him that this is *not* a prelude to an attack of the Buddy-blues; then quickly continues, "My other resolution is that I'm going to stop denying that that infuriating accusation is true: Women *do* mix drinks too strong, damn it! I suppose it's part of our terrible anxiety to please. So let's begin the new regime as of now, shall we? You come and mix your own drink and mine too— and I'd like a vodka and tonic, please."

She has obviously had at least a couple already. Her hands fumble as she lights a cigarette. (The Indonesian ashtray is full, as usual, of lipstick-marked stubs.) Then she leads the way into the kitchen with her curious rolling gait which is nearly a limp, suggesting arthritis and the kind of toughness that goes with it.

"It *was* sweet of you to come tonight, Geo."

He grins suitably, says nothing.

"You broke your other appointment, didn't you?"

"I did not! I told you on the phone—these people canceled at the last minute—"

"Oh, Geo dear, come off it! You know, I sometimes think, about you, whenever you do something really sweet, you're ashamed of it afterwards! You knew jolly well how badly I needed you tonight, so you broke that appointment. I could tell you were fibbing, the minute you opened your mouth! You and I can't pull the wool over each other's eyes. *I* found that out, long ago. Haven't *you*—after all these years?"

"I certainly should have," he agrees, smiling and thinking what an absurd and universally accepted bit of nonsense it is that your best friends must necessarily be the ones who best understand you. As if there weren't far too much understanding in the world already; above all, that understanding between lovers, celebrated in song and story, which is actually such torture that no two of them can bear it without frequent separations or fights. Dear old Charley, he thinks, as he fixes their snorts in her cluttered, none-too-clean kitchen, how could I have gotten through these last years without your wonderful lack of perception? How many times, when Jim and I had been quarreling and came to visit you—sulking, avoiding each other's eyes, talking to each other only through you—did you somehow bring us together again by the sheer power of your unawareness that anything was wrong?

And now, as George pours the vodka (giving her a light one, to slow her down) and the Scotch (giving himself a heavier one, to catch up on), he begins to feel this utterly mysterious unsensational thing—not bliss, not ecstasy, not joy—just plain happiness. *Das Glueck, le bonheur, la felicidad*—they have given it all three genders, but one has to admit, however grudgingly, that the Spanish are right; it is usually feminine, that's to say, woman-created. Charley creates it astonishingly often; this doubtless is something else she isn't aware of, since she can do it even when she herself is miserable. As for George, his felicidad is sublimely selfish; he can enjoy it unperturbed while Charley is in the midst of Buddy-blues or a Fred-crisis (one is brewing this evening, obviously). However, there are unlucky occasions when you get her blues without your felicidad, and it's a graveyard bore. But not this evening. This evening he is going to enjoy himself.

Charlotte, meanwhile, has peeked into the oven and then closed its door again, announcing, "Twenty more minutes" with the absolute confidence of a great chef, which by God she isn't.

As they walk back into the living room with their drinks, she tells him, "Fred called me—late last night." This is said in her flat, underplayed crisis-tone.

"Oh?" George manages to sound sufficiently surprised. "Where is he now?"

"Palo Alto." Charlotte sits down on the couch under the paper fish, with conscious drama, as though she has said, "Siberia."

"Palo Alto—he was there before, wasn't he?"

"Of course he was. That's where that girl lives. He's with her, naturally. . . . I *must* learn not to say 'that girl.' She's got a perfectly good name, and I can hardly pretend I don't know it: Loretta Marcus. Anyhow, it's none of my business who Fred's with or what she does with Fred. Her mother doesn't seem to care. Well, never mind any of that. . . . We had a long talk. This time, he really was quite sweet and reasonable about the whole situation. At least, I could feel how hard he was trying to be . . . Geo, it's no good our going on like this. He *has* made up his mind, really and truly. He wants a complete break."

Her voice is trembling ominously. George says without conviction, "He's awfully young, still."

"He's awfully old for his age. Even two years ago he could have looked after himself if he'd had to. Just because he's a minor, I can't treat him like a child—I mean, and use the law to make him come back. Besides, then, he'd *never* forgive me—"

"He's changed his mind before this."

"Oh, I know. And I know you think he hasn't behaved well to me, Geo. I don't blame you for thinking that. I mean, it's natural for you to take my side. And then, you've never had any children of your own. You don't mind my saying that, Geo dear? Oh, I'm sorry—"

"Don't be silly, Charley."

"Even if you had had children, it wouldn't really be the same. This mother and son thing—I mean, especially when you've had to bring him up without a father—that's really hell. I mean, you try and you try—but everything you do or say seems to turn out wrong. I smother him—he said that to me once. At first I couldn't understand— I just couldn't accept it—but now I do—I've got to—and I honestly *think* I do—he must live his own life—right away from me—even if he begs me to, I simply mustn't see him for a long long while—I'm sorry, Geo—I didn't mean to do this—I'm so—sorry—"

George moves closer to her on the couch, puts one arm around her, squeezes her sobbing plumpness gently, without speaking. He is not cold; he is not unmoved. He is truly sorry for Charley and this mess—and yet—la felicidad remains intact; he is very much at his ease. With his free hand, he helps himself to a sip of his drink, being careful not to let the movement be felt through the engaged side of his body.

But how very strange to sit here with Charley sobbing and re-member that night when the long-distance call came through from Ohio. An uncle of Jim's whom he'd never met—trying to be sym-pathetic, even admitting George's right to a small honorary share in the sacred family grief—but then, as they talked, becoming a bit chilled by George's laconic *Yes, I see, yes,* his curt *No, thank you,* to the funeral invitation—deciding no doubt that this much talked of room-mate hadn't been such a close friend, after all. . . . And then, at least five minutes after George had put down the phone, when the first shock wave hit, when the meaningless news suddenly meant exactly what it said, his blundering gasping run up the hill in the dark, his blind stumbling on the steps, banging at Charley's door, crying blub-bering howling on her shoulder, in her lap, all over her; and Charley squeezing him, stroking his hair, telling him the usual stuff one tells. . . . Late next afternoon, as he shook himself out of the daze of the sleeping pills she'd given him, he felt only disgust: I betrayed you, Jim; I betrayed our life together; I made you into a sob story for a skirt. But that was just hysteria, part of the second shock wave. It soon passed. And meanwhile Charley, bless her silly heart, took the situation

over more and more completely—cooking his meals and bringing them
down to the house while he was out, the dishes wrapped in tinfoil
ready to be reheated; leaving him notes urging him to call her at any
hour he felt the need, the deader of night the better; hiding the truth
from her friends with such visibly sealed lips that they must surely
have suspected Jim had fled the state after some sex scandal—until at
last she had turned Jim's death into something of her own creation
entirely, a roaring farce. (George is grinning to himself, now.) Oh yes
indeed, he is glad that he ran to her that night. That night, in purest
ignorance, she taught him a lesson he will never forget—namely, that
you can't betray (that idiotic expression!) a Jim, or a life with a Jim,
even if you try to.

By now, Charlotte has sobbed herself into a calm. After a couple
of sniffs, she says "sorry" again, and stops.

"I keep wondering just when it began to go wrong."

"Oh, Charley, for Heaven's sake, what good does that do?"

"Of course, if Buddy and I had stayed together—"

"No one can say that was your fault."

"It's always both people's."

"Do you hear from him nowadays?"

"Oh yes, every so often. They're still in Scranton. He's out of a
job. And Debbie just had another baby—that's their third—another
daughter. I can't think how they manage. I keep trying to stop him
sending any more money, even though it is for Fred. But he's so
obstinate, poor lamb, when he thinks something's his duty. Well, from
now on, I suppose he and Fred will have to work that out between
them. I'm out of the picture altogether—"

There is a bleak little pause. George gives her an encouraging pat
on the shoulder. "How about a couple of quick ones before that stew?"

"I think that's a positively brilliant idea!" She laughs quite gaily.
But then, as he takes the glass from her, she strokes his hand with a
momentary return to pathos, "you're so damned good to me, Geo."
Her eyes fill with tears. However, he can decently pretend that he
hasn't noticed them, so he walks away.

If I'd been the one the truck hit, he says to himself, as he enters
the kitchen, Jim would be right here, this very evening, walking

through this doorway, carrying these two glasses. Things are as simple as that.

"So here we are," Charlotte says, "just the two of us. Just you and me."

They are drinking their coffee after dinner. The stew turned out quite a success, though not noticeably different from all Charlotte's other stews, its relationship to Borneo being almost entirely literary.

"Just the two of us," she repeats.

George smiles at her vaguely, not sure yet if this is a lead-in to something, or only sententious-sentimental warmth arising from the wine. They had about a bottle and a half between them.

But then, slowly, thoughtfully, as though this were a mere bit of irrelevant feminine musing, she adds, "I suppose, in a day or two, I must get around to cleaning out Fred's room."

A pause.

"I mean, until I've done that, I won't feel that everything's really over. You have to do something, to convince yourself. You know what I mean?"

"Yes, Charley. I think so."

"I shall send Fred anything he needs, of course. The rest I can store away. There's heaps of space under the house."

"Are you planning to rent his room?" George asks—because, if she *is* leading up to something, they may as well get to it.

"Oh no, I couldn't possibly do that. Well, not to a stranger, anyhow. One couldn't offer him any real privacy. He'd have to be part of the family—oh dear, I *must* stop using that expression, it's only force of habit. . . . Still, *you* understand, Geo. It would have to be someone I knew most awfully well—"

"I can see that."

"You know, you and I—it's funny—we're really in the same boat now. Our houses are kind of too big for us, and yet they're too small."

"Depending on which way you look at it."

"Yes. . . . Geo darling—if I ask you something—it's not that I'm trying to pry or anything—"

"Go ahead."

"Now that—well, now that some time has gone by—do you still feel that you want to live alone?"

"I never wanted to live alone, Charley."

"Oh, I *know*! Forgive me. I never meant—"

"I know you didn't. That's perfectly all right."

"Of course, I know how you must feel about that house of yours. . . . You've never thought of moving, have you?"

"No—not seriously."

"No—" (This is a bit wistful.) "I suppose you wouldn't. I suppose—as long as you stay there—you feel closer to Jim. Isn't that it?"

"Maybe that's it."

She reaches over and gives his hand a long squeeze of deep understanding. Then, stubbing out her cigarette (brave, now, for both of them), she says brightly, "Would you like to get us some drinks, Geo?"

"The dishes, first."

"Oh, but darling, let's leave them, please! I'll wash them in the morning. I mean, I'd *like* to. It gives me something to do these days. There's so little—"

"No arguments, Charley! If you won't help me, I'll do them alone."

"Oh, *Geo*!"

And now, half an hour later, they're back in the living room again, with fresh drinks in their hands.

"How can you pretend you don't love it?" she is asking him, with a teasing, coquettish reproachfulness. "And you miss it—you wish you were back there—you *know* you do!" This is one of her favorite themes.

"I'm not pretending anything, Charley, for Heaven's sake! You keep ignoring the fact that I *have* been back there, several times; and you haven't. I'm absolutely willing to admit that I like it better every time I do go. In fact, right now I think it's probably the most extraordinary country in the world—because it's such a marvelous mixup. Everything's changed, and yet nothing has. I don't believe I ever told you this—last year, in the middle of the summer, when Jim and I were over there, you remember, we made a trip through the Cotswolds.

Well, one morning we were on this little branch-line train, and we stopped at a village which was right out of a Tennyson poem—sleepy meadows all around, and lazy cows, and moaning doves, and immemorial elms, and the Elizabethan manor house showing through the trees. And there, on the platform, were two porters dressed just the same way porters have been dressed since the nineteenth century. Only they were Negroes from Trinidad. And the ticket collector at the gate was Chinese. I nearly died of joy. I mean, it was the one touch that had been lacking, all these years. It finally made the whole place perfect—"

"I'm not sure how I should like that part of it," says Charlotte. Her romanticism has received a jolt, as he knew it would. Indeed, he has told this story to tease her. But she won't be put off. She wants more. She is just in the mood for tipsy daydreaming. "And then you went up North, didn't you," she prompts him, "to look at the house you were born in?"

"Yes."

"Tell me about it!"

"Oh, Charley—I've told you dozens of times!"

"Tell me again—*please*, Geo!"

She is as persistent as a child; and George can seldom refuse her, especially after he's had a few drinks.

"It used to be a farmhouse, you know. It was built in 1649—the year they beheaded Charles the First—"

"1649! Oh, Geo—just *think* of it!"

"There are several other farms in the neighborhood much older than that. Of course, it's had a lot of alterations. The people who live there now—he's a television producer in Manchester—have practically rebuilt the inside of it. Put in a new staircase and an extra bathroom and modernized the kitchen. And the other day they wrote me that they now have central heating."

"How horrible! There ought to be a law against ruining beautiful old houses. This craze for bringing things up to date—I suppose they've caught it from this bloody country."

"Don't be a goose, Charley darling! The place was all but uninhabitable the way it was. It's built of that local stone which seems to suck up every drop of moisture in the air. And there's plenty, in that ghastly climate. Even in summer the walls used to be clammy; and in winter, if you went into a room where the fire hadn't been lighted for a few days, it was cold as death. The cellar actually smelt like a tomb. Mold was always forming on the books, and the wallpaper kept peeling off, and the mounts of the pictures were spotted with damp. . . ."

"Whatever you say about it, darling, you always make it sound so marvelously romantic. Exactly like *Wuthering Heights!*"

"Actually, it's almost suburban nowadays. You walk down a short lane and there you are on the main road, with buses running every twenty minutes into Manchester."

"But didn't you tell me the house is on the edge of the moors?"

"Well, yes—so it is. That's what's so odd about it. It's kind of in two worlds. When you look out from the back—from the room I was born in, as a matter of fact—that view literally hasn't changed since I was a boy. You still see hardly any houses—just the open hills, and the stone walls running over them, and a few little whitewashed dots of farms. And of course the trees around the old farmyard were planted long, long before I was born, to shelter the house—there's a lot of wind up there, on the ridge—great big beech trees—they make a sort of seething sound, like waves—that's one of the earliest sounds I remember. I sometimes wonder if that's why I always have had this thing about wanting to live near the ocean—"

Something is happening to George. To please Charley, he has started to make magic; and now the magic is taking hold of him. He is quite aware of this—but what's the harm? It's fun. It adds a new dimension to being drunk. Just as long as there's no one to hear him but Charley! She is sighing deeply now with sympathy and delight— the delight of an addict when someone else admits he's hooked, too.

"There's a little pub high up on the moors, the very last house in the village—actually it's on the old coaching road over the hills, which hardly anyone uses now. Jim and I used to go there in the evenings. It's called The Farmer's Boy. The bar parlor has one of those low, very heavy-looking ceilings, you know, with warped oak beams; and there's a big open fireplace. And some foxes' masks mounted on the wall. And an engraving of Queen Victoria riding a pony in the Highlands—"

Charlotte is so delighted that she actually claps her hands. "Geo! Oh, I can just see it all!"

"One night we were there, they stayed open extra late, because it was Jim's birthday—that is, they shut the outside door and went right on serving drinks. We felt marvelously cozy, and we drank pints and pints of Guinness, far more than we wanted, just because it was illegal. And then there was a 'character'—that was how they all described him—'Oh, he's a character, he is!' named Rex, who was a kind of a rustic beat. He worked as a farm laborer, but only when he absolutely had to. He started talking in a very superior tone to impress us. He told Jim, 'You Yanks are living in a world of fantasy'! But then he got much more friendly, and when we were walking back to the inn where we were staying, absolutely plastered by this time, Rex and I discovered something in common: we both knew Newbolt's *Vitae Lampada* by heart, we'd learnt it at school. So of course we began roaring out, 'Play up, play up, and play the game!' And when we got to the second verse, about the sands of the desert being sodden red, I said, 'The colonel's jammed and the gatling's dead,' and Rex thought that was the joke of the year, and Jim sat right down on the road, and buried his face in his hands and uttered a terrible groan—"

"You mean, he wasn't enjoying himself?"

"Jim not enjoying himself? He was having the ball of his life! For a while I thought I'd never get him out of England again. And, you know, he fell wildly in love with that pub? The rest of the house is very attractive, I must admit. There's an upstairs sitting room which you could really make something out of. And quite a big garden. Jim wanted us to buy it and live there, and run it together."

"What a marvelous idea! Oh, what a shame you couldn't have!"

"Actually, it wouldn't have been utterly impossible. We made some inquiries. I think we could have persuaded them to sell. And no doubt Jim would have picked up pub-running, the way he did everything else. Of course, there'd have been an awful lot of red tape, and permits, and stuff. . . . Oh yes, we talked about it. We even used to say we'd go back this year and look into the whole thing some more—"

"Do you think—I mean, if Jim—would you *really* have bought it and settled down there?"

"Oh, who knows? We were always making plans like that. We hardly ever told other people about them, even you. Maybe that was because we knew in our hearts they were crazy. But then again, we did do some crazy things, didn't we? Well, we'll never know, now. . . . Charlotte, dear, we are both in need of a drink."

He is suddenly aware of Charlotte saying, "I suppose, for a man, it *is* different. . . ."

(*What's* different? Can he have dozed off for a couple of seconds? George shakes himself awake.)

". . . You know, I used to think that about Buddy? He could have lived anywhere. He could have traveled hundreds of miles across nowhere and then suddenly just pitched his tent and called it some-where, and it *would* have been somewhere, simply because he said so. After all, I mean, isn't that what the pioneers all did in this country, not so long ago? It must have been in Buddy's blood—though it certainly can't be any longer. Debbie would never put up with that sort of thing. No, Geo, cross my heart, I am honestly not being bitchy! I wouldn't have put up with it either, in the long run. Women are like that—we've simply got to hang on to our roots. We *can* be trans-planted, yes—but it has to be done by a man, and when he's done it, he has to stay with us and wither—I mean water—I mean, the new roots wither if they aren't watered. . . ." Her voice has thickened. Now she gives her head an abrupt shake, just as George did a few moments ago. "Am I making any sense at all?"

"Yes, Charley. Aren't you trying to tell me you've decided to go back?"

"You mean, go back home?"

"Are you sure it *is* home, still?"

"Oh dear—I'm not sure of anything—but—now Fred doesn't need me any more—will you tell me, Geo, what am I doing here?"

"You've got a lot of friends."

"Certainly I have. Friends. And they're real dears. The Peabodys and the Garfeins, especially, and Jerry and Flora, and I am very fond of Myrna Custer. But none of them *need* me. There isn't anyone who'd make me feel guilty about leaving them. . . . Now, Geo, be absolutely honest—is there anyone, *anyone at all*, I ought to feel guilty about leaving behind?"

There's me. No, he refuses to say it. Such flirting is unworthy of them, even when drunk. "Feeling guilty's no reason for staying *or* going," he tells her, firmly but kindly. "The point is, do you *want* to go? If you want to go, you should go. Never mind anybody else."

Charlotte nods sadly. "Yes, I suppose you're right."

George goes into the kitchen, fixes another round. (They seem to be drinking up much faster, now. This one really should be the last.) When he comes out again, she's sitting with her hands clasped, gazing in front of her. "I think I shall go back, Geo. I dread it—but I'm beginning to think I really shall."

"Why do you dread it?"

"In a way, I dread it. There's Nan, for one thing."

"You wouldn't have to live with her, would you?"

"I wouldn't have to. But I would. I'm sure I would."

"But, Charley—I've always had the impression that you loathe each other."

"Not *exactly* loathe. Anyhow, in a family, that's not really what matters. I mean, it can be beside the point. That's hard to explain to you, Geo, because you never had any family, did you, after you were quite young? No, I wouldn't say loathe. Though, of course, when I first got to know Buddy—when she found out we were sleeping together, that is—Nan did rather hate me. I mean, she hated my luck. Of course, in those days, Buddy *was* a dreamboat. Any sister might have felt jealous. But that wasn't the biggest part of it. What she really minded was that Buddy was a G.I. and that he was going to take me back to live in the States when we were married. Nan simply longed to come over here, you see—so many girls did, after wartime England and the shortages and everything—but she'd have died rather than admit it. She felt she was being disloyal to England even to want to come. I do believe she'd have far sooner admitted to being jealous of me with Buddy! Isn't that a laugh?"

"She knows you and Buddy have split up, of course?"

"Oh yes, I had to tell her at once, right after it happened. Otherwise, I'd have been so afraid she'd find out for herself, in some uncanny way, and that would have been too shaming. So I wrote to her about it, and she wrote back, such a beastly, quietly triumphing letter, saying Now I suppose you'll *have* to come back here—back to the country you deserted; that was what she implied. So of course I flew right off the handle—you know *me*!—and answered saying I was blissfully happy here, and that never never would I set foot on her dreary little island again. Oh, and then—I've never told you any of this, because it embarrassed me so—after I wrote *that* letter, I felt most terribly guilty, so I started sending her things: you know, deli- catessen from those luxury shops in Beverly Hills, all sorts of cheeses and things in bottles and jars. As a matter of fact, living in this so- called land of plenty, I could hardly afford them! And I was such an utter idiot, I didn't once stop to think how tactless I was being! Actually, I was playing right into Nan's hands. I mean, she let me go on sending all this stuff for a while—which she ate, I presume—and then *really* torpedoed me. Asked hadn't we heard in America that the war had been over quite some time, and that Bundles for Britain were out of date?"

"Charming creature!"

"No, Geo—underneath all that, Nan really loves me. It's just she wants me to see things her way. You know, she's two years older; that meant a lot when we were children. I've always thought of her as being sort of like a road—I mean, she *leads* somewhere. With her, I'll never lose my way. . . . Do you know what I'm trying to say?"

"No."

"Well, never mind. There's another thing about going back home—it's the past; and that's all tied up with Nan, too. Sort of going back to the place where I turned off the road, do you see?"

"No. I don't see."

"But, Geo—the *past*! Surely you can't pretend you don't know what I mean by that?"

"The past is just something that's over."

"Oh really—how *can* you be so tiresome!"

"No, Charley, I mean it. The past is over. People make believe that it isn't, and they show you things in museums. But that's not the past. You won't find the past in England. Or anywhere else, for that matter."

"Oh, you're tiresome!"

"Listen, why not just go back there on a visit? See Nan if you want to. But, for Christ's sake, don't commit yourself."

"No—if I go back at all, I've got to go back for good."

"*Why?*"

"I can't stand any more indecision. I've got to burn my boats, this time. I thought I'd done that when I came over here with Buddy. But, this time, I've got to—"

"Oh, for Christ's sake!"

"I know I'll find it all changed. I know there'll be a lot of things I'll hate. I know I'll miss all these supermarkets and labor-savers and conveniences. Probably I'll keep catching one cold after another, after living in this climate. And I expect you're quite right—I *shall* be miserable, living with Nan. I can't help any of that. At least, when I'm there, I shall know *where I am.*"

"Never in my born days have I heard such utter drooling masochism!"

"Oh yes, I know it sounds like that. And perhaps it is! Do you suppose masochism's our way of being patriotic? Or do I mean that the other way round? What fun! Darling, shouldn't we have another tiny drink? Let's drink to the masochism of Old England!"

"I don't think so, darling. Time for our beds."

"Geo—*you're leaving!*"

"I must, Charley."

"But when shall I see you?"

"Very soon. That is, unless you're taking off for England right away."

"Oh, don't tease me! You know perfectly well I'm not! It'd take me ages just to get ready. Perhaps I never will go at all. How could I ever face all that packing and the saying goodbye, and the *effort*? No—perhaps I never will—"

"We'll talk more about it. A lot more. . . . Good night, Charley dear."

She rises as he bends forward to kiss her. They bump awkwardly and very nearly topple over and roll on the floor. He steadies her, unsteadily.

"I should hate so to leave you, Geo."

"Then don't."

"The way you say that! I don't believe you care if I go or if I stay."

"Of course I care!"

"Truly?"

"Truly!"

"Geo?"

"Yes, Charley?"

"I don't think Jim would want me to leave you here alone."

"Then don't leave me."

"No—I'm dead serious! You remember when you and I drove up to San Francisco? In September, it must have been, last year, just after you got back from England—"

"Yes."

"Jim couldn't come up with us that day. I forget why. He flew up the next day and joined us. Well, anyhow, just as you and I were getting into the car, Jim said something to me. Something I've never forgotten. . . . Did I ever tell you this?"

"I don't believe so." (She has told him at least six times; always when very drunk.)

"He said to me, You two take care of each other."

"He did?"

"Yes he did. Those were his exact words. And, Geo, I believe he didn't just mean take care. He meant something *more*—"

"What did he mean?"

"That was less than two months, wasn't it, before he left for Ohio. I believe he said *take care*, because he *knew*—"

Swaying a little, she regards him earnestly but dimly, as though she were peering up at him, fishlike, through all the liquor she has drunk. "Do *you* believe that, Geo?"

"How can we tell what he knew, Charley? As for our taking care of each other, we can be certain he'd have wanted us to do that." George puts his hands on her shoulders. "So now let's both tell each other to get some sleep, shall we?"

"No, wait—" She's like a child, stalling off bedtime with questions. "Do you suppose that pub is still for sale?"

"I expect so. That's an idea! Why don't we buy it, Charley? What do you say? We could get drunk and earn money at the same time. That'd be more fun than living with Nan!"

"Oh darling, how lovely! Do you suppose we really *could* buy it? No—you're not serious, are you? I can see you aren't. But don't ever say you aren't. Let's make plans about it, like you and Jim used to. He'd like us to make plans, wouldn't he?"

"Sure he would. . . . Good night, Charley."

"Good night, Geo, my love—" As they embrace, she kisses him full on the mouth. And suddenly sticks her tongue right in. She has done this before, often. It's one of those drunken long shots which just might, at least theoretically, once in ten thousand tries, throw a relationship right out of its orbit and send it whizzing off on another. Do women ever stop trying? No. But, because they never stop, they learn to be good losers. When, after a suitable pause, he begins to draw back, she doesn't attempt to cling to him. And now she accepts his going with no more resistance. He kisses her on the forehead. She is like a child who has at last submitted to being tucked into her cot.

"Sleep tight."

George turns, swings open the house door, takes one stride and— *oops!*—very very nearly falls headfirst down the steps—all of them— oh, and, unthinkably, much farther—ten, fifty, one hundred million feet into the bottomless black night. Only his grip on the door handle saves him.

He turns groggily, with a punching heart, to grin back at Charlotte; but luckily she has wandered away off somewhere. She hasn't seen him do this asinine thing. Which is truly providential because, if she *had* seen him, she would have insisted on his staying the night; which would have meant, well, at the very least, such a late breakfast that it would have been brunch; which would have meant more drinks; which would have meant siesta and supper, and more and more and more drinks to follow. . . . This has actually happened, before now.

But this time he has escaped. And now he closes the house door with the care of a burglar, sits himself down on the top step, takes a deep breath, and gives himself a calm stern talking-to. You are drunk. Oh, you stupid old thing, how dare you get so drunk? Well, now, listen: We are going to walk down those steps very slowly, and when we are at the bottom we are going straight home and upstairs and right into bed, without even brushing our teeth. All right, that's understood? Now, here we go. . . .

Well and good.

How to explain, then, that, with his foot actually on the bridge over the creek, George suddenly turns, chuckles to himself, and with the movement of a child wriggling free of a grownup—old guardian Cortex—runs off down the road, laughing, toward the ocean?

As he trots out of Camphor Tree Lane on to Las Ondas, he sees the round green porthole lights of The Starboard Side, down on the corner of the ocean highway across from the beach, shining to welcome him.

The Starboard Side has been here since the earliest days of the colony. Its bar, formerly a lunch counter, served the neighbors with their first post-prohibition beers, and the mirror behind it was sometimes honored by the reflection of Tom Mix. But its finest hours came later. That summer of 1945! The war as good as over. The blackout no more than an excuse for keeping the lights out at a gangbang. A sign over the bar said, "In case of a direct hit, we close immediately." Which was meant to be funny, of course. And yet, out across the bay, in deep water under the cliffs of Palos Verdes, lay a real Japanese submarine full of real dead Japanese, depth-bombed after they had sunk two or three ships in sight of the Californian coast.

You pushed aside the blackout curtain and elbowed your way through a jam-packed bar crowd, scarcely able to breathe or see for smoke. Here, in the complete privacy of the din and the crowd, you and your pickup yelled the preliminary sex advances at each other. You could flirt but you couldn't fight; there wasn't even room to smack someone's face. For that, you had to step outside. Oh, the bloody battles and the sidewalk vomitings! The punches flying wide, the heads crashing backwards against the fenders of parked cars! Huge diesel-dikes slugging it out, grimmer far than the men. The siren-wailing arrival of the police; the sudden swoopings of the shore patrol. Girls dashing down from their apartments to drag some gorgeous endangered young drunk upstairs to safety and breakfast served next morning in bed like a miracle of joy. Hitchhiking servicemen delayed at this corner for hours, nights, days; proceeding at last on their journey with black eyes, crab-lice, clap, and only the dimmest memory of their hostess or host.

And then the war's end and the mad spree of driving up and down the highway on the instantly derationed gas, shedding great black chunks of your recaps all the way to Malibu. And then the beach-months of 1946. The magic squalor of those hot nights, when the whole shore was alive with tongues of flame, the watchfires of a vast naked barbarian tribe—each group or pair to itself and bothering no one, yet all a part of the life of the tribal encampment—swimming in the darkness, cooking fish, dancing to the radio, coupling without shame on the sand. George and Jim (who had just met) were out there among them evening after evening, yet not often enough to satisfy the sad fierce appetite of memory, as it looks back hungrily on that glorious Indian summer of lust.

The hitchhiking servicemen are few now and mostly domesticated, going back and forth between the rocket base and their homes and wives. Beach fires are forbidden, except in designated picnic areas where you must eat sitting up on benches at communal tables, and mustn't screw at all. But, though so much of the glory has faded, nevertheless—thanks to the persecuted yet undying old gods of disorder—this last block of Las Ondas is still a bad neighborhood. Respectable people avoid it instinctively. Realtors deplore it. Property values are low here. The motels are new but cheaply stuck together and already slum-sordid; they cater to one-night stands. And, though the charcoal remnants of those barbarian orgy-fires have long since been ground into the sand, this stretch of the shore is still filthy with trash; high-school gangs still daub huge scandalous words on its beach-wall; and seashells are still less easy to find here than discarded rubbers.

The glory has faded, too, from The Starboard Side; only a true devotee like George can still detect even a last faint gleam of it. The place has been stripped of its dusty marine trophies and yellow group photographs. Right after the New Year it's to be what they dare to call redecorated: that's to say, desecrated, in readiness for next summer's mob of blank-faced strangers. Already there is a new juke-box; and a new television fixed high up on the wall, so you can turn half right, rest your elbow on the bar and go into a cow-daze, watching it. This is what most of the customers are doing, as George enters.

He makes unsteadily but purposefully for his favorite little table in the corner, from which the TV screen is invisible. At the table next to him, two other unhypnotized nonconformists, an elderly couple who belong to the last handful of surviving colonists, are practicing their way of love: a mild quarrelsome alcoholism which makes it possible for them to live in a play-relationship, like children. *You old bag, you old prick, you old bitch, you old bastard*: rage without resentment, abuse without venom. This is how it will be for them till the end. Let's hope they will never be parted, but die in the same hour of the same night, in their beer-stained bed.

And now George's eyes move along the bar, stop on a figure seated alone at the end nearest the door. The young man isn't watching the TV; indeed, he is quite intent upon something he is writing on the back of an envelope. As he writes, he smiles to himself and rubs the side of his large nose with his forefinger. It is Kenny Potter.

At first, George doesn't move; seems hardly to react at all. But then a slow intent smile parts his lips. He leans forward, watching Kenny with the delight of a naturalist who has identified a rosy finch out of the high sierras on a tree in a city park. After a minute he rises, crosses almost stealthily to the bar and slips onto the stool beside Kenny.

"Hello, there," he says.

Kenny turns quickly, sees who it is, laughs loudly, crumples the envelope and tosses it over the bar into a trash container. "Hello, sir."

"What did you do that for?"

"Oh. Nothing."

"I disturbed you. You were writing."

"It was nothing. Only a poem."

"And now it's lost to the world!"

"I'll remember it. Now I've written it down."

"Would you say it for me?"

This sends Kenny into convulsions of laughter. "It's crazy. It's"— he gulps down his giggles—"it's a—a *haiku*!"

"Well, what's so crazy about a haiku?"

"I'd have to count the syllables first."

But Kenny obviously isn't going to count them now. So George says, "I didn't expect to see you in this neck of the woods. Don't you live over on the other side of town, near campus?"

"That's right. Only sometimes I like to get way away from there."

"But imagine your happening to pick on this particular bar!"

"Oh, that was because one of the kids told me you're in here a lot."

"You mean, you came out here to see me?" Perhaps George says this a little too eagerly. Anyhow, Kenny shrugs it off with a teasing smile.

"I thought I'd see what kind of a joint it was."

"It's nothing now. It used to be quite something, though. And I've gotten accustomed to coming here. You see, I live very close."

"Camphor Tree Lane?"

"How in the world did you know that?"

"Is it supposed to be a secret?"

"Why no—of course not! I have students come over to see me now and then. I mean, about their work—" George is immediately aware that this sounds defensive and guilty as hell. Has Kenny noticed? He is grinning; but then he has been grinning all the time. George adds, rather feebly, "You seem to know an awful lot about me and my habits. A lot more than I know about any of you—"

"There isn't much to know about us, I guess!" Kenny gives him a teasing, challenging look. "What would you like to know about us, sir?"

"Oh, I'll think of something. Give me time. Say, what are you drinking?"

"Nothing!" Kenny giggles. "He hasn't even noticed me yet." And, indeed, the bartender is absorbed in a TV wrestling match.

"Well, what'll you have?"

"What are you having, sir?"

"Scotch."

"Okay," Kenny says, in a tone which suggests that he would have agreed just as readily to buttermilk. George calls the bartender—very loudly, so he can't pretend not to have heard—and orders. The bartender, always a bit of a bitch, demands to see Kenny's I.D. So they go through all of that. George says stuffily to the bartender, "You ought to know me by this time. Do you really think I'd be such an idiot as to try to buy drinks for a minor?"

"We have to check," says the bartender, through a skin inches thick. He turns his back on them and moves away. George feels a brief spurt of powerless rage. He has been made to look like an ass—and in front of Kenny, too.

While they are waiting for the drinks, he asks, "How did you get here? In your car?"

"I don't have one. Lois drove me."

"Where is she now, then?"

"Gone home, I guess."

George senses something not quite in order. But, whatever it is, Kenny doesn't seem worried about it. He adds vaguely, "I thought I'd walk around for a while."

"But how'll you get back?"

"Oh, I'll manage."

(A voice inside George says, *You could invite him to stay the night at your place. Tell him you'll drive him back in the morning.* What in hell do you think I am? George asks it. *It was merely a suggestion,* says the voice.)

The drinks arrive. George says to Kenny, "Look, why don't we sit over there, at the table in the corner? That damned television keeps catching my eye."

"All right."

It *would* be fun, George thinks, if the young were just a little less passive. But that's too much to ask. You have to play it their way, or not at all. As they take their chairs, facing each other, George says, "I've still got my pencil sharpener," and, bringing it out of his pocket, he tosses it down on the table, as though shooting craps.

Kenny laughs. "I already lost mine!"

And now an hour, maybe, has passed. And they are both drunk: Kenny fairly, George very. But George is drunk in a good way, and one that he seldom achieves. He tries to describe to himself what this kind of drunkenness is like. Well—to put it very crudely—it's like Plato; it's a dialogue. A dialogue between two people. Yes, but not a Platonic dialogue in the hair-splitting, word-twisting, one-up-to-me sense; not a mock-humble bitching match; not a debate on some dreary set theme. You can talk about anything and change the subject as often as you like. In fact, what really matters is not what you talk about, but the being together in this particular relationship. George can't imagine having a dialogue of this kind with a woman, because women can only talk in terms of the personal. A man of his own age would do, if there was some sort of polarity; for instance, if he was a Negro. You and your dialogue-partner have to be somehow opposites. Why? Because you have to be symbolic figures—like, in this case, Youth and Age. Why do you have to be symbolic? Because the dialogue is by its nature impersonal. It's a symbolic encounter. It doesn't involve either party personally. That's why, in a dialogue, you can say absolutely anything. Even the closest confidence, the deadliest secret, comes out objectively as a mere metaphor or illustration which could never be used against you.

George would like to explain all of this to Kenny. But it is so complicated, and he doesn't want to run the risk of finding that Kenny can't understand him. More than anything, he wants Kenny to understand, wants to be able to believe that Kenny knows what this dialogue is all about. And really, at this moment, is seems possible that Kenny *does* know. George can almost feel the electric field of the dialogue surrounding and irradiating them. *He* certainly feels irradiated. As for Kenny, he looks quite beautiful. *Radiant with rapport* is the phrase which George finds to describe him. For what shines out of Kenny isn't mere intelligence or any kind of switched-on charm. There the two of them sit, smiling at each other—oh, far more than that—fairly beaming with mutual insight.

"Say something," he commands Kenny.

"Do I have to?"

"Yes."

"What'll I say?"

"Anything. Anything that seems to be important, right now."

"That's the trouble. I don't know what is important and what isn't. I feel like my head is stopped up with stuff that doesn't matter—I mean, matter to me."

"Such as—"

"Look, I don't mean to be personal, sir—but—well, the stuff our classes are about—"

"That doesn't matter to you?"

"Jesus Christ, sir—I *said* I wasn't being personal! Yours are a whole lot better than most; we all think that. And you do try to make these books fit in with what's going on nowadays, only, it's not your fault, but—we always seem to end up getting bogged down in the past; like this morning, with Tithonus. Look, I don't want to pan the past; maybe it'll mean a whole lot to me when I'm older. All I'm saying is, the past doesn't really matter to most kids my age. When we talk like it does, we're just being polite. I guess that's because we don't have any pasts of our own—except stuff we want to forget, like things in high school, and times we acted like idiots—"

"Well, fine! I can understand that. You don't need the past, yet. You've got the present."

"Oh, but the present's a real drag! I just despise the present—I mean, the way it is right now—I mean, tonight's an exception, of course— What are you laughing at, sir?"

"Tonight—*sí!* The present—*no!*" George is getting noisy. Some people at the bar turn their heads. "Drink to tonight!" He drinks, with a flourish.

"Tonight—*sí!*" Kenny laughs and drinks.

"Okay," says George. "The past—no help. The present—no good. Granted. But there's one thing you can't deny; you're stuck with the future. You can't just sneeze that off."

"I guess we are. What's left of it. There may not be much, with all these rockets—"

"Death."

"Death?"

"That's what I said."

"Come again, sir. I don't get you."

"I said death. I said, do you think about death a lot?"

"Why, no. Hardly at all. Why?"

"The future—that's where death is."

"Oh—yeah. Yeah—maybe you've got a point there." Kenny grins. "You know something? Maybe the other generations before us used to think about death a lot more than we do. What I mean is, kids must have gotten mad, thinking how they'd be sent out to some corny war and killed, while their folks stayed home and acted patriotic.

But it won't be like that any more. We'd all be in this thing together."

"You could still get mad at the older people. Because of all those extra years they'll have had before they get blown up."

"Yes, that's right, I could, couldn't I? Maybe I will. Maybe I'll get mad at you, sir."

"Kenneth—"

"Sir?"

"Just as a matter of the purest sociological interest, why do you persist in calling me sir?"

Kenny grins teasingly. "I'll stop if you want me to."

"I didn't ask you to stop. I asked you why."

"Why don't you like it? None of you do, though, I guess."

"You mean, none of us old folks?" George smiles a no-hard-feelings smile. Nevertheless, he feels that the symbolic relationship is starting to get out of hand. "Well, the usual explanation is that we don't like being reminded—"

Kenny shakes his head decisively. "No."

"What do you mean, 'No'?"

"You're not like that."

"Is that supposed to be a compliment?"

"Maybe. The point is, I *like* calling you sir."

"You do?"

"What's so phony nowadays is all this familiarity. Pretending there isn't any difference between people—well, like you were saying about minorities, this morning. If you and I are no different, what do we have to give each other? How can we ever be friends?"

He *does* understand, George thinks, delighted. "But two young people can be friends, surely?"

"That's something else again. They can, yes, after a fashion. But there's always this thing of competition, getting in the way. All young people are kind of competing with each other, do you know that?"

"Yes, I suppose so—unless they're in love."

"Maybe they are even then. Maybe that's what's wrong with—" Kenny breaks off abruptly. George watches him, expecting to hear some confidence about Lois. But it doesn't come. For Kenny is obviously following some quite different train of thought. He sits smiling in silence for a few moments and—yes, actually—he is blushing! "This sounds as corny as hell, but—"

"Never mind. Go ahead."

"I sometimes wish—I mean, when you read those Victorian novels—I'd have hated living in those days, all except for one thing—oh, hell—I can't say it!" He breaks off, blushing and laughing.

"Don't be silly!"

"When I say it, it's so corny, it's the end! But—I'd have liked living when you could call your father sir."

"Is your father alive?"

"Oh, sure."

"Why don't you call him sir, then? Some sons do, even nowadays."

"Not my father. He isn't the type. Besides, he isn't around. He ran out on us a couple of years ago. . . . Hell!"

"What's the matter?"

"Whatever made me tell you all that? Am I drunk or something?"

"No more drunk than I am."

"I must be stoned."

"Look—if it bothers you—let's forget you told me."

"*I* won't forget."

"Oh yes, you will. You'll forget if I tell you to forget."

"Will I?"

"You bet you will!"

"Well, if you say so—okay."

"Okay, *sir*."

"Okay, *sir!*" Kenny suddenly beams. He is really pleased—so pleased that his own pleasure embarrasses him. "Say, you know—when I came over here—I mean, when I thought I might just happen to run into you this evening—there was something I wanted to ask you. I just remembered what it was"—he downs the rest of his drink in one long swallow—"it's about experience. They keep telling you, when you're older, you'll have experience—and that's supposed to be so great. What would you say about that, sir? Is it really any use, would you say?"

"What kind of experience?"

"Well—places you've been to, people you've met. Situations you've been through already, so you know how to handle them when they come up again. All that stuff that's supposed to make you wise, in your later years."

"Let me tell you something, Kenny. For other people, I can't speak—but, personally, I haven't gotten wise on anything. Certainly, I've been through this and that; and when it happens again, I say to myself, Here it is again. But that doesn't seem to help me. In my opinion, I, personally, have gotten steadily sillier and sillier and sillier—and that's a fact."

"No kidding, sir? You can't mean that! You mean, sillier than when you were young?"

"Much, much sillier."

"I'll be darned. Then experience is no use at all? You're saying it might just as well not have happened?"

"No. I'm not saying that. I only mean, you can't *use* it. But if you don't try to—if you just realize it's there and you've got it—then it can be kind of marvelous."

"Let's go swimming," says Kenny abruptly, as if bored by the whole conversation.

"All right."

Kenny throws his head right back and laughs wildly. "Oh—that's terrific!"

"What's terrific?"

"It was a test. I thought you were bluffing, about being silly. So I said to myself, I'll suggest doing something wild, and if he objects— if he even hesitates—then I'll know it was all a bluff. You don't mind my telling you that, do you, sir?"

"Why should I?"

"Oh, that's terrific!"

"Well, I'm not bluffing—so what are we waiting for? *You* weren't bluffing, were you?"

"Hell, no!"

They jump up, pay, run out of the bar and across the highway, and Kenny vaults the railing and drops down, about eight feet, onto the beach. George, meanwhile, is clambering over the rail, a bit stiffly. Kenny looks up, his face still lit by the boardwalk lamps: "Put your feet on my shoulders, sir." George does so, drunk-trustful, and Kenny, with the deftness of a ballet dancer, supports him by ankles and calves, lowering him almost instantly to the sand. During the descent, their bodies rub against each other, briefly but roughly. The electric field of the dialogue is broken. Their relationship, whatever it now is, is no longer symbolic. They turn and begin to run toward the ocean.

Already the lights seem far, far behind. They are bright but they cast no beams; perhaps they are shining on a layer of high fog. The waves ahead are barely visible. Their blackness is immensely cold and wet. Kenny is tearing off his clothes with wild whooping cries. The last remaining minim of George's caution is aware of the lights and the possibility of cruise cars and cops, but he doesn't hesitate, he is no longer able to; this dash from the bar can only end in the water. He strips himself clumsily, tripping over his pants. Kenny, stark naked now, has plunged and is wading straight in, like a fearless native warrior, to attack the waves. The undertow is very strong. George flounders for a while in a surge of stones. As he finally struggles through and feels sand under his feet, Kenny comes body-surfing out of the night and shoots past him without a glance—a water-creature absorbed in its element.

As for George, these waves are much too big for him. They seem truly tremendous, towering up, blackness unrolling itself out of blackness, mysteriously and awfully sparkling, then curling over in a thundering slap of foam which is sparked with phosphorus. George has sparks of it all over his body, and he laughs with delight to find himself bejeweled. Laughing, gasping, choking, he is too drunk to be afraid; the salt water he swallows seems as intoxicating as whiskey. From time to time he catches tremendous glimpses of Kenny, arrowing down some toppling foam-precipice. Then, intent upon his own rites of purification, George staggers out once more, wide-open-armed, to receive the stunning baptism of the surf. Giving himself to it utterly, he washes away thought, speech, mood, desire, whole selves, entire lifetimes; again and again he returns, becoming always cleaner, freer, less. He is perfectly happy by himself; it's enough to know that Kenny and he are the sole sharers of the element. The waves and the night and the noise exist only for their play. Meanwhile, no more than two hundred yards distant, the lights shine from the shore and the cars flick past up and down the highway, flashing their long beams. On the dark hillsides you can see lamps in the windows of dry homes, where the dry are going dryly to their dry beds. But George and Kenny are refugees from dryness; they have escaped across the border into the water-world, leaving their clothes behind them for a customs fee.

And now, suddenly, here is a great, an apocalyptically great wave, and George is way out, almost out of his depth, standing naked and tiny before its presence, under the lip of its roaring upheaval and the towering menace of its fall. He tries to dive through it—even now he feels no real fear—but instead he is caught and picked up, turned over and over and over, flapping and kicking toward a surface which may be either up or down or sideways, he no longer knows.

And now Kenny is dragging him out, groggy-legged. Kenny's hands are under George's armpits and he is laughing and saying like a nanny, "That's enough for now!" And George, still water-drunk, gasps, "I'm all right," and wants to go straight back into the water. But Kenny says, "Well, *I'm* not—I'm cold," and nannylike he towels George, with his own shirt, not George's, until George stops him because his back is sore. The nanny-relationship is so convincing at this moment that George feels he could curl up and fall immediately asleep right here, shrunk to child-size within the safety of Kenny's bigness. Kenny's body seems to have grown gigantic since they left the water. Everything about him is larger than life: the white teeth of his grin, the wide dripping shoulders, the tall slim torso with its heavy-hung sex, and the long legs, now beginning to shiver.

"Can we go back to your place, sir?" he asks.

"Sure. Where else?"

"Where else?" Kenny repeats, seeming to find this very amusing. He picks up his clothes and turns, still naked, toward the highway and the lights.

"Are you crazy?" George shouts after him.

"What's the matter?" Kenny looks back, grinning.

"You're going to walk home like that? Are you crazy? They'd call the cops!"

Kenny shrugs his shoulders good-humoredly. "Nobody would have seen us. We're invisible—didn't you know?"

But he gets into his clothes now, and George does likewise. As they start up the beach again, Kenny puts his arm around George's shoulder. "You know something, sir? They ought not to let you out on your own, ever. You're liable to get into real trouble."

Their walk home sobers George quite a lot. By the time they reach the house, he no longer sees the two of them as wild water-creatures but as an elderly professor with wet hair bringing home an exceedingly wet student in the middle of the night. George becomes self-conscious and almost curt. "The bathroom's upstairs. I'll get you some towels."

Kenny reacts to the formality at once. "Aren't you taking a shower, too, sir?" he asks, in a deferential, slightly disappointed tone.

"I can do that later. I wish I had some clothes your size to lend you. You'll have to wrap up in a blanket, while we dry your things on the heater. It's rather a slow process, I'm afraid, but that's the best we can do."

"Look, sir—I don't want to be a nuisance. Why don't I go now?"

"Don't be an idiot. You'd get pneumonia."

"My clothes'll dry on me. I'll be all right."

"Nonsense! Come on up and I'll show you where everything is."

George's refusal to let him leave appears to have pleased Kenny. At any rate, he makes a terrific noise in the shower, not so much singing as a series of shouts. He is probably waking up the neighbors, George thinks, but who cares? George's spirits are up again; he feels excited, amused, alive. In his bedroom, he undresses quickly, gets into his thick white terry-cloth bathrobe, hurries downstairs again, puts on the kettle and fixes some tuna fish and tomato sandwiches on rye. They are all ready, set out on a tray in the living room when Kenny comes down, wearing the blanket awkwardly, saved-from-shipwreck style.

Kenny doesn't want coffee or tea; he would rather have beer, he says. So George gets him a can from the icebox and unwisely pours himself a biggish Scotch. He returns to find Kenny looking around the room as though it fascinates him.

"You live here all by yourself, sir?"

"Yes," says George, and adds with a shade of irony, "Does that surprise you?"

"No. One of the kids said he thought you did."

"As a matter of fact, I used to share this place with a friend."

But Kenny shows no curiosity about the friend. "You don't even have a cat or a dog or anything?"

"You think I should?" George asks, a bit aggressive. The poor old guy doesn't have anything to love, he thinks Kenny is thinking.

"Hell, no! Didn't Baudelaire say they're liable to turn into demons and take over your life?"

"Something like that. This friend of mine had lots of animals, though, and they didn't seem to take *us* over. Of course, it's different when there's two of you. We often used to agree that neither one of us would want to keep on the animals if the other wasn't there. . . ."

No. Kenny is absolutely not curious about any of this. Indeed, he is concentrating on taking a huge bite out of his sandwich. So George asks him, "Is it all right?"

"I'll say!" He grins at George with his mouth full, then swallows and adds, "You know something, sir? I believe you've discovered the secret of the perfect life!"

"I have?" George has just gulped nearly a quarter of his Scotch to drown out a spasm which started when he talked about Jim and the animals. Now he feels the alcohol coming back on him with a rush. It is exhilarating, but it is coming much too fast.

"You don't realize how many kids my age just dream about the kind of setup you've got here. I mean, what more can you want? I mean, you don't have to take orders from anybody. You can do any crazy thing that comes into your head."

"And that's your idea of the perfect life?"

"Sure it is!"

"Honestly?"

"What's the matter, sir? Don't you believe me?"

"What I don't quite understand is, if you're so keen on living alone—how does Lois fit in?"

"Lois? What's she got to do with it?"

"Now, look, Kenny—I don't mean to be nosy—but, rightly or wrongly, I got the idea that you and she might be, well, considering—"

"Getting married? No. That's out."

"Oh?"

"She says she won't marry a Caucasian. She says she can't take people in this country seriously. She doesn't feel anything we do here *means* anything. She wants to go back to Japan and teach."

"She's an American citizen, isn't she?"

"Oh, sure. She's a Nisei. But, just the same, she and her whole family got shipped up to one of those internment camps in the Sierras, right after the war began. Her father had to sell his business for peanuts, give it away, practically, to some sharks who were grabbing all the Japanese property and talking big about avenging Pearl Harbor! Lois was only a small kid, then, but you can't expect anyone to forget a thing like that. She says they were all treated as enemy aliens; no one even gave a damn which side they were on. She says the Negroes were the only ones who acted decently to them. And a few pacifists. Christ, she certainly has the right to hate our guts! Not that she does, actually. She always seems to be able to see the funny side of things."

"And how do you feel about her?"

"Oh, I like her a lot."

"And she likes you, doesn't she?"

"I guess so. Yes, she does. A lot."

"But don't you *want* to marry her?"

"Oh sure. I guess so. If she were to change her attitude. But I doubt if she will. And, anyhow, I'm in no rush about marrying anyone. There's a lot of things I want to do, first—" Kenny pauses, regarding George with his most teasing, penetrating grin. "You know what I think, sir?"

"What do you think?"

"I don't believe you're that much interested whether I marry Lois or not. I think you want to ask me something different. Only you're not sure how I'll take it."

"What do I want to ask you?"

This is getting positively flirty, on both sides. Kenny's blanket, under the relaxing influence of the talk and beer, has slipped, baring an arm and a shoulder and turning itself into a classical Greek garment, the chlamys worn by a young disciple—the favorite, surely—of some philosopher. At this moment, he is utterly, dangerously charming.

"You want to know if Lois and I—if we make out together."

"Well, do you?"

Kenny laughs triumphantly. "So I was right!"

"Maybe. Maybe not. . . . Do you?"

"We did, once."

"Why only once?"

"It wasn't so long ago. We went to a motel. It's down the beach, as a matter of fact, quite near here."

"Is that why you drove out here tonight?"

"Yes—partly. I was trying to talk her into going there again."

"And that's what the argument was about?"

"Who says we had an argument?"

"You left her to drive home alone, didn't you?"

"Oh well, that was because . . . No, you're right—she didn't want to. She hated that motel the first time, and I don't blame her. The office and the desk clerk and the register—all that stuff they put you through. And of course they know damn well what the score is. It all makes the thing much too important and corny, like some big sin or something. And the way they look at you! Girls mind all that much more than we do—"

"So now she's called the whole thing off?"

"Hell, no, it's not that bad! It's not that she's against it, you understand. Not on principle. In fact, she's definitely—well, anyhow, I guess we can work something out. We'll have to see. . . ."

"You mean, maybe you can find some place that isn't so public and embarrassing?"

"That'd be a big help, certainly." Kenny grins, yawns, stretches himself. The chlamys slips off his other shoulder. He pulls it back over both shoulders as he rises, turning it into a blanket again and himself into a gawky twentieth-century American boy comically stranded without his clothes. "Look, sir, it's getting as late as all hell. I have to be going."

"Where, may I ask?"

"Why, back across town."

"In what?"

"I can get a bus, can't I?"

"They won't start running for another two hours, at least."

"Just the same . . ."

"Why don't you stay here? Tomorrow I'll drive you."

"I don't think I . . ."

"If you start wandering around this neighborhood in the dark, now the bars are shut, the police will stop you and ask what you're doing. And you aren't exactly sober, if you don't mind my saying so. They might even take you in."

"Honestly, sir, I'll be all right."

"I think you're out of your mind. However, we'll discuss that in a minute. First—sit down. I've got something I want to tell you."

Kenny sits down obediently, without further protest. Perhaps he is curious to know what George's next move will be.

"Now listen to this very carefully. I am about to make a simple statement of fact. Or facts. No comment is required from you. If you like, you can decide that this doesn't concern you at all. Is that clear?"

"Yes, sir."

"There's a woman I know who lives near here—a very close friend of mine. We have supper together at least one day a week; often, more than that. Matter of fact, we had supper tonight. Now—it never makes any difference to her which day I pick. So what I've decided is this— and, mind, it has nothing whatsoever to do with you, *necessarily*— from now on, I shall go to her place for supper each week on the same night. *Invariably, on the same night*. Tonight, that is. Is that much clear? No, don't answer. Go right on listening, because I'm just coming to the point. These nights, when I have supper with my friend, *I shall never, under any circumstances*, return here before midnight. Is that clear? No—listen! This house is never locked, because anyone could get into it anyway just by breaking a panel in the glass door. Upstairs, in my study, you must have noticed that there's a couch bed? I keep it made up with clean sheets on it, just on the once-in-a-blue-moon chance that I'll get an unexpected guest—such as you are going to be tonight, for instance. . . . No—listen carefully! If that bed were ever used while I was out, and straightened up afterwards, I'd never be any the wiser. And if my cleaning woman were to notice anything, she'd merely put the sheets out to go to the laundry; she'd suppose I'd had a guest and forgotten to tell her. . . . All right! I've made a decision and now I've told you about it. Just as I might tell you I'd decided to water the garden on a certain day of the week. I have also told you a few facts about this house. You can make a note of them. Or you can forget them. That's all."

George looks straight at Kenny. Kenny smiles back at him faintly. But he is—yes, just a little bit—embarrassed.

"And now get me another drink."

"Okay, sir." Kenny rises from his chair with noticeable eagerness, as if glad of this breaking of tension. He picks up George's glass and goes into the kitchen. George calls after him, "And get yourself one, too!"

Kenny puts his head around the corner, grinning. "Is that an order, sir?"

"You're damn right it is!"

"I suppose you've decided I'm a dirty old man?"

While Kenny was getting the drinks from the kitchen, George felt himself entering a new phase. Now, as Kenny takes his seat again, he is, though he cannot have realized it yet, in the presence of a George transformed: a formidable George, who articulates thickly but clearly, with a menace behind his words. An inquisitorial George, seated in judgment and perhaps about to pronounce sentence. An oracular George, who may shortly begin to speak with tongues.

This isn't at all like their drunkenness at The Starboard Side. Kenny and he are no longer in the symbolic dialogue-relationship; this new phase of communication is very much person-to-person. Yet, paradoxically, Kenny seems farther away, not closer; he has receded far beyond the possible limits of an electric field. Indeed, it is only now and then that George can see him clearly, for the room has become dazzlingly bright, and Kenny's face keeps fading into the brightness. Also, there is a loud buzzing in George's ears, so loud that he can't be certain if Kenny answered his question or not.

"You needn't say anything," George tells Kenny (thus dealing with either possibility), "because I admit it—oh, hell, yes, of course I admit it—I *am* a dirty old man. Ninety-nine per cent of all old men are dirty. That is, if you want to talk that language; if you insist on that kind of dreariness. I'm not protesting against what you choose to call me or don't. I'm protesting against an attitude—and I'm only doing that for your sake, not mine. . . .

"Look—things are quite bad enough anyhow, nowadays—we're in quite enough of a mess, semantically and every other way—without getting ourselves entangled in these dreary categories. I mean, what is this life of ours supposed to be *for*? Are we to spend it identifying each other with catalogues, like tourists in an art gallery? Or are we to try to exchange *some* kind of a signal, however garbled, before it's too late? *You* answer *me* that!

"It's all very fine and easy for you young things to come to me on campus and tell me I'm cagey. Merciful Christ—*cagey*! Don't you even know better than that? Don't you have a glimmering of how I must feel—longing to *speak*?

"You asked me about experience. So I told you. Experience isn't any *use*. And yet, in quite another way, it *might* be. If only we weren't all such miserable fools and prudes and cowards. Yes, you too, my boy. And don't you dare deny it! What I said just now, about the bed in the study—that shocked you. Because you were determined to be shocked. You utterly refused to understand my motives. Oh God, don't you *see*? That bed—what that bed *means*—that's what experience *is*!

"Oh well, I'm not blaming you. It'd be a miracle if you *did* understand. Never mind. Forget it. Here am I. Here are you—in that damned blanket. Why don't you take it right off, for Christ's sake? What made me say that? I suppose you're going to misunderstand that, too? Well, if you do, I don't give a damn. The point is—here am I and here are you—and for once there's no one to disturb us. This may never happen again. I mean that literally! And the time is *desperately* short. All right, let's put the cards on the table. Why are you here in this room at this moment? *Because you want me to tell you something!* That's the true reason you came all the way across town tonight. You may have honestly believed it was to get Lois in bed with you. Mind you, I'm not saying one word against her. She's a truly beautiful angel. But you can't fool a dirty old man; he isn't sentimental about Young Love; he knows just how much it's worth—a great deal, but not everything. No, my dear Kenneth. You came here this evening to see *me*—

whether you realize it or not. Some part of you knew quite well that Lois would refuse to go to that motel again; and that that would give you an excuse to send her home and get yourself stranded out here. I expect that poor girl is feeling terrible about it all, right now, and crying into her pillow. You must be very sweet to her when you see her again. . . .

"But I'm getting off the point. The point is, you came to ask me about something that really *is* important. So why be ashamed and deny it? You see, I know you through and through. I know *exactly* what you want. You want me to tell you *what I know.*

"Oh, Kenneth, Kenneth, believe me—there's nothing I'd rather do! I want *like hell* to tell you. But I can't. I quite literally can't. Because, don't you see, *what I know is what I am?* And I can't tell you that. You have to find it out for yourself. I'm like a book you have to read. A book can't read itself to you. It doesn't even know what it's about. I don't know what I'm about.

"You could know what I'm about. You could. But you can't be bothered to. Look—you're the only boy I ever met on that campus I really believe could. That's what makes it so tragically futile. Instead of trying to know, you commit the inexcusable triviality of saying 'he's a dirty old man,' and turning this evening, which might be the most precious and unforgettable of your young life, into a *flirtation!* You don't like that word, do you? But it's the word. It's the enormous tragedy of everything nowadays: flirtation. Flirtation instead of fucking, if you'll pardon my coarseness. All any of you ever do is flirt, and wear your blankets off one shoulder, and complain about motels. And miss the one thing that might really—and, Kenneth, I do not say this casually—*transform your entire life*—"

For a moment, Kenny's face is quite distinct. It grins, dazzlingly. Then his grin breaks up, is refracted, or whatever you call it, into rainbows of light. The rainbows blaze. George is blinded by them. He shuts his eyes. And now the buzzing in his ears is the roar of Niagara.

Half an hour, an hour, later—not long, anyway—George blinks and is awake.

Night, still. Dark. Warm. Bed. *Am in bed!* He jerks up, propped on his elbow. Clicks on the bedside lamp. His hand does this; arm in sleeve; pajama sleeve. *Am in pajamas!* Why? How?

Where is he?

George staggers out of bed, dizzy, a bit sickish, startled wide awake. Ready to lurch into the front room. No—wait. Here's paper propped against lamp:

> *Thought maybe I'd better split, after all. I like to wander around at night. If those cops pick me up, I won't tell them where I've been— I promise! Not even if they twist my arm!*
>
> *That was great, this evening. Let's do it again, shall we? Or don't you believe in repeating things?*
>
> *Couldn't find pajamas you already used, so took these clean ones from the drawer. Maybe you sleep raw? Didn't want to take a chance, though. Can't have you getting pneumonia, can we?*
>
> *Thanks for everything,*
> *Kenneth*

George sits on the bed, reading this. Then, with slight impatience, like a general who has just glanced through an unimportant dispatch, he lets the paper slide to the floor, stands up, goes into the bathroom, empties his bladder, doesn't glance in the mirror, doesn't even turn on the light, returns to bed, gets in, switches off bed lamp.

Little teaser, his mind says, but without the least resentment. Just as well he didn't stay.

But, as he lies on his back in the dark, there is something that keeps him from sleep: a tickle in the blood and the nerves of the groin. The alcohol itches in him, down there.

Lying in the dark, he conjures up Kenny and Lois in their car, makes them drive into Camphor Tree Lane, park further down the street, in case a neighbor should be watching, hurry discreetly across the bridge, get the door open—it sticks, she giggles—bump against the living-room furniture—a tiny Japanese cry of alarm—tiptoe upstairs without turning on the lights. . . .

No—it won't work. George tries several times, but he just cannot make Lois go up those stairs. Each time he starts her up them, she dematerializes, as it were. (And now he knows, with absolute certainty, that Kenny will never be able to persuade her even to enter this house.)

But the play has begun, now, and George isn't about to stop it. Kenny must be provided with a partner. So George turns Lois into the sexy little gold cat, the Mexican tennis player. No trouble about getting *him* upstairs! He and Kenny are together in the front room, now. George hears a belt drop to the floor. They are stripping themselves naked.

The blood throbs deep down in George's groin. The flesh stirs and swells up, suddenly hard hot. The pajamas are pulled off, tossed out of bed.

George hears Kenny whisper to the Mexican, *Come on, kid!* Making himself invisible, he enters the front room. He finds the two of them just about to lie down together. . . .

No. That won't work, either. George doesn't like Kenny's attitude. He isn't taking his lust seriously; in fact, he seems to be on the verge of giggles. Quick—we need a substitute! George hastily turns Kenny into the big blond boy from the tennis court. Oh, much better! Perfect! Now they can embrace. Now the fierce hot animal play can begin. George hovers above them, watching; then he begins passing in and out of their writhing, panting bodies. He is either. He is both at once. Ah—it is so good! Ah—ah . . . !

You old idiot, George's mind says. But he is not ashamed of himself. He speaks to the now slack and sweating body with tolerant good humor, as if to an old greedy dog which has just gobbled down a chunk of meat far bigger than it really wanted. Well, maybe you'll let us sleep, now? His hand feels for a handkerchief from under the pillow, wipes his belly dry.

As sleep begins to wash lightly over him, he asks himself, Shall I mind meeting Kenny's eye in class on Monday?

No. Not a bit. Even if he has told Lois (which I doubt): I undressed him, I put him to bed, he was drunk as a skunk. For then he will have told her about the swimming, too: You should have seen him in that water—as crazy as a kid! They ought not to let you out on your own, I said to him.

George smiles to himself, with entire self-satisfaction. Yes, I *am* crazy, he thinks. That is my secret; my strength.

And I'm about to get much crazier, he announces. Just watch me, all of you! Do you know what? I'm flying to Mexico for Christmas! You dare me to? I'll make reservations first thing in the morning!

He falls asleep, still smiling.

Partial surfacings, after this. Partial emergings, just barely breaking the sheeted calm of the water. Most of George remaining submerged in sleep.

Just barely awash, the brain inside its skull on the pillow cognizes darkly; not in its daytime manner. It is incapable of decision now. But, perhaps for this very reason, it can become aware, in this state, of certain decisions apparently not yet made. Decisions that are like codicils which have been secretly signed and witnessed and put away in a most private place to await the hour of their execution.

Daytime George may even question the maker of these decisions; but he will not be allowed to remember its answers in the morning.

What if Kenny has been scared off? What if he doesn't come back? Let him stay away. George doesn't need him, or any of these kids. He isn't looking for a son.

What if Charlotte goes back to England?

He can do without her, if he must. He doesn't need a sister.

Will George go back to England?

No. He will stay here.

Because of Jim?

No. Jim is in the past, now. He is of no use to George any more.

But George remembers him so faithfully.

George makes himself remember. He is afraid of forgetting. Jim is my life, he says. But he will have to forget, if he wants to go on living. Jim is death.

Then why will George stay here?

This is where he found Jim. He believes he will find another Jim here. He doesn't know it, but he has started looking already.

Why does George believe he will find him?

He only knows that he must find him. He believes he will because he must.

But George is getting old. Won't it very soon be too late?

Never use those words to George. He won't listen. He daren't listen. Damn the future. Let Kenny and the kids have it. Let Charley keep the past. George clings only to Now. It is Now that he must find another Jim. Now that he must love. Now that he must live. . . .

Meanwhile, here we have this body known as George's body, asleep on this bed and snoring quite loud. The dampness of the ocean air affects its sinuses; and anyhow, it snores extra loud after drinking. Jim used to kick it awake, turn it over on its side, sometimes get out of bed in a fury and go to sleep in the front room.

But *is* all of George altogether present here?

Up the coast a few miles north, in a lava reef under the cliffs, there are a lot of rock pools. You can visit them when the tide is out. Each pool is separate and different, and you can, if you are fanciful, give them names, such as George, Charlotte, Kenny, Mrs. Strunk. Just as George and the others are thought of, for convenience, as individual entities, so you may think of a rock pool as an entity; though, of course, it is not. The waters of its consciousness—so to speak—are swarming with hunted anxieties, grim-jawed greeds, dartingly vivid intuitions, old crusty-shelled rock-gripping obstinacies, deep-down sparkling undiscovered secrets, ominous protean organisms motioning mysteriously, perhaps warningly, toward the surface light. How can such a variety of creatures coexist at all? Because they have to. The rocks of the pool hold their world together. And, throughout the day of the ebb tide, they know no other.

But that long day ends at last; yields to the nighttime of the flood. And, just as the waters of the ocean come flooding, darkening over the pools, so over George and the others in sleep come the waters of that other ocean—that consciousness which is no one in particular but which contains everyone and everything, past, present and future, and extends unbroken beyond the uttermost stars. We may surely suppose that, in the darkness of the full flood, some of these creatures are lifted from their pools to drift far out over the deep waters. But do they ever bring back, when the daytime of the ebb returns, any kind of catch with them? Can they tell us, in any manner, about their journey? Is there, indeed, anything for them to tell—except that the waters of the ocean are not really other than the waters of the pool?

Within this body on the bed, the great pump works on and on, needing no rest. All over this quietly pulsating vehicle the skeleton crew make their tiny adjustments. As for what goes on topside, they know nothing of this but danger signals, false alarms mostly: red lights flashed from the panicky brain stem, curtly contradicted by green all clears from the level-headed cortex. But now the controls are on automatic. The cortex is drowsing; the brain stem registers only an occasional nightmare. Everything seems set for a routine run from here to morning. The odds are enormously against any kind of accident. The safety record of this vehicle is outstanding.

Just let us suppose, however . . .

Let us take the particular instant, years ago, when George walked into The Starboard Side and set eyes for the first time on Jim, not yet demobilized and looking stunning beyond words in his Navy uniform. Let us then suppose that, at that same instant, deep down in one of the major branches of George's coronary artery, an unimaginably gradual process began. Somehow—no doctor can tell us exactly why—the inner lining begins to become roughened. And, one by one, on the roughened surface of the smooth endothelium, ions of calcium, carried by the bloodstream, begin to be deposited. . . . Thus, slowly, invisibly, with the utmost discretion and without the slightest hint to those old fussers in the brain, an almost indecently melodramatic situation is contrived: the formation of the atheromatous plaque.

Let us suppose this, merely. (The body on the bed is still snoring.) This thing is wildly improbable. You could bet thousands of dollars against its happening, tonight or any night. And yet it *could*, quite possibly, be about to happen—within the next five minutes.

Very well—let us suppose that this is the night, and the hour, and the appointed minute.

Now—

The body on the bed stirs slightly, perhaps; but it does not cry out, does not wake. It shows no outward sign of the instant, annihilating shock. Cortex and brain stem are murdered in the blackout with the speed of an Indian strangler. Throttled out of its oxygen, the heart clenches and stops. The lungs go dead, their power line cut. All over the body, the arterials contract. Had this blockage not been absolute, had the occlusion occurred in one of the smaller branches of the artery, the skeleton crew could have dealt with it; they are capable of engineering miracles. Given time, they could have rigged up bypasses, channeled out new collateral communications, sealed off the damaged area with a scar. But there is no time at all. They die without warning at their posts.

For a few minutes, maybe, life lingers in the tissues of some outlying regions of the body. Then, one by one, the lights go out and there is total blackness. And if some part of the nonentity we called George has indeed been absent at this moment of terminal shock, away out there on the deep waters, then it will return to find itself homeless. For it can associate no longer with what lies here, unsnoring, on the bed. This is now cousin to the garbage in the container on the back porch. Both will have to be carted away and disposed of, before too long.